# PostGIS Cookbook

Over 80 task-based recipes to store, organize, manipulate, and analyze spatial data in a PostGIS database

**Paolo Corti**

**Thomas J Kraft**

**Stephen Vincent Mather**

**Bborie Park**

[PACKT] open source ✳
PUBLISHING   community experience distilled

BIRMINGHAM - MUMBAI

# PostGIS Cookbook

First published: February 2014

Production Reference: 2310114

Published by Packt Publishing Ltd.
Livery Place
35 Livery Street
Birmingham B3 2PB, UK.

ISBN 978-1-84951-866-6

www.packtpub.com

Cover Image by Charles E. Mather (matherc@yahoo.com)

# Credits

**Authors**
Paolo Corti
Thomas J Kraft
Stephen Vincent Mather
Bborie Park

**Reviewers**
Jorge Arévalo
Andrea Flesca

**Acquisition Editor**
Mary Jasmine Nadar

**Content Development Editor**
Azharuddin Sheikh

**Technical Editors**
Vrinda Nitesh Bhosale
Rahul Nair
Anita Nayak
Humera Shaikh

**Copy Editors**
Tanvi Gaitonde
Dipti Kapadia
Kirti Pai
Shambhavi Pai

**Project Coordinator**
Mary Alex

**Proofreaders**
Stephen Copestake
Lauren Harkins

**Graphics**
Abhinash Sahu

**Indexers**
Rekha Nair
Tejal Soni

**Production Coordinator**
Shantanu Zagade

**Cover Work**
Shantanu Zagade

# About the Authors

**Paolo Corti** is based in Rome, Italy. He is an environmental engineer with more than 15 years of experience in the GIS sector. After working with proprietary solutions for some years, he has proudly switched to open-source technologies and Python for almost a decade.

He has been working as a developer and analyst for organizations such as the EU Joint Research Center, UN World Food Program, and the Italian Government.

Currently, he is working within the GeoNode project, for which he is a core developer, in the context of emergency preparedness and response.

He is an OSGeo Charter member and writes a blog on open-source GIS at http://www.paolocorti.net/.

---

I would like to thank the PostGIS Steering Committee and everyone else who makes PostGIS such a beautiful project.

A special thanks must go to the co-authors of this book: they have been brilliant mates always ready to give me suggestions and help.

A mention is needed here to some geospatial minds that are great source of inspiration for me: Paul Ramsey, Sandro Santilli, Frank Warmerdam, and Even Rouault.

Last, but not least, I would like to thank my wife Renata and my family for their support and patience.

---

**Thomas J Kraft** is currently a Planning Technician at Cleveland Metroparks after beginning as a GIS intern in 2011.

He graduated with Honors from Cleveland State University in 2012, majoring in Environmental Science with an emphasis on GIS.

When not in front of a computer, he enjoys his weekends landscaping and the outdoors in general.

I'd like to thank the co-authors of this book, who are some of the most knowledgeable and motivated professionals in the field. It's truly an honor to have been involved in this process.

I'd like to give special acknowledgements to Stephen Mather (also a co-author) for introducing me to the world of open-source GIS and my girlfriend, Sandy, for keeping me on the straight and narrow.

**Stephen Vincent Mather** has worked in the geospatial industry for 15 years, having always had a flair for geospatial analyses in general, especially those at the intersection of Geography and Ecology. His work in open-source geospatial databases started 5 years ago with PostGIS and he immediately began using PostGIS as an analytic tool, attempting a range of innovative and sometimes bleeding-edge techniques (although he admittedly prefers the cutting edge). His geospatial career has spanned a variety of interesting and novel natural-resource projects, everything from the movement of ice sheets in Antarctica to hiking viewsheds and mobile trail applications to help park users find trails, picnic areas, and restrooms.

Stephen is currently the GIS manager for Cleveland Metroparks in Cleveland, Ohio. He manages a small geospatial shop that specializes in high-end cartography, curating and generating data, geospatial web development, and analyses for natural-resource management, largely with open-source software.

Stephen is also a Mennonite technologist, aka a straw-hat hacker, interested in creating fair and open data and infrastructure for better governance and humanitarian purposes. He is heavily involved in the Cleveland Civic Hacking movement as he works with the public to help them get engaged with geospatial data. In his spare time, he builds guitars really, really slowly.

Thanks go out to those who form my geospatial pedigree: Gordon Longsworth (and his advisor Ian Mcharg), Kevin Czajkowski, Karl Schneider, and Ken Jezek, as well as to the geospatial minds who inspire me, including Martin Davis.

A special thanks goes to the blessings that are my two beautiful and bright children and my wife (who is equally so), all of whom exhibit endless patience and love. They are three people who both structure my life and fill its interstitial spaces with the glow of their love.

**Bborie Park** has been breaking (and subsequently fixing) computers for most of his life. His primary interest involves developing end-to-end pipelines for spatial datasets. He is an active contributor to the PostGIS project and is a member of the PostGIS Steering Committee. He happily resides with his wife Nicole in the San Francisco Bay Area.

I would like to thank my wife Nicole, who patiently tolerated many hours, days, and weeks of my working when I should have been relaxing. I would also like to thank the PostGIS community and Steering Committee for accepting and providing feedback for my contributions to the project.

# About the Reviewers

**Jorge Arévalo** is a computer engineer from Universidad Autónoma de Madrid, UAM. He started developing web applications with JS, PHP, and Python. In 2010, he began collaborating with PostGIS and GDAL projects after participating in GSoC 2009, creating the PostGIS Raster GDAL driver. He currently works as a freelance Web/GIS developer and collaborates with the `geomati.co` group in projects, such as gvSIG CE or QGIS. He also writes a blog about GIS at `http://www.libregis.org`.

**Andrea Flesca** is an Italian electronic engineer working in the software world for Selex ES, a primary Italian electronic systems and software provider. After extensive experience with software development and over the past several years, he has dealt with GIS systems and Enterprise Architectures. He's Technical Head for systems integration.

Andrea loves rock music and knows how to prepare a great tiramisu.

# www.PacktPub.com

## Support files, eBooks, discount offers and more

You might want to visit www.PacktPub.com for support files and downloads related to your book.

Did you know that Packt offers eBook versions of every book published, with PDF and ePub files available? You can upgrade to the eBook version at www.PacktPub.com and as a print book customer, you are entitled to a discount on the eBook copy. Get in touch with us at service@packtpub.com for more details.

At www.PacktPub.com, you can also read a collection of free technical articles, sign up for a range of free newsletters and receive exclusive discounts and offers on Packt books and eBooks.

http://PacktLib.PacktPub.com

Do you need instant solutions to your IT questions? PacktLib is Packt's online digital book library. Here, you can access, read and search across Packt's entire library of books.

## Why Subscribe?

- Fully searchable across every book published by Packt
- Copy and paste, print and bookmark content
- On demand and accessible via web browser

## Free Access for Packt account holders

If you have an account with Packt at www.PacktPub.com, you can use this to access PacktLib today and view nine entirely free books. Simply use your login credentials for immediate access.

# Table of Contents

# Preface

How close is the nearest hospital from my children's school? Where were the property crimes in my city for the last three months? What is the shortest route from my home to my office? What route should I prescribe for my company's delivery truck so as to maximize equipment utilization and minimize fuel consumption? Where should the next fire station should be built so as to minimize the response time?

People ask these questions and others like them every day all over this planet. Answering these questions require a mechanism capable of thinking in two or more dimensions. Historically, a Desktop GIS application was used to formulate an answer for each question. This method—though completely functional—is incapable of answering many questions at once. In addition, this method is typically unable to effectively manage and operate on massive spatial datasets, such as all of the roads of Europe for 2013 in one dataset, or allow tasks to be automated instead of significant pointing and clicking.

Once scalability, support for large datasets, and a direct input mechanism are required or desired, most users explore using a spatial database. There are several spatial database software available, some proprietary and others open source. PostGIS is an open source spatial database software and is probably the most accessible of all spatial database software.

PostGIS runs as an extension to provide spatial capabilities to PostgreSQL databases. In this capacity, PostGIS permits the inclusion of spatial data alongside data typically found in a database. By having all of the data together, questions such as "What is the rank of all of the police stations after taking into account the distance for each response time?" are possible. New or enhanced capabilities are possible by building upon the core functions provided by PostGIS and the inherent extensibility of PostgreSQL.

*PostGIS Cookbook* uses a problem-solving approach to help you acquire a solid understanding of PostGIS. Hopefully, this book provides answers to some common spatial questions and gives you the inspiration and confidence to use and enhance PostGIS in finding solutions to challenging spatial problems.

# What this book covers

*Chapter 1, Moving Data In and Out of PostGIS*, covers the processes available for importing and exporting spatial and nonspatial data to and from PostGIS. These processes include the use of utilities provided by PostGIS and third parties, such as GDAL/OGR.

*Chapter 2, Structures that Work*, discusses how to organize PostGIS data using mechanisms available through PostgreSQL. These mechanisms are used to normalize potentially unclean and unstructured import data.

*Chapter 3, Working with Vector Data – The Basics*, introduces PostGIS operations commonly done on vectors, known as geometries and geographies in PostGIS. Operations covered include the processing of invalid geometries, determining relationships between geometries, and simplifying complex geometries.

*Chapter 4, Working with Vector Data – Advanced Recipes*, dives into advanced topics for analyzing geometries. You will learn how to make use of KNN filters to increase the performance of proximity queries, create polygons from LiDAR data, and compute Voronoi cells usable in neighborhood analyses.

*Chapter 5, Working with Raster Data*, presents a realistic workflow for operating on rasters in PostGIS. You will learn how to import a raster, modify the raster, conduct analysis on the raster, and export the raster in standard raster formats.

*Chapter 6, Working with pgRouting*, introduces the pgRouting extension that brings graph traversal and analysis capabilities to PostGIS. The recipes in this chapter answer the real-world questions of conditionally navigating from point A to point B and accurately modeling complex routes, such as waterways.

*Chapter 7, Into the Nth Dimension*, covers tools and techniques used to process and analyze multi-dimensional spatial data in PostGIS, including LiDAR-sourced point cloud. Topics covered include the loading of point clouds into PostGIS, creating 2.5D and 3D geometries from point clouds, and the application of several photogrammetry principles.

*Chapter 8, PostGIS Programming*, shows how to use the Python language to write applications that operate on and interact with PostGIS. The applications written include methods to read and write external datasets to and from PostGIS, as well as a basic geocoding engine using OpenStreetMap datasets.

*Chapter 9, PostGIS and the Web*, presents the use of OGC and REST web services to deliver PostGIS data and services to the Web. This chapter discusses providing OGC WFS and WMS services with MapServer and GeoServer and consuming them from clients such as OpenLayers and Leaflet. It then shows how to build a web application with GeoDjango.

*Chapter 10, Maintenance, Optimization, and Performance Tuning*, takes a step back from PostGIS and focuses on the capabilities of the PostgreSQL database server. By leveraging the tools provided by PostgreSQL, you can ensure the long-term viability of your spatial and nonspatial data and maximize the performance of various PostGIS operations.

*Chapter 11*, *Using Desktop Clients*, shows how spatial data in PostGIS can be consumed and manipulated by various open source desktop GIS applications. Several applications are discussed so as to highlight the different approaches to interact with spatial data and help you find the right tool for the task.

# What you need for this book

Before going further with this book, you will want to install the latest versions of PostgreSQL and PostGIS (9.3 and 2.1, respectively). You may also want to install pgAdmin (1.18), if you prefer a graphical SQL tool. For most computing environments (Windows, Linux, OSX), installers and packages include all of the required dependencies of PostGIS. The minimum required dependencies for PostGIS are PROJ.4, GEOS, libjson, and GDAL.

A basic understanding of the SQL language is required to understand and adapt the code found in this book's recipes.

# Who this book is for

This book is written for those who are looking for the best method to solve their spatial problems using PostGIS. These problems can be as simple as finding the nearest restaurant to a specific location or as complex as finding the shortest and/or most efficient route from point A to point B.

For those who are just starting out with PostGIS or even spatial datasets, this book is structured to help readers become comfortable and proficient at running spatial operations in the database. For experienced users, the book provides opportunities to dive into advanced topics such as point clouds, raster map-algebra, and PostGIS programming.

# Conventions

In this book, you will find a number of styles of text that distinguish between different kinds of information. Here are some examples of these styles, and an explanation of their meaning.

Code words in text, database table names, folder names, filenames, file extensions, pathnames, dummy URLs, and user input are shown as follows: "We will import the `firenews.csv` file that stores a series of web news collected from various RSS feeds".

A block of code is set as follows:

```
SELECT ROUND(SUM(chp02.proportional_sum(ST_Transform(a.geom,3734),
b.geom, b.pop))) AS population FROM
    nc_walkzone AS a, census_viewpolygon as b
    WHERE ST_Intersects(ST_Transform(a.geom, 3734), b.geom)
    GROUP BY a.id;
```

When we wish to draw your attention to a particular part of a code block, the relevant lines or items are set in bold:

```
SELECT ROUND(SUM(chp02.proportional_sum(ST_Transform(a.geom,3734),
b.geom, b.pop))) AS population FROM
    nc_walkzone AS a, census_viewpolygon as b
    WHERE ST_Intersects(ST_Transform(a.geom, 3734), b.geom)
    GROUP BY a.id;
```

Any command-line input or output is written as follows:

```
> raster2pgsql -s 4322 -t 100x100 -F -I -C -Y C:\postgis_cookbook\data\
chap5\PRISM\us_tmin_2012.*.asc chap5.prism | psql -d postgis_cookbook
```

**New terms** and **important words** are shown in bold. Words that you see on the screen, in menus or dialog boxes for example, appear in the text like this: "clicking the **Next** button moves you to the next screen".

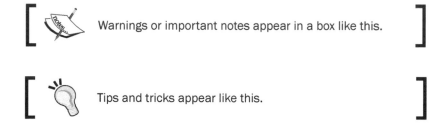

Warnings or important notes appear in a box like this.

Tips and tricks appear like this.

# Reader feedback

Feedback from our readers is always welcome. Let us know what you think about this book—what you liked or may have disliked. Reader feedback is important for us to develop titles that you really get the most out of.

To send us general feedback, simply send an e-mail to feedback@packtpub.com and mention the book title via the subject of your message.

If there is a topic that you have expertise in and you are interested in either writing or contributing to a book, see our author guide on www.packtpub.com/authors.

# Customer support

Now that you are the proud owner of a Packt book, we have a number of things to help you to get the most from your purchase.

# Downloading the example code

You can download the example code files for all Packt books you have purchased from your account at http://www.packtpub.com. If you purchased this book elsewhere, you can visit http://www.packtpub.com/support and register to have the files e-mailed directly to you.

# Errata

Although we have taken every care to ensure the accuracy of our content, mistakes do happen. If you find a mistake in one of our books—maybe a mistake in the text or the code—we would be grateful if you would report this to us. By doing so, you can save other readers from frustration and help us improve subsequent versions of this book. If you find any errata, please report them by visiting http://www.packtpub.com/submit-errata, selecting your book, clicking on the **errata submission form** link, and entering the details of your errata. Once your errata are verified, your submission will be accepted and the errata will be uploaded on our website, or added to any list of existing errata, under the Errata section of that title. Any existing errata can be viewed by selecting your title from http://www.packtpub.com/support.

# Piracy

Piracy of copyright material on the Internet is an ongoing problem across all media. At Packt, we take the protection of our copyright and licenses very seriously. If you come across any illegal copies of our works, in any form on the Internet, please provide us with the location address or website name immediately so that we can pursue a remedy.

Please contact us at copyright@packtpub.com with a link to the suspected pirated material.

We appreciate your help in protecting our authors and our ability to bring you valuable content.

# Questions

You can contact us at questions@packtpub.com if you are having a problem with any aspect of the book, and we will do our best to address it.

# 1
# Moving Data In and Out of PostGIS

In this chapter, we will cover:

- ▶ Importing nonspatial tabular data (CSV) using PostGIS functions
- ▶ Importing nonspatial tabular data (CSV) using GDAL
- ▶ Importing shapefiles with shp2pgsql
- ▶ Importing and exporting data with the ogr2ogr GDAL command
- ▶ Handling batch importing and exporting of datasets
- ▶ Exporting data to the shapefile with the pgsql2shp PostGIS command
- ▶ Importing OpenStreetMap data with the osm2pgsql command
- ▶ Importing raster data with the raster2pgsql PostGIS command
- ▶ Importing multiple rasters at a time
- ▶ Exporting rasters with the gdal_translate and gdalwarp GDAL commands

## Introduction

In this chapter, we will show you a set of recipes covering different tools and methodologies to import and export geographic data from the PostGIS spatial database.

## Importing nonspatial tabular data (CSV) using PostGIS functions

There are a couple of alternative approaches to import a **Comma Separated Values** (**CSV**) file, which stores attributes and geometries in PostGIS. In this recipe, we will use the approach of importing such a file using the PostgreSQL COPY command and a couple of PostGIS functions.

## Getting ready

We will import the `firenews.csv` file that stores a series of web news collected from the various RSS feeds related to forest fires in Europe in the context of the **European Forest Fire Information System** (**EFFIS**), available at `http://effis.jrc.ec.europa.eu/`.

For each news feed, there are attributes like `place name`, `size` of the fire in hectares, `URL`, and so on. Most importantly, there are the `x` and `y` fields that give the position of the geolocalized news in decimal degrees (in the WGS 84 spatial reference system, SRID = 4326).

## How to do it...

The steps you need to follow to complete this recipe are as shown:

1. Inspect the structure of the CSV file, `firenews.csv`, which you can find within the book dataset (if you are on Windows, open the CSV file with an editor such as Notepad).

**Downloading the example code**

You can download the example code files for all Packt books you have purchased from your account at `http://www.packtpub.com`. If you purchased this book elsewhere, you can visit `http://www.packtpub.com/support` and register to have the files e-mailed directly to you.

```
$ cd ~/postgis_cookbook/data/chp01/
$ head -n 5 firenews.csv
```

The output of the preceding command is as shown:

```
x,y,place,size,update,startdate,enddate,title,url-
8.2499,42.37657,Avión,52,2011/03/07,2011/03/05,2011/03/06,D
os incendios calcinan 74 hectáreas el fin de semana,http://www.
laregion.es/noticia/145578/incendios/calcinan/hectareas/semana/
-8.1013,42.13924,Quintela de Leirado,22,2011/03/07,2011/03/
06,2011/03/06,Dos incendios calcinan 74 hectáreas el fin de
semana,http://www.laregion.es/noticia/145578/incendios/calcinan/
hectareas/semana/
3.48159,43.99156,Arrigas,4,2011/03/06,2011/03/05,2011/03/05,"À
Arrigas, la forêt sous la menace d'un feu",http://www.midilibre.
com/articles/2011/03/06/NIMES-A-Arrigas-la-foret-sous-la-menace-d-
39-un-feu-1557923.php5
6.1672,44.96038,Vénéon,9,2011/03/06,2011/03/06,2011/03/06,Isè
re Spectaculaire incendie dans la vallée du Vénéon,http://www.
ledauphine.com/isere-sud/2011/03/06/isere-spectaculaire-incendie-
dans-la-vallee-du-veneon
```

2. Connect to PostgreSQL and create the following table:

```
$ psql -U me -d postgis_cookbook
postgis_cookbook=> CREATE TABLE chp01.firenews
(
    x float8,
    y float8,
    place varchar(100),
    size float8,
    update date,
    startdate date,
    enddate date,
    title varchar(255),
    url varchar(255),
    the_geom geometry(POINT, 4326)
);
```

> We are using the psql client for connecting to PostgreSQL, but you can use your favorite one, for example, pgAdmin.
>
> Using the psql client, we will not show the host and port options as we will assume that you are using a local PostgreSQL installation on the standard port.
>
> If that is not the case, please provide those options!

3. Copy the records from the CSV file to the PostgreSQL table using the COPY command (if you are on Windows, use an input directory such as c:\temp instead of /tmp) as follows:

```
postgis_cookbook=> COPY chp01.firenews (x, y, place, size, update,
startdate, enddate, title, url) FROM '/tmp/firenews.csv' WITH CSV
HEADER;
```

> Make sure that the firenews.csv file is in a location accessible from the PostgreSQL process user. For example, in Linux, copy the file to the /tmp directory.
>
> If you are on Windows, you most likely will need to set the encoding to UTF-8 before copying:
>
> ```
> postgis_cookbook=# set client_encoding to 'UTF-8';
> ```

4. Check if all of the records have been imported from the CSV file to the PostgreSQL table:

```
postgis_cookbook=> SELECT COUNT(*) FROM chp01.firenews;
```

The output of the preceding command is as follows:

```
count
-------
3006
(1 row)
```

5. Check if a record related to this new table is in the PostGIS `geometry_columns` metadata view:

```
postgis_cookbook=# SELECT f_table_name, f_geometry_column, coord_
dimension, srid, type FROM geometry_columns where f_table_name =
'firenews';
 f_table_name | f_geometry_column | coord_dimension | srid | type
--------------+-------------------+-----------------+------+-----
 --
 firenews     | the_geom          |        2        | 4326 | POINT
(1 row)
```

> Before PostGIS 2.0, you had to create a table containing spatial data in two distinct steps; in fact, the `geometry_columns` view was a table that needed to be manually updated. For that purpose, you had to use the `AddGeometryColumn` function to create the column. For example, for this recipe:
>
> ```
> postgis_cookbook=> CREATE TABLE chp01.firenews
> (
>     x float8,
>     y float8,
>     place varchar(100),
>     size float8,
>     update date,
>     startdate date,
>     enddate date,
>     title varchar(255),
>     url varchar(255)
> )
> WITHOUT OIDS;
> postgis_cookbook=> SELECT AddGeometryColumn('chp01',
> 'firenews', 'the_geom', 4326, 'POINT', 2);
> chp01.firenews.the_geom SRID:4326 TYPE:POINT DIMS:2
> ```

In PostGIS 2.0, you can still use the AddGeometryColumn function if you wish; however, you need to set its use_typmod parameter to false.

6.  Now, import the points in the geometric column using the ST_MakePoint or ST_PointFromText functions (use one of the following two update commands):

    ```
    postgis_cookbook=> UPDATE chp01.firenews SET the_geom = ST_
    SetSRID(ST_MakePoint(x,y), 4326);
    ```

    ```
    postgis_cookbook=> UPDATE chp01.firenews SET the_geom = ST_
    PointFromText('POINT(' || x || ' ' || y || ')', 4326);
    ```

7.  Check how the geometry field has been updated in some records from the table:

    ```
    postgis_cookbook=# SELECT place, ST_AsText(the_geom) AS wkt_geom
    FROM chp01.firenews ORDER BY place LIMIT 5;
    ```

    The output of the preceding comment is as follows:

    ```
    place                            | wkt
    -----------------------------------------------------------------
    Abbaslik                         | POINT(29.95...
    Abeledos, Montederramo           | POINT(-7.48...
    Abreiro                          | POINT(-7.28...
    Abrunheira, Montemor-o-Velho     | POINT(-8.72...
    Achaia                           | POINT(21.89...
    (5 rows)
    ```

8.  Finally, create a spatial index for the geometric column of the table:

    ```
    postgis_cookbook=> CREATE INDEX idx_firenews_geom ON chp01.
    firenews USING GIST (the_geom);
    ```

## How it works...

This recipe showed you how to load nonspatial tabular data (in CSV format) in PostGIS using the COPY PostgreSQL command.

After creating the table and copying the CSV file rows to the PostgreSQL table, you updated the geometric column using one of the geometry constructor functions that PostGIS provides (ST_MakePoint and ST_PointFromText for bi-dimensional points).

These geometry constructors (in this case, ST_MakePoint and ST_PointFromText) must always provide the **spatial reference system identifier** (**SRID**) together with the point coordinates to define the point geometry.

Each geometric field added in any table in the database is tracked with a record in the `geometry_columns` PostGIS metadata view. In the previous PostGIS version (< 2.0), the `geometry_fields` view was a table and needed to be manually updated, possibly with the convenient `AddGeometryColumn` function.

For the same reason, to maintain the updated `geometry_columns` view, when dropping a geometry column or removing a spatial table in the previous PostGIS versions, there were the `DropGeometryColumn` and `DropGeometryTable` functions. With PostGIS 2.0, you don't need to use these functions any more, but you can safely remove the column or the table with the standard `ALTER TABLE DROP COLUMN` and `DROP TABLE` SQL commands.

In the last step of the recipe, you have created a spatial index on the table to improve performances. Please be aware that as in the case of alphanumerical database fields, indexes improve performances only when reading data using the `SELECT` command. In this case, you are making a number of updates on the table (`INSERT`, `UPDATE`, and `DELETE`); depending on the scenario, it could be less time consuming to drop and recreate the index after the updates.

# Importing nonspatial tabular data (CSV) using GDAL

As an alternative approach to the previous recipe, you will import a CSV file to PostGIS using the `ogr2ogr` GDAL command and the **GDAL OGR virtual format**. The **Geospatial Abstraction Library** (**GDAL**), is a translator library for raster geospatial data formats. OGR is the related library that provides similar capabilities for vector data formats.

This time, as an extra step, you will import only a part of the features in the file and you will reproject them to a different spatial reference system.

## Getting ready

You will import the `Global_24h.csv` file to the PostGIS database from NASA's **Earth Observing System Data and Information System** (**EOSDIS**).

You can download the file from the EOSDIS website at `http://firms.modaps.eosdis.nasa.gov/active_fire/text/Global_24h.csv`, or copy it from the dataset directory of the book for this chapter.

This file represents the active hotspots detected by the **Moderate Resolution Imaging Spectroradiometer** (**MODIS**) satellites in the world for the last 24 hours. For each row, there are the coordinates of the hotspot (latitude, longitude) in decimal degrees (in the WGS 84 spatial reference system, SRID = 4326), and a series of useful fields such as the `acquisition date`, `acquisition time`, and `satellite type`, just to name a few.

You will import only the active fire data scanned by the satellite type marked as "T" (Terra MODIS), and you will project it using the Spherical Mercator projection coordinate system (EPSG:3857, sometimes marked as EPSG:900913, where the number 900913 represents Google in 1337 speak, as it was first widely used by Google Maps).

## How to do it...

The steps you need to follow to complete this recipe are as follows:

1. Analyze the structure of the Global_24h.csv CSV file (in Windows, open the CSV file with an editor such as Notepad).

   ```
   $ cd ~/postgis_cookbook/data/chp01/
   $ head -n 5 Global_24h.csv
   latitude,longitude,brightness,scan,track,acq_date,acq_time,satellite,confidence,version,bright_t31,frp
   -23.386,-46.197,307.5,1.1,1,2012-08-20, 0140,T,54,5.0,285.7,16.5
   -22.952,-47.574,330.1,1.2,1.1,2012-08-20, 0140,T,100,5.0,285.2,53.9
   -23.726,-56.108,333.3,4.7,2,2012-08-20, 0140,T,100,5.0,283.5,404.1
   -23.729,-56.155,311.8,4.7,2,2012-08-20, 0140,T,61,5.0,272,143.1
   ```

2. Create a GDAL virtual data source composed of just one layer derived from the Global_24h.csv file. To do so, create a text file named global_24h.vrt in the same directory where the CSV file is and edit it as follows:

   ```
   <OGRVRTDataSource>
     <OGRVRTLayer name="Global_24h">
       <SrcDataSource>Global_24h.csv</SrcDataSource>
       <GeometryType>wkbPoint</GeometryType>
       <LayerSRS>EPSG:4326</LayerSRS>
       <GeometryField encoding="PointFromColumns"
         x="longitude" y="latitude"/>
     </OGRVRTLayer>
   </OGRVRTDataSource>
   ```

3. With the ogrinfo command, check if the virtual layer is correctly recognized by GDAL. For example, analyze the schema of the layer and the first of its features (fid=1):

   ```
   $ ogrinfo global_24h.vrt Global_24h -fid 1
   INFO: Open of `global_24h.vrt'using driver `VRT' successful.
   Layer name: Global_24h
   ```

```
Geometry: Point
Feature Count: 30326
Extent: (-155.284000, -40.751000) - (177.457000, 70.404000)
Layer SRS WKT:
GEOGCS["WGS 84",    DATUM["WGS_1984",    ...
latitude: String (0.0)
longitude: String (0.0)
frp: String (0.0)
OGRFeature(Global_24h):1
latitude (String) = -23.386
longitude (String) = -46.197
frp (String) = 16.5
POINT (-46.197 -23.386)
```

4.  You can also try to open the virtual layer with a Desktop GIS supporting a GDAL/ OGR virtual driver such as **Quantum GIS** (**QGIS**). In the following screenshot, the `Global_24h` layer is displayed together with the shapefile of the countries that you can find in the dataset directory of the book:

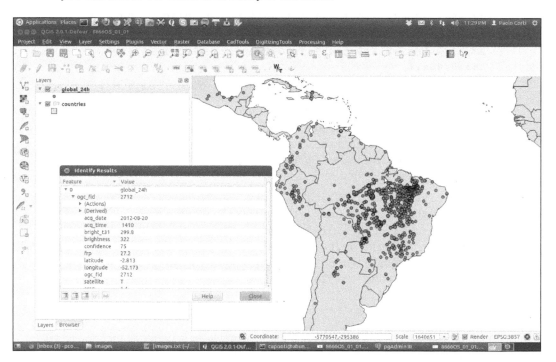

5. Now, export the virtual layer as a new table in PostGIS using the `ogr2ogr` GDAL/OGR command. You need to use the `-f` option to specify the output format, the `-t_srs` option to project the points to the `EPSG:3857` spatial reference, the `-where` option to load only the records from the MODIS Terra satellite type, and the `-lco` layer creation option to provide the schema where you want to store the table:

```
$ ogr2ogr -f PostgreSQL -t_srs EPSG:3857 PG:"dbname='postgis_
cookbook' user='me' password='mypassword'" -lco SCHEMA=chp01
global_24h.vrt -where "satellite='T'" -lco GEOMETRY_NAME=the_geom
```

6. Check how the `ogr2ogr` command created the table as shown in the following command:

```
$ pg_dump -t chp01.global_24h --schema-only -U me postgis_cookbook
CREATE TABLE global_24h (
    ogc_fid integer NOT NULL,
    the_geom public.geometry(Point,3857),
    latitude character varying,
    longitude character varying,
    brightness character varying,
    scan character varying,
    track character varying,
    acq_date character varying,
    acq_time character varying,
    satellite character varying,
    confidence character varying,
    version character varying,
    bright_t31 character varying,
    frp character varying
);
```

7. Now, check the record that should appear in the `geometry_columns` metadata view:

```
postgis_cookbook=# SELECT f_geometry_column, coord_dimension,
srid, type FROM geometry_columns WHERE f_table_name =
'global_24h';
 f_geometry_column | coord_dimension | srid  | type
-------------------+-----------------+-------+-------
 the_geom          |               2 |  3857 | POINT
(1 row)
```

8. Check how many records have been imported in the table:

```
postgis_cookbook=# select count(*) from chp01.global_24h;
count
-------
9190
(1 row)
```

9. Note how the coordinates have been projected from `EPSG:4326` to `EPSG:3857`:

```
postgis_cookbook=# SELECT ST_AsEWKT(the_geom) FROM chp01.
global_24h LIMIT 1;
st_asewkt
------------------------------------------------------
SRID=3857;POINT(-5142626.51617686 -2678766.03496892)
(1 row)
```

## How it works...

As mentioned in the GDAL documentation:

> *"OGR Virtual Format is a driver that transforms features read from other drivers based on criteria specified in an XML control file."*

GDAL supports the reading and writing of nonspatial tabular data stored as a CSV file, but we need to use a virtual format to derive the geometry of the layers from attribute columns in the CSV file (the longitude and latitude coordinates for each point). For this purpose, you need to at least specify in the driver the path to the CSV file (the `SrcDataSource` element), the geometry type (the `GeometryType` element), the spatial reference definition for the layer (the `LayerSRS` element), and the way the driver can derive the geometric information (the `GeometryField` element).

There are many other options and reasons for using OGR virtual formats; if you are interested in having a better understanding, please refer to the GDAL documentation available at `http://www.gdal.org/ogr/drv_vrt.html`.

After a virtual format is correctly created, the original flat nonspatial dataset is spatially supported by GDAL and the software based on GDAL. This is the reason why we can manipulate these files with GDAL commands such as `ogrinfo` and `ogr2ogr`, and with Desktop GIS software such as QGIS.

Once we have verified that GDAL can correctly read the features from the virtual driver, we can easily import them in PostGIS using the popular `ogr2ogr` command-line utility. The `ogr2ogr` command has a plethora of options, so refer to its documentation at `http://www.gdal.org/ogr2ogr.html` for a more in-depth discussion.

In this recipe, you have just seen some of these options, such as:

- ▸ **-where option**: Used to export just a selection of the original feature class
- ▸ **-t_srs option**: Used to reproject the data to a different spatial reference system
- ▸ **-lco layer creation option**: Used to provide the schema where we would want to store the table (without it, the new spatial table would be created in the `public` schema) and the name of the geometry field in the output layer

# Importing shapefiles with shp2pgsql

If you need to import a shapefile in PostGIS, you have at least a couple of options such as the `ogr2ogr` GDAL command, as you have seen previously, or the `shp2pgsql` PostGIS command.

In this recipe, you will load a shapefile in the database using the `shp2pgsql` command, analyze it with the `ogrinfo` command, and display it in the QGIS Desktop software.

## How to do it...

The steps you need to follow to complete this recipe are as follows:

1. Create a shapefile from the virtual driver created in the previous recipe using the `ogr2ogr` command (note that in this case, you do not need to specify the `-f` option, as the shapefile is the default output format for the `ogr2ogr` command):

   ```
   $ ogr2ogr global_24h.shp global_24h.vrt
   ```

2. Generate the SQL dump file for the shapefile using the `shp2pgsql` command. You are going to use the `-G` option to generate a PostGIS spatial table using the geography type, and the `-I` option to generate the spatial index on the geometric column:

   ```
   $ shp2pgsql -G -I global_24h.shp chp01.global_24h_geographic >
   global_24h.sql
   ```

3. Analyze the `global_24h.sql` file (in Windows, use a text editor such as Notepad):

   ```
   $ head -n 20 global_24h.sql
   SET CLIENT_ENCODING TO UTF8;
   SET STANDARD_CONFORMING_STRINGS TO ON;
   BEGIN;
   CREATE TABLE "chp01"."global_24h_geographic" (gid serial PRIMARY
   KEY,
   ```

```
"latitude" varchar(80),
"longitude" varchar(80),
"brightness" varchar(80),
...
"frp" varchar(80),
"geog" geography(POINT,4326));
INSERT INTO "chp01"."global_24h_geographic" ("latitude","long
itude","brightness","scan","track","acq_date","acq_time","sat
ellite","confidence","version","bright_t31","frp",geog) VALUES
('-23.386','-46.197','307.5','1.1','1','2012-08-20','0140','T','
54','5.0','285.7','16.5','0101000000F0A7C64B371947C0894160E5D0623
7C0');
...
```

4. Run the `global_24h.sql` file in PostgreSQL:

   ```
   $ psql -U me -d postgis_cookbook -f global_24h.sql
   ```

> If you are on Linux, you may concatenate the commands from the last two steps in a single line in the following manner:
>
> ```
> $ shp2pgsql -G -I global_24h.shp chp01.global_24h_
> geographic | psql -U me -d postgis_cookbook
> ```

5. Check if the metadata record is visible in the `geography_columns` view (and not in the `geometry_columns` view as with the `-G` option of the `shp2pgsql` command, we have opted for a `geography` type):

   ```
   postgis_cookbook=# SELECT f_geography_column,   coord_dimension,
   srid, type FROM geography_columns   WHERE f_table_name =
   'global_24h_geographic';
    f_geography_column | coord_dimension | srid  | type
   --------------------+-----------------+-------+-------
    geog               |               2 | 4326  | Point
   ```

6. Analyze the new PostGIS table with `ogrinfo` (use the `-fid` option just to display one record from the table):

   ```
   $ ogrinfo PG:"dbname='postgis_cookbook' user='me'
   password='mypassword'" chp01.global_24h_geographic -fid 1
   INFO: Open of `PG:dbname='postgis_cookbook' user='me'
   password='mypassword''
   using driver `PostgreSQL' successful.
   Layer name: chp01.global_24h_geographic
   Geometry: Point
   Feature Count: 30326
   Extent: (-155.284000, -40.751000) - (177.457000, 70.404000)
   Layer SRS WKT:
   ```

```
(unknown)
FID Column = gid
Geometry Column = the_geom
latitude: String (80.0)
longitude: String (80.0)
brightness: String (80.0)
...
frp: String (80.0)
OGRFeature(chp01.global_24h_geographic):1
  latitude (String) = -23.386
  longitude (String) = -46.197
  brightness (String) = 307.5
  ...
  frp (String) = 16.5
  POINT (-46.197 -23.386)
```

7. Now open QGIS and try to add the new layer to the map. Navigate to **Layer** | **Add PostGIS layers** and provide the connection information, and then add the layer to the map as shown in the following screenshot:

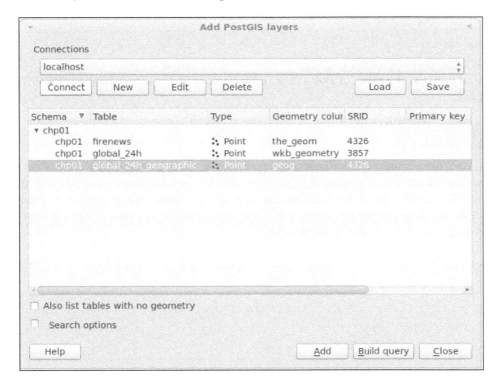

## How it works...

The PostGIS command, shp2pgsql, allows the user to import a shapefile in the PostGIS database. Basically, it generates a PostgreSQL dump file that can be used to load data by running it from within PostgreSQL.

The SQL file will be generally composed of the following sections:

 ▶ The CREATE TABLE section (if the -a option is not selected, in which case, the table should already exist in the database)

 ▶ The INSERT INTO section (one INSERT statement for each feature to be imported from the shapefile)

 ▶ The CREATE INDEX section (if the -I option is selected)

Unlike ogr2ogr, there is no way to make spatial or attribute selections (-spat, -where ogr2ogr options) for features in the shapefile to import.

On the other hand, with the shp2pgsql command, it is possible to import the m coordinate of the features too (ogr2ogr only supports x, y, and z at the time of writing).

To have a complete list of the shp2pgsql command options and their meaning, just type the command name in the shell (or in the command windows, if you are on Windows) and check the output.

## There's more...

If you do not prefer using the command-line utilities, you can still export your shapefiles, even multiple ones all at once, by using shp2pgsql-gui, which is a GUI software that can also be used as a plugin in pgAdmin. From its interface, you can select the shapefiles to import in PostGIS and select all the parameters that the shp2pgsql command allows the user to specify as shown in the following screenshot:

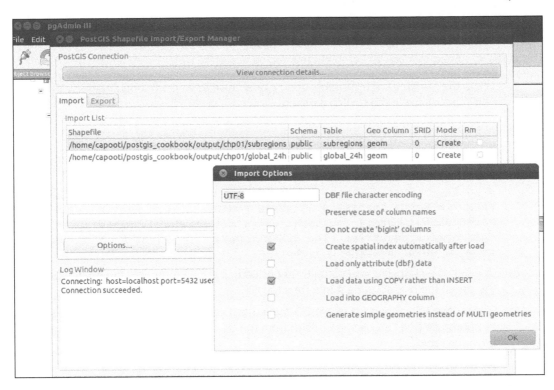

PostGIS 2.0 onward, `shp2pgsql-gui` is also a GUI for the `pgsql2shp` command (there will be a recipe about it later). It allows the user to select one or more PostGIS tables and export them to shapefiles. The GUI lets the user specify all the options that can be used in the `pgsql2shp` command.

There are other GUI tools to manage data in and out of PostGIS, generally integrated in the GIS Desktop software. In the last chapter of this book, we will take a look at the most popular ones.

# Importing and exporting data with the ogr2ogr GDAL command

In this recipe, you will use the popular `ogr2ogr` GDAL command for importing and exporting vector data from PostGIS.

Firstly, you will import a shapefile in PostGIS using the most significant options of the `ogr2ogr` command. Then, still using `ogr2ogr`, you will export the results of a spatial query performed in PostGIS to a couple of GDAL-supported vector formats.

## How to do it...

The steps you need to follow to complete this recipe are as follows:

1. Unzip the `TM_WORLD_BORDERS-0.3.zip` archive to your working directory. You can find this archive in the book's dataset.

2. Import the world countries shapefile (`TM_WORLD_BORDERS-0.3.shp`) in PostGIS using the `ogr2ogr` command. Using some of the `ogr2ogr` options, you will import only the features from `SUBREGION=2` (Africa), and the `ISO2` and `NAME` attributes, and rename the feature class to `africa_countries`:

```
$ ogr2ogr -f PostgreSQL -sql "SELECT ISO2, NAME AS country_name
FROM 'TM_WORLD_BORDERS-0.3' WHERE REGION=2" -nlt MULTIPOLYGON
PG:"dbname='postgis_cookbook' user='me' password='mypassword'"
-nln africa_countries -lco SCHEMA=chp01 -lco GEOMETRY_NAME=the_
geom TM_WORLD_BORDERS-0.3.shp
```

3. Check if the shapefile was correctly imported in PostGIS, querying the spatial table in the database or displaying it in a Desktop GIS.

4. Query PostGIS to get a list of the 50 active hotspots with the highest brightness temperature (the `bright_t31` field) from the `global_24h` table created in the previous recipe:

```
postgis_cookbook=# SELECT
ST_AsText(the_geom) AS the_geom, bright_t31
FROM chp01.global_24h
ORDER BY bright_t31 DESC LIMIT 100;
```

The output of the preceding command is as follows:

```
                the_geom                 | bright_t31
-------------------------------------------------------
 POINT(-13361233.2019535 4991419.20457202) | 360.6
 POINT(-13161080.7575072 8624445.64118912) | 359.6
 POINT(-13359897.3680639 4991124.84275376) | 357.4
 ...
(100 rows)
```

5. You want to figure out in which African countries these hotspots are located. For this purpose, you can do a spatial join with the `africa_countries` table produced in the previous step:

```
postgis_cookbook=# SELECT
ST_AsText(f.the_geom) AS the_geom,    f.bright_t31, ac.iso2,
ac.country_name
FROM chp01.global_24h as f
JOIN chp01.africa_countries as ac
ON ST_Contains(ac.the_geom, ST_Transform(f.the_geom,    4326))
ORDER BY f.bright_t31 DESC
LIMIT 100;
```

The output of the preceding command is as follows:

```
    the_geom   | bright_t31 | iso2 |  country_name
-----------------------------------------------------------

  POINT(229...)| 316.1      | AO   | Angola
  POINT(363...)| 315.4      | TZ   | United Republic ofTanzania
  POINT(229...)| 315        | AO   | Angola

...

(100 rows)
```

6.  You will now export the result of this query to a vector format supported by GDAL, such as GeoJSON, in the WGS 84 spatial reference using `ogr2ogr`:

```
$ ogr2ogr -f GeoJSON -t_srs EPSG:4326 warmest_hs.geojson
PG:"dbname='postgis_cookbook' user='me' password='mypassword'"
-sql "SELECT f.the_geom as the_geom, f.bright_t31, ac.iso2,
ac.country_name FROM chp01.global_24h as f JOIN chp01.africa_
countries as ac ON ST_Contains(ac.the_geom, ST_Transform(f.the_
geom, 4326)) ORDER BY f.bright_t31 DESC LIMIT 100"
```

7.  Open the GeoJSON file and inspect it with your favorite Desktop GIS. The following screenshot shows you how it looks with QGIS:

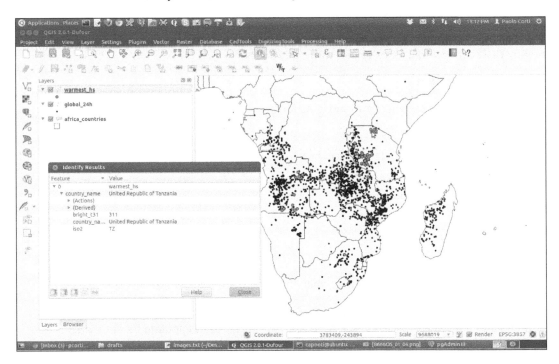

8. Export the previous query to a CSV file. In this case, you have to indicate how the geometric information must be stored in the file; this is done using the `-lco GEOMETRY` option:

```
$ ogr2ogr -t_srs EPSG:4326 -f CSV -lco GEOMETRY=AS_XY -lco
SEPARATOR=TAB warmest_hs.csv PG:"dbname='postgis_cookbook'
user='me' password='mypassword'" -sql "SELECT f.the_geom,
f.bright_t31, ac.iso2, ac.country_name FROM chp01.global_24h as
f JOIN chp01.africa_countries as ac ON ST_Contains(ac.the_geom,
ST_Transform(f.the_geom, 4326)) ORDER BY f.bright_t31 DESC  LIMIT
100"
```

## How it works...

GDAL is an open source library that comes together with several command-line utilities, which let the user translate and process raster and vector geo datasets in a plethora of formats. In the case of vector datasets, there is a GDAL sublibrary for managing vector datasets named OGR (therefore, when talking about vector datasets in the context of GDAL, we can also use the expression **OGR dataset**).

When you are working with an OGR dataset, two of the most popular OGR commands are `ogrinfo`, which lists many kinds of information from an OGR dataset, and `ogr2ogr`, which converts the OGR dataset from one format to the other.

It is possible to retrieve a list of the supported OGR vector formats using the `-formats` option on any OGR commands, for example, with `ogr2ogr`:

```
$ ogr2ogr --formats
```

The output of the preceding command is as follows:

```
Supported Formats:
  -> "ESRI Shapefile" (read/write)
  -> "MapInfo File" (read/write)
  -> "UK .NTF" (readonly)
  -> "SDTS" (readonly)
  -> "TIGER" (read/write)
  ...
```

Note that some formats are read-only, while the others are read/write.

PostGIS is one of the supported read/write OGR formats, so it is possible to use the OGR API or any OGR commands (such as `ogrinfo` and `ogr2ogr`) to manipulate its datasets.

The `ogr2ogr` command has many options and parameters; in this recipe, you have seen some of the most notable ones such as `-f`—to define the output format, `-t_srs`—to reproject/transform the dataset, and `-sql`—to define an (eventually spatial) query in the input OGR dataset.

When using `ogrinfo` and `ogr2ogr` together with the desired option and parameters, you have to define the datasets. When specifying a PostGIS dataset, you need a connection string that is defined as follows:

```
PG:"dbname='postgis_cookbook' user='me' password='mypassword'"
```

## See also

You can find more information about the `ogrinfo` and `ogr2ogr` commands on the GDAL website available at `http://www.gdal.org`.

If you need more information about the PostGIS driver, you should check its related documentation page available at `http://www.gdal.org/ogr/drv_pg.html`.

# Handling batch importing and exporting of datasets

In many GIS workflows, there is a typical scenario where subsets of a PostGIS table must be deployed to external users in a filesystem format (most typically, shapefiles or a spatialite database). Often, there is also the reverse process, where datasets received from different users have to be uploaded to the PostGIS database.

In this recipe, we will simulate both of these data flows. You will first create the data flow for processing the shapefiles out of PostGIS, and then the reverse data flow for uploading the shapefiles.

You will do it using the power of bash scripting and the `ogr2ogr` command.

## Getting ready

If you didn't follow all the other recipes, be sure to import the hotspots and the countries dataset in PostGIS. The following is how to do it with `ogr2ogr` (you should import both the datasets in their original SRID, 4326, to make spatial operations faster):

1.  Import in PostGIS the `Global_24h.csv` file using the `global_24.vrt` virtual driver you created in a previous recipe:

    ```
    $ ogr2ogr -f PostgreSQL PG:"dbname='postgis_cookbook' user='me'
    password='mypassword'" -lco SCHEMA=chp01 global_24h.vrt -lco
    OVERWRITE=YES -lco GEOMETRY_NAME=the_geom -nln hotspots
    ```

2. Import the countries shapefile using `ogr2ogr`:

```
$ ogr2ogr -f PostgreSQL -sql "SELECT ISO2, NAME AS country_
name FROM 'TM_WORLD_BORDERS-0.3'" -nlt MULTIPOLYGON
PG:"dbname='postgis_cookbook' user='me' password='mypassword'"
-nln countries -lco SCHEMA=chp01 -lco OVERWRITE=YES -lco GEOMETRY_
NAME=the_geom TM_WORLD_BORDERS-0.3.shp
```

In case you already imported the hotspots dataset using the 3857 SRID, you can use the new PostGIS 2.0 method that allows the user to modify the geometry type column of an existing spatial table. You can update the SRID definition for the hotspots table in this way thanks to the support of typmod on geometry objects:

```
postgis_cookbook=# ALTER TABLE hotspots
ALTER COLUMN the_geom
SET DATA TYPE geometry(Point, 4326)
USING ST_Transform(the_geom, 4326);
```

## How to do it...

The steps you need to follow to complete this recipe are as follows:

1. Check how many hotspots there are for each distinct country by using the following query:

```
postgis_cookbook=> SELECT c.country_name, MIN(c.iso2) as iso2,
count(*) as hs_count
```

```
FROM chp01.hotspots as hs JOIN chp01.countries as c ON ST_
Contains(c.the_geom, hs.the_geom) GROUP BY c.country_name ORDER BY
c.country_name;
```

The output of the preceding command is as follows:

```
country_name | iso2 | hs_count
--------------------------------------------
Albania      | AL   | 66
Algeria      | DZ   | 361
...
Yemen        | YE   | 6
Zambia       | ZM   | 1575
Zimbabwe     | ZW   | 179
(103 rows)
```

2.  Using the same query, generate a CSV file using the PostgreSQL `COPY` command or the `ogr2ogr` command (in the first case, make sure that the Postgre service user has full write permission to the output directory). If you are following the `COPY` approach and using Windows, be sure to replace `/tmp/hs_countries.csv` with a different path:

```
$ ogr2ogr -f CSV hs_countries.csv PG:"dbname='postgis_cookbook'
user='me' password='mypassword'" -lco SCHEMA=chp01 -sql "SELECT
c.country_name, MIN(c.iso2) as iso2, count(*) as hs_count FROM
chp01.hotspots as hs JOIN chp01.countries as c ON ST_Contains(c.
the_geom, hs.the_geom) GROUP BY c.country_name ORDER BY c.country_
name"

postgis_cookbook=> COPY (SELECT c.country_name, MIN(c.iso2) as
iso2, count(*) as hs_count

   FROM chp01.hotspots as hs

   JOIN chp01.countries as c

   ON ST_Contains(c.the_geom, hs.the_geom)

   GROUP BY c.country_name

   ORDER BY c.country_name) TO '/tmp/hs_countries.csv' WITH CSV
HEADER;
```

3.  If you are using Windows, go to step 5. With Linux, create a bash script named `export_shapefiles.sh` that iterates each record (country) in the `hs_countries.csv` file and generates a shapefile with the corresponding hotspots exported from PostGIS for that country:

```
#!/bin/bash
while IFS="," read country iso2 hs_count
do
   echo "Generating shapefile $iso2.shp for country $country
     ($iso2) containing $hs_count features."
ogr2ogr out_shapefiles/$iso2.shp
PG:"dbname='postgis_cookbook' user='me' password='mypassword'"
-lco SCHEMA=chp01 -sql "SELECT ST_Transform(hs.the_geom, 4326),
hs.acq_date, hs.acq_time, hs.bright_t31 FROM
chp01.hotspots as hs JOIN chp01.countries as c ON
ST_Contains(c.the_geom, ST_Transform(hs.the_geom, 4326)) WHERE
c.iso2 = '$iso2'"
done < hs_countries.csv
```

4. Give execution permissions to the bash file, and then run it after creating an output directory (`out_shapefiles`) for the shapefiles that will be generated by the script. Then, go to step 7:

```
chmod 775 export_shapefiles.sh

mkdir out_shapefiles

$ ./export_shapefiles.sh

Generating shapefile AL.shp for country Albania (AL) containing 66
features.

Generating shapefile DZ.shp for country Algeria (DZ) containing
361 features.

...

Generating shapefile ZM.shp for country Zambia (ZM) containing
1575 features.

Generating shapefile ZW.shp for country Zimbabwe (ZW) containing
179 features.
```

If you get the output as `ERROR: function getsrid(geometry) does not exist LINE 1: SELECT getsrid("the_geom") FROM (SELECT,...`, you will need to load the legacy support in PostGIS, for example, in a Debian Linux box:

```
psql -d postgis_cookbook -f /usr/share/
postgresql/9.1/contrib/postgis-2.1/legacy.sql
```

5. If you are using Windows, create a batch file named `export_shapefiles.bat`, that iterates each record (country) in the `hs_countries.csv` file and generates a shapefile with the corresponding hotspots exported from PostGIS for that country:

```
@echo off
for /f "tokens=1-3 delims=, skip=1" %%a in (hs_countries.csv) do (
    echo "Generating shapefile %%b.shp for country %%a (%%b)
containing %%c features"
    ogr2ogr out_shapefiles/%%b.shp PG:"dbname='postgis_cookbook'
user='me' password='mypassword'" -lco SCHEMA=chp01 -sql "SELECT
ST_Transform(hs.the_geom, 4326), hs.acq_date, hs.acq_time,
hs.bright_t31 FROM chp01.hotspots as hs JOIN chp01.countries as c ON
ST_Contains(c.the_geom, ST_Transform(hs.the_geom, 4326)) WHERE
c.iso2 = '%%b'"
)
```

6. Run the batch file after creating an output directory (`out_shapefiles`) for the shapefiles that will be generated by the script:

```
>mkdir out_shapefiles
>export_shapefiles.bat
"Generating shapefile AL.shp for country Albania (AL) containing
66 features"
"Generating shapefile DZ.shp for country Algeria (DZ) containing
361 features"
...
"Generating shapefile ZW.shp for country Zimbabwe (ZW) containing
179 features"
```

7. Try to open a couple of these output shapefiles in your favorite Desktop GIS. The following screenshot shows you how they look in QGIS:

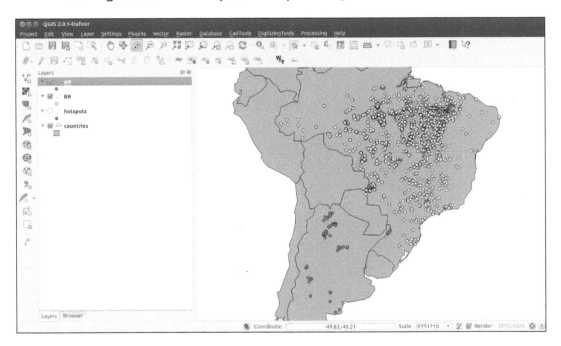

8. Now, you will do the round trip, uploading all of the generated shapefiles to PostGIS. You will upload all of the features for each shapefile and include the upload datetime and the original shapefile name. First, create the following PostgreSQL table, where you will upload the shapefiles:

```
postgis_cookbook=# CREATE TABLE chp01.hs_uploaded
(
  ogc_fid serial NOT NULL,
  acq_date character varying(80),
  acq_time character varying(80),
```

```
bright_t31 character varying(80),
iso2 character varying,
upload_datetime character varying,
shapefile character varying,
the_geom geometry(POINT, 4326),
CONSTRAINT hs_uploaded_pk PRIMARY KEY (ogc_fid)
);
```

9. If you are using Windows, go to step 11. With Linux, create another bash script named `import_shapefiles.sh`:

```
#!/bin/bash
for f in `find out_shapefiles -name \*.shp -printf "%f\n"`
do
  echo "Importing shapefile $f to chp01.hs_uploaded PostGIS
    table..." #, ${f%.*}"
  ogr2ogr -append -update  -f PostgreSQL
  PG:"dbname='postgis_cookbook' user='me'
  password='mypassword'" out_shapefiles/$f -nln
  chp01.hs_uploaded -sql "SELECT acq_date, acq_time,
  bright_t31, '${f%.*}' AS iso2, '`date`' AS upload_datetime,
  'out_shapefiles/$f' as shapefile FROM ${f%.*}"
done
```

10. Assign the execution permission to the bash script and execute it:

```
$ chmod 775 import_shapefiles.sh
```

```
$ ./import_shapefiles.sh
```

```
Importing shapefile DO.shp to chp01.hs_uploaded PostGIS table...
Importing shapefile ID.shp to chp01.hs_uploaded PostGIS table...
Importing shapefile AR.shp to chp01.hs_uploaded PostGIS table...
...
```

11. If you are using Windows, create a batch script named `import_shapefiles.bat`:

```
@echo off
for %%I in (out_shapefiles\*.shp)
do (
  echo Importing shapefile %%~nxI to chp01.hs_uploaded
    PostGIS table...
  ogr2ogr -append -update  -f PostgreSQL
  PG:"dbname='postgis_cookbook' user='me'
  password='mypassword'" out_shapefiles/%%~nxI -nln
  chp01.hs_uploaded -sql "SELECT acq_date, acq_time,
  bright_t31, '%%~nI' AS iso2, '%date%' AS upload_datetime,
  'out_shapefiles/%%~nxI' as shapefile FROM %%~nI"
)
```

12. Run the batch script:

```
>import_shapefiles.bat

Importing shapefile AL.shp to chp01.hs_uploaded PostGIS table...

Importing shapefile AO.shp to chp01.hs_uploaded PostGIS table...

Importing shapefile AR.shp to chp01.hs_uploaded PostGIS table...

...
```

13. Check some of the records that have been uploaded to the PostGIS table by using SQL:

```
postgis_cookbook=# SELECT upload_datetime, shapefile, ST_
AsText(the_geom) FROM chp01.hs_uploaded WHERE ISO2='AT';

upload_datetime        |        shapefile        |        st_astext
----------------------------+-----------------------+----------
-----------
 Sun Aug 26 01:58:44 CEST 2012 | out_shapefiles/AT.shp |
POINT(14.333 48.279)
 Sun Aug 26 01:58:44 CEST 2012 | out_shapefiles/AT.shp |
POINT(14.347 48.277)
 Sun Aug 26 01:58:44 CEST 2012 | out_shapefiles/AT.shp |
POINT(14.327 48.277)
 ...

(8 rows)
```

14. Check the same query with `ogrinfo` as well:

```
$ ogrinfo PG:"dbname='postgis_cookbook' user='me'
password='mypassword'" chp01.hs_uploaded -where "iso2='AT'"

INFO: Open of `PG:dbname='postgis_cookbook' user='me'
password='mypassword''
  using driver `PostgreSQL' successful.
Layer name: chp01.hs_uploaded

Geometry: Point

Feature Count: 8

Extent: (-155.284000, -40.751000) - (177.457000, 70.404000)

Layer SRS WKT:

GEOGCS["WGS 84",

    ...

FID Column = ogc_fid

Geometry Column = the_geom

acq_date: String (80.0)

acq_time: String (80.0)

bright_t31: String (80.0)
```

```
iso2: String (0.0)
upload_datetime: String (0.0)
shapefile: String (0.0)
OGRFeature(chp01.hs_uploaded):6413
  acq_date (String) = 2012-08-20
  acq_time (String) = 0110
  bright_t31 (String) = 292.7
  iso2 (String) = AT
  upload_datetime (String) = Sun Aug 26 01:58:44 CEST 2012
  shapefile (String) = out_shapefiles/AT.shp
  POINT (14.333 48.279)
...
```

## How it works...

You could implement both the data flows (processing shapefiles out from PostGIS, and then into it again) thanks to the power of the `ogr2ogr` GDAL command.

You have been using this command in different forms and with the most important input parameters in other recipes, so you should now have a good understanding of it.

Here, it is worth mentioning the way OGR lets you export the information related to the current datetime and the original shapefile name to the PostGIS table. Inside the `import_shapefiles.sh` (Linux, OS X) or the `import_shapefiles.bat` (Windows) scripts, the core is the line with the `ogr2ogr` command (here is the Linux version):

```
 ogr2ogr -append -update  -f PostgreSQL PG:"dbname='postgis_cookbook'
user='me' password='mypassword'" out_shapefiles/$f -nln chp01.hs_uploaded
-sql "SELECT acq_date, acq_time, bright_t31, '${f%.*}' AS iso2, '`date`'
AS upload_datetime, 'out_shapefiles/$f' as shapefile FROM ${f%.*}"
```

Thanks to the `-sql` option, you can specify the two additional fields—getting their values from the system date command and the filename that is being iterated from the script.

# Exporting data to the shapefile with the pgsql2shp PostGIS command

In this recipe, you will export a PostGIS table to a shapefile using the `pgsql2shp` command that is shipped with any PostGIS distribution.

## How to do it...

The steps you need to follow to complete this recipe are as follows:

1. In case you still haven't done it, export the countries shapefile to PostGIS using the `ogr2ogr` or the `shp2pgsql` commands. The `shp2pgsql` approach is as shown:

   ```
   $ shp2pgsql -I -d -s 4326 -W LATIN1 -g the_geom countries.shp
   chp01.countries > countries.sql
   ```

   ```
   $ psql -U me -d postgis_cookbook -f countries.sql
   ```

2. The `ogr2ogr` approach is as follows:

   ```
   $ ogr2ogr -f PostgreSQL PG:"dbname='postgis_cookbook' user='me'
   password='mypassword'" -lco SCHEMA=chp01 countries.shp -nlt
   MULTIPOLYGON -lco OVERWRITE=YES -lco GEOMETRY_NAME=the_geom
   ```

3. Now, query PostGIS in order to get a list of countries grouped by the `subregion` field. For this purpose, you will merge the geometries for features having the same `subregion` code using the `ST_Union` PostGIS geometric processing function:

   ```
   postgis_cookbook=> SELECT MIN(subregion) AS subregion,
       ST_Union(the_geom) AS the_geom, SUM(pop2005) AS pop2005
       FROM chp01.countries GROUP BY subregion;
   ```

4. Export the results of this query by using the `pgsql2shp` PostGIS command:

   ```
   $ pgsql2shp -f subregions.shp -h localhost -u me -P mypassword
   postgis_cookbook "SELECT MIN(subregion) AS subregion, ST_
   Union(the_geom) AS the_geom, SUM(pop2005) AS pop2005 FROM chp01.
   countries GROUP BY subregion;"

   Initializing...

   Done (postgis major version: 2).

   Output shape: Polygon

   Dumping: X [23 rows].
   ```

5. Open the shapefile and inspect it with your favorite Desktop GIS. This is how it looks in QGIS after applying a graduated classification symbology style based on the aggregated population for each subregion.

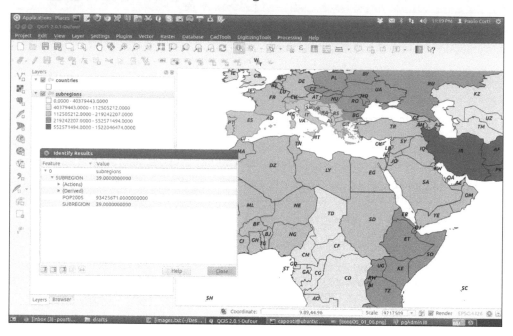

## How it works...

You have exported the results of a spatial query to a shapefile using the `pgsql2shp` PostGIS command. The spatial query you have used aggregates fields using the `SUM` PostgreSQL function for summing country populations in the same subregion, and the `ST_Union` PostGIS function to aggregate the corresponding geometries as a geometric union.

The `pgsql2shp` command allows you to export PostGIS tables and queries to shapefiles. The options you need to specify are quite similar to the ones you use to connect to PostgreSQL with `psql`. To have a full list of these options, just type `pgsql2shp` in your command prompt and read the output.

# Importing OpenStreetMap data with the osm2pgsql command

In this recipe, you will import **OpenStreetMap (OSM)** data to PostGIS using the `osm2pgsql` command.

You will first download a sample dataset from the OSM website, and then you will import it using the `osm2pgsql` command.

You will add the imported layers in a GIS Desktop software and generate a view to get subdatasets, using the `hstore` PostgreSQL additional module to extract features based on their tags.

## Getting ready

We need the following in place before we can proceed with the steps required for the recipe:

1. Install `osm2pgsql`. If you are using Windows, follow the instructions available at `http://wiki.openstreetmap.org/wiki/Osm2pgsql`. If you are on Linux, you can install it from the preceding website or from packages. For example, for Debian distributions, use the following:

   ```
   $ sudo apt-get install osm2pgsql
   ```

2. For more information about the installation of the `osm2pgsql` command for the other Linux distributions, Mac OS X, and MS Windows, please refer to the `osm2pgsql` web page available at `http://wiki.openstreetmap.org/wiki/Osm2pgsql`.

3. Although, it's most likely that you will need to compile `osm2pgsql` yourself as the one that is installed with your package manager could already be obsolete. In my Linux Mint 12 box, this was the case (it was `osm2pgsql` v0.75), so I have installed Version 0.80 following the instructions on the `osm2pgsql` web page. You can check the installed version just by typing the following command:

   ```
   $ osm2pgsql

   osm2pgsql SVN version 0.80.0 (32bit id space)
   ```

4. We will create a different database only for this recipe, as we will use this OSM database in other chapters. For this purpose, create a new database named `rome` and assign privileges to your user:

   ```
   postgres=# CREATE DATABASE rome OWNER me;

   postgres=# \connect rome;

   rome=# create extension postgis;
   ```

5. You will not create a different schema in this new database, though, as the `osm2pgsql` command can only import OSM data in the public schema at the time of writing.

6. Be sure that your PostgreSQL installation supports `hstore`. If not, download and install it; for example, in Debian-based Linux distributions, you will need to install the `postgresql-contrib-9.1` package. Then, add the `hstore` support to the `rome` database using the `CREATE EXTENSION` syntax:

   ```
   $ sudo apt-get update

   $ sudo apt-get install postgresql-contrib-9.1

   $ psql -U me -d romerome=# CREATE EXTENSION hstore;
   ```

## How to do it...

The steps you need to follow to complete this recipe are as follows:

1. Download a .osm file from the openstreetmap.org website:

    1. Go to the openstreetmap.org website.

    2. Select the area of interest for which you want to export data. You should not select a large area, as the live export from the website is limited to 50,000 nodes.

     If you want to export larger areas, you should consider downloading the whole database, built daily at planet.osm (250 GB uncompressed and 16 GB compressed). At planet.osm, you may also download extracts that contain OpenstreetMap Data for individual continents, countries, and metropolitan areas.

    3. If you want to get the same dataset used for this recipe, just copy and paste the following URL in your browser: http://www.openstreetmap.org/export?lat=41.88745&lon=12.4899&zoom=15&layers=M; or, get it from the book datasets (chp01/map.osm file).

    4. Click on the **Export** link.

    5. Select **OpenStreetMap XML Data** as the output format.

    6. Download the map.osm file to your working directory.

2. Run osm2pgsql to import the OSM data in the PostGIS database. Use the -hstore option, as you wish to add tags with an additional hstore (key/value) column in the PostgreSQL tables:

```
$ osm2pgsql -d rome -U me --hstore map.osm

osm2pgsql SVN version 0.80.0 (32bit id space)
Using projection SRS 900913 (Spherical Mercator)
Setting up table: planet_osm_point
...
All indexes on planet_osm_polygon created in 1s
Completed planet_osm_polygon
Osm2pgsql took 3s overall
```

3. At this point, you should have the following geometry tables in your database:

```
rome=# SELECT f_table_name, f_geometry_column, coord_dimension,
srid, type FROM geometry_columns;
```

The output of the preceding command is as shown below:

```
    f_table_name    | f_geometry_column | coord_dimension |   srid
  |   type
------------------+-------------------+-----------------+-------
--+-----------
   planet_osm_roads | way               |               2 | 900913
  | LINESTRING
   planet_osm_point | way               |               2 | 900913
  | POINT
   planet_osm_polygon | way             |               2 | 900913
  | GEOMETRY
   planet_osm_line  | way               |               2 | 900913
  | LINESTRING
  (4 rows)
```

4.  Note that the `osm2pgsql` command imports everything in the public schema. If you did not deal differently with the command's input parameter, your data is imported in the Mercator Projection (`900913`).

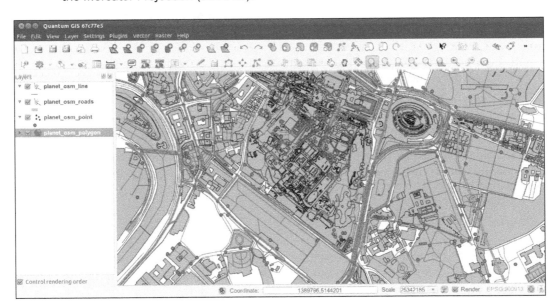

5.  Open the PostGIS tables and inspect them with your favorite Desktop GIS. The preceding screenshot shows how it looks in QGIS. All the different thematic features are mixed at this time, so it looks a bit confusing.

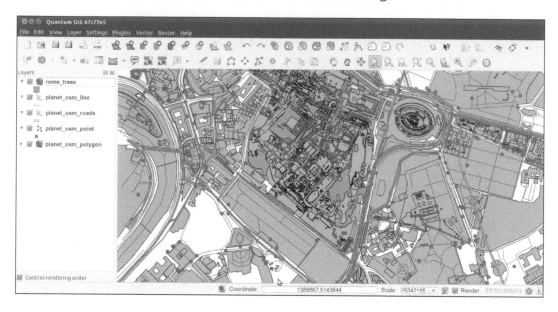

6.  Generate a PostGIS view that extracts all the polygons tagged with `trees` as `land cover`. For this purpose, create the following view:

```
rome=# CREATE VIEW rome_trees AS
  SELECT way, tags FROM planet_osm_polygon
  WHERE (tags -> 'landcover') = 'trees';
```

7.  Open the view with a Desktop GIS that supports PostGIS views, such as QGIS, and add your `rome_trees` view. The preceding screenshot shows you how it looks.

## How it works...

OpenStreetMap is a popular collaborative project for creating a free map of the world. Every user participating in the project can edit data; at the same time, it is possible for everyone to download those datasets in `.osm` datafiles (an XML format) under the terms of the **Open Data Commons Open Database License** (**ODbL**) at the time of writing.

The `osm2pgsql` command is a command-line tool that can import `.osm` datafiles (eventually zipped) to the PostGIS database. For using the command, it is enough to give the PostgreSQL connection parameters and the `.osm` file to import.

It is possible to import only features having certain tags in the spatial database, as defined in the `default.style` configuration file. You can decide to comment in or out from this file the OSM tagged features that you would like to import or not. The command by default exports all the nodes and ways to linestring, point, and geometry PostGIS geometries.

It is highly recommended to enable the `hstore` support in the PostgreSQL database and use the `-hstore` option of `osm2pgsql` when importing the data. Having enabled this support, the OSM tags for each feature will be stored in an `hstore` PostgreSQL data type, which is optimized for storing (and retrieving) sets of key/values pairs in a single field. This way it will be possible to query the database as follows

```
SELECT way, tags FROM planet_osm_polygon
  WHERE (tags -> 'landcover') = 'trees';
```

# Importing raster data with the raster2pgsql PostGIS command

PostGIS 2.0 now has full support for raster datasets, and it is possible to import raster datasets using the `raster2pgsql` command.

In this recipe, you will import a raster file to PostGIS using the `raster2pgsql` command. This command, included in any PostGIS distribution from Version 2.0 onward, is able to generate an sql dump to be loaded in PostGIS for any GDAL raster-supported format (in the same fashion that the command `shp2pgsql` does for shapefiles).

After loading the raster to PostGIS, you will inspect it both with SQL commands (analyzing the raster metadata information contained in the database), and with the `gdalinfo` command-line utility (to understand the way the input `raster2pgsql` parameters have been reflected in the PostGIS import process).

You will finally open the raster in a Desktop GIS and try a basic spatial query-mixing vector and raster tables.

## Getting ready

We need the following in place before we can proceed with the steps required for the recipe:

1. From the `worldclim.org` website, download the current raster data (`http://www.worldclim.org/current`) for min and max temperatures (only the raster for max temperatures will be used for this recipe). Alternatively, use the ones provided in the book datasets (`data/chp01`). Each of the two archives (`data/tmax_10m_bil.zip` and `data/tmin_10m_bil.zip`) contain 12 rasters in the BIL format, one for each month. You can look for more information at `http://www.worldclim.org/formats`.

2. Extract the two archives to a directory named `worldclim` in your working directory.

3. Rename each raster dataset to a name format having two digits for the month, for example, `tmax1.bil` and `tmax1.hdr` will become `tmax01.bil` and `tmax01.hdr`.

4. If you still haven't loaded the countries shapefile to PostGIS from a previous recipe, do it using the `ogr2ogr` or `shp2pgsql` commands. The following is the `shp2pgsql` syntax:

```
$ shp2pgsql -I -d -s 4326 -W LATIN1 -g the_geom countries.shp
chp01.countries > countries.sql
$ psql -U me -d postgis_cookbook -f countries.sql
```

## How to do it...

The steps you need to follow to complete this recipe are as follows:

1. Get information about one of the rasters using the `gdalinfo` command-line tool as follows:

```
$ gdalinfo worldclim/tmax09.bil
Driver: EHdr/ESRI .hdr Labelled
Files: worldclim/tmax9.bil
       worldclim/tmax9.hdr
Size is 2160, 900
Coordinate System is:
GEOGCS["WGS 84",
  DATUM["WGS_1984",
    SPHEROID["WGS 84",6378137,298.257223563,
      AUTHORITY["EPSG","7030"]],
    TOWGS84[0,0,0,0,0,0,0],
    AUTHORITY["EPSG","6326"]],
  PRIMEM["Greenwich",0,
    AUTHORITY["EPSG","8901"]],
  UNIT["degree",0.0174532925199433,
  AUTHORITY["EPSG","9108"]],
AUTHORITY["EPSG","4326"]]
Origin = (-180.000000000000057,90.000000000000000)
Pixel Size = (0.166666666666667,-0.166666666666667)
Corner Coordinates:
  Upper Left   (-180.0000000,  90.0000000) (180d 0' 0.00"W, 90d
    0' 0.00"N)
  Lower Left   (-180.0000000, -60.0000000) (180d 0' 0.00"W, 60d
    0' 0.00"S)
  Upper Right  ( 180.0000000,  90.0000000) (180d 0' 0.00"E, 90d
    0' 0.00"N)
```

```
Lower Right ( 180.0000000, -60.0000000) (180d 0' 0.00"E, 60d
    0' 0.00"S)
Center     (   0.0000000, 15.0000000) (  0d 0' 0.00"E, 15d
    0' 0.00"N)
Band 1 Block=2160x1 Type=Int16, ColorInterp=Undefined
Min=-153.000 Max=441.000
NoData Value=-9999
```

2. The `gdalinfo` command provides a series of useful information about the raster, for example, the GDAL driver being used to read it, the files composing it (in this case, two files with a `.bil` and `.hdr` extension), the size in pixels (2160 x 900), the spatial reference (WGS 84), the geographic extents, the origin and the pixel size (needed to correctly georeference the raster), and for each raster band (just one in the case of this file), some statistical information like the min and max value (-153.000 and 441.000, corresponding to a temperature of -15.3 °C and 44.1 °C. Values are expressed as temperature * 10 in °C, according to the documentation available at `worldclim.org`).

3. Use the `raster2pgsql` file to generate the `.sql` dump file and then import the raster in PostGIS:

```
$ raster2pgsql -I -C -F -t 100x100 -s 4326 worldclim/tmax01.bil
chp01.tmax01 > tmax01.sql

$ psql -d postgis_cookbook -U me -f tmax01.sql
```

If you are in Linux, you may pipe the two commands in a unique line:

```
$ raster2pgsql -I -C -M -F -t 100x100 worldclim/tmax1.bil chp01.
tmax01 | psql -d postgis_cookbook -U me -f tmax01.sql
```

4. Check how the new table has been created in PostGIS:

```
$ pg_dump -t chp01.tmax01 --schema-only -U me postgis_cookbook
...
CREATE TABLE tmax01 (
    rid integer NOT NULL,
    rast public.raster,
    filename text,
    CONSTRAINT enforce_height_rast CHECK ((public.st_height(rast)
= 100)),
    CONSTRAINT enforce_max_extent_rast CHECK (public.st_
coveredby(public.st_convexhull(rast), '0103...'::public.
geometry)),
    CONSTRAINT enforce_nodata_values_rast CHECK (((public._
raster_constraint_nodata_values(rast))::numeric(16,10)[] =
'{0}'::numeric(16,10)[])),
```

```
        CONSTRAINT enforce_num_bands_rast CHECK ((public.st_
numbands(rast) = 1)),

        CONSTRAINT enforce_out_db_rast CHECK ((public._raster_
constraint_out_db(rast) = '{f}'::boolean[])),

        CONSTRAINT enforce_pixel_types_rast CHECK ((public._raster_
constraint_pixel_types(rast) = '{16BUI}'::text[])),

        CONSTRAINT enforce_same_alignment_rast CHECK (public.st_
samealignment(rast, '01000...'::public.raster)),

        CONSTRAINT enforce_scalex_rast CHECK
(((public.st_scalex(rast))::numeric(16,10) =
0.166666666666667::numeric(16,10))),

        CONSTRAINT enforce_scaley_rast CHECK
(((public.st_scaley(rast))::numeric(16,10) =
(-0.166666666666667)::numeric(16,10))),

        CONSTRAINT enforce_srid_rast CHECK ((public.st_srid(rast) =
0)),

        CONSTRAINT enforce_width_rast CHECK ((public.st_width(rast) =
100))
);
```

5.  Check if a record for this PostGIS raster appears in the `raster_columns` metadata view, and note the main metadata information that has been stored there such as schema, name, raster column name (default is raster), SRID, scale (for x and y), block size (for x and y), band numbers (1), band types (`16BUI`), zero data values (0), and db storage type (`out_db` is false, as we have stored the raster bytes in the database; you could have used the `-R` option to register the raster as an out-of-db filesystem):

```
postgis_cookbook=# SELECT * FROM raster_columns;
```

6.  If you have followed this recipe from the beginning, you should now have 198 rows in the raster table, with each row representing one raster block size (100 x 100 pixels blocks, as indicated with the `-t raster2pgsql` option):

```
postgis_cookbook=# SELECT count(*) FROM chp01.tmax01;
```

The output of the preceding command is as follows:

```
 count
-------
   198
(1 row)
```

7. Try to open the raster table with `gdalinfo`. You should see the same information you got from `gdalinfo` when you were analyzing the original BIL file. The only difference is the block size, as you moved to a smaller one (100x100) from the original (2160x900). That's why the original file has been split into several datasets (198):

```
gdalinfo PG":host=localhost port=5432 dbname=postgis_cookbook
user=me password=mypassword schema='chp01' table='tmax01'"
```

8. The `gdalinfo` command reads the PostGIS raster as being composed of multiple raster subdatasets (198, one for each row in the table). You still have the possibility of reading the whole table as a single raster, using the `mode=2` option in the PostGIS raster connection string (`mode=1` is the default). Check the difference:

```
gdalinfo PG":host=localhost port=5432 dbname=postgis_cookbook
user=me password=mypassword schema='chp01' table='tmax01' mode=2"
```

9. You can easily obtain a visual representation of those blocks by converting the extent of all the 198 rows in the `tmax01` table (each representing a raster block) to a shapefile using `ogr2ogr`:

```
$ ogr2ogr temp_grid.shp PG:"host=localhost port=5432
dbname='postgis_cookbook' user='me' password='mypassword'" -sql
"SELECT rid, filename, ST_Envelope(rast) as the_geom FROM chp01.
tmax01"
```

10. Now, try to open the raster table with QGIS (at the time of writing, one of the few Desktop GIS tools had support for it) together with the blocks shapefile generated in the previous steps (`temp_grid.shp`). You should see something like the following screenshot:

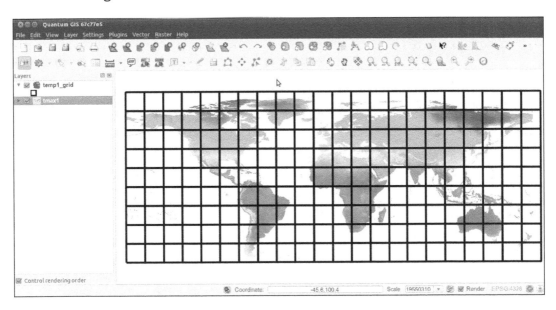

If you are using QGIS, you need the PostGIS raster QGIS plugin to read and write the PostGIS raster. This plugin makes it possible to add single rows of the `tmax01` table as a single raster or the whole table. Try to add a couple of rows.

11. As the last bonus step, you will select the 10 countries with the lowest average max temperature in January (using the centroid of the polygon representing the country):

```
SELECT * FROM (
   SELECT c.name, ST_Value(t.rast, ST_Centroid(c.the_geom))/10 as
tmax_jan FROM chp01.tmax01 AS t
   JOIN chp01.countries AS c
   ON ST_Intersects(t.rast, ST_Centroid(c.the_geom))
) AS foo
ORDER BY tmax_jan LIMIT 10;
```

The output is as follows:

```
name                                              | tmax_jan
--------------------------------------------------+----------
Greenland                                         |    -29.8
  ...
Korea                                             |     -8.5
Democratic People's Republic of Kyrgyzstan        |     -7.9
Finland                                           |     -6.8
(10 rows)
```

## How it works...

The `raster2pgsql` command is able to load any raster formats supported by GDAL in PostGIS. You can have a format list supported by your GDAL installation by typing the following command:

```
$ gdalinfo -formats
```

In this recipe, you have been importing one raster file using some of the most common `raster2pgsql` options:

```
$ raster2pgsql -I -C -F -t 100x100 -s 4326 worldclim/tmax01.bil chp01.
tmax01 > tmax01.sql
```

The `-I` option creates a GIST spatial index for the raster column. The `-C` option will create the standard set of constraints after the rasters have been loaded. The `-F` option will add a column with the filename of the raster that has been loaded. This is useful when you are appending many raster files to the same PostGIS raster table. The `-s` option sets the raster's SRID.

If you decide to include the -t option, then you will cut the original raster in tiles, each inserted as a single row in the raster table. In this case, you decided to cut the raster in 100x100 tiles, resulting in 198 table rows in the raster table.

Another important option is -R, which will register the raster as out-of-db; in such a case, only the metadata will be inserted in the database, while the raster will be out of the database.

The raster table contains an identifier for each row, the raster itself (eventually one of its tiles, if using the -t option), and eventually the original filename, if you used the -F option, as in this case.

You can analyze the PostGIS raster using SQL commands or the gdalinfo command. Using SQL, you can query the raster_columns view for getting the most significant raster metadata (spatial reference, band number, scale, block size, and so on).

With gdalinfo, you can access the same information, using a connection string with the following syntax:

```
gdalinfo PG":host=localhost port=5432 dbname=postgis_cookbook user=me
password=mypassword schema='chp01' table='tmax01' mode=2"
```

The mode parameter is not influential if you loaded the whole raster as a single block (for example, if you did not specify the -t option). But, as in the use case of this recipe, if you split it in tiles, gdalinfo will see each tile as a single subdataset with the default behavior (mode-1). If you want GDAL to consider the raster table as a unique raster dataset, you have to specify the mode option and explicitly set it to 2.

# Importing multiple rasters at a time

This recipe will guide you through the import of multiple rasters at a time.

You will first import some different single band rasters to a unique single band raster table using the raster2pgsql command.

Then, you will try an alternative approach, merging the original single band rasters in a virtual raster, having one band for each of the original rasters, and then load the multiband raster to a raster table. For accomplishing this, you will use the GDAL gdalbuildvrt command and then load the data to PostGIS with raster2pgsql.

## Getting ready

Be sure to have all the original raster datasets you have been using for the previous recipe.

## How to do it...

The steps you need to follow to complete this recipe are as follows:

1.  Import all the maximum average temperature rasters in a single PostGIS raster table using `raster2pgsql` and then `psql` (eventually, pipe the two commands if you are in Linux):

    ```
    $ raster2pgsql -d -I -C -M -F -t 100x100 -s 4326 worldclim/tmax*.
    bil chp01.tmax_2012 > tmax_2012.sql
    ```

    ```
    $ psql -d postgis_cookbook -U me -f tmax_2012.sql
    ```

2.  Check how the table was created in PostGIS, querying the `raster_columns` table. Here we are querying only some significant fields:

    ```
    postgis_cookbook=# SELECT r_raster_column, srid,
    ROUND(scale_x::numeric, 2) AS scale_x, ROUND(scale_y::numeric,
    2) AS scale_y, blocksize_x, blocksize_y, num_bands, pixel_
    types, nodata_values, out_db FROM raster_columns where r_table_
    schema='chp01' AND  r_table_name ='tmax_2012';

     r_raster_column | srid | scale_x | scale_y | blocksize_x |
    blocksize_y | num_bands | pixel_types | nodata_values | out_db
    -----------------+------+---------+---------+-------------+------
    ------+-----------+-------------+---------------+--------
     rast            | 4326 |   0.17  |  -0.17  |       100    |
    100 |         1 | {16BUI}     | {0}         | {f}
    (1 row)
    ```

3.  Check some raster statistics using the `ST_MetaData` function:

    ```
    SELECT rid, (foo.md).*

        FROM (SELECT rid, ST_MetaData(rast) As md FROM chp01.
    tmax_2012) As foo;
    ```

     Note that there is a different metadata for each raster record loaded in the table.

4.  If you now query the table, you would be able to derive the month for each raster row only from the `original_file` column. In the table, you have imported 198 distinct records (raster) for each of the 12 original files (we divided them into 100x100 blocks, if you remember). Test this with the following query:

    ```
    postgis_cookbook=# SELECT COUNT(*) AS num_raster, MIN(filename) as
    original_file FROM chp01.tmax_2012

    GROUP BY filename ORDER BY filename;

     num_raster | original_file
    ------------+---------------
    ```

```
198 | tmax01.bil
198 | tmax02.bil
198 | tmax03.bil
198 | tmax04.bil
198 | tmax05.bil
198 | tmax06.bil
198 | tmax07.bil
198 | tmax08.bil
198 | tmax09.bil
198 | tmax10.bil
198 | tmax11.bil
198 | tmax12.bil
```

(12 rows)

5. With this approach, using the `filename` field, you could use the `ST_Value` PostGIS raster function to get the average monthly maximum temperature of a certain geographic zone for the whole year:

```
SELECT REPLACE(REPLACE(filename, 'tmax', ''), '.bil', '') AS
month,
                 (ST_VALUE(rast, ST_SetSRID(ST_Point(12.49, 41.88),
4326))/10) AS tmax
                 FROM chp01.tmax_2012
                 WHERE rid IN (
                         SELECT rid FROM chp01.tmax_2012
                         WHERE ST_Intersects(ST_Envelope(rast), ST_
SetSRID(ST_Point(12.49, 41.88), 4326))
                         )
                 ORDER BY month;
```

```
month | tmax
-------+------
 01    | 11.8
 02    | 13.2
 03    | 15.3
 04    | 18.5
 05    | 22.9
 06    | 27
 07    | 30
 08    | 29.8
```

```
09    | 26.4
10    | 21.7
11    | 16.6
12    | 12.9
(12 rows)
```

6. A different approach is to store each month value in a different raster band. The `raster2pgsql` command doesn't let you load to different bands in an existing table. But, you can use GDAL by combining the `gdalbuildvrt` and the `gdal_translate` commands. First, use `gdalbuildvrt` to create a new virtual raster composed of 12 bands, one for each month:

   ```
   $ gdalbuildvrt -separate tmax_2012.vrt worldclim/tmax*.bil
   ```

7. Analyze the `tmax_2012.vrt` xml file with a text editor. It should have a virtual band (`VRTRasterBand`) for each physical raster pointing to it:

   ```
   <VRTDataset rasterXSize="2160" rasterYSize="900">
     <SRS>GEOGCS...</SRS>
     <GeoTransform> -1.8000000000000006e+02,
       1.6666666666666699e-01,  ...</GeoTransform>
     <VRTRasterBand dataType="Int16" band="1">
     <NoDataValue>-9.99900000000000E+03</NoDataValue>
     <ComplexSource>
     <SourceFilename
       relativeToVRT="1">worldclim/tmax01.bil</SourceFilename>
     <SourceBand>1</SourceBand>
     <SourceProperties RasterXSize="2160" RasterYSize="900"
       DataType="Int16" BlockXSize="2160" BlockYSize="1" />
       <SrcRect xOff="0" yOff="0" xSize="2160" ySize="900" />
       <DstRect xOff="0" yOff="0" xSize="2160" ySize="900" />
       <NODATA>-9999</NODATA>
     </ComplexSource>
     </VRTRasterBand>
     <VRTRasterBand dataType="Int16" band="2">
     . . .
   ```

8. Now, with `gdalinfo`, analyze this output virtual raster to check if it is effectively composed of 12 bands:

   ```
   $ gdalinfo tmax_2012.vrt
   ```

   The output of the preceding command is as follows:

   ```
   Driver: VRT/Virtual Raster
   Files: tmax_2012.vrt
           worldclim/tmax01.bil
   ```

```
        worldclim/tmax02.bil

        . . .

        worldclim/tmax12.bil

    Size is 2160, 900

    Coordinate System is:

    GEOGCS["WGS 84",

        DATUM["WGS_1984",

            . . .

    Band 1 Block=128x128 Type=Int16, ColorInterp=Undefined

      Min=-478.000 Max=418.000

      NoData Value=-9999

    Band 2 Block=128x128 Type=Int16, ColorInterp=Undefined

      Min=-421.000 Max=414.000

      NoData Value=-9999

    . . .
```

9.  Import the virtual raster composed of 12 bands, each referring to one of the 12 original rasters, to a PostGIS raster table composed of 12 bands. For this purpose, you can use the `raster2pgsql` command:

```
$ raster2pgsql -d -I -C -M -F -t 100x100 -s 4326 tmax_2012.vrt
chp01.tmax_2012_multi > tmax_2012_multi.sql

$ psql -d postgis_cookbook -U me -f tmax_2012_multi.sql
```

10. Query the `raster_columns` view to get some indicators for the imported raster. Note as the num_bands is now 12:

```
    postgis_cookbook=# SELECT r_raster_column, srid, blocksize_x,
blocksize_y, num_bands, pixel_types from raster_columns where r_
table_schema='chp01' AND  r_table_name ='tmax_2012_multi';

 r_raster_column | srid | blocksize_x | blocksize_y | num_bands |
pixel_types

-----------------+------+-------------+-------------+-----------+-
--------------------------------------------------------------------
--------

 rast            | 4326 |         100 |         100 |        12 |
{16BSI,16BSI,16BSI,16BSI,16BSI,16BSI,16BSI,16BSI,16BSI,16BSI,16BSI
,16BSI}
```

11. Now, let's try to produce the same output of the query with the previous approach. This time, given the table structure, we keep the results in a single row:

```
postgis_cookbook=# SELECT
(ST_VALUE(rast, 1, ST_SetSRID(ST_Point(12.49, 41.88), 4326))/10)
AS jan,
(ST_VALUE(rast, 2, ST_SetSRID(ST_Point(12.49, 41.88), 4326))/10)
AS feb,
(ST_VALUE(rast, 3, ST_SetSRID(ST_Point(12.49, 41.88), 4326))/10)
AS mar,
(ST_VALUE(rast, 4, ST_SetSRID(ST_Point(12.49, 41.88), 4326))/10)
AS apr,
(ST_VALUE(rast, 5, ST_SetSRID(ST_Point(12.49, 41.88), 4326))/10)
AS may,
(ST_VALUE(rast, 6, ST_SetSRID(ST_Point(12.49, 41.88), 4326))/10)
AS jun,
(ST_VALUE(rast, 7, ST_SetSRID(ST_Point(12.49, 41.88), 4326))/10)
AS jul,
(ST_VALUE(rast, 8, ST_SetSRID(ST_Point(12.49, 41.88), 4326))/10)
AS aug,
(ST_VALUE(rast, 9, ST_SetSRID(ST_Point(12.49, 41.88), 4326))/10)
AS sep,
(ST_VALUE(rast, 10, ST_SetSRID(ST_Point(12.49, 41.88), 4326))/10)
AS oct,
(ST_VALUE(rast, 11, ST_SetSRID(ST_Point(12.49, 41.88), 4326))/10)
AS nov,
(ST_VALUE(rast, 12, ST_SetSRID(ST_Point(12.49, 41.88), 4326))/10)
AS dec
FROM chp01.tmax_2012_multi WHERE rid IN (SELECT rid FROM chp01.
tmax_2012_multi
WHERE ST_Intersects(rast, ST_SetSRID(ST_Point(12.49, 41.88),
4326)));
```

The output of the preceding command is as follows:

```
jan | feb | mar | apr | may | jun | jul | aug | sep | oct | nov |
dec
----+-----+-----+-----+-----+-----+-----+-----+-----+-----+-----+-
---
11.8| 13.2| 15.3| 18.5| 22.9| 27  | 30  | 29.8| 26.4| 21.7|
16.6|12.9
(1 row)
```

## How it works...

You can import raster datasets in PostGIS using the `raster2pgsql` command.

 The GDAL PostGIS raster so far does not support writing operations; therefore, for now, you cannot use GDAL commands such as `gdal_translate` and `gdalwarp`.

This is going to change in the near future, so you may have such an extra option when you are reading this chapter.

In a scenario where you have multiple rasters representing the same variable at a time, as in this recipe, it makes sense to store all of the original rasters as a single table in PostGIS. In this recipe, we have the same variable (average maximum temperature) represented by a single raster for each month. You have seen that you could proceed in two different ways:

1. Append each single raster (representing a different month) to the same PostGIS single band raster table and derive the information related to the month from the value in the filename column (added to the table using the `-F raster2pgsql` option).

2. Generate a multiband raster using `gdalbuildvrt` (one raster with 12 bands, one for each month), and import it in a single multiband PostGIS table using the `raster2pgsql` command.

# Exporting rasters with the gdal_translate and gdalwarp GDAL commands

In this recipe, you will see a couple of main options for exporting PostGIS rasters to different raster formats. They are both provided as command-line tools, `gdal_translate` and `gdalwarp`, by GDAL.

## Getting ready

You need the following in place before you can proceed with the steps required for the recipe:

1. You need to have gone through the previous recipe and imported the tmax 2012 datasets (12 `.bil` files) as a single multiband (12 bands) raster in PostGIS.

2. You must have the PostGIS raster format enabled in GDAL. For this purpose, check the output of the following command:

```
$ gdalinfo --formats | grep -i postgis
```

The output of the preceding command is as follows:

```
PostGISRaster (rw): PostGIS Raster driver
```

3. You should have already learned how to use the GDAL PostGIS raster driver in the previous two recipes. You need to use a connection string composed of the following parameters:

```
$ gdalinfo PG:"host=localhost port=5432 dbname='postgis_cookbook'
user='me' password='mypassword' schema='chp01'password='mypasswo
rd' schema='chp01' table='tmax_2012_multi' mode='2'"
```

4. Refer to the previous two recipes for more information about the preceding parameters.

## How to do it...

The steps you need to follow to complete this recipe are as follows:

1. As an initial test, you will export the first six months of the tmax for 2012 (the first six bands in the `tmax_2012_multi` PostGIS raster table) using the `gdal_translate` command:

```
$ gdal_translate -b 1 -b 2 -b 3 -b 4 -b 5 -b 6
PG:"host=localhost port=5432 dbname='postgis_cookbook' user='me'
password='mypassword' schema='chp01' table='tmax_2012_multi'
mode='2'" tmax_2012_multi_123456.tif
```

2. As the second test, you will export all of the bands, but only for the geographic area containing Italy. Use the `ST_Extent` command for getting the geographic extent of that zone:

```
postgis_cookbook=# SELECT ST_Extent(the_geom) FROM chp01.countries
WHERE name = 'Italy';
```

The output of the preceding command is as follows:

```
                          st_extent
-----------------------------------------------------------------
 BOX(6.61975999999999 36.649162,18.514999 47.0947189999999)
(1 row)
```

3. Now use the `gdal_translate` command with the `-projwin` option for obtaining the desired purpose:

```
$ gdal_translate -projwin 6.619 47.095 18.515 36.649
PG:"host=localhost port=5432 dbname='postgis_cookbook' user='me'
password='mypassword' schema='chp01' table='tmax_2012_multi'
mode='2'" tmax_2012_multi.tif
```

4. There is another GDAL command, `gdalwarp`, that is still a convert utility with reprojection and advanced warping functionalities. You can use it, for example, to export a PostGIS raster table, reprojecting it to a different spatial reference system. This will convert the PostGIS raster table to GeoTiff and reproject it from `EPSG:4326` to `EPSG:3857`:

```
gdalwarp -t_srs EPSG:3857 PG:"host=localhost port=5432
dbname='postgis_cookbook' user='me' password='mypassword'
schema='chp01' table='tmax_2012_multi' mode='2'" tmax_2012_
multi_3857.tif
```

## How it works...

Both `gdal_translate` and `gdalwarp` can transform rasters from the PostGIS raster to all the GDAL-supported formats. To have a complete list of the supported formats, you can use the `--formats` option of one of the GDAL's command line as follows:

```
$ gdalinfo --formats
```

For both these GDAL commands, the default output format is GeoTiff; if you need a different format, you must use the `-of` option and assign to it one of the outputs produced by the previous command line.

In this recipe, you have tried some of the most common options for these two commands. As they are complex tools, you may try some more command options as a bonus step.

## See also

To have a better understanding, you should check out the excellent documentation on the GDAL website:

▸ The information about the `gdal_translate` command is available at http://www.gdal.org/gdal_translate.html

▸ The information about the `gdalwarp` command is available at http://www.gdal.org/gdalwarp.html

# 2
# Structures that Work

In this chapter, we will cover:

- ▶ Using geospatial views
- ▶ Using triggers to populate a geometry column
- ▶ Structuring spatial data with table inheritance
- ▶ Extending inheritance – table partitioning
- ▶ Normalizing imports
- ▶ Normalizing internal overlays
- ▶ Using polygon overlays for proportional census estimates

## Introduction

This chapter focuses on ways to structure data using the functionality provided by the combination of PostgreSQL and PostGIS. These will be useful approaches for structuring and cleaning up imported data, converting tabular data into spatial data "on the fly" as it is entered, and maintaining relationships between tables and datasets using functionality endemic to the powerful combination of PostgreSQL and PostGIS. There are three categories of techniques by which we will leverage these functionalities: automatic population and modification of data using views and triggers, object orientation using PostgreSQL table inheritance, and using PostGIS functions (stored procedures) to reconstruct and normalize problematic data.

Automatic population of data is where this chapter begins. By leveraging PostgreSQL views and triggers, we can create ad hoc and flexible solutions to create connections between and within the tables. By extension, and for more formal or structured cases, PostgreSQL provides table inheritance and table partitioning that allow for explicit hierarchical relationships between tables. This can be useful in cases where an object inheritance model enforces data relationships that either represent the data better, thereby resulting in greater efficiencies, or reduce the administrative overhead of maintaining and accessing the datasets over time. With PostGIS extending that functionality, the inheritance can apply not just to the commonly used table attributes, but can also leverage spatial relationships between tables, resulting in greater query efficiency with very large datasets. Finally, we will explore PostGIS SQL patterns that provide table normalization of data inputs, so datasets that come from flat filesystems or are not normalized can be converted to a form we would expect in a database.

# Using geospatial views

Views in PostgreSQL allow for ad hoc representation of data and data relationships in alternate forms. In this recipe, we'll be using views to allow for the automatic creation of point data based on tabular inputs. We can imagine a case where the input stream of data is non-spatial, but includes longitude and latitude or some other coordinates. We would like to automatically show this data as points in space.

## Getting ready

We can create a view as a representation of spatial data pretty easily. The syntax for creating a view is similar to creating a table; for example:

```
CREATE VIEW viewname AS
    SELECT...
```

In the preceding command line, our SELECT query manipulates the data for us. Let's start with a small dataset. In this case, we will start with some random points.

First, we create the table from which the view will be constructed as follows:

```
-- Drop the table in case it exists
DROP TABLE IF EXISTS chp02.xwhyzed CASCADE;
CREATE TABLE chp02.xwhyzed
-- This table will contain numeric x, y, and z values
(
  x numeric,
  y numeric,
  z numeric
)
WITH (OIDS=FALSE);
```

```
ALTER TABLE chp02.xwhyzed OWNER TO postgres;
-- We will be disciplined and ensure we have a primary key
ALTER TABLE chp02.xwhyzed ADD COLUMN gid serial;
ALTER TABLE chp02.xwhyzed ADD PRIMARY KEY (gid);
```

Now let's populate this with data for testing using the following query:

```
INSERT INTO chp02.xwhyzed (x, y, z)
  VALUES (random()*5, random()*7, random()*106);
INSERT INTO chp02.xwhyzed (x, y, z)
  VALUES (random()*5, random()*7, random()*106);
INSERT INTO chp02.xwhyzed (x, y, z)
  VALUES (random()*5, random()*7, random()*106);
INSERT INTO chp02.xwhyzed (x, y, z)
  VALUES (random()*5, random()*7, random()*106);
```

## How to do it...

Now to create the view, we will use the following query:

```
-- Ensure we don't try to duplicate the view
DROP VIEW IF EXISTS chp02.xbecausezed;
-- Retain original attributes, but also create a point
   attribute from x and y
CREATE VIEW chp02.xbecausezed AS
  SELECT x, y, z, ST_MakePoint(x,y)
  FROM chp02.xwhyzed;
```

## How it works...

Our view is really a simple transformation of the existing data using PostGIS's ST_MakePoint function. The ST_MakePoint function takes the input of two numbers to create a PostGIS point; in this case, our view simply uses our x and y values to populate the data. Any time there is an update to the table to add a new record with x and y values, the view will populate a point, which is really useful for data that is constantly being updated.

There are two disadvantages to this approach. The first is that we have not declared our spatial reference system in the view, so any software consuming these points will not know the coordinate system we are using—that is, whether it is a geographic (latitude/longitude) or a planar coordinate system. We will address this problem shortly. The second problem is that many software systems accessing these points may not automatically detect and use the spatial information from the table. This problem is addressed in the *Using triggers to populate a geometry column* recipe.

**Spatial Reference ID** (**SRID**) allows us to specify the coordinate system for a given dataset. The numbering system is a simple integer value to specify a given coordinate system. SRID is derived originally from the **European Petroleum Survey Group** (**EPSG**) and now maintained by the Surveying & Positioning Committee of the International Association of **Oil & Gas Producers** (**OGP**). Useful tools for SRIDs are Spatial Reference (`http://spatialreference.org`) and Prj2EPSG (`http://prj2epsg.org/search`).

## There's more...

To address the first problem mentioned in the *How it works...* section, we can simply wrap our existing `ST_MakePoint` function in another function specifying the SRID using `ST_SetSRID`, as shown in the following query:

```
-- Ensure we don't try to duplicate the view
DROP VIEW IF EXISTS chp02.xbecausezed;
-- Retain original attributes, but also create a point
   attribute from x and y
CREATE VIEW chp02.xbecausezed AS
  SELECT x, y, z, ST_SetSRID(ST_MakePoint(x,y), 3734) -- Add ST_SetSRID
  FROM chp02.xwhyzed;
```

## See also

 ▸ The *Using triggers to populate a geometry column* recipe

# Using triggers to populate a geometry column

In this recipe, we imagine that we have ongoing updates to our database, which needs spatial representation; however, in this case, we want a hard-coded geometry column to be updated each time an `INSERT` operation takes place on the database, converting our *x* and *y* values to geometry as they are inserted in the database.

The advantage of this approach is that the geometry is then registered in the `geometry_columns` view, and therefore this approach works reliably with more PostGIS client types than creating a geospatial view. This also provides the advantage of allowing for a spatial index that can significantly speed up a variety of queries. The disadvantage for users using PostgreSQL versions lower than Version 9.0 is that, without a `WHERE` clause within the trigger, every time an insert takes place, the trigger will be calculated on all points to create geometry. This method could be very expensive on large datasets. However, for users of PostgreSQL 9.0 and later, a `WHERE` clause makes this trigger perform quickly, as we can constrain the trigger to only those rows that have no geometry yet populated.

## Getting ready

We will start by creating another table of random points with x, y, and z values, as shown in the following query:

```
DROP TABLE IF EXISTS chp02.xwhyzed1 CASCADE;
CREATE TABLE chp02.xwhyzed1
(
  x numeric,
  y numeric,
  z numeric
)
WITH (OIDS=FALSE);
ALTER TABLE chp02.xwhyzed1 OWNER TO postgres;
ALTER TABLE chp02.xwhyzed1 ADD COLUMN gid serial;
ALTER TABLE chp02.xwhyzed1 ADD PRIMARY KEY (gid);

INSERT INTO chp02.xwhyzed1 (x, y, z)
  VALUES (random()*5, random()*7, random()*106);
INSERT INTO chp02.xwhyzed1 (x, y, z)
  VALUES (random()*5, random()*7, random()*106);
INSERT INTO chp02.xwhyzed1 (x, y, z)
  VALUES (random()*5, random()*7, random()*106);
INSERT INTO chp02.xwhyzed1 (x, y, z)
  VALUES (random()*5, random()*7, random()*106);
```

## How to do it...

Now we need a geometry column to populate. By default, the geometry column will be populated with null values. We populate a geometry column using the following query:

```
SELECT AddGeometryColumn ('chp02','xwhyzed1','geom',3734,'POINT',2);
```

We now have a column called `the_geom` with an SRID of `3734`, that is, a point geometry type in two dimensions. Since we have x, y, z data, we could, in principle, populate a 3D point table using a similar approach.

Since all the geometry values are currently null, we will populate them using an `UPDATE` statement as follows:

```
UPDATE chp02.xwhyzed1
  SET geom = ST_SetSRID(ST_MakePoint(x,y), 3734);
```

The query here is simple when broken down. We update the table `xwhyzed1` and set the `the_geom` column using `ST_MakePoint`, construct our point using the x and y columns, and wrap it in an `ST_SetSRID` function in order to apply the appropriate spatial reference information. So far we have just set the table up. Now we need to create a trigger in order to continue to populate this information once the table is in use. The first part of the trigger is a newly populated geometry function using the following query:

```
CREATE OR REPLACE FUNCTION chp02.xyz_pop_geom()
  RETURNS TRIGGER AS $popgeom$

BEGIN
  IF(TG_OP='INSERT') THEN

  UPDATE chp02.xwhyzed1
    SET geom = ST_SetSRID(ST_MakePoint(x,y), 3734)
      WHERE geom IS NULL
    ;

  END IF;
  RETURN NEW;
END;

$popgeom$ LANGUAGE plpgsql;
```

In essence, we have created a function that does exactly what we did manually: it updates the table's geometry column with the combination of `ST_SetSRID` and `ST_MakePoint`. The one exception here is that we've added a `WHERE` clause that allows us to apply this only to rows that have no geometry populated. This is the performant choice.

## There's more...

While we have a function created, we have not yet applied it as a trigger to the table. Let us do that here as follows:

```
CREATE TRIGGER popgeom_insert
  AFTER INSERT ON chp02.xwhyzed1
  FOR EACH STATEMENT EXECUTE PROCEDURE chp02.xyz_pop_geom();
```

Now, any inserts into our table should be populated with new geometry records. Let us do a test insert using the following query:

```
INSERT INTO chp02.xwhyzed1 (x, y, z)
  VALUES (random()*5, random()*7, random()*106);
```

## Extending further...

So far we've implemented an `insert` trigger. What if the value changes for a particular row? In that case, we will require a separate update trigger. We'll change our original function to test the UPDATE case, and we'll use WHEN in our trigger to constrain updates to the column being changed.

Also note that the following function is written with the assumption that the user wants to always update the changing geometries based on the changing values:

```
CREATE OR REPLACE FUNCTION chp02.xyz_pop_geom()
  RETURNS TRIGGER AS $popgeom$

BEGIN
  IF(TG_OP='INSERT') THEN

  UPDATE chp02.xwhyzed1
    SET geom = ST_SetSRID(ST_MakePoint(x,y), 3734)
      WHERE geom IS NULL
    ;

  ELSIF(TG_OP='UPDATE') THEN
  UPDATE chp02.xwhyzed1
    SET geom = ST_SetSRID(ST_MakePoint(x,y), 3734)
    ;

  END IF;
  RETURN NEW;
END;
```

```
$popgeom$ LANGUAGE plpgsql;

CREATE TRIGGER popgeom_insert
  AFTER INSERT ON chp02.xwhyzed1
  FOR EACH ROW
  EXECUTE PROCEDURE chp02.xyz_pop_geom();

CREATE TRIGGER popgeom_update
  AFTER UPDATE ON chp02.xwhyzed1
  FOR EACH ROW
  WHEN (OLD.X IS DISTINCT FROM NEW.X AND OLD.Y IS DISTINCT FROM
    NEW.Y)
  EXECUTE PROCEDURE chp02.xyz_pop_geom();
```

## See also

 ▸   The *Using geospatial views* recipe

# Structuring spatial data with table inheritance

An unusual and useful property of PostgreSQL databases is that they allow for object inheritance models as they apply to tables. This means that we can have parent/child relationships between tables and leverage that to structure out data in meaningful ways. In our example, we will apply this to hydrology data. This data can be points, lines, polygons, or more complex structures, but they have one commonality; they are explicitly linked in a physical sense and inherently related and are all about water. Water/hydrology is an excellent natural system to model this way, as our ways of modeling it spatially can be quite mixed depending on scales, details, the data collection process, and a host of other factors.

## Getting ready

The data we will be using is hydrology data that has been modified from engineering "blue lines" (see the following screenshot), that is, hydrologic data that is very detailed and meant to be used at scales approaching 1:600. The data in their original application aided in detailed digital terrain modeling.

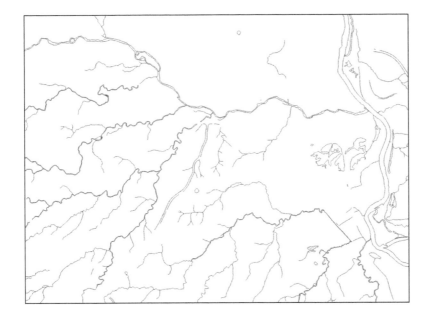

While useful in itself, the data was further manipulated, separating the linear features from area features, with additional polygonization of area features as shown in the following screenshot:

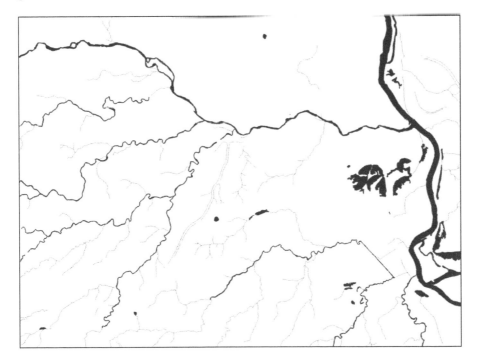

Finally, the data was classified into basic waterway categories as follows:

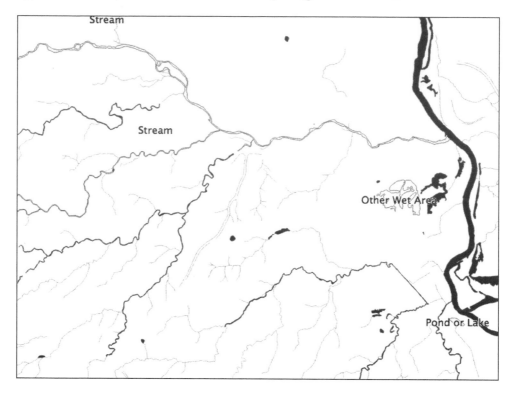

In addition, a process was undertaken to generate centerlines for polygon features such as streams, which are effectively linear features, as follows:

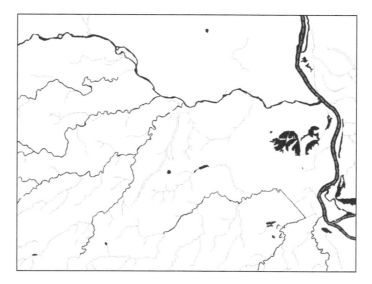

Hence, we have three separate but related datasets:

- ▸ cuyahoga_hydro_polygon
- ▸ cuyahoga_hydro_polyline
- ▸ cuyahoga_river_centerlines

Now, let us look at the structure of the tabular data. The `ogrinfo` utility can help us with this as shown in the following command that is run on the command line:

```
> ogrinfo cuyahoga_hydro_polygon.shp -al -so
INFO: Open of `cuyahoga_hydro_polygon.shp'
      using driver `ESRI Shapefile' successful.


Layer name: cuyahoga_hydro_polygon
Geometry: Polygon
Feature Count: 6237
Extent: (1694482.287974, 552986.308029) - (2947684.750393,
1200045.105669)
Layer SRS WKT:
PROJCS["NAD_1983_StatePlane_Ohio_North_FIPS_3401_Feet",
    GEOGCS["GCS_North_American_1983",

    PARAMETER["Latitude_Of_Origin",39.66666666666666],
    UNIT["Foot_US",0.3048006096012192]]
Name: String (30.0)
AREA: Real (19.11)
PERIMETER: Real (19.11)
hyd_type: String (50.0)
geom_type: String (15.0)
```

Executing this command on each of the shapefiles, we see the following fields that are common to all the shapefiles:

- ▸ name
- ▸ hyd_type
- ▸ geom_type

It is by understanding our common fields that we can apply inheritance to completely structure our data.

## How to do it...

Now that we know our common fields, creating an inheritance model is easy. First, we will create a parent table with the fields common to all the tables, using the following query:

```
CREATE TABLE chp02.hydrology (
  gid SERIAL PRIMARY KEY,
  "name"      text,
  hyd_type    text,
  geom_type   text,
  the_geom    geometry
);
```

If you are paying attention, you will note that we also added a geometry field as all of our shapefiles implicitly have this commonality. To establish inheritance for a given table, we need to declare only the additional fields that the child table contains, using the following query:

```
CREATE TABLE chp02.hydrology_centerlines (
  "length"    numeric
) INHERITS (chp02.hydrology);

CREATE TABLE chp02.hydrology_polygon (
  area      numeric,
  perimeter    numeric
) INHERITS (chp02.hydrology);

CREATE TABLE chp02.hydrology_linestring (
  sinuosity    numeric
) INHERITS (chp02.hydrology_centerlines);
```

Now we are ready to load our data using the following commands:

- shp2pgsql -s 3734 -a -i -I -W LATIN1 -g the_geom cuyahoga_hydro_polygon chp02.hydrology_polygon | psql -U me -d postgis_cookbook

- shp2pgsql -s 3734 -a -i -I -W LATIN1 -g the_geom cuyahoga_hydro_polyline chp02.hydrology_linestring | psql -U me -d postgis_cookbook

- shp2pgsql -s 3734 -a -i -I -W LATIN1 -g the_geom cuyahoga_river_centerlines chp02.hydrology_centerlines | psql -U me -d postgis_cookbook

If we view our parent table, we will see all the records in all the child tables. A viewing of any of the child tables will just reveal the specific table of interest.

## How it works...

PostgreSQL table inheritance allows us to enforce essentially hierarchical relationships between tables. In this case, we leverage inheritance to allow for commonality between related datasets. Now, if we want to query data from these tables, we can query directly from the parent table as follows, depending on whether we want a mix of geometries or just a targeted dataset.

```
SELECT * FROM chp02.hydrology
```

From any of the child tables, we could use the following query:

```
SELECT * FROM chp02.hydrology_polygon
```

## See also

It is possible to extend this concept in order to leverage and optimize storage and querying by using the CHECK constrains in conjunction with inheritance. For more info, see the *Extending inheritance – table partitioning* recipe.

# Extending inheritance – table partitioning

Table partitioning is an approach specific to PostgreSQL that extends inheritance to model tables that typically do not vary from each other in the available fields, but where the child tables represent logical partitioning of the data based on a variety of factors, be it time, value ranges, classifications, or, in our case, spatial relationships. The advantages of partitioning include improved query performance due to smaller indexes and targeted scans of data, bulk loads, and deletes that bypass the costs of maintenance functions like VACUUM. It can thus be used to put commonly used data on a faster and more expensive storage, and the remaining data on a slower and cheaper storage. In combination with PostGIS, we get the novel power of spatial partitioning, which is a really powerful feature for large datasets.

## Getting ready

We could use many examples of large datasets that could benefit from partitioning. In our case, we will use a contour dataset. Contours are useful ways to represent terrain data, as they are well established in use, and thus commonly interpreted. Contours can also be used to compress terrain data into linear representations, thus allowing them to be shown in conjunction with other data easily.

The problem is, the storage of contour data can be quite expensive. Two-foot contours for a single US county can take 20 to 40 GB, and storing such data for a larger area such as a region or nation can become quite prohibitive from the standpoint of accessing the appropriate portion of the dataset in an efficient way.

## How to do it...

The first step in this case may be to prepare the data. If we had a monolithic contour table called `cuy_contours_2`, we could choose to clip the data to a series of rectangles that would serve as our table partitions; in this case, `chp02.contour_clip`, using the following query:

```
CREATE TABLE chp02.contour_2_cm_only AS
  SELECT contour.elevation, contour.gid, contour.div_10,
    contour.div_20, contour.div_50,
  contour.div_100, cc.id, ST_Intersection(contour.the_geom,
    cc.the_geom) AS the_geom FROM
    chp02.cuy_contours_2 AS contour, chp02.contour_clip as cc
    WHERE ST_Within(contour.the_geom,cc.the_geom
      OR
    ST_Crosses(contour.the_geom,cc.the_geom);
```

We are performing two tests here in our query. We are using `ST_Within`, which tests whether a given contour is entirely within our area of interest. If so, we perform an intersection; the resultant geometry should just be the geometry of the contour.

The `ST_Crosses` function checks whether the contour crosses the boundary of the geometry we are testing. This should capture all the geometries lying partially inside and partially outside our areas. These are the ones that we will truly intersect to get the resultant shape.

In our case, it is easier and we don't require the previous step. Our contour shapes are already individual shapefiles clipped to rectangular boundaries, as shown in the following screenshot:

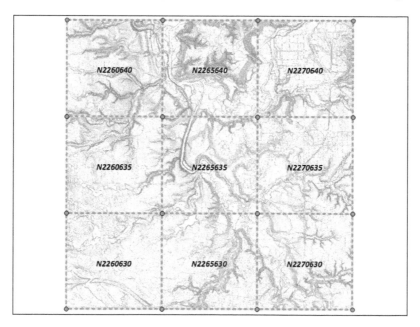

Since the data is already clipped into the chunks needed for our partitions, we can just continue to create the appropriate partitions.

Much as with inheritance, we start by creating our parent table using the following query:

```
CREATE TABLE chp02.contours
(
  gid serial NOT NULL,
  elevation integer,
  __gid double precision,
  the_geom geometry(MultiLineStringZM,3734),
  CONSTRAINT contours_pkey PRIMARY KEY (gid)
)
WITH (
  OIDS=FALSE
);
```

Here again, we maintain our constraints such as `PRIMARY KEY` and specify the geometry type (`MultiLineStringZM`), not because these will propagate to the child tables, but for any client software accessing the parent table to anticipate such constraints.

Now we may begin to create tables that inherit from our parent table. In the process, we will create a `CHECK` constraint specifying the limits of our associated geometry using the following query:

```
CREATE TABLE chp02.contour_N2260630
  (CHECK (ST_CoveredBy(the_geom,ST_GeomFromText('POLYGON((2260000
    630000, 2260000 635000,
  2265000 635000, 2265000 630000, 2260000 630000))',3734)
  ))) INHERITS (chp02.contours);
```

We can complete with similar `CREATE TABLE` queries for our remaining tables, as follows:

```
CREATE TABLE chp02.contour_N2260635
  (CHECK ( ST_CoveredBy(the_geom,ST_GeomFromText('POLYGON
    ((2260000 635000, 2260000 640000,
  2265000 640000, 2265000 635000, 2260000 635000))', 3734)
  ))) INHERITS (chp02.contours);
CREATE TABLE chp02.contour_N2260640
  (CHECK ( ST_CoveredBy(the_geom,ST_GeomFromText
    ('POLYGON((2260000 640000, 2260000 645000,
    2265000 645000, 2265000 640000, 2260000 640000))', 3734)
  ))) INHERITS (chp02.contours);
CREATE TABLE chp02.contour_N2265630
```

```
  (CHECK ( ST_CoveredBy(the_geom,ST_GeomFromText
     ('POLYGON((2265000 630000, 2265000 635000,

  2270000 635000, 2270000 630000, 2265000 630000))', 3734)

  ))) INHERITS (chp02.contours);
CREATE TABLE chp02.contour_N2265635

  (CHECK ( ST_CoveredBy(the_geom,ST_GeomFromText
     ('POLYGON((2265000 635000, 2265000 640000,

  2270000 640000, 2270000 635000, 2265000 635000))', 3734)

  ))) INHERITS (chp02.contours);
CREATE TABLE chp02.contour_N2265640

  (CHECK ( ST_CoveredBy(the_geom,ST_GeomFromText
     ('POLYGON((2265000 640000, 2265000 645000,

  2270000 645000, 2270000 640000, 2265000 640000))', 3734)

  ))) INHERITS (chp02.contours);
CREATE TABLE chp02.contour_N2270630

  (CHECK ( ST_CoveredBy(the_geom,ST_GeomFromText
     ('POLYGON((2270000 630000, 2270000 635000,

  2275000 635000, 2275000 630000, 2270000 630000))', 3734)

  ))) INHERITS (chp02.contours);
CREATE TABLE chp02.contour_N2270635

  (CHECK ( ST_CoveredBy(the_geom,ST_GeomFromText
     ('POLYGON((2270000 635000, 2270000 640000,

  2275000 640000, 2275000 635000, 2270000 635000))', 3734)

  ))) INHERITS (chp02.contours);
CREATE TABLE chp02.contour_N2270640

  (CHECK ( ST_CoveredBy(the_geom,ST_GeomFromText
     ('POLYGON((2270000 640000, 2270000 645000,

  2275000 645000, 2275000 640000, 2270000 640000))', 3734)

  ))) INHERITS (chp02.contours);
```

Next we can load our contours into each of our child tables using the following command. If we wanted to, we could even implement a trigger on the parent table, which would place each insert into its correct child table, though this might incur performance costs. In loading our contours, we use the -a flag to specify that we want to append the data.

```
shp2pgsql -s 3734 -a -i -I -W LATIN1 -g the_geom N2260630 chp02.contour_
N2260630 | psql -U me -d postgis_cookbook
```

## How it works...

The CHECK constraint in combination with inheritance is all it takes to build table partitioning. In this case, we're using a bounding box as our CHECK constraint and simply inheriting the columns from the parent table. Now that we have this in place, queries against the parent table will check our CHECK constraints first before employing a query. This also allows us to place any of our lesser-used contour tables on cheaper and slower storage, thus allowing for cost-effective optimizations of large datasets. This structure is also beneficial for rapidly changing data as updates can be applied to an entire area; the entire table for that area can be efficiently dropped and repopulated without traversing across the dataset.

Unfortunately, some of the promises of table partitioning, such as being able to bypass spatial indexes by using ranges, are not yet available.

## See also

For more on table inheritance in general, particularly the flexibility associated with the usage of alternate columns in the child table, see the previous recipe, *Structuring spatial data with table inheritance*.

# Normalizing imports

Often data used in a spatial database is imported from other sources. As such it may not be in a form that is useful for our current application. In such a case, it may be useful to write functions that will aid in transforming the data into a form that is more useful for our application. This is particularly the case when going from flat file formats, such as shapefiles, to relational databases such as PostgreSQL.

> A shapefile is a de facto as well as formal standard for the storage of spatial data, and is probably the most common delivery format for vector spatial data. A shapefile, in spite of its name, is never just one file, but a collection of files. It consists of at least *.shp (which contains geometry), *.shx (an index file), and *.dbf (which contains the tabular information for the shapefile). It is a powerful and useful format but, as a flat file, it is inherently nonrelational. Each geometry is associated in a one-to-one relationship with each row in a table.

There are many structures that might serve as a proxy for relational stores in a shapefile. We will explore one here—a single field with delimited text for multiple relations. This is a not-too-uncommon hack to encode multiple relationships into a flat file. The other common approach is to create multiple fields to store what in a relational arrangement would be a single field.

## Getting ready

The dataset we will be working with is a trails dataset that has linear extents for a set of trails in a park system. The data is the typical data that comes from the GIS world—as a flat shapefile, there are no explicit relational constructs in the data.

First, we load the data using the following command:

```
shp2pgsql -s 3734 -d -i -I -W LATIN1 -g the_geom trails chp02.trails |
psql -U me -d postgis_cookbook
```

Looking at the linear data in a Desktop GIS, we see some categories for trail use:

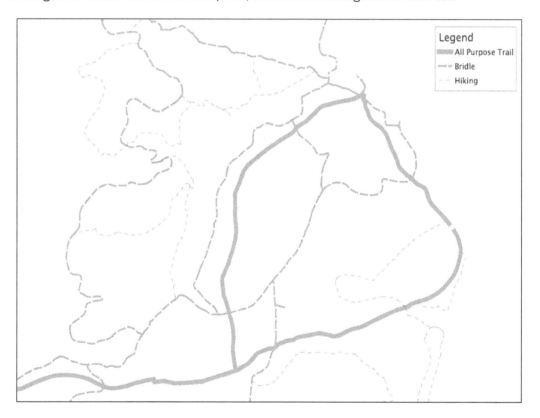

We want to retain this information as well as the name. Unfortunately, the `label_name` field is a messy field with a variety of related names concatenated with an ampersand (&), as shown in the following query:

```
SELECT DISTINCT label_name FROM chp02.trails
  WHERE label_name LIKE '%&%' LIMIT 10;
```

It will return the following output:

```
                        label_name
- - - - - - - - - - - - - - - - - - - - - - - - - - - - - - - - - - - - - - - - -
 All Purpose Trail & Buckeye Trail & Sagamore Creek Loop Trail
 Hemlock Loop Trail & Prairie Loop Trail & Wildflower Loop Trail
 NC1 & NC2
 Hinckley Hills Loop Trail & HI3
 All Purpose Trail & North Ravine Loop Trail
 BR3 & BR4 & Buckeye Trail
 Bridle Trail & Hemlock Loop Trail
 Hemlock Trail & NC2
 Hinckley Hills Loop Trail & HI1
 Lake Isaac Trail & Lake to Lake Trail
(10 rows)
```

This is where the normalization of our table will begin.

## How to do it...

The first thing we need to do is find all the fields that don't have ampersands and use those as our unique list of available trails. In our case, we can do this, as every trail has at least one segment that is uniquely named and not associated with another trail name. This approach will not work with all datasets, so be careful in understanding your data before applying this approach to that data. To select the fields without ampersands, we use the following query:

```
SELECT DISTINCT label_name, res
  FROM chp02.trails
  WHERE label_name NOT LIKE '%&%';
```

It will return the following output:

```
            label_name                |          res
- - - - - - - - - - - - - - - - - - - + - - - - - - - - - - - - - - - - -
South Quarry Loop Trail               | Mill Stream Run
                                        Reservation
Buckeye Trail                         | Hinckley Reservation
Bridle Connector Trail                | Rocky River
                                        Reservation
West Channel Pond Loop Trail          | Rocky River
                                        Reservation
Green Milkweed Trail                  | Mill Stream Run
                                        Reservation
All Purpose Trail                     | Euclid Creek
                                        Reservation
```

| | |
|---|---|
| Connector Trail | Bradley Woods Reservation |
| North Chagrin Reservation Bridle Trail | North Chagrin Reservation |
| Connector Trail | Garfield Park Reservation |
| BR2 | Brecksville Reservation |
| Connector Trail | Rocky River Reservation |
| Buckeye Trail | South Chagrin Reservation |

For sanity, we will also sort these entries as follows:

```
SELECT DISTINCT label_name, res
  FROM chp02.trails
  WHERE label_name NOT LIKE '%&%'
  ORDER BY label_name, res;
```

Next, we want to search for all the records that match any of these unique trail names. This will give us the list of records that will serve as relations. The first step in doing this search is to append the percent (%) signs to our unique list in order to build a string on which we can search using a LIKE query:

```
SELECT '%' || label_name || '%' AS label_name, label_name as
  label, res FROM
  (
  SELECT DISTINCT label_name, res
    FROM chp02.trails
    WHERE label_name NOT LIKE '%&%'
    ORDER BY label_name, res
  ) AS label;
```

Finally, we'll use this in the context of a WITH block to do the normalization itself. This will provide us with a table of unique IDs for each segment in our first column, along with the associated label column. For good measure, we will do this as a CREATE TABLE procedure as shown in the following query:

```
CREATE TABLE chp02.trails_names AS
  WITH labellike AS
(
SELECT '%' || label_name || '%' AS label_name, label_name as
  label, res FROM
  (
  SELECT DISTINCT label_name, res
    FROM chp02.trails
```

```
    WHERE label_name NOT LIKE '%&%'
    ORDER BY label_name, res
  ) AS label
)
SELECT t.gid, ll.label, ll.res
  FROM chp02.trails AS t, labellike AS ll
  WHERE t.label_name LIKE ll.label_name
  AND
  t.res = ll.res
  ORDER BY gid;
```

Now that we have a table of the relations, we need a table of the geometries associated with `gid`. This, in comparison, is quite easy, as shown in the following query:

```
CREATE TABLE chp02.trails_geom AS
  SELECT gid, the_geom
  FROM chp02.trails;
```

## How it works...

In this example, we have generated a unique list of possible records in conjunction with a search for the associated records, in order to build table relationships. In one table, we have the geometry and a unique ID of each spatial record; in another table, we have the names associated with each of those unique IDs. Now we can explicitly leverage those relationships.

First, we need to establish our unique IDs as primary keys with the following query:

```
ALTER TABLE chp02.trails_geom ADD PRIMARY KEY (gid);
```

Now we can use that PRIMARY KEY as a FOREIGN KEY in our trails_names table with the following query:

```
ALTER TABLE chp02.trails_names ADD FOREIGN KEY (gid) REFERENCES chp02.
trails_geom(gid)
```

This step isn't strictly necessary, but does enforce referential integrity for queries such as the following:

```
SELECT geo.gid, geo.geom, names.label FROM
  chp02.trails_geom AS geo, chp02.trails_names AS names
  WHERE geo.gid = names.gid
```

## There's more...

If we had multiple fields we wanted to normalize, we could write `CREATE TABLE` queries for each of them.

It is interesting to note that the approach framed in this recipe is not limited to cases where we have a delimited field. This approach can provide a relatively generic solution to the problem of normalizing flat files. For example, if we have a case where we have multiple fields to represent relational info, such as `label1`, `label2`, `label3`, or similar multiple attribute names to a single record, we can write a simple query to concatenate them together before feeding that info into our query.

# Normalizing internal overlays

Data from an external source can have not just table structure issues, but also topological issues endemic to the geospatial data itself. Take, for example, the problem of data with overlapping polygons. If our dataset has polygons that overlap with internal overlays, queries for area, perimeter, and other metrics may not produce predictable or consistent results.

There are a few approaches that can solve the problem of polygon datasets with internal overlays. The general approach presented here was originally proposed by *Kevin Neufeld* of *Refractions Research*.

Over the course of writing our query, we will also produce a solution for converting polygons to linestrings.

## Getting ready

First, we'll load our dataset using the following command:

```
shp2pgsql -s 3734 -d -i -I -W LATIN1 -g the_geom cm_usearea_polygon
chp02.use_area | psql -U me -d postgis_cookbook
```

## How to do it...

Now that the data is loaded into a table in the database, we can leverage PostGIS to flatten and get the union of the polygons, such that we have a normalized dataset. The first step in doing so using this approach will be to convert the polygons to linestrings. We can then node those linestrings and convert them back to polygons, representing the union of all the polygon inputs. We will perform the following tasks:

1. Converting polygons to linestrings.
2. Converting linestrings back to polygons.

3. Finding center points of resultant polygons.
4. Use resultant points to query tabular relationships.

## Converting polygons to linestrings

To accomplish this, we'll need to extract just the portions of the polygons we want using ST_ExteriorRing, convert those parts to points using ST_DumpPoints, and then connect those points back into lines like a "connect-the-dots" coloring book using ST_MakeLine.

Breaking it down further, ST_ExteriorRing (the_geom) will grab just the outer boundary of our polygons. But ST_ExteriorRing returns polygons, so we need to take that output and create a line from it. The easiest way to do this is to convert it to points using ST_DumpPoints and then connect those points. By default, the Dump function returns an object called a geometry_dump, which is not just simple geometry but the geometry in combination with an array of integers. The easiest way to return the geometry alone is to leverage the object notation to extract just the geometry portion of geometry_dump as follows:

**(ST_DumpPoints(geom)).geom**

Piecing the geometry back together with ST_ExteriorRing is done using the following query:

**SELECT (ST_DumpPoints(ST_ExteriorRing(geom))).geom**

This should give us a listing of points in order from the exterior rings of all the points from which we want to construct our lines using ST_MakeLine, as shown in the following query:

```
SELECT ST_MakeLine(geom) FROM (
  SELECT (ST_DumpPoints(ST_ExteriorRing(geom))).geom
    ) AS linpoints
```

Since the preceding approach is a process we may want to use in many other places, it might be prudent to create a function from this using the following query:

```
CREATE OR REPLACE FUNCTION chp02.polygon_to_line(geometry)
  RETURNS geometry AS
$BODY$

    SELECT ST_MakeLine(geom) FROM (
      SELECT (ST_DumpPoints(ST_ExteriorRing(
        (ST_Dump($1)).geom
        ))).geom

          ) AS linpoints
$BODY$
  LANGUAGE sql VOLATILE;
ALTER FUNCTION chp02.polygon_to_line(geometry)
  OWNER TO me;
```

Now that we have the `polygon_to_line` function, we still need to force the noding of overlapping lines in our particular use. The `ST_Union` function will aid in this as shown in the following query:

```
SELECT ST_Union(geom) AS geom FROM (
  SELECT chp02.polygon_to_line(geom) AS geom FROM
    chp02.use_area
    ) AS unioned
;
```

## Converting linestrings back to polygons

Now we can polygonize this result using `ST_Polygonize`, as shown in the following query:

```
SELECT ST_Polygonize(geom) AS geom FROM (
  SELECT ST_Union(geom) AS geom FROM (
    SELECT chp02.polygon_to_line(geom) AS geom FROM
    chp02.use_area
  ) AS unioned
) as polygonized;
```

The `ST_Polygonize` function will create a single multi polygon, so we need to explode this into multiple single polygon geometries if we are to do anything useful with it. While we are at it, we might as  well do the following within a `CREATE  TABLE` statement:

```
CREATE TABLE chp02.use_area_alt AS (
  SELECT (ST_Dump(the_geom)).geom AS the_geom FROM (
    SELECT ST_Polygonize(the_geom) AS the_geom FROM (
      SELECT ST_Union(the_geom) AS the_geom FROM (
    SELECT chp02.polygon_to_line(the_geom) AS the_geom FROM
      chp02.use_area
      ) AS unioned
    ) as polygonized
  ) AS exploded
);
```

We will be performing spatial queries against this geometry, so we should create an index in order to ensure our query performs well, as shown in the following query:

```
CREATE INDEX chp02_use_area_alt_the_geom_gist
  ON chp02.use_area_alt
  USING gist(the_geom);
```

## Finding center points of resultant polygons

In order to extract the appropriate table information from the original geometry and apply that back to our resultant geometries, we will perform a point-in-polygon query. For that, we first need to calculate centroids on the resultant geometry:

```
CREATE TABLE chp02.use_area_alt_p AS
  SELECT ST_SetSRID(ST_PointOnSurface(the_geom), 3734) AS
    the_geom FROM
    chp02.use_area_alt;
ALTER TABLE chp02.use_area_alt_p ADD COLUMN gid serial;
ALTER TABLE chp02.use_area_alt_p ADD PRIMARY KEY (gid);
```

And, as always, create a spatial index using the following query:

```
CREATE INDEX chp02_use_area_alt_p_the_geom_gist
  ON chp02.use_area_alt_p
  USING gist(the_geom);
```

## Using resultant points to query tabular relationships

The centroids then structure our point-in-polygon (ST_Intersects) relationship between the original tabular information and resultant polygons, using the following query:

```
CREATE TABLE chp02.use_area_alt_relation AS
SELECT points.gid, cu.location FROM
  chp02.use_area_alt_p AS points,
  chp02.use_area AS cu
    WHERE ST_Intersects(points.the_geom, cu.the_geom);
```

## How it works...

Our essential approach here is to look at the underlying topology of the geometry and reconstruct a topology that is nonoverlapping, and then use the centroids of that new geometry to construct a query that establishes the relationship to the original data.

## There's more...

At this stage, we can optionally establish a framework for referential integrity using a foreign key as follows:

```
ALTER TABLE chp02.use_area_alt_relation ADD FOREIGN KEY (gid) REFERENCES
chp02.use_area_alt_p (gid);
```

# Using polygon overlays for proportional census estimates

PostgreSQL functions abound for the aggregation of tabular data, including sum, count, min, max, and so on. PostGIS as a framework does not explicitly have spatial equivalents of these, but this does not prevent us from building functions using the aggregates in concert with PostGIS's spatial functionality.

In this recipe, we will explore spatial summarization with the United States Census data. US Census data, by nature, is aggregated data. This is done intentionally to protect the privacy of citizens. But when it comes to doing analyses with this data, the aggregate nature of the data can become problematic. There are some tricks to disaggregate data. Amongst the simplest of these is the use of a proportional sum based on area, which we will do in this exercise.

## Getting ready

The problem at hand is that a proposed trail has been drawn in order to provide services for the public. This example could apply to road construction or even finding sites for commercial properties for the purpose of provisioning services.

First, perform a quick data load using the following commands:

```
shp2pgsql -s 3734 -d -i -I -W LATIN1 -g the_geom census chp02.trail_
census | psql -U me -d postgis_cookbook
shp2pgsql -s 3734 -d -i -I -W LATIN1 -g the_geom trail_alignment_
proposed_buffer chp02.trail_buffer | psql -U me -d postgis_cookbook
shp2pgsql -s 3734 -d -i -I -W LATIN1 -g the_geom trail_alignment_proposed
chp02.trail_alignment_prop | psql -U me -d postgis_cookbook
```

The preceding commands will produce the following output:

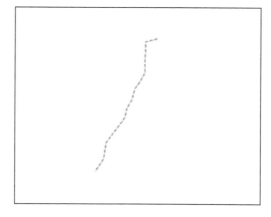

In our case, we want to know the population within 1 mile of the trail, assuming that people living within 1 mile of the trail are the ones most likely to use it and, thus, most likely to be served by it.

To find the population near this proposed trail, we overlay census block group population density information. Illustrated in the next screenshot is a 1 mile buffer around the proposed trail overlayed on census information:

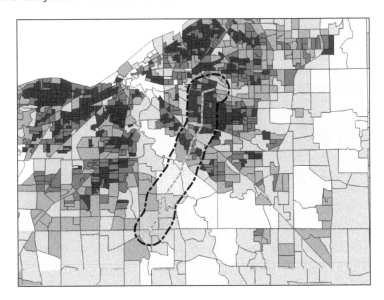

One of the things we might note about this census data is the wide range of census densities and census block group size. An approach to calculate the population would be to simply select all census clocks that intersect our area, as shown in the following screenshot:

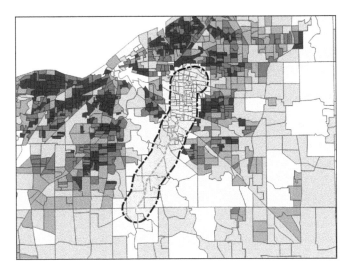

This is a simple procedure that gives us an estimate of 130,288 people living within 1 mile of the trail. But, looking at the shape of the selection, we can see that we are over-estimating the population by taking the entirety of the block groups in our estimate.

Similarly, if we just used the block groups whose centroids lay within 1 mile of our proposed trail alignment, we would underestimate the population.

Instead, we will make some useful assumptions. Block groups are designed to be moderately homogenous within the block group. Assuming that this holds true for our data, we can assume that, for a given block group, if 50 percent of the block group is within our target area, we can attribute half of the population of that block group to our estimate. Apply this to all our block groups, sum them, and we have a refined estimate that is likely to be better than pure intersects or centroid queries. Thus, we employ a proportional sum.

## How to do it...

As the problem of a proportional sum is a generic problem, we will write the underlying proportioning as a function. A function takes inputs and returns a value. In our case, we want our proportioning function to take two geometries, that is, the geometry of our buffered trail and block groups as well as the value we want proportioned, and we want it to return the proportioned value.

```
CREATE OR REPLACE FUNCTION chp02.proportional_sum(geometry,
  geometry, numeric)
  RETURNS numeric AS
$BODY$
-- SQL here
$BODY$
  LANGUAGE sql VOLATILE;
```

Now for the purpose of our calculation, for any given intersection of buffered area and block group, we want to find the proportion that the intersection is over the overall block group. Then this value should be multiplied by the value we want to scale.

In SQL, the function looks like the following query:

```
SELECT $3 * areacalc FROM
  (
  SELECT (ST_Area(ST_Intersection($1, $2)) / ST_Area($2))::
    numeric AS areacalc
  ) AS areac
;
```

The preceding query in its full form looks as follows:

```
CREATE OR REPLACE FUNCTION chp02.proportional_sum(geometry,
  geometry, numeric)
  RETURNS numeric AS
$BODY$
    SELECT $3 * areacalc FROM
    (
        SELECT (ST_Area(ST_Intersection($1,
          $2))/ST_Area($2))::numeric AS areacalc
    ) AS areac
;
$BODY$
  LANGUAGE sql VOLATILE;
```

## How it works...

Since we have written the query as a function, the query uses the SELECT statement to loop through all available records and give us a proportioned population. An astute reader will note that we have not yet done any work on summarization; we have only worked on the proportionality portion of the problem. We can do the summarization upon calling the function using PostgreSQL's built-in aggregate functions. What is neat about this approach is that we need not just apply a sum, but could also calculate other aggregates such as min or max. In the following example, we will just apply a sum:

```
SELECT ROUND(SUM(chp02.proportional_sum(a.the_geom, b.the_geom,
  b.pop))) FROM
  chp02.trail_buffer AS a, chp02.trail_census as b
  WHERE ST_Intersects(a.the_geom, b.the_geom)
  GROUP BY a.gid;
```

The value returned is quite different (population of 96,081), which is more likely to be accurate.

# 3
# Working with Vector Data – The Basics

In this chapter, we will cover the following recipes:

- ▶ Working with GPS data
- ▶ Fixing invalid geometries
- ▶ GIS analysis with spatial joins
- ▶ Simplifying geometries
- ▶ Measuring distances
- ▶ Merging polygons using a common attribute
- ▶ Computing intersections
- ▶ Clipping geometries to deploy data
- ▶ Simplifying geometries with PostGIS topology

## Introduction

In this chapter, you will work with a set of PostGIS functions and vector datasets. You will first take a look at how to use PostGIS with **GPS data**—you will import such datasets using `ogr2ogr`, and then compose polylines from point geometries using the `ST_MakeLine` function.

Then, you will see how PostGIS manages and helps you find and fix invalid geometries with functions such as `ST_MakeValid`, `ST_IsValid`, `ST_IsValidReason`, and `ST_IsValidDetails`.

We will then learn about one of the most powerful elements of a spatial database—spatial joins. PostGIS provides you with a rich set of operators, such as ST_Intersects, ST_Contains, ST_Covers, ST_Crosses, and ST_DWithin, for this purpose.

After that, you will use the ST_Simplify and ST_SimplifyPreverveTopology functions to simplify (generalize) geometries when you don't need too many details. While this function works well on linear geometries, topological anomalies may be introduced for polygonal ones. In such cases, you should consider using an external GIS tool such as GRASS.

You will then have a tour of PostGIS functions to make distance measurements— ST_Distance, ST_DistanceSphere, ST_DistanceSpheroid are on the way.

One of the recipes explained in this chapter will guide you through the typical GIS workflow to merge polygons based on a common attribute; you will use the ST_Union function for this purpose.

You will then learn how to clip geometries using the ST_Intersection function, before deep diving into the new **PostGIS topology** support in the last recipe.

# Working with GPS data

In this recipe, you will work with GPS data. This kind of data is typically saved in a .gpx file. You will import a bunch of .gpx files to PostGIS from RunKeeper, a popular social network for runners.

If you have an account on RunKeeper, you can export your .gpx files and process them by following the instructions in this recipe. Otherwise, you can use the RunKeeper .gpx files included in the runkeeper-gpx.zip file, located in the chp03 directory included in the code bundle available with this book.

You will first create a bash script for importing the .gpx files to a PostGIS table, using ogr2ogr. After the import is completed, you will try to write a couple of SQL queries and test some very useful functions, such as ST_MakeLine to generate polylines from point geometries, ST_Length to compute distance, and ST_Intersects to perform a spatial join operation.

## Getting ready

Extract the data/chp03/runkeeper-gpx.zip file to working/chp03/runkeeper_gpx. In case you haven't been through *Chapter 1, Moving Data In and Out of PostGIS*, be sure to have the countries dataset in the PostGIS database.

## How to do it...

First, be sure of the format of the `.gpx` files that you need to import to PostGIS. Open one of them and check the file structure—each file must be in the XML format composed of just one `<trk>` element that contains just one `<trkseg>` element that contains many `<trkpt>` elements (the points stored from the runner's GPS device). Import these points to a PostGIS `Point` table.

1. Create a new schema named `chp03` to store the data for all of the recipes in this chapter using the following command:

   ```
   postgis_cookbook=# create schema chp03;
   ```

2. Create the `chp03.rk_track_points` table in PostgreSQL by executing the following command lines:

   ```
   postgis_cookbook=# CREATE TABLE chp03.rk_track_points
   (
      fid serial NOT NULL,
      the_geom geometry(Point,4326),
      ele double precision,
      "time" timestamp with time zone,
      CONSTRAINT activities_pk PRIMARY KEY (fid)
   ),
   ```

3. Create the following script to import all of the `.gpx` files in the `chp03.rk_track_points` table using the GDAL `ogr2ogr` command.

   The following is the Linux version (name it `working/chp03/import_gpx.sh`):

   ```bash
   #!/bin/bash
   for f in `find runkeeper_gpx -name \*.gpx -printf "%f\n"`
   do
        echo "Importing gpx file $f to chp03.rk_track_points PostGIS
   table..." #, ${f%.*}"
        ogr2ogr -append -update  -f PostgreSQL PG:"dbname='postgis_
   cookbook' user='me' password='mypassword'" runkeeper_gpx/$f -nln
   chp03.rk_track_points -sql "SELECT ele, time FROM track_points"
   done
   ```

The following is the Windows version (name it `working/chp03/import_gpx.bat`):

```
@echo off
for %%I in (runkeeper_gpx\*.gpx*) do (
    echo Importing gpx file %%~nxI to chp03.rk_track_points
PostGIS table...
    ogr2ogr -append -update -f PostgreSQL PG:"dbname='postgis_
cookbook' user='me' password='mypassword'" runkeeper_gpx/%%~nxI
-nln chp03.rk_track_points -sql "SELECT ele, time FROM track_
points"
)
```

4. In Linux, don't forget to assign execution permission to it before running it. Run the following script:

```
$ chmod 775 import_gpx.sh
```

```
$ ./import_gpx.sh
```

```
Importing gpx file 2012-02-26-0930.gpx to chp03.rk_track_points
PostGIS table...
```

```
Importing gpx file 2012-02-29-1235.gpx to chp03.rk_track_points
PostGIS table...
```

```
...
```

```
Importing gpx file 2011-04-15-1906.gpx to chp03.rk_track_points
PostGIS table...
```

In Windows, just double-click on the `.bat` file or run it from the command prompt using the following command:

```
> import_gpx.bat
```

5. Now, create a polyline table containing a single runner's track details, using the `ST_MakeLine` function. Assume that on each distinct day the runner had just one training. In this table, you should include the start and end times of the track details as follows:

```
postgis_cookbook=# SELECT
ST_MakeLine(the_geom) AS the_geom,
    run_date::date,
    MIN(run_time) as start_time,
    MAX(run_time) as end_time
    INTO chp03.tracks
    FROM (
```

```
SELECT the_geom,
    "time"::date as run_date,
    "time" as run_time
    FROM chp03.rk_track_points
    ORDER BY run_time
) AS foo GROUP BY run_date;
```

6. Before querying the created tables, don't forget to add spatial indexes to both of the tables to improve their performance, as follows:

```
postgis_cookbook=# CREATE INDEX rk_track_points_geom_idx ON chp03.
rk_track_points USING gist(the_geom);
```

```
postgis_cookbook=# CREATE INDEX tracks_geom_idx ON chp03.tracks
USING gist(the_geom);
```

7. If you try to open both the spatial tables on a Desktop GIS on any given day, you should see that the points from the rk_track_points table compose a single polyline geometry record in the tracks table, as shown in the following screenshot:

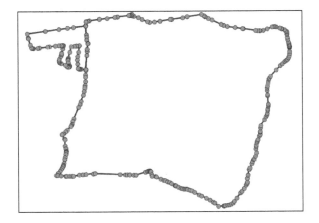

8. Now, query the tracks table to get a report of the total distance run (in km) by the runner for each month. For this purpose, use the ST_Length function, as shown in the following query:

```
postgis_cookbook=# SELECT
    EXTRACT(year FROM run_date) AS run_year,
    EXTRACT(MONTH FROM run_date) as run_month,
    SUM(ST_Length(geography(the_geom)))/1000 AS distance
FROM chp03.tracks
GROUP BY run_year, run_month;
```

```
run_year    | run_month  |    distance
------------+------------+------------------
       2010 |     5      | 67.9277530981487

       ...

       2012 |     7      | 38.8795349962323
       2012 |     8      | 72.0557697278750
```

(28 rows)

9. Using a spatial join between the `tracks` and `countries` tables and again using the `ST_Length` function as follows, you will get a report of the distance run (in km) by the runner, per country:

```
postgis_cookbook=# SELECT
    c.name,
    SUM(ST_Length(geography(t.the_geom)))/1000 AS run_distance
FROM chp03.tracks AS t
JOIN chp01.countries AS c
ON ST_Intersects(t.the_geom, c.the_geom)
GROUP BY c.name
ORDER BY run_distance DESC;
 country_name        |    run_distance
---------------------+------------------
 Italy               | 2628.78393844143
 ...
 Greece              | 18.1060004468414
```

(4 rows)

## How it works...

The `.gpx` files store all of the points' details in the WGS 84 spatial reference system; therefore, we created the `rk_track_points` table with SRID (4326).

After creating the `rk_track_points` table, we imported all of the `.gpx` files in the `runkeeper_gpx` directory using a bash script. The bash script iterates all of the files with the extension `*.gpx` in the `runkeeper_gpx` directory. For each of these files, the script runs the `ogr2ogr` command, importing the `.gpx` files to PostGIS using the GPX GDAL driver (for more details go to `http://www.gdal.org/ogr/drv_gpx.html`).

In the GDAL's abstraction, a `.gpx` file is an OGR data source composed of several layers, as follows:

```
$ ogrinfo -so 2012-08-29-1930.gpx
Had to open data source read-only
INFO: Open of '2012-08-29-1930.gpx'
       using driver `GPX' successful.
1: waypoints (Point)
2: routes (Line String)
3: tracks (Multi Line String)
4: route_points (Point)
5: track_points (Point)
```

In the `.gpx` files (OGR data sources), you have just the `tracks` and `track_points` layers. As a shortcut, you could have imported just the `tracks` layer using `ogr2ogr`, but you would need to start using some PostGIS functions from the `track_points` layer in order to generate the `tracks` layer itself. This is why in the `ogr2ogr` section in the bash script, we import the point geometries from the `track_` points layer, plus a couple of useful attributes, such as elevation and timestamp, to the `rk_track_points` PostGIS table.

Once the records were imported, we fed a new polylines table named `tracks` using a subquery and select all of the point geometries and their dates and times from the `rk_track_points` table, grouped by date, and with the geometries aggregated using the `ST_MakeLine` function. This function was able to create linestrings from point geometries (for more details, go to `http://www.postgis.org/docs/ST_MakeLine.html`).

You should not forget to sort the points in the subquery by `datetime`; otherwise, you will obtain an irregular linestring, jumping from one point to the other and not following the correct order.

After loading the `tracks` table, we tested the two spatial queries.

At first, you got a month-by-month report of the total distance run by the runner. For this purpose, you selected all of the track records grouped by date (year and month), with the total distance obtained by summing up the lengths of the single tracks (obtained with the `ST_Length` function). To get the year and the month from the `run_date` function, you used the PostgreSQL `EXTRACT` function; be aware that if you measure the distance using geometries in the WGS 84 system, you will obtain it in degree units. For this reason, you have to project the geometries to a planar metric system designed for the specific region from where the data will be projected.

For large-scale areas, such as in our case where we have points that span all around Europe, as shown in the last query results, a good option is to use the geography data type introduced with PostGIS 1.5. The calculations may be slower, but they are much more accurate than in other systems. This is the reason why you casted the geometries to the geography data type before making measures.

The last spatial query used a spatial join with the ST_Intersects function to get the name of the country where each track was run by the runner (with the assumption that the runner didn't run cross-border tracks). To get the total distance run per country is just a matter of aggregating the selection on the country_name field and aggregating the track distances with the PostgreSQL SUM operator.

# Fixing invalid geometries

You will often find **invalid geometries** in your PostGIS database. These invalid geometries could compromise the functioning of PostGIS itself and any external tool using it, such as QGIS and MapServer. PostGIS, being compliant with the OGC Simple Features Specification, must manage and work with valid geometries.

Luckily, PostGIS 2.0 offers you the ST_MakeValid function that, together with the ST_IsValid, ST_IsValidReason, and ST_IsValidDetails functions, is the ideal toolkit for inspecting and fixing geometries within the database. In this recipe, you will learn how to fix a common case of invalid geometry.

## Getting ready

Unzip the data/TM_WORLD_BORDERS-0.3.zip file into your working directory—working/chp3. Import the shapefile in PostGIS with the shp2pgsql command, as follows:

```
$ shp2pgsql -s 4326 -g the_geom -W LATIN1 -I TM_WORLD_BORDERS-
0.3.shp chp03.countries > countries.sql
$ psql -U me -d postgis_cookbook -f countries.sql
```

## How to do it...

The steps you need to perform to complete this recipe are as follows:

1. First, investigate whether or not any geometry is invalid in the imported table. As you can see in the following query, using the ST_IsValid and ST_IsValidReason functions, we find four invalid geometries that are all invalid for the same reason—ring self-intersection:

   ```
   postgis_cookbook=# SELECT gid, name, ST_IsValidReason(the_geom)
       FROM chp03.countries
       WHERE ST_IsValid(the_geom)=false;
   ```

```
gid  |  name  |  st_isvalidreason
-----+--------+-----------------------------------------------
 24  | Canada | Ring Self-intersection[-53.756367 48.5032620000001]
 33  | Chile  | Ring Self-intersection[-70.917236 -54.708618]
155  | Norway | Ring Self-intersection[5.33694400000002 61.592773]
175  | Russia | Ring Self-intersection[143.661926 49.31221]

(4 rows)
```

2. Now, concentrate on just one of the invalid geometries, for example, in the multipolygon geometry representing Russia. Create a table containing just the ring generating the invalidity by selecting the table using the point coordinates given in the ST_IsValidReason response in the previous step:

```
postgis_cookbook=# SELECT * INTO chp03.invalid_geometries
 FROM (

 SELECT 'broken'::varchar(10) as status,
 ST_GeometryN(the_geom, generate_series(1, ST_NRings(the_
geom)))::geometry(Polygon,4326) as the_geom
 FROM chp03.countries

 WHERE name = 'Russia') AS foo

 WHERE ST_Intersects(the_geom, ST_SetSRID(ST_
Point(143.661926,49.31221), 4326));
```

> ST_MakeValid requires GEOS 3.3.0 or higher; check whether or not your system has its support using the PostGIS_full_version function as follows:
>
> ```
> postgis_cookbook=# SELECT PostGIS_full_version();
>     postgis_full_version
> ----------------------------------------
>  POSTGIS="2.0.1 r9979" GEOS="3.3.5-CAPI-1.7.5"
> PROJ="Rel. 4.7.1, 23 September 2009" GDAL="GDAL 2.0dev,
> released 2011/12/29" LIBXML="2.7.8" TOPOLOGY RASTER
> (1 row)
> ```

3. Now, using the ST_MakeValid function, add a new record in the previously created table with the valid version of the same geometry:

```
postgis_cookbook=# INSERT INTO chp03.invalid_geometries
    VALUES ('repaired', (SELECT ST_MakeValid(the_geom)

FROM chp03.invalid_geometries));
```

4. Open this geometry on your Desktop GIS; the invalid geometry has just one self-intersecting ring that produces a hole in its internal. While this is accepted in the ESRI shapefile format specification (that was the original dataset you imported), the OGC standard does not allow for the self-intersecting ring, so neither does PostGIS.

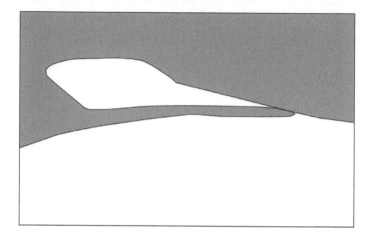

5. Now, in the `invalid_geometries` table, you have the invalid and valid version of the polygon. It is easy to figure out that the self-intersection ring was removed by `ST_MakeValid` by adding one supplementary ring to the original polygon, which resulted in a valid geometry, according to the OGC standard:

```
postgis_cookbook=# SELECT status, ST_NRings(the_geom) FROM chp03.
invalid_geometries;

  status   | st_nrings
-----------+-----------
  broken   |         1
  repaired |         2
(2 rows)
```

6. Now that you have identified the problem and its solution, don't forget to fix all of the other invalid geometries in the `countries` table by executing the following code:

```
postgis_cookbook=# UPDATE chp03.countries
    SET the_geom = ST_MakeValid(the_geom)
    WHERE ST_IsValid(the_geom) = false;
```

A smart way to not have invalid geometries in the database at all is by adding a CHECK constraint on the table to check for validity. This will increase the computation time when updating or inserting new geometries, but will keep your dataset valid. For example, in the countries table, this can be implemented as follows:

```
ALTER TABLE chp03.countries
    ADD CONSTRAINT geometry_valid_check
    CHECK (ST_IsValid(the_geom));
```

Many times in this recipe, though, you will need to remove such a constraint in order to be able to import records from a different source. After making validations with the ST_MakeValid function, you can safely add the constraint again.

## How it works...

There are a series of reasons why an invalid geometry could result in your database; for example, rings composing polygons must be closed and cannot self intersect or share more than one point with another ring.

After importing the country shapefile using the ST_IsValid and ST_IsValidReason functions, you will have figured out that four of the imported geometries are invalid all because their polygons have self-intersecting rings.

At this point, a good way to investigate the invalid multipolygon geometry is by decomposing the polygon to its component rings and checking out the invalid ones. For this purpose, we have exported the geometry of the ring causing the invalidity, using the ST_GeometryN function, which is able to extract the *nth* ring from the polygon. We coupled this function with the useful PostgreSQL generate_series function to iterate all of the rings composing the geometry, selecting the desired one using the ST_Intersects function.

As expected, the reason why this ring generates the invalidity is that it is self-intersecting and produces a hole in the polygon. While this is adherent with the shapefile specification, it isn't so with the OGC specification.

By running the ST_MakeValid function, PostGIS has been able to make the geometry valid, generating a second ring. Remember that the ST_MakeValid function is available only with the latest PostGIS compiled with the latest GEOS (3.3.0+). If that is not the setup for your working box and you cannot upgrade (upgrading is always recommended), you can follow the techniques discussed in a very popular, excellent presentation by Paul Ramsey at http://blog.opengeo.org/2010/09/08/tips-for-the-postgis-power-user/.

# GIS analysis with spatial joins

Joins for regular SQL tables have the real power in a relational database and spatial joins are one of the most impressive features of a spatial database engine such as PostGIS.

Basically, it is possible to correlate information from different layers on the basis of the geometric relation of each feature from the input layers. In this recipe, we will take a tour of some common use cases of spatial joins.

## Getting ready

1.  First, import some data to be used as a test bed in PostGIS. Download the `.kmz` file containing the information about 2012 global earthquakes from the USGS website at `http://earthquake.usgs.gov/earthquakes/eqarchives/epic/kml/2012_Earthquakes_ALL.kmz`. Save it in the `working/chp03` directory (alternatively, you can use the copy of this file included in the code bundle provided with this book).

2.  A `.kmz` file is a collection of `.kml` files packaged with the ZIP compressor. Therefore, after unzipping the file (you may need to change the `.kmz` file extension to `.zip`), you may notice that it is composed of just a single `.kml` file. This file, which is in the GDAL abstraction, constitutes an OGR KML data source composed of nine different layers and containing 3D point geometries. Each layer contains earthquake data for each distinct earthquake magnitude:

    ```
    $ ogrinfo 2012_Earthquakes_ALL.kml

    Had to open data source read-only.

    INFO: Open of `2012_Earthquakes_ALL.kml'
          using driver `KML' successful.

    1: Magnitude 8 (3D Point)

    2: Magnitude 7 (3D Point)

    ...

    8: Magnitude 1 (3D Point)

    9: Magnitude None (3D Point)
    ```

3.  Import all of those layers in a PostGIS table named `chp03.earthquakes` simultaneously by executing one of the following scripts, using the `ogr2ogr` command.

    The following is the Linux version (name it `import_eq.sh`):

    ```
    #!/bin/bash

    for ((i = 1; i < 9 ; i++)) ; do

      echo "Importing earthquakes with magnitude $i to chp03.
    earthquakes PostGIS table..."
    ```

```
ogr2ogr -append -f PostgreSQL -nln chp03.earthquakes
PG:"dbname='postgis_cookbook' user='me' password='mypassword'"
2012_Earthquakes_ALL.kml -sql "SELECT name, description, CAST($i
AS integer) AS magnitude FROM 'Magnitude $i'"
done
```

The following is the Windows version (name it `import_eq.bat`):

```
@echo off
for /l %%i in (1, 1, 9) do (
  echo "Importing earthquakes with magnitude %%i to chp03.
earthquakes PostGIS table..."
  ogr2ogr -append -f PostgreSQL -nln chp03.earthquakes
PG:"dbname='postgis_cookbook' user='me' password='mypassword'"
2012_Earthquakes_ALL.kml -sql "SELECT name, description, CAST(%%i
AS integer) AS magnitude FROM 'Magnitude %%i'"
)
```

4. Execute the following script (for Linux, you need to add `execute` permissions to it):

```
$ chmod 775 import_eq.sh
$ ./import_eq.sh
Importing earthquakes with magnitude 1 to chp03.earthquakes
PostGIS table...
Importing earthquakes with magnitude 2 to chp03.earthquakes
PostGIS table...
...
```

5. To maintain consistency with the book's conventions, rename the geometric column `wkb_geometry` (the default geometry output name in `ogr2ogr`) to `the_geom`, as illustrated in the following command:

```
postgis_cookbook=# ALTER TABLE chp03.earthquakes RENAME wkb_
geometry  TO the_geom;
```

6. Download the `cities` shapefile for USA from the `nationalatlas.gov` website at `http://dds.cr.usgs.gov/pub/data/nationalatlas/citiesx020_nt00007.tar.gz` (this archive is also included in the code bundle provided with this book), and import it in PostGIS by executing the following code:

```
$ ogr2ogr -f PostgreSQL -s_srs EPSG:4269 -t_srs EPSG:4326 -lco
GEOMETRY_NAME=the_geom -nln chp03.cities PG:"dbname='postgis_
cookbook' user='me' password='mypassword'" citiesx020.shp
```

7. Download the `states` shapefile for USA from the `nationalatlas.gov` website at `http://dds.cr.usgs.gov/pub/data/nationalatlas/statesp020_nt00032.tar.gz` (this archive is also included in the code bundle provided with this book) and import it in PostGIS by executing the following code:

```
$ ogr2ogr -f PostgreSQL -s_srs EPSG:4269 -t_srs EPSG:4326 -lco
GEOMETRY_NAME=the_geom -nln chp03.states -nlt MULTIPOLYGON
PG:"dbname='postgis_cookbook' user='me' password='mypassword'"
statesp020.shp
```

## How to do it...

In this recipe, you will see for yourself the power of spatial SQL by solving a series of typical problems using spatial joins.

1. First, query PostGIS to get the number of registered earthquakes in 2012 by state:

```
postgis_cookbook=# SELECT s.state, COUNT(*) AS hq_count
FROM chp03.states AS s
    JOIN chp03.earthquakes AS e
    ON ST_Intersects(s.the_geom, e.the_geom)
    GROUP BY s.state
    ORDER BY hq_count DESC;
    state        | hq_count
-------------- --+---------
 Alaska        |      569
 California    |      467
 Hawaii        |       93
 ...
 South Dakota  |        1
(33 rows)
```

2. Now, to make it just a bit more complex, query PostGIS to get the number of earthquakes, grouped per magnitude, that are no further than 200 km from the cities in the USA that have more than 1,000,000 inhabitants; execute the following code:

```
postgis_cookbook=# SELECT c.name, e.magnitude, count(*) as hq_
count FROM chp03.cities AS c
    JOIN chp03.earthquakes AS e
    ON ST_DWithin(geography(c.the_geom), geography(e.the_geom),
200000)
    WHERE c.pop_2000 > 1000000
    GROUP BY c.name, e.magnitude
```

```
ORDER BY c.name, e.magnitude, hq_count;
    name     | magnitude | hq_count
-------------+-----------+---------
 Chicago     |         2 |        1
 Chicago     |         3 |        1
 Dalla       |         2 |       12
 ...
 San Diego   |         4 |       20
 San Diego   |         5 |        2
(18 rows)
```

3. As a variant of the previous query, executing the following code gives you a complete list of earthquakes, along with their distance from the city (in meters):

```
postgis_cookbook=# SELECT c.name, e.magnitude,
    ST_Distance(geography(c.the_geom), geography(e.the_geom)) AS
distance FROM chp03.cities AS c
    JOIN chp03.earthquakes AS e
    ON ST_DWithin(geography(c.the_geom), geography(e.the_geom),
200000)
    WHERE c.pop_2000 > 1000000
    ORDER BY distance;
    name      | magnitude |     distance
--------------+-----------+------------------
 Dallas       |         2 | 10801.3253855616
 Los Angeles  |         3 | 13740.7943591606
 ...
 San Diego    |         2 | 199062.753724934
 Los Angeles  |         2 | 199390.900371205
(488 rows)
```

4. Now, ask PostGIS for the city count and the total population in each state by executing the following code:

```
postgis_cookbook-# SELECT s.state, COUNT(*) AS city_count,
SUM(pop_2000) AS pop_2000 FROM
    chp03.states AS s
    JOIN chp03.cities AS c
    ON ST_Intersects(s.the_geom, c.the_geom)
    WHERE c.pop_2000 > 0 -- NULL values is -9999 on this field!
    GROUP BY s.state
```

```
        ORDER BY pop_2000 DESC;
          state          | city_count | pop_2000
    ---------------------+------------+----------
      California         |        470 | 27380349
      Texas              |       1182 | 15738629
      New York           |        613 | 12139544
      ...
      Wyoming            |         96 |   334624
      Delaware           |         56 |   214413
      Vermont            |         48 |   154831
    (51 rows)
```

5. As a final test, use a spatial join to update an existing table. You need to add the information in the `state_fips` field to the `earthquake` table, from the `states` table. First, to host that kind of information, you need to create a column, as shown in the following command:

```
postgis_cookbook-# ALTER TABLE chp03.earthquakes ADD COLUMN state_
fips character varying(2);
```

6. Then, you can update the new column using a spatial join, as follows:

```
postgis_cookbook-# UPDATE chp03.earthquakes AS e
    SET state_fips = s.state_fips
    FROM chp03.states AS s
    WHERE ST_Intersects(s.the_geom, e.the_geom);
```

## How it works...

Spatial joins are one of the key features that unleash the spatial power of PostGIS. For a regular join, it is possible to relate entities from two distinct tables using a common field. For a spatial join, it is possible to relate features from two distinct spatial tables using any spatial relationship function, such as `ST_Contains`, `ST_Covers`, `ST_Crosses`, and `ST_DWithin`.

In the first query, we used the `ST_Intersects` function to join the earthquake points to their respective containing state. We grouped the query by the `state` column to obtain the number of earthquakes in the state.

In the second query, we used the `ST_DWithin` function to relate each city to the earthquake points within a 200 km distance from it. We filtered out the cities with a population of less than 1 million inhabitants and grouped them by city name and earthquake magnitude to get a report of the number of earthquakes per city and magnitude.

The third query is similar to the second one, except it doesn't group per city and magnitude. The distance is computed using the ST_Distance function. Note that as feature coordinates are stored in WGS 84, you need to cast the geometric column to a spheroid and use the spheroid to get the distance in meters. Alternatively, you could project the geometries to a planar system that is accurate for the area we are studying in this recipe (in this case, the *ESPG:2163, US National Atlas Equal Area* would be a good choice) using the ST_Transform function. However, in the case of large areas like the one we've dealt with in this recipe, casting to geography is generally the best option, as it gives more accurate results.

The fourth query uses the ST_Intersects function. In this case, we grouped by the state column and used two aggregation SQL functions (SUM and COUNT) to get the desired results.

Finally, in the last query, you update a spatial table using the results of a spatial join. The concept behind this is like that of the previous query, except that it is in the context of an UPDATE SQL command.

# Simplifying geometries

There will be many times when you will need to generate a less detailed and lighter version of a vector dataset, as you may not need too-detailed features for several reasons. Think about a case where you are going to publish the dataset to a website and performance is a concern, or maybe you need to deploy the dataset to a colleague who does not need too much detail because he or she is using it for a large-area map. In all of these cases, GIS tools provide you the implementation of **simplification algorithms** that reduce unwanted details from a given dataset. Basically, these algorithms reduce the vertex numbers comprised in a certain tolerance, which is expressed in units measuring distance.

For this purpose, PostGIS provides you the ST_Simplify and ST_SimplifyPreserveTopology functions. In many cases, they are the right solutions for simplification tasks, but in some cases, especially for polygonal features, they are not the best option out there and you will need a different GIS tool such as GRASS, or the new PostGIS topology support.

## How to do it...

The steps you need to complete this recipe are as follows:

1. Set the PostgreSQL search_path variable so that all of your newly created database objects will be stored in the chp03 schema, using the following code:

```
postgis_cookbook=# SET search_path TO chp03,public;
```

2. Suppose you need a less-detailed version of the `states` layer for your mapping website or to deploy to a client; you could consider using the `ST_SimplifyPreserveTopology` function, as follows:

```
postgis_cookbook=# CREATE TABLE states_simplify_topology AS

    SELECT ST_SimplifyPreserveTopology(ST_Transform(
        the_geom, 2163), 500) FROM states;
```

3. The previous command works quickly, using some variant of the Douglas-Peucker algorithm, and effectively reduces the vertex number. But the resulting polygons, in some cases, are not adjacent any more. If you zoom in at any polygon border, you should notice something similar to that which is shown in the following screenshot. There are holes and overlaps along the shared border between two polygons. This is because PostGIS is using the OGC Simple Features Specification model, which doesn't implement topology, so the function just removes the redundant vertex without taking the adjacent polygons into consideration:

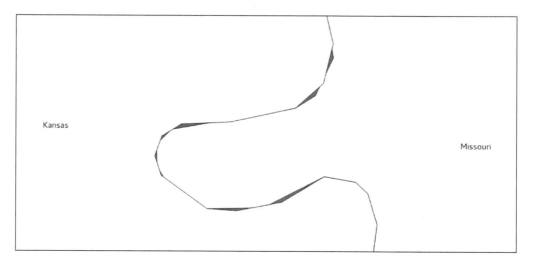

4. It looks like the `ST_SimplifyPreserveTopology` function, while working well with linear features, produces topological anomalies with polygons. In the event that you want topological simplification, another approach is to utilize the following code suggested by Paul Ramsey (`http://gis.stackexchange.com/questions/178/simplifying-adjacent-polygons`), and improved in a Webspaces blog post (`http://webspaces.net.nz/page.php?view=polygon-dissolve-and-generalise`):

```
SET search_path TO chp03, public;

-- first project the spatial table to a planar system (recommended
for simplification operations)

CREATE TABLE states_2163 AS SELECT ST_Transform(the_geom,
2163)::geometry(MultiPolygon, 2163) AS the_geom, state FROM states;
```

```
-- now decompose the geometries from multipolygons (2895) using the ST_Dump function
```

```
CREATE TABLE polygons AS SELECT (ST_Dump(the_geom)).geom AS the_
geom FROM states_2163;
```

```
-- now decompose from polygons (2895) to rings (3150) using the
ST_DumpRings function
```

```
CREATE TABLE rings AS SELECT (ST_DumpRings(the_geom)).geom AS the_
geom FROM polygons;
```

```
-- now decompose from rings (3150) to linestrings (3150) using the
ST_Boundary function
```

```
CREATE TABLE ringlines AS SELECT(ST_boundary(the_geom)) AS the_
geom FROM rings;
```

```
-- now merge all linestrings (3150) in a single merged linestring
(this way duplicate linestrings at polygon borders disappear)
```

```
CREATE TABLE mergedringlines AS SELECT ST_Union(the_geom) AS the_
geom FROM ringlines;
```

```
-- finally simplify the linestring with a tolerance of 150 meters
```

```
CREATE TABLE simplified_ringlines AS SELECT ST_
SimplifyPreserveTopology(the_geom, 150) AS the_geom FROM
mergedringlines;
```

```
-- now compose a polygons collection from the linestring using the
ST_Polygonize function
```

```
CREATE TABLE simplified_polycollection AS SELECT ST_
Polygonize(the_geom) AS the_geom FROM simplified_ringlines;
```

```
-- here you generate polygons (2895) from the polygons collection
using ST_Dumps
```

```
CREATE TABLE simplified_polygons AS SELECT ST_Transform((ST_
Dump(the_geom)).geom, 4326)::geometry(Polygon,4326) AS the_geom
FROM simplified_polycollection;
```

```
-- time to create an index, to make next operations faster CREATE
INDEX simplified_polygons_gist ON simplified_polygons USING GIST
(the_geom);
```

```
-- now copy the state name attribute from old layer with a spatial
join using the ST_Intersects and ST_PointOnSurface function
```

```
CREATE TABLE simplified_polygonsattr AS SELECT new.the_geom,
old.state FROM simplified_polygons new, states old WHERE ST_
Intersects(new.the_geom, old.the_geom) AND ST_Intersects(ST_
PointOnSurface(new.the_geom), old.the_geom);
```

```
-- now make the union of all polygons with a common name
```

```
CREATE TABLE states_simplified AS SELECT ST_Union(the_geom) AS
the_geom, state FROM simplified_polygonsattr GROUP BY state;
```

5. This approach seems to work smoothly, but if you try to increment the simplifying tolerance from 150 to let's say, 500 meters, you will again end up with topological anomalies (test this yourself). A better approach would be to use the PostGIS topology (you will do this in a following recipe) or an external GIS tool that is able to manage topological operations the way GRASS can. For this recipe, you will use the GRASS approach.

6. Install GRASS on your system if you don't already have it. Then, create a directory to contain the GRASS database (in GRASS jargon, a GISDBASE), as follows:

```
$ mkdir grass_db
```

7. Now, start GRASS by typing grass in the Linux command prompt or by double-clicking on the **GRASS GUI** icon in Windows (**Start | All Programs | OSGeo4W | GRASS GIS 6.4.3 | GRASS 6.4.3 GUI**). You will be prompted to select grass_db as the GIS data directory. Select the one you created in the previous step.

8. Using the **Location Wizard** button, create a location named postgis_cookbook with the title PostGIS Cookbook (GRASS uses subdirectories named locations, where all of the data are kept in the same coordinate system, map projection, and geographical boundaries).

9. When creating the new location, select the EPSG with SRID 2163 as the spatial reference system (you need to select the **Select EPSG code of spatial reference system** option under **Choose method for creating a new location**).

10. Now **start GRASS** by clicking on the Start GRASS button. The program's command line will start:

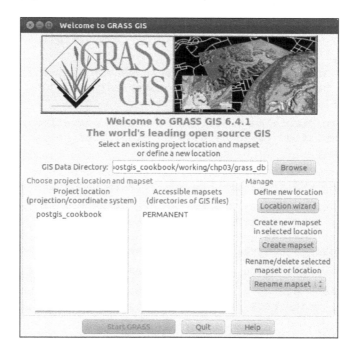

11. Import the `states` PostGIS spatial table to the GRASS location. To do so, use the `v.in.ogr` GRASS command, which will then use the OGR PostgreSQL driver (in fact, the PostGIS connection string syntax is the same):

```
GRASS 6.4.1 (postgis_cookbook):~ > v.in.ogr
dsn=PG:"dbname='postgis_cookbook' user='me' password='mypassword'"
layer=chp03.states_2163 out=states
```

12. GRASS will import the OGR PostGIS table and simultaneously build the topology for this layer, which is composed of points, lines, areas, and so on. The `v.info` command can be used in combination with the `-c` option to check the attributes table and get more information on the imported layer, as follows:

```
GRASS 6.4.1 (postgis_cookbook):~ > v.info states

+--------------------------------------------------------+
| Layer:          states                                 |
| Mapset:         PERMANENT                               |
| Location:       postgis_cookbook                       |
| Database: /home/capooti/postgis_cookbook/working/      |
| chp03/grass_db                                         |
| Title:                                                 |
| Map scale:      1:1                                     |
| Map format:     native                                 |
| Name of creator: capooti                               |
| Organization:                                          |
| Source date:    Tue Sep 18 18:18:38 2012               |
|-------------------------------------- ---------------|
|   Type of Map:  vector (level: 2)                      |
|                                                        |
|   Number of points:      0    Number of areas:   2895 |
|   Number of lines:       0    Number of islands: 2818 |
|   Number of boundaries:  3034 Number of faces:   0    |
|   Number of centroids:   2895 Number of kernels: 0    |
|   Map is 3D:                                           |
|   Number of dblinks:                                   |
|                                                        |
|        Projection: x,y                                 |
|             N:   3910267.02926988    S: -2360476.09035623 |
|             E:   3745267.23502577    W: -5761129.11796747 |
|                                                        |
```

```
|   Digitization threshold: 0
|   Comments:
|
+---------------------------------------------------------- --+
```

13. Now, you can simplify the polygon geometries using the `v.generalize` GRASS command with a tolerance (threshold) of 500 meters. If you are using the same dataset used in this recipe, you will end up with 47.191 vertices from the original 346.914 vertices, composing 1.919 polygons (areas) from the original 2.895 polygons:

```
GRASS 6.4.1 (postgis_cookbook):~ > v.generalize input=states
output=states_generalized_from_grass method=douglas threshold=500
-c
```

14. Export the results back to PostGIS using the `v.out.ogr` command (the `v.in.ogr` counterpart), as follows:

```
GRASS 6.4.1 (postgis_cookbook):~ > v.out.ogr input=states_
generalized_from_grass type=area dsn=PG:"dbname='postgis_cookbook'
user='me' password='mypassword'" olayer=chp03.states_simplified_
from_grass format=PostgreSQL
```

15. Now, open a Desktop GIS and check for differences between the geometry simplification performed by the `ST_SimplifyPreserveTopology` PostGIS function and GRASS. There should be no holes or overlaps at shared polygon borders. In the following screenshot, the original layer boundaries are in red, the boundaries built by `ST_SimplifyPreserveTopology` are in blue, and those built by GRASS are in green:

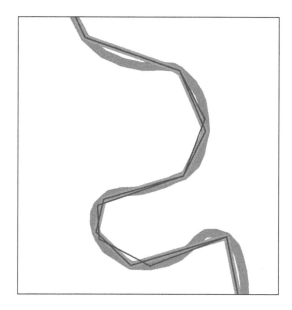

## How it works...

The ST_Simplify PostGIS function is able to simplify and generalize either a (simple or multi) linear or polygonal geometry using the Douglas-Peucker algorithm (for more details, go to http://en.wikipedia.org/wiki/Ramer%E2%80%93Douglas%E2%80%93Peucker_algorithm). Since it can create invalid geometries in some cases, it is recommended that you use its evolved version—the ST_SimplifyPreserveTopology function—that will produce only valid geometries.

While the functions are working well with (multi) linear geometries, in the case of (multi) polygons, they will most likely create topological anomalies, such as overlaps and holes, at shared polygon borders.

To get a valid, topologically simplified dataset, there are the following two choices at the time of this writing:

▶ Performing the simplified process on an external GIS tool such as GRASS

▶ Using the new PostGIS topological support

While you will see the new PostGIS topological features in a following recipe, in this one, you have been using GRASS to perform the simplification process.

We opened GRASS, created a GIS data directory and a project location, and then imported in the GRASS location the polygonal PostGIS table using the v.ogr.in command, based on GDAL/OGR, as the name suggests.

Until this point, you have been using the GRASS v.generalize command to perform the simplification of the dataset using a tolerance (threshold) expressed in meters.

After simplifying the dataset, you have imported it back to PostGIS using the v.ogr.out GRASS command and then opened the derived spatial table in a Desktop GIS to see whether or not the process was performed in a topologically correct way.

# Measuring distances

In this recipe, we will check out the PostGIS functions needed for distance measurements (ST_Distance and its variants) and find out how considering the earth's curvature makes a big difference when measuring distances between distant points.

## Getting ready

You should import the shapefile representing the cities from the USA that we generated in a previous recipe (the PostGIS table named `chp03.cities`). In case you haven't already done so, download that shapefile from the `nationalatlas.gov` website at `http://dds.cr.usgs.gov/pub/data/nationalatlas/citiesx020_nt00007.tar.gz` (this archive is also included in the code bundle available with this book) and import it to PostGIS:

```
$ ogr2ogr -f PostgreSQL -s_srs EPSG:4269 -t_srs EPSG:4326 -lco GEOMETRY_
NAME=the_geom -nln chp03.cities PG:"dbname='postgis_cookbook' user='me'
password='mypassword'" citiesx020.shp
```

## How to do it...

The steps you need to perform to complete this recipe are as follows:

1. First, use the `ST_Distance` function to calculate the distances between cities in the USA that have more than 1,000,000 inhabitants using the Spherical Mercator planar projection coordinate system (EPSG:900913, EPSG:3857, or EPSG:3785; all of these SRID representations are equivalent). Use the `ST_Transform` function as follows to convert the point coordinates from lon lat degrees (as the coordinates are originally in EPSG:4326) to a planar metric system, if you want the results in meters:

   ```
   postgis_cookbook=# SELECT c1.name, c2.name,
   ST_Distance(ST_Transform(c1.the_geom, 900913),
   ST_Transform(c2.the_geom, 900913))/1000 AS distance_900913
   FROM chp03.cities AS c1
   CROSS JOIN
   chp03.cities AS c2
   WHERE c1.pop_2000 > 1000000 AND c2.pop_2000 > 1000000 AND c1.name
   < c2.name
   ORDER BY distance_900913 DESC;
        name      |     name      | distance_900913
   --------------+--------------+------------------
    Los Angeles  | New York     | 5012.39789777705
    New York     | San Diego    | 4930.76973825481
    Los Angeles  | Philadelphia |  4865.7736877805
    ...
    Los Angeles  | San Diego    | 215.396531218742
    New York     | Philadelphia | 170.272806220365
   (36 rows)
   ```

2. Now, write the same query as we did in the previous recipe, but in a more compact expression and by using PostgreSQL **Common Table Expression** (**CTE**):

```
WITH cities AS (
    SELECT name, the_geom FROM chp03.cities
    WHERE pop_2000 > 1000000 )
SELECT c1.name, c2.name,
ST_Distance(ST_Transform(c1.the_geom, 900913), ST_Transform(c2.
the_geom, 900913))/1000 AS distance_900913
FROM cities c1 CROSS JOIN cities c2
where c1.name < c2.name
ORDER BY distance_900913 DESC;
```

3. For large distances such as the ones in this case, it is not correct to use a planar spatial reference system, but you should make the calculations taking into consideration the earth's curvature. For example, the previously used Mercator planar system, while it is very good to use for map outputs, is very bad for measuring distances and areas, as it assesses directions. For this purpose, it would be better to use a spatial reference system that is able to measure distance. You can also use the `ST_Distance_Sphere` or `ST_Distance_Spheroid` functions (the first being quicker, but less accurate, as it performs calculations on a sphere and not a spheroid). An even better option is converting the geometries to the geography data type, `ST_Distance`, as it will automatically make the calculations using the spheroid. Note that this is exactly equivalent to using `ST_DistanceSpheroid`. Try to check the difference between the various approaches, using the same query as before:

```
WITH cities AS (
    SELECT name, the_geom FROM chp03.cities
    WHERE pop_2000 > 1000000 )
SELECT c1.name, c2.name,
ST_Distance(ST_Transform(c1.the_geom, 900913), ST_Transform(c2.
the_geom, 900913))/1000 AS d_900913,
ST_Distance_Sphere(c1.the_geom, c2.the_geom)/1000 AS d_4326_
sphere,
ST_Distance_Spheroid(c1.the_geom, c2.the_geom, 'SPHEROID["G
RS_1980",6378137,298.257222101]')/1000 AS d_4326_spheroid,
ST_Distance(geography(c1.the_geom), geography(c2.the_geom))/1000
AS d_4326_geography
FROM cities c1 CROSS JOIN cities c2
where c1.name < c2.name
ORDER BY d_900913 DESC;
    name    |    name    | d_900913 | d_4326_sphere | d_4326_
spheroid | d_4326_geography
```

```
---------------+---------------+-----------+----------------+--------
---------+-----------------
   Los Angeles  | New York      | 5012.3..  |    3935.7..    |
3944.4..  |    3944.4..
   New York     | San Diego     | 4930.7..  |    3906.8..    |
3915.0..  |    3915.0..
   ...
   New York     | Philadelphia  | 170.2..   |    129.6..     |
129.7..   |    129.7..
   (36 rows)
```

4. You can easily verify from the output that there is a big difference with using the planar system (EPSG:900913, as in the `d_900913` column) when confronted with systems that take into consideration the curvature of the earth.

## How it works...

If you need to compute the minimum Cartesian distance between two points, you can use the PostGIS `ST_Distance` function. This function accepts the two-point geometries as input parameters, and these geometries must be specified in the same **spatial reference system**.

If the two input geometries are using different spatial references, you can use the `ST_Transform` function on one or both of them to make them consistent with a single spatial reference system.

To get better results, you should consider the earth's curvature, which is mandatory when measuring large distances, and use the `ST_Distance_Sphere` or the `ST_Distance_Spheroid` functions. Alternatively, use `ST_Distance`, but cast the input geometries to the **geography spatial data type**, which is optimized for this kind of operation. The geography type stores the geometries in the WGS 84 lon lat degrees, but it always returns the measurements in meters.

In this recipe, you have used PostgreSQL CTE, which is a handy way to provide a subquery in the context of the main query. You can consider a CTE as a temporary table used only within the scope of the main query.

# Merging polygons using a common attribute

There are many cases in GIS workflows where you need to merge a polygonal dataset based on a common attribute. A typical example is merging the European administrative areas (that you can see at `http://en.wikipedia.org/wiki/Nomenclature_of_Territorial_Units_for_Statistics`), starting from the NUTS level 4 to obtain the subsequent levels up to the NUTS level 1, using the NUTS code or merging the USA counties layer using the state code to obtain the states layer.

PostGIS lets you perform this kind of processing operation with the ST_Union function.

## Getting ready

Download the USA counties shapefile from the nationalatlas.gov website at
http://dds.cr.usgs.gov/pub/data/nationalatlas/co2000p020_nt00157.tar.
gz (this archive is also included in the code bundle provided with this book) and import it in
PostGIS as follows:

```
$ ogr2ogr -f PostgreSQL -s_srs EPSG:4269 -t_srs EPSG:4326 -lco GEOMETRY_
NAME=the_geom -nln chp03.counties -nlt MULTIPOLYGON PG:"dbname='postgis_
cookbook' user='me' password='mypassword'" co2000p020.shp
```

## How to do it...

The steps you need to perform to complete this recipe are as follows:

1. First, check the imported table by running the following commands:

   ```
   postgis_cookbook=# SELECT county, fips, state_fips FROM chp03.
   counties ORDER BY county;
                    county         | fips  | state_fips
   ----------------------------------+-----  ---+-----------
        Abbeville County            | 45001 | 45
        Acadia Parish               | 22001 | 22
        Accomack County             | 51001 | 51
   ...
        Zapata County               | 48505 | 48
        Zavala County               | 48507 | 48
        Ziebach County              | 46137 | 46
   (6138 rows)
   ```

2. Now, perform the merging operation based on the state_fips field, using the
   ST_Union PostGIS function:

   ```
   postgis_cookbook=# CREATE TABLE chp03.states_from_counties AS
   SELECT ST_Multi(ST_Union(the_geom)) as the_geom, state_fips FROM
   chp03.counties
   GROUP BY state_fips;
   ```

3.  The following screenshot shows how the output PostGIS layer looks in a Desktop GIS: the aggregate counties have successfully composed their respective state (thick blue border):

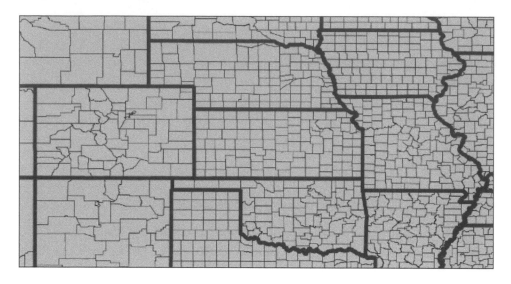

## How it works...

You have been using the ST_Union PostGIS function to make a polygon merge on a common attribute. This function can be used as an aggregate PostgreSQL function (such as SUM, COUNT, MIN, and MAX) on the layer's geometric field, using the common attribute in the GROUP BY clause.

Note that ST_Union can also be used as a nonaggregate function to perform the union of two geometries (which are the two input parameters).

## Computing intersections

One typical GIS geoprocessing workflow is to compute intersections generated by intersecting linear geometries.

PostGIS offers a rich set of functions for solving this particular type of problem and you will have a look at them in this recipe.

## Getting ready

Download the `rivers` dataset from the following `naturalearthdata.com` website (or use the ZIP file included in the code bundle provided with this book):

```
http://www.naturalearthdata.com/http//www.naturalearthdata.com/
download/10m/physical/10m-rivers-lake-centerlines.zip
```

Extract the shapefile to your working directory, `chp03/working`. Import the shapefile in PostGIS using `shp2pgsql` as follows:

```
$ shp2pgsql -I -W LATIN1 -s 4326 -g the_geom ne_10m_rivers_lake_
centerlines.shp chp03.rivers > rivers.sql
$ psql -U me -d postgis_cookbook -f rivers.sql
```

## How to do it...

The steps you need to perform to complete this recipe are as follows:

1.  First, perform a self-spatial join with your `MultiLineString` dataset with the PostGIS `ST_Intersects` function and find intersections in the join context with the `ST_Intersection` PostGIS function. The following is the basic query, resulting in 1448 records being selected:

    ```
    postgis_cookbook=# SELECT r1.gid AS gid1, r2.gid AS gid2,
        ST_AsText(ST_Intersection(r1.the_geom, r2.the_geom)) AS the_
    geom
        FROM chp03.rivers r1
        JOIN chp03.rivers r2
        ON ST_Intersects(r1.the_geom, r2.the_geom)
        WHERE r1.gid != r2.gid;
    ```

2.  You may hastily assume that all of the intersections are single points, but this is not the case—if you check the geometry type of the geometric intersections using the `ST_GeometryType` function, you have three different cases of intersection, resulting in the following geometries:

    - An `ST_POINT` geometry for a simple intersection between two linear geometries.

    - An `ST_MultiPoint` geometry, if two linear geometries intersect each other at more points.

    - An `ST_GeometryCollection` geometry in cases where the two `MultiLineString` objects intersect and share part of the line. In such a case, the geometry collection is composed of `ST_Point` and/or `ST_Line` geometries.

3. You can check the different cases with a query, shown as follows:

```
postgis_cookbook=# SELECT COUNT(*),
    ST_GeometryType(ST_Intersection(r1.the_geom, r2.the_geom)) AS
geometry_type
    FROM chp03.rivers r1
    JOIN chp03.rivers r2
    ON ST_Intersects(r1.the_geom, r2.the_geom)
    WHERE r1.gid != r2.gid
    GROUP BY geometry_type;
 count |      geometry_type
-------+-----------------------
     4 | ST_GeometryCollection
   356 | ST_MultiPoint
  1088 | ST_Point
(3 rows)
```

4. First, try to compute the intersection for just the first two cases (intersections composed of the `ST_Point` and `ST_MultiPoint` geometries). Just generate a table with the `Point` and `MultiPoint` geometries, excluding the records that have an intersection composed of a geometric collection. By executing the following commands, 1444 of the 1448 records are imported (the four records with geometry collections are ignored using the `ST_GeometryType` function):

```
postgis_cookbook=# CREATE TABLE chp03.intersections_simple AS
    SELECT r1.gid AS gid1, r2.gid AS gid2,
      ST_Multi(ST_Intersection(r1.the_geom,
      r2.the_geom))::geometry(MultiPoint, 4326) AS the_geom
    FROM chp03.rivers r1
    JOIN chp03.rivers r2
    ON ST_Intersects(r1.the_geom, r2.the_geom)
    WHERE r1.gid != r2.gid
    AND ST_GeometryType(ST_Intersection(r1.the_geom,
      r2.the_geom)) != 'ST_GeometryCollection';
```

5. In case you want to import the points from the geometry collection, too (but just the points, ignoring the eventual linestrings), one way to go is by using the `ST_CollectionExtract` function in the context of a `SELECT CASE` PostgreSQL conditional statement; this way you can import all the 1448 intersections, as follows:

```
postgis_cookbook=# CREATE TABLE chp03.intersections_all AS
    SELECT gid1, gid2, the_geom::geometry(MultiPoint, 4326) FROM (
    SELECT r1.gid AS gid1, r2.gid AS gid2,
```

```
CASE
    WHEN ST_GeometryType(ST_Intersection(r1.the_geom,
        r2.the_geom)) != 'ST_GeometryCollection' THEN
    ST_Multi(ST_Intersection(r1.the_geom,
        r2.the_geom))
    ELSE ST_CollectionExtract(ST_Intersection(r1.the_geom,
        r2.the_geom), 1)
END AS the_geom
FROM chp03.rivers r1
JOIN chp03.rivers r2
ON ST_Intersects(r1.the_geom, r2.the_geom)
WHERE r1.gid != r2.gid
) AS only_multipoints_geometries;
```

6. You may see the difference between the two processes, counting the total number of points in each of the generated tables, as follows:

```
postgis_cookbook=# SELECT SUM(ST_NPoints(the_geom)) FROM chp03.
intersections_simple; --2268 points per 1444 records
```

```
postgis_cookbook=# SELECT SUM(ST_NPoints(the_geom)) FROM chp03.
intersections_all; --2282 points per 1448 records
```

7. In the following screenshot (taken from QGIS), you may notice the generated intersections with both approaches. In the case of the intersection_all layer, you will notice that some more intersections have been computed (in red).

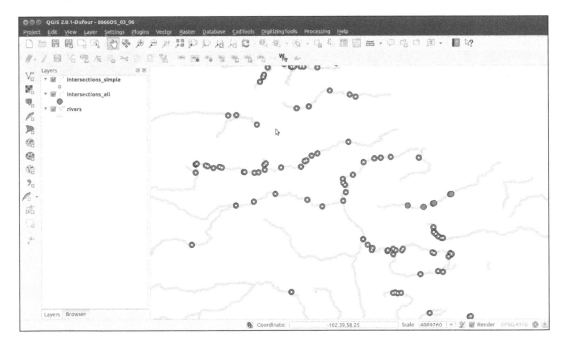

## How it works...

We have been using a spatial self join of a linear PostGIS spatial layer to find intersections generated by the features of that layer.

For generating the spatial self join, we used the ST_Intersects function. This way we found all of the pair features having at least one intersection in their respective geometries.

In the same self spatial join context, we found out the intersections using the ST_Intersection function.

The problem is that the computed intersections are not always single points. In fact, two intersecting lines can produce the origin for a single-point geometry (ST_Point) if the two lines just intersect once. But, the two intersecting lines can produce the origin for a point collection (ST_MultiPoint) or even a geometric collection, if the two lines intersect at more points and/or share common parts.

As our target was to compute all of the point intersections (ST_Point and ST_MultiPoint) using the ST_GeometryType function, we filtered out the values using a SQL SELECT CASE construct where the feature had a GeometryCollection geometry, for which we extracted just the points (and not the eventual linestrings) using the ST_CollectionExtract function (parameter type = 1) from the composing collections.

We finally compared the two result sets, both with plain SQL and a Desktop GIS: the intersecting points computed filtering out the geometric collections from the output geometries and the intersecting points computed from all of the geometries generated from the intersections, including the GeometryCollection features.

# Clipping geometries to deploy data

A common GIS use case is clipping a big dataset into small portions (subsets), with maybe each representing an area of interest. In this recipe, you will export from a PostGIS layer representing the rivers in the world one distinct shapefile composed of rivers for each world's country. For this purpose, you will use the ST_Intersection function.

## Getting ready

Be sure that you have imported in PostGIS the same river dataset (a shapefile) that was used in the previous recipe.

## How to do it...

The steps you need to perform to complete this recipe are as follows:

1. First, you will create a view to clip the river geometries for each country using the `ST_Intersection` and `ST_Intersects` functions. Name the view `rivers_clipped_by_country`:

```
postgis_cookbook=> CREATE VIEW chp03.rivers_clipped_by_country AS

    SELECT r.name, c.iso2, ST_Intersection(r.the_geom,
      c.the_geom)::geometry(Geometry,4326) AS the_geom
    FROM chp03.countries AS c

    JOIN chp03.rivers AS r

    ON ST_Intersects(r.the_geom, c.the_geom);
```

2. Create a directory named `rivers`, as follows:

```
mkdir working/chp03/rivers
```

3. Create the following scripts to export a `rivers` shapefile for each country.

   The following is the Linux version (name it `export_rivers.sh`):

```
#!/bin/bash
for f in `ogrinfo PG:"dbname='postgis_cookbook' user='me'
password='mypassword'" -sql "SELECT DISTINCT(iso2) FROM chp03.
countries ORDER BY iso2" | grep iso2 | awk '{print $4}'`
do
    echo "Exporting river shapefile for $f country..."
    ogr2ogr rivers/rivers_$f.shp PG:"dbname='postgis_cookbook'
user='me' password='mypassword'" -sql "SELECT * FROM chp03.rivers_
clipped_by_country WHERE iso2 = '$f'"
done
```

   The following is the Windows version (name it `export_rivers.bat`):

```
FOR /F "tokens=*" %%f IN ('ogrinfo PG:"dbname=postgis_cookbook
user=me password=mypassword" -sql "SELECT DISTINCT(iso2) FROM
chp03.countries ORDER BY iso2" ^| grep iso2 ^| awk "{print $4}"')
DO (
   echo "Exporting river shapefile for %%f country..."
   ogr2ogr rivers/rivers_%%f.shp PG:"dbname='postgis_cookbook'
user='me' password='mypassword'" -sql "SELECT * FROM chp03.rivers_
clipped_by_country WHERE iso2 = '%%f'"
)
```

**For Windows users**

The script uses the `grep` and `awk` Linux commands, so you will need to download their Windows versions from `http://unxutils.sourceforge.net/`. There's the chance that you already have them installed in your system if you have installed OSGeo4W—a binary distribution of a broad set of open-source, geospatial software for Win32 environments. You can find it at `http://trac.osgeo.org/osgeo4w/`.

You could eventually skip the creation of the `rivers_clipped_by_country` view and perform the query in the `ogr2ogr` statement in the script, as shown in the following command (`ogr2ogr` passes the content of the `-sql` option directly to PostGIS):

```
ogr2ogr rivers/rivers_$f.shp PG:"dbname='postgis_
cookbook' user='me' password='mypassword'" -sql "SELECT
r.name, c.iso2, ST_Intersection(r.the_geom, c.the_geom)
AS the_geom FROM chp03.countries AS c JOIN chp03.rivers
AS r ON ST_Intersects(r.the_geom, c.the_geom) WHERE
c.iso2 = '$f'"
```

4. Now, run the following script (in Linux, you need to assign `execute` permissions to the script beforehand):

```
$ chmod 775 rivers.sh
$ ./export_rivers.sh
Exporting river shapefile for AD country...
Exporting river shapefile for AE country...
...
Exporting river shapefile for ZM country...
Exporting river shapefile for ZW country...
```

5. Check the output with `ogrinfo` or a Desktop GIS. The following screenshot shows how the output looks in QGIS; we have added the original PostGIS `chp03.rivers` layer and a couple of the generated shapefiles:

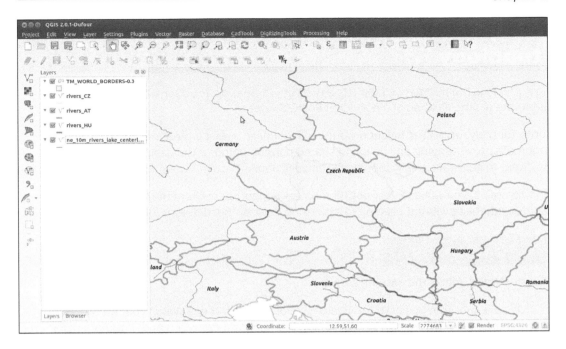

## How it works...

You can use the `ST_Intersection` function to clip one dataset from another. In this recipe, you first created a view, where you performed a spatial join between a polygonal layer (countries) and a linear layer (rivers) using the `ST_Intersects` function. In the context of the spatial join, you have used the `ST_Intersection` function to generate a clip of the rivers in every country.

You have then created a bash script in which you iterated every single country and pulled out to a shapefile the clipped rivers for that country using `ogr2ogr` and the previously created view as the input layer.

For iterating the countries in the script, you have been using `ogrinfo` with the `-sql` option, using a SQL `SELECT DISTINCT` statement. You have used a combination of the `grep` and `awk` Linux commands, piped together to get every single country code. The `grep` command is a utility for searching plain-text datasets for lines matching a regular expression, while `awk` is an interpreted programming language designed for text processing and typically used as a data extraction and reporting tool.

# Simplifying geometries with PostGIS topology

In a previous recipe, we used the `ST_SimplifyPreserveTopology` function to try to generate a simplification of a polygonal PostGIS layer.

Unfortunately, while that function works well for linear layers, it produces topological anomalies (overlapping and holes) in shared polygon borders. You used an external toolset (`GRASS`) to generate a valid topological simplification.

In this recipe, you will use the PostGIS topology support to perform the same task within the spatial database without needing to export the dataset to a different toolset.

## Getting ready

To get started, follow the ensuing steps:

1. Be sure that you have the PostGIS topology support enabled in your database instance. This support is packaged as a separate extension and, if you are using PostgreSQL 9.1 or newer versions, you can install it using the following SQL `CREATE EXTENSION` command:

   ```
   postgis_cookbook=# CREATE EXTENSION postgis_topology;
   ```

2. Download the administrative area archive for Hungary from the `gadm.org` website at `http://gadm.org/country` (or use the copy included in the code bundle provided with this book).

3. Extract the `HUN_adm1.shp` shapefile from the archive to your working directory, `working/chp03`.

4. Import the shapefile to PostGIS using a tool such as `ogr2ogr` or `shp2pgsql`, as follows:

   ```
   ogr2ogr -f PostgreSQL -t_srs EPSG:3857 -nlt MULTIPOLYGON -lco
   GEOMETRY_NAME=the_geom -nln chp03.hungary PG:"dbname='postgis_
   cookbook' user='me' password='mypassword'" HUN_adm1.shp
   ```

5. After the import process is completed, you can check the count using the following command; note that this spatial table consists of 20 multipolygons, each representing one administrative area in Hungary:

   ```
   postgis_cookbook=# SELECT COUNT(*) FROM chp03.hungary;
   count
   -------
   20
   (1 row)
   ```

# How to do it...

The steps you need to perform to complete this recipe are as follows:

1. All functions and tables associated with the topology module are installed in a schema named `topology`, so let's add it to the search path to avoid prefixing it before every topology function or object:

   ```
   postgis_cookbook=# SET search_path TO chp03, topology, public;
   ```

2. Now, you will use the `CreateTopology` function to create a new topology schema named `hu_topo`, in which you will import the 20 administrative areas from the `hungary` table. In PostGIS topology, all of the topology entities and relations needed for one topology schema are stored in a single PostgreSQL schema using the same spatial references system. You will name this schema `hu_topo` and use the EPSG:3857 spatial reference (the one used in the original shapefile):

   ```
   postgis_cookbook=# SELECT CreateTopology('hu_topo', 3857);
   ```

3. Note how a record has been added to the `topology.topology` table:

   ```
   postgis_cookbook=# SELECT * FROM topology.topology;
    id |        name        | srid | precision | hasz
   ----+--------------------+------+-----------+------
     1 | hu_regions_topo    | 3857 |         0 | f
   (1 rows)
   ```

4. Also note that four tables and one view that are needed for storing and managing the topology have been generated in the schema named `hu_topo`, created from the `CreateTopology` function:

   ```
   postgis_cookbook=# \dtv hu_topo.*
               List of relations
     Schema  |    Name     |  Type  | Owner
   ----------+-------------+--------+------
    hu_topo  | edge        | view   |   me
    hu_topo  | edge_data   | table  |   me
    hu_topo  | face        | table  |   me
    hu_topo  | node        | table  |   me
    hu_topo  | relation    | table  |   me
   (5 rows)
   ```

5. Check the initial information for the created topology using the `topologysummary` function, as follows; all of the topologic entities (nodes, edges, faces, and so on) are still not initialized:

```
postgis_cookbook=# SELECT topologysummary('hu_topo');
                    topologysummary

-----------------------------------------------------
 Topology hu_topo (1), SRID 3857, precision 0      +
 0 nodes, 0 edges, 0 faces, 0 topogeoms in 0 layers+
(1 row)
```

6. Create a new PostGIS table for storing the topological administrative boundaries, as follows:

```
postgis_cookbook=# CREATE TABLE chp03.hu_topo_polygons(gid serial
primary key, name_1 varchar(75));
```

7. Add a topological geometry column to this table using the `AddTopoGeometryColumn` function:

```
postgis_cookbook=# SELECT AddTopoGeometryColumn('hu_topo',
'chp03', 'hu_topo_polygons', 'the_geom_topo', 'MULTIPOLYGON') As
layer_id;
```

8. Insert the polygons from the nontopological `hungary` spatial table to the topological table, using the `toTopoGeom` function, as follows:

```
postgis_cookbook=> INSERT INTO chp03.hu_topo_polygons(name_1, the_
geom_topo)
    SELECT name_1, toTopoGeom(the_geom, 'hu_topo', 1)
    FROM chp03.hungary;
    Query returned successfully: 20 rows affected, 10598 ms
execution time.
```

9. Now, run the following code to check out how the content of the topology schema has been modified by the `toTopoGeom` function; you would expect to have 20 faces, one for each Hungarian administrative area; but instead, there are 97:

```
postgis_cookbook=# SELECT topologysummary('hu_topo');
                     topologysummary

------------------------------------------------------------
 Topology hu_topo (1), SRID 3857, precision 0             +
 209 nodes, 304 edges, 97 faces, 60 topogeoms in 1 layers+
 Layer 1, type Polygonal (3), 60 topogeoms              +
  Deploy: chp03.hu_topo_polygons.the_geom_topo            +
```

10. The problem is easily identifiable by analyzing the `hu_topo.face` table or using a Desktop GIS. If you sort the polygons from this table by area, using the `ST_Area` function, you will notice after the details of the first polygon, which has one null area (used by the topology screenshot in the next step) and 20 large areas (each representing one administrative area), that there are 77 very small polygons generated by topological anomalies (polygon overlaps and holes):

```
postgis_cookbook=# SELECT row_number() OVER (ORDER BY ST_Area(mbr)
DESC) as rownum, ST_Area(mbr)/100000 AS area FROM hu_topo.face
ORDER BY area DESC;
 rownum  |        area
---------+--------------------
       1 |
       2 |   366365.476705923
       3 |   313236.739489454
...
      21 |   20662.4948917497
      22 |   8.12994437170007
      23 |   6.72174611815608
...
      97 |  0.0164102556404216
      98 |  0.014788623905157
(98 rows)
```

11. You can eventually look at the built topology elements (nodes, edges, faces, and topogeoms) using a Desktop GIS. The following screenshot shows how they look in QGIS:

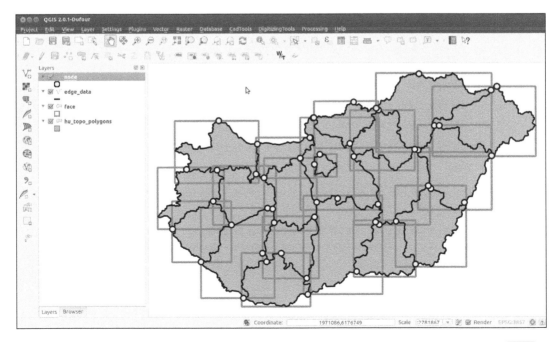

12. Now, you will rebuild the topology using a small tolerance value—1 meter—as an additional parameter to the `CreateTopology` function, in order to get rid of the unnecessary faces (the tolerance will collapse the vertex together, eliminating the small polygons). First, drop your topology schema with the `DropTopology` function, and the topological table with the `DROP TABLE` command, and rebuild both of them using a topology tolerance of 1 meter, as follows:

```
postgis_cookbook=# SELECT DropTopology('hu_topo');

postgis_cookbook=# DROP TABLE chp03.hu_topo_polygons;

postgis_cookbook=# SELECT CreateTopology('hu_topo',
  3857, 1);

postgis_cookbook=# CREATE TABLE chp03.hu_topo_polygons(
  gid serial primary key, name_1 varchar(75));

postgis_cookbook=# SELECT AddTopoGeometryColumn('hu_topo',
  'chp03', 'hu_topo_polygons', 'the_geom_topo',
  'MULTIPOLYGON') As layer_id;

postgis_cookbook=# INSERT INTO chp03.hu_topo_polygons(name_1, the_
geom_topo)
        SELECT name_1, toTopoGeom(the_geom, 'hu_topo', 1)
        FROM chp03.hungary;
```

13. Now, if you check the information related to the topology using the `topologysummary` function as follows, you can see that there is one face per administrative boundary and the previous 77 faces generated by topological anomalies have been eliminated:

```
postgis_cookbook=# SELECT topologysummary('hu_topo');
                      topologysummary
--------------------------------------------------------
 Topology hu_topo (2), SRID 3857, precision 1          +
 52 nodes, 70 edges, 20 faces, 20 topogeoms in 1 layers+
 Layer 1, type Polygonal (3), 20 topogeoms             +
   Deploy: chp03.hu_topo_polygons.the_geom_topo        +
(1 row)
```

14. Finally, simplify the polgyons of the `topo_polygons` table using a tolerance of 500 meters, as follows:

```
postgis_cookbook=# SELECT ST_ChangeEdgeGeom('hu_topo',
  edge_id, ST_SimplifyPreserveTopology(geom, 500))
  FROM hu_topo.edge;
```

15. Now, it's time to update the original `hungary` table using a join with the `hu_topo_polygons` table by running the following commands:

```
postgis_cookbook=# UPDATE chp03.hungary hu
    SET the_geom = hut.the_geom_topo
    FROM chp03.hu_topo_polygons hut
    WHERE hu.name_1 = hut.name_1;
```

16. The simplification process should have worked smoothly and produced a valid topological dataset. The following screenshot shows how this looks:

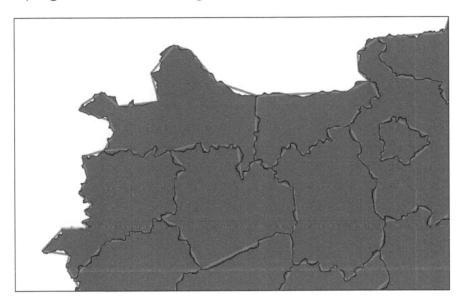

## How it works...

We created a new PostGIS topology schema using the `CreateTopology` function. This function creates a new PostgreSQL schema where all of the topological entities are stored.

We can have more topological schemas within the same spatial database, each being contained in a different PostgreSQL schema. The PostGIS `topology.topology` table manages all of the metadata for all of the topological schemas.

Each topological schema is composed of a series of tables and views to manage the topological entities (such as edge, edge_data, face, node, and topogeoms) and their relations.

We can have a quick look at the description of a single topological schema using the `topologysummary` function, which summarizes the main metadata information—name, SRID, precision; the number of nodes, edges, faces, topogeoms, and topological layers; and, for each topological layer, the geometry type and the number of topogeoms.

After creating the topology schema, we created a new PostGIS table and added to it a topological geometry column (`topogeom` in PostGIS topology jargon) using the `AddTopoGeometryColumn` function.

We then used the `ST_ChangeEdgeGeom` function to alter the geometries for the topological edges, using the `ST_SimplifyPreserveTopology` function with a tolerance of 500 meters, and checked that this function, used in the context of a topological schema, produces topologically correct results for polygons, too.

# 4

# Working with Vector Data – Advanced Recipes

In this chapter, we will cover:

- ▶ Improving proximity filtering with KNN
- ▶ Improving proximity filtering with KNN – advanced
- ▶ Rotating geometries
- ▶ Improving ST_Polygonize
- ▶ Translating, scaling, and rotating geometries – advanced
- ▶ Generating detailed building footprints from LiDAR
- ▶ Using external scripts to embed new functionality in order to calculate a Voronoi diagram
- ▶ Using external scripts to embed other libraries in order to calculate a Voronoi diagram – advanced

## Introduction

Beyond being a spatial database with the capacity to store and query spatial data, PostGIS is a very powerful analytical tool. What this means to the user is a tremendous capacity to expose and encapsulate deep spatial analyses right within a PostgreSQL database.

The recipes in this chapter can roughly be divided into three main sections:

- ▸ Highly optimized queries::
    - ❑ Improving proximity filtering with KNN
    - ❑ Improving proximity filtering with KNN – advanced

- ▸ Using the database to create and modify geometries:
    - ❑ Rotating geometries
    - ❑ Improving ST_Polygonize
    - ❑ Translating, scaling, and rotating geometries – advanced
    - ❑ Generating detailed building footprints from LiDAR

- ▸ Using external libraries to aid advanced analyses:
    - ❑ Using external scripts to embed new functionality in order to calculate a Voronoi diagram
    - ❑ Using external scripts to embed other libraries in order to calculate a Voronoi diagram – advanced

# Improving proximity filtering with KNN

The basic question that we seek to answer in this recipe is the fundamental distance question, "Which are the closest (name what you are searching for) to me?", for example, "Which are the five coffee shops closest to me?" It turns out that while it is a fundamental question, it's not always easy to answer, though we will make this possible in this recipe. We will approach this with two approaches. The first way in which we'll approach this is in a simple heuristic, which will allow us to come to a solution quickly. Then, we'll take advantage of the deeper PostGIS functionality to make the solution faster and more general with a **K-Nearest Neighbor** (**KNN**) approach.

A concept that we need to understand from the outset is that of a spatial index. A spatial index, like other database indexes, functions like a book index. It is a special construct to make looking for things inside our table easier, much in the way a book index helps us find content in a book faster. In the case of a spatial index, it helps us find faster where things are in space. Therefore, by using a spatial index in our geographic searches, we can speed up our searches by many orders of magnitude.

 To learn more about spatial indexes, see `http://en.wikipedia.org/wiki/Spatial_index#Spatial_index`.

## Getting ready

We will start by loading our data. Our data are the address records from Cuyahoga County, Ohio, USA.

```
shp2pgsql -s 3734 -d -i -I -W LATIN1 -g the_geom CUY_ADDRESS_POINTS
chp04.knn_addresses | psql -U me -d postgis_cookbook
```

As this dataset may take a while to load, you can alternatively load a subset.

```
shp2pgsql -s 3734 -d -i -I -W LATIN1 -g the_geom CUY_ADDRESS_POINTS_
subset chp04.knn_addresses | psql -U me -d postgis_cookbook
```

We specified the -I flag in order to request a spatial index be created upon the import of this data.

Let us start by seeing how many records we are dealing with:

```
SELECT COUNT(*) FROM chp04.knn_addresses;
--484958
```

We have, in this address table, almost half a million address records, which is not an insubstantial number against which to perform a query.

## How to do it...

KNN is an approach to searching for an arbitrary number of points closest to a given point. Without the right tools, this can be a very slow process that requires testing the distance between the point of interest and all the possible neighbors. The problem with this approach is that the search becomes exponentially slower as the number of points increases. Let's start with this naïve approach and then improve upon it.

Suppose we were interested in finding 10 records closest to the geographic location, -81.738624, 41.396679. The naïve approach would be to transform this value into our local coordinate system and compare the distance to each point in the database from the search point, order those values by distance, and limit the search to the first 10 closest records (it is not recommended that you run the following query—it could run indefinitely)

```
SELECT ST_Distance(searchpoint.the_geom, addr.the_geom) AS dist, * FROM
    chp04.knn_addresses addr,
    (SELECT ST_Transform(ST_SetSRID(ST_MakePoint(-81.738624, 41.396679),
4326), 3734) AS the_geom) searchpoint
    ORDER BY ST_Distance(searchpoint.the_geom, addr.the_geom)
    LIMIT 10;
```

This is a fine approach for smaller datasets. This is a logical, simple, fast approach for relatively small numbers of records. This approach scales very poorly, however, getting exponentially slower with the addition of records, and with 500,000 points, this would take a very long time.

An alternative is to only compare my point to the ones I know are close by setting a search distance. So, for example, in the following diagram, we have a star that represents my current location, and I want to know the 10 closest addresses. The grid in the diagram is a 100 foot grid, so I can search for the points within 200 feet, then measure the distance to each of these points, and return the closest 10 points to my search location.

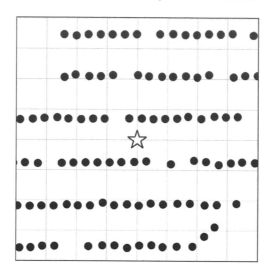

So far, our approach to answering this question is to limit the search using the ST_DWithin operator to only search for records within a certain distance. ST_DWithin uses our spatial index, so the initial distance search is fast and the list of returned records should be short enough to do the same pair-wise distance comparison we did earlier in this section. In our case here, we could limit the search to within 200 feet as follows.

```
SELECT ST_Distance(searchpoint.the_geom, addr.the_geom) AS dist, * FROM
    chp04.knn_addresses addr,
    (SELECT ST_Transform(ST_SetSRID(ST_MakePoint(-81.738624, 41.396679),
4326), 3734) AS the_geom) searchpoint
    WHERE ST_DWithin(searchpoint.the_geom, addr.the_geom, 200)
    ORDER BY ST_Distance(searchpoint.the_geom, addr.the_geom)
    LIMIT 10;
```

This approach performs well so long as our search window, ST_DWithin, is the right size for the data. The problem with this approach is that, in order to optimize it, we need to know how to set a search window that is about the right size. Any larger than the right size and the query will run more slowly than we'd like. Any smaller than the right size and we might not get all the points back that we need. Inherently, we don't know this ahead of time, so we can only hope for the best guess.

In this same dataset, if we apply the same query in another location, the output will return no points because the 10 closest points are further than 200 feet away. We can see this in the following diagram:

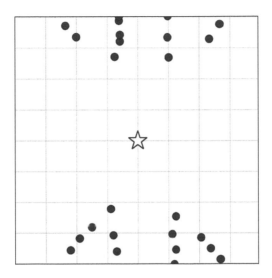

Fortunately, for PostGIS 2.0, we can leverage the distance operators (<-> and <#>) to do indexed nearest-neighbor searches. This makes for very fast KNN searches that don't require us to guess ahead of time how far away we need to search. Why are the searches fast? The spatial index helps, of course, but in the case of the distance operator, we are using the structure of the index itself, which is hierarchical, to very quickly sort our neighbors.

When used in an ORDER BY clause, the distance operator uses the index:

```
SELECT ST_Distance(searchpoint.the_geom, addr.the_geom) AS dist, * FROM
  chp04.knn_addresses addr,
  (SELECT ST_Transform(ST_SetSRID(ST_MakePoint(-81.738624, 41.396679),
4326), 3734) AS the_geom) searchpoint
  ORDER BY addr.the_geom <-> searchpoint.the_geom
  LIMIT 10;
```

This approach requires no *a priori* knowledge of how far the nearest neighbors might be. It also scales very well, returning thousands of records in not more than the time it takes to return a few records. It is sometimes slower than using ST_DWithin, depending on how small our search distance is and how large the dataset we are dealing with. But the tradeoff is that we don't need to make a guess as to our correct search distance and for large queries, it can be much faster than the naïve approach.

## How it works...

What makes this magic possible is that PostGIS uses an R-Tree index. This means that the index itself is sorted hierarchically based on spatial information. As demonstrated, we can leverage the structure of the index in sorting distances from a given arbitrary location and, thus, use the index to directly return the sorted records. This means that the structure of the spatial index itself helps us answer such fundamental questions quickly and inexpensively.

 More information about KNN and R-tree can be found at http://workshops.boundlessgeo.com/postgis-intro/knn.html and https://en.wikipedia.org/wiki/R-tree.

## See also

▸ The *Improving proximity filtering with KNN – advanced* recipe

# Improving proximity filtering with KNN – advanced

In the preceding recipe, we wanted to answer the simple question of which are the nearest 10 locations to a given point, a simple question with a surprisingly sophisticated answer. Now that we have addressed the preceding question, the question is how do we approach this problem when we want to traverse an entire dataset and test each record for its nearest neighbors?

Our problem is as follows: for each point in our table, we are interested in the angle to the nearest object in another table. A case demonstrating this scenario is if we want to represent address points as building-like squares rotated to align with an adjacent road, similar to the historic **United States Geological Survey** (**USGS**) quadrangle maps, as shown in the following screenshot:

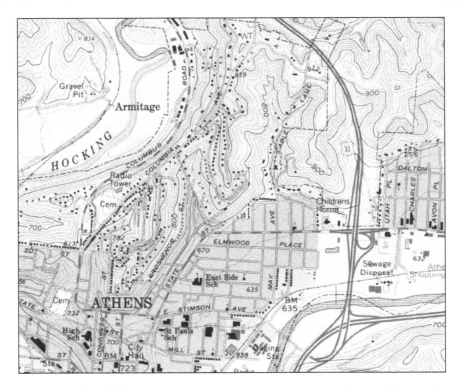

For larger buildings, USGS Quads show the buildings' footprints but, for residential buildings below their minimum threshold, the points are just rotated squares—a nice cartographic effect that could easily be replicated with address points.

## Getting ready

As in the previous recipe, we will start off by loading our data. Our data are the address records from Cuyahoga County, Ohio, USA. If you have not loaded the data yet, run the following command:

```
shp2pgsql -s 3734 -d -i -I -W LATIN1 -g the_geom CUY_ADDRESS_POINTS
chp04.knn_addresses | psql -U me -d postgis_cookbook
```

As this dataset may take a while to load, you can alternatively load a subset using the following command:

```
shp2pgsql -s 3734 -d -i -I -W LATIN1 -g the_geom CUY_ADDRESS_POINTS_
subset chp04.knn_addresses | psql -U me -d postgis_cookbook
```

If you loaded this in the previous recipe, there is no need to reload the data. The address points will serve as a proxy for our building structures. However, to align our structure to the nearby streets, we will need a `streets` layer. We will use Cuyahoga County's street centerline data for this:

```
shp2pgsql -s 3734 -d -i -I -W LATIN1 -g the_geom CUY_STREETS chp04.knn_
streets | psql -U me -d postgis_cookbook
```

Before we commence, however, we have to consider another aspect of using indexes, which we need not have considered in our previous KNN recipe. When our KNN approach used only points, our indexing was exact—the bounding box of a point is effectively a point. As bounding boxes are what indexes are built around, our indexing estimates of distance perfectly reflected the actual distances between our points. In the case of nonpoint geometries, as is our example here, the bounding box is an approximation of the lines to which we will be comparing our points. Put another way, what this means is that our nearest neighbor may not be our *very* nearest neighbor, but is likely our approximately nearest neighbor, or one of our nearest neighbors.

In practice, we apply a heuristic approach—we simply gather slightly more than the number of nearest neighbors we are interested in and then sort them based on the actual distance in order to gather only the number we are interested in. In this way, we only need to sort a small number of records.

## How to do it...

Insofar as KNN is a nuanced approach to these problems, forcing KNN to run on all the records in a dataset takes what I like to call a venerable and age-old approach. In other words, it requires a bit of a hack.

 More on the general solution to using KNN within a function can be found in Alexandre Neto's post on the PostGIS users list at the following link:

http://lists.osgeo.org/pipermail/postgis-users/2012-May/034017.html

In SQL, of course, the typical way to loop is to use a `SELECT` statement. For our case, we don't have a function that does KNN looping; we simply have an operator that allows us to efficiently order our returning records by distance from a given record. The workaround is to write a temporary function and, thus, be able to use `SELECT` to loop through the records for us. The cost is the creation and deletion of the function, plus the work done by the query, and the combination of costs is well worth the "hackiness" of the approach.

First, consider the following function:

```
CREATE OR REPLACE FUNCTION chp04.angle_to_street (geometry) RETURNS
double precision AS $$


WITH index_query as
                (SELECT ST_Distance($1,road.the_geom) as dist,
                                degrees(ST_Azimuth($1, ST_
ClosestPoint(road.the_geom, $1))) as azimuth
                FROM   chp04.knn_streets As road
                ORDER BY $1 <#> road.the_geom limit 5)


SELECT azimuth
                FROM index_query
                ORDER BY dist
LIMIT 1;


$$ LANGUAGE SQL;
```

Now, we can use this function quite easily:

```
CREATE TABLE chp04.knn_address_points_rot AS
                SELECT addr.*, chp04.angle_to_street(addr.the_geom)
                FROM
                                chp04.knn_addresses  addr;
```

If you have loaded the whole address dataset, this will take a while.

If we choose to, we can optionally drop the function so that extra functions are not left in our database.

```
DROP FUNCTION chp04.angle_to_street (geometry);
```

If we render this with rotation in a desktop package such as Quantum GIS (QGIS), we will get a pleasant effect shown as follows:

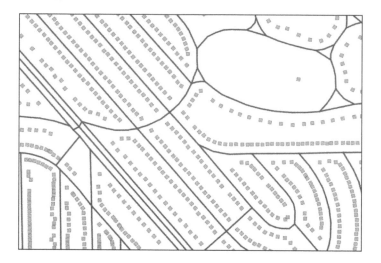

## How it works...

Our function is simple, KNN magic aside. As an input to the function, we allow geometry as shown in the following code:

```
CREATE OR REPLACE FUNCTION chp04.angle_to_street (geometry) RETURNS
double precision AS $$
```

The preceding function returns a floating-point value.

We then use a `WITH` statement to create a temporary table that returns the five closest lines to our point of interest. Remember, as the index uses bounding boxes, we don't really know which line is the very closest, so we gather a few extra points and then filter them based on distance. This idea is implemented in the following query:

```
WITH index_query as
            (SELECT ST_Distance($1,road.geom) as dist,
                        degrees(ST_Azimuth($1, ST_
ClosestPoint(road.geom, $1))) as azimuth
            FROM street_centerlines As road
            ORDER BY $1 <#> road.geom LIMIT 5)
```

Note that we are actually returning two columns. The first column is dist in which we calculate the distance to the nearest five road lines. Note that this operation is performed after the ORDER BY and LIMIT functions have been used as filters, so this does not take much computation. Then, we use ST_Azimuth to calculate the angle from our point to the closest points (ST_ClosestPoint) on each of our nearest five lines. In summary, what returns with our temporary index_query table is the distance to the nearest five lines and the respective rotation angles to the nearest five lines.

If we recall, however, we were not looking for the angle to the nearest five but to the true nearest road line. For this, we order the results by distance and further use LIMIT 1:

```
SELECT azimuth
        FROM index_query
        ORDER BY dist
        LIMIT 1;
```

## See also

▸  The *Improving proximity filtering with KNN* recipe

# Rotating geometries

Among the many functions that PostGIS provides, geometry manipulation is a very powerful addition. In this recipe, we will explore a simple example of using the ST_Rotate function to rotate geometries. We will use a function from the *Improving proximity filtering with KNN – advanced* recipe to calculate our rotation values.

## Getting ready

ST_Rotate has a few variants: ST_RotateX, ST_RotateY, and ST_RotateZ, with the ST_Rotate function serving as an alias for ST_RotateZ. Thus, for two-dimensional cases, ST_Rotate is a typical use case.

In the *Improving proximity filtering with KNN – advanced* recipe, our function calculated the angle to the nearest road from a building's centroid or address point. We can symbolize that building's point according to that rotation factor as a square symbol but, more interestingly, we can explicitly build the area of that footprint in real space and rotate it to match our calculated rotation angle.

## How to do it...

Recall our function from the *Improving proximity filtering with KNN – advanced* recipe:

```
CREATE OR REPLACE FUNCTION chp04.angle_to_street (geometry) RETURNS
double precision AS $$

WITH index_query as
                (SELECT ST_Distance($1,road.the_geom) as dist,
                            degrees(ST_Azimuth($1, ST_
ClosestPoint(road.the_geom, $1))) as azimuth
            FROM  chp04.knn_streets As road
            ORDER BY $1 <#> road.the_geom limit 5)

SELECT azimuth
            FROM index_query
            ORDER BY dist
LIMIT 1;

$$ LANGUAGE SQL;
```

This function will calculate the geometry's angle to the nearest road line. Now, to construct geometries using this calculation, run the following function:

```
CREATE TABLE chp04.tsr_building AS

SELECT ST_Rotate(ST_Envelope(ST_Buffer(the_geom, 20)), radians(90 -
chp04.angle_to_street(addr.the_geom)), addr.the_geom)
    AS the_geom FROM
    chp04.knn_addresses addr
    LIMIT 500
;
```

## How it works...

In the first step, we are taking each of the points and first applying a buffer to them of 20 feet:

```
ST_Buffer(the_geom, 20)
```

Then, we calculate the envelope of the buffer, providing us with a square around that buffered area. This is a quick and easy way to create a square geometry of a specified size from a point:

```
ST_Envelope(ST_Buffer(the_geom, 20))
```

Finally, we use `ST_Rotate` to rotate the geometry to the appropriate angle. Here is where the query becomes harder to read. The `ST_Rotate` function takes three arguments:

```
ST_Rotate(geometry to rotate, angle, origin around which to rotate)
```

The geometry we are using is the newly calculated square. The angle is the one we calculate using our `chp04.angle_to_street` function. Finally, the origin around which we rotate is the input point itself, resulting in the following portion of our query:

```
ST_Rotate(ST_Envelope(ST_Buffer(the_geom, 20)), radians(90 -chp04.angle_
to_street(addr.the_geom)), addr.the_geom);
```

This gives us some really nice cartography as shown in the following screenshot:

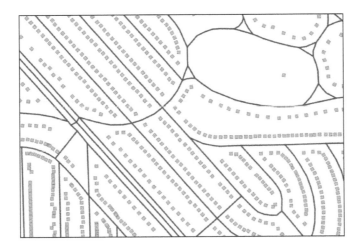

## See also

-   The *Improving proximity filtering with KNN – advanced* recipe
-   The *Translating, scaling, and rotating geometries – advanced* recipe

# Improving ST_Polygonize

In this short recipe, we will be using a common coding pattern, in use when geometries are being constructed with ST_Polygonize, and formalizing it into a function for re-use.

ST_Polygonize is a very useful function. Pass a set of "unioned" lines or an array of lines to ST_Polygonize, and the function will construct polygons from the input. ST_Polygonize does so aggressively insofar as it will construct all possible polygons from the inputs. One frustrating aspect of the function, however, is that it does not return a multipolygon, but instead returns a GeometryCollections. GeometryCollections can be problematic in third-party tools for interacting with PostGIS as so many third-party tools don't have mechanisms in place for recognizing and displaying GeometryCollections.

The pattern we will formalize here is the commonly recommended approach for changing GeometryCollections into mulipolygons when it is appropriate to do so. This approach will be useful not only for ST_Polygonize, which we will use in the subsequent recipe, but can also be adapted for other cases where a function returns GeometryCollections that are, for all practical purposes, multipolygons. Hence, this is why it merits its own dedicated recipe.

## Getting ready

The basic pattern for handling GeometryCollections is to use ST_Dump to convert them to a dump type, extract the geometry portion of the dump, collect the geometry, and then convert this collection into a multipolygon. The dump type is a special PostGIS type that is a combination of the geometries and an index number for the geometries. It's typical to use ST_Dump to convert from a GeometryCollection to a dump type and then do further processing on the data from there. Rarely is a dump object used directly, but it is typically an intermediate type of data.

## How to do it...

We expect this function to take a geometry and return a geometry:

```
CREATE OR REPLACE FUNCTION chp04.polygonize_to_multi (geometry) RETURNS
geometry AS $$
```

For readability, we will use a WITH statement to construct the series of transformations of geometry. First, we will polygonize:

```
WITH polygonized AS (
    SELECT ST_Polygonize($1) AS the_geom
    ),
```

Then, we will dump:

```
dumped AS (
SELECT (ST_Dump(the_geom)).geom AS the_geom FROM
    polygonized
)
```

Now, we can collect and construct a multipolygon from our result:

```
SELECT ST_Multi(ST_Collect(the_geom)) FROM
    dumped
;
```

Put together into a single function:

```
CREATE OR REPLACE FUNCTION chp04.polygonize_to_multi (geometry) RETURNS
geometry AS $$

    WITH polygonized AS (
        SELECT ST_Polygonize($1) AS the_geom
        ),
    dumped AS (
    SELECT (ST_Dump(the_geom)).geom AS the_geom FROM
        polygonized
    )
      SELECT ST_Multi(ST_Collect(the_geom)) FROM
        dumped
;
$$ LANGUAGE SQL;
```

Now, we can polygonize directly from a set of closed lines and skip the typical intermediate step when we use the `ST_Polygonize` function of having to handle a GeometryCollection.

## See also

▶ The *Translating, scaling, and rotating geometries – advanced* recipe

# Translating, scaling, and rotating geometries – advanced

Often, in a spatial database, we are interested in making explicit the representation of geometries that are implicit in the data. In the example that we will use here, the explicit portion of the geometry is a single-point coordinate where a field survey plot has taken place. In the following screenshot, this explicit location is the red dot. The implicit geometry is the actual extent of the field survey, which includes 10 subplots arranged in a 5 x 2 array and rotated according to a bearing. These subplots are the purple squares in the following screenshot:

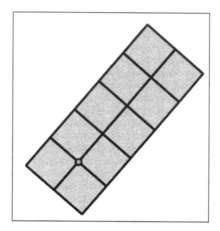

## Getting ready

There are a number of ways for us to approach this problem. In the interest of simplicity, we will first construct our grid and then rotate it in place. Also, we could, in principle, use an ST_Buffer function in combination with ST_Extent to construct the squares in our resultant geometry. But, as ST_Extent uses floating-point approximations of the geometry for efficiency sake, this could result in some mismatches at the edges of our subplots.

The approach we will use for the construction of the subplots is to construct the grid with a series of ST_MakeLine and use ST_Union to *flatten* or node the results. This ensures that we have all of our lines properly intersecting each other. ST_Polygonize will then construct our multipolygon geometry for us. We will leverage this function through our wrapper from the *Improving ST_Polygonize* recipe.

Our plots are 10 units on a side, in a 5 x 2 array. As such, we can imagine a function to which we pass our plot origin, and the function returns a multipolygon of all the subplot geometries. One additional element to consider is that the orientation of the layout of our plots is rotated to a bearing. We expect the function to actually use two inputs, so origin and rotation will be the variables that we will pass to our function.

## How to do it...

We can consider geometry and a float value as the inputs, and we want the function to return geometry:

```
CREATE OR REPLACE FUNCTION chp04.create_grid (geometry, float) RETURNS
geometry AS $$
```

In order to construct the subplots, we will require three lines running parallel to the x axis:

```
WITH middleline AS (
        SELECT ST_MakeLine(ST_Translate($1, -10, 0), ST_Translate($1,
40.0, 0)) AS the_geom
        ),
    topline AS (
        SELECT ST_MakeLine(ST_Translate($1, -10, 10.0), ST_Translate($1,
40.0, 10)) AS the_geom
        ),
    bottomline AS (
        SELECT ST_MakeLine(ST_Translate($1, -10, -10.0), ST_Translate($1,
40.0, -10)) AS the_geom
        ),
```

And, we will require six lines running parallel to the y axis:

```
    oneline AS (
        SELECT ST_MakeLine(ST_Translate($1, -10, 10.0), ST_Translate($1,
-10, -10)) AS the_geom
        ),
    twoline AS (
        SELECT ST_MakeLine(ST_Translate($1, 0, 10.0), ST_Translate($1, 0,
-10)) AS the_geom
        ),
    threeline AS (
        SELECT ST_MakeLine(ST_Translate($1, 10, 10.0), ST_Translate($1,
10, -10)) AS the_geom
        ),
    fourline AS (
        SELECT ST_MakeLine(ST_Translate($1, 20, 10.0), ST_Translate($1,
20, -10)) AS the_geom
        ),
    fiveline AS (
        SELECT ST_MakeLine(ST_Translate($1, 30, 10.0), ST_Translate($1,
30, -10)) AS the_geom
        ),
    sixline AS (
        SELECT ST_MakeLine(ST_Translate($1, 40, 10.0), ST_Translate($1,
40, -10)) AS the_geom
        ),
```

To use these for polygon construction, we will require them to have nodes where they cross and touch. A UNION ALL function will combine these lines in a single record; ST_Union will provide the geometric processing necessary to construct the nodes of interest and will combine our lines into a single entity ready for chp04.polygonize_to_multi:

```
combined AS (
    SELECT ST_Union(the_geom) AS the_geom FROM
        (
    SELECT the_geom FROM middleline
        UNION ALL
    SELECT the_geom FROM topline
        UNION ALL
    SELECT the_geom FROM bottomline
        UNION ALL
    SELECT the_geom FROM oneline
        UNION ALL
    SELECT the_geom FROM twoline
        UNION ALL
    SELECT the_geom FROM threeline
        UNION ALL
    SELECT the_geom FROM fourline
        UNION ALL
    SELECT the_geom FROM fiveline
        UNION ALL
    SELECT the_geom FROM sixline
        ) AS alllines
    )
```

But we have not created polygons yet, just lines. The final step, using our polygonize_to_multi function finishes the work for us:

```
    SELECT chp04.polygonize_to_multi(ST_Rotate(the_geom, $2, $1)) AS
the_geom FROM combined
;
```

The combined query is as follows:

```
CREATE OR REPLACE FUNCTION chp04.create_grid (geometry, float) RETURNS
geometry AS $$

    WITH middleline AS (
        SELECT ST_MakeLine(ST_Translate($1, -10, 0), ST_Translate($1,
40.0, 0)) AS the_geom
        ),
    topline AS (
        SELECT ST_MakeLine(ST_Translate($1, -10, 10.0), ST_Translate($1,
40.0, 10)) AS the_geom
        ),
    bottomline AS (
        SELECT ST_MakeLine(ST_Translate($1, -10, -10.0), ST_Translate($1,
40.0, -10)) AS the_geom
        ),
    oneline AS (
        SELECT ST_MakeLine(ST_Translate($1, -10, 10.0), ST_Translate($1,
-10, -10)) AS the_geom
        ),
    twoline AS (
        SELECT ST_MakeLine(ST_Translate($1, 0, 10.0), ST_Translate($1, 0,
-10)) AS the_geom
        ),
    threeline AS (
        SELECT ST_MakeLine(ST_Translate($1, 10, 10.0), ST_Translate($1,
10, -10)) AS the_geom
        ),
    fourline AS (
        SELECT ST_MakeLine(ST_Translate($1, 20, 10.0), ST_Translate($1,
20, -10)) AS the_geom
        ),
    fiveline AS (
        SELECT ST_MakeLine(ST_Translate($1, 30, 10.0), ST_Translate($1,
30, -10)) AS the_geom
        ),
    sixline AS (
```

```
       SELECT ST_MakeLine(ST_Translate($1, 40, 10.0), ST_Translate($1,
40, -10)) AS the_geom
       ),
   combined AS (
       SELECT ST_Union(the_geom) AS the_geom FROM
          (
       SELECT the_geom FROM middleline
          UNION ALL
       SELECT the_geom FROM topline
          UNION ALL
       SELECT the_geom FROM bottomline
          UNION ALL
       SELECT the_geom FROM oneline
          UNION ALL
       SELECT the_geom FROM twoline
          UNION ALL
       SELECT the_geom FROM threeline
          UNION ALL
       SELECT the_geom FROM fourline
          UNION ALL
       SELECT the_geom FROM fiveline
          UNION ALL
       SELECT the_geom FROM sixline
          ) AS alllines
       )
       SELECT chp04.polygonize_to_multi(ST_Rotate(the_geom, $2, $1)) AS
the_geom FROM combined
;
$$ LANGUAGE SQL;
```

## How it works...

This function, shown in the preceding section, essentially draws the geometry from a single input point and rotation value. It does this using nine instances of ST_MakeLine. Typically, one might use ST_MakeLine in combination with ST_MakePoint to accomplish this. We bypass this need, however, by having the function consume a point geometry as an input. We can, therefore, use ST_Translate to move this point geometry to the endpoints of the lines of interest in order to construct our lines with ST_MakeLine.

One final step, of course, is to test the use of our new geometry constructing function:

```
CREATE TABLE chp04.tsr_grid AS

-- embed inside the function
    SELECT chp04.create_grid(ST_SetSRID(ST_MakePoint(0,0), 3734), 0) AS
the_geom
        UNION ALL
    SELECT chp04.create_grid(ST_SetSRID(ST_MakePoint(0,100), 3734),
0.274352 * pi()) AS the_geom
        UNION ALL
    SELECT chp04.create_grid(ST_SetSRID(ST_MakePoint(100,0), 3734),
0.824378 * pi()) AS the_geom
        UNION ALL
    SELECT chp04.create_grid(ST_SetSRID(ST_MakePoint(0,-100), 3734),
0.43587 * pi()) AS the_geom
        UNION ALL
    SELECT chp04.create_grid(ST_SetSRID(ST_MakePoint(-100,0), 3734), 1 *
pi()) AS the_geom
;
```

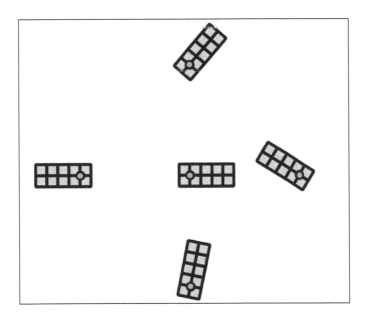

## See also

▸ The *Improving ST_Polygonize* recipe

▸ The *Improving proximity filtering with KNN – advanced* recipe

# Generating detailed building footprints from LiDAR

Frequently, with spatial analyses, we receive data in one form that seems quite promising but need it in another more extensive form. LiDAR is an excellent solution for such problems. LiDAR data is laser-scanner either from an airborne platform, such as a fixed-wing plane or helicopter, or from a ground unit. LiDAR devices typically return a cloud of points referencing absolute or relative positions in space. As a raw dataset, they are often not as useful as they are once they have been processed. Many LiDAR datasets are classified into land cover types. So, a LiDAR dataset, in addition to having data that contains x, y, and z values for all the points sampled across a space, will often contain LiDAR points that are classified as ground, vegetation, tall vegetation, buildings, and so on.

As useful as this is, the data is intensive, that is, it has discreet points, rather than extensive, as polygon representations of such data would be. This recipe was developed as a simple method to use PostGIS to transform the intensive LiDAR samples of buildings into extensive building footprints.

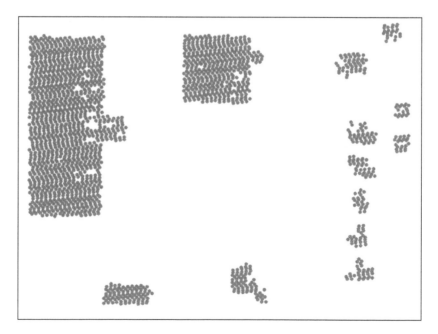

## Getting ready

The LiDAR dataset we will use is a 2006 collection, which was classified into ground, tall vegetation (> 20 feet), buildings, and others. One characteristic of the analysis that follows is that we assume the classification to be correct, and so we are not revisiting the quality of the classification or attempting to improve it within PostGIS.

A characteristic of the LiDAR dataset is that a sample point exists for relatively flat surfaces at approximately no fewer than 1 point for every 5 feet. This will inform how we manipulate the data.

First, let us load our dataset using the following command:

```
shp2pgsql -s 3734 -d -i -I -W LATIN1 -g the_geom lidar_buildings chp04.
lidar_buildings | psql -U me -d postgis_cookbook
```

## How to do it...

The simplest way to convert point data to polygon data would be to buffer the points by their known separation:

```
ST_Buffer(the_geom, 5)
```

We can imagine, however, that such a simplistic approach might look strange:

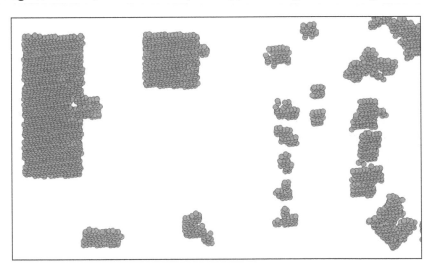

As such, it would be good to perform a union of these geometries in order to dissolve the internal boundaries.

```
ST_Union(ST_Buffer(the_geom, 5))
```

Now, we can see the start of some simple building footprints:

While this is marginally better, the result is quite "lumpy." We will use the `ST_Simplify_PreserveTopology` function to simplify the polygons and then grab just the external ring to remove the internal holes.

```
CREATE TABLE chp04.lidar_buildings_buffer AS


WITH lidar_query AS
(SELECT ST_ExteriorRing(ST_SimplifyPreserveTopology((ST_Dump(ST_Union(ST_
Buffer(the_geom, 5)))).geom, 10)) AS the_geom FROM
  chp04.lidar_buildings)


SELECT chp04.polygonize_to_multi(the_geom) AS the_geom from lidar_query;
```

Now, we have simplified versions of our buffered geometries:

There are two things to note here. The larger the building, relative to the density of the sampling, the better it looks. We might query to eliminate smaller buildings, which are likely to degenerate when using this approach, depending on the density of our LiDAR data.

If we want to further improve upon this, we can refine our lines and make them orthogonal (square up) using the in-progress project, `pg-orthogonalize`, which we might use in lieu of the simplification step we covered in this section:

```
https://github.com/smathermather/pg-orthogonalize
```

## How it works...

To put it informally, our buffering technique effectively lumps together or clusters adjacent samples. This is possible only because we have regularly sampled data. But that is OK. The density and scan patterns for the LiDAR data are typical of such datasets, so we can expect this approach to be applicable to other datasets.

The `ST_Union` function converts these discreet buffered points into a single record with dissolved internal boundaries. To complete the clustering, we simply need to use `ST_Dump` to convert these boundaries back to discreet polygons such that we can utilize individual building footprints. Finally, we simplify the pattern with `ST_SimplifyPreserveTopology` and extract the external ring outside of these polygons, using `ST_ExteriorRing`, which removes the holes inside the building footprints. Since `ST_ExteriorRing` returns a line, we have to reconstruct our polygon. We use `chp04.polygonize_to_multi`, a function we wrote in the *Improving ST_Polygonize* recipe to handle just such occasions.

# Using external scripts to embed new functionality in order to calculate a Voronoi diagram

PostgreSQL provides a variety of ways to embed functionality that otherwise is not native to either the database or the database extensions in use.

In our case, for the purposes of this recipe, we are interested in applying a space-filling technique called a Voronoi diagram. The following screenshot shows a Voronoi diagram generated from a set of address points. Note how the points from which the diagram was generated are equidistant to the lines that divide them. Packed soap bubbles viewed from above form a similar network of shapes.

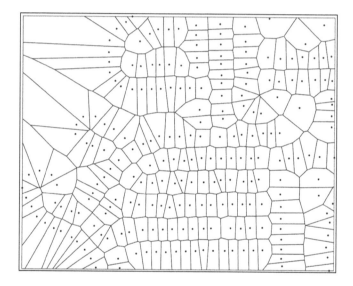

Voronoi diagrams are a space-filling approach that is useful for a variety of spatial analysis problems. We can use these to create space-filling polygons around points, the edges of which are equidistant from all the surrounding points.

 More information about Voronoi diagrams can be found at the following link:
http://en.wikipedia.org/wiki/Voronoi_diagram

Unfortunately, there is no native PostGIS function for generating Voronoi diagrams in stock versions of PostGIS. But, with some creativity, we can still create a Voronoi diagram. We will do so using a Python function adapted by *Darrell Fuhriman* and *Carson Farmer* and written by *Steven Fortune*.

## Getting ready

The first step in this exercise is to download and load the function by *Mr. Fuhriman*. The code can be accessed from the following address:

```
http://geogeek.garnix.org/2012/04/faster-voronoi-diagrams-in-postgis.
html
```

The first three lines of code are an example of the use of the function. We can comment these out before running the SQL against our database.

```
/*CREATE OR REPLACE FUNCTION voronoi(table_name text) returns SETOF
record as $$
  SELECT * from voronoi($1, 'the_geom') as (id integer,the_geom
geometry);
$$ LANGUAGE SQL;
*/
```

And simply run this code against the database in question.

Now, we will create a small arbitrary point dataset to feed into our function around which to calculate the Voronoi diagram.

```
DROP TABLE IF EXISTS chp04.voronoi_test_points;
CREATE TABLE chp04.voronoi_test_points
(
 x numeric,
 y numeric
)
WITH (OIDS=FALSE);

ALTER TABLE chp04.voronoi_test_points ADD COLUMN gid serial;
ALTER TABLE chp04.voronoi_test_points ADD PRIMARY KEY (gid);

INSERT INTO chp04.voronoi_test_points (x, y)
    VALUES (random() * 5, random() * 7);
INSERT INTO chp04.voronoi_test_points (x, y)
    VALUES (random() * 2, random() * 8);
INSERT INTO chp04.voronoi_test_points (x, y)
    VALUES (random() * 10, random() * 4);
INSERT INTO chp04.voronoi_test_points (x, y)
```

```
        VALUES (random() * 1, random() * 15);
INSERT INTO chp04.voronoi_test_points (x, y)
        VALUES (random() * 4, random() * 9);
INSERT INTO chp04.voronoi_test_points (x, y)
        VALUES (random() * 8, random() * 3);
INSERT INTO chp04.voronoi_test_points (x, y)
        VALUES (random() * 5, random() * 3);
INSERT INTO chp04.voronoi_test_points (x, y)
        VALUES (random() * 20, random() * 0.1);
INSERT INTO chp04.voronoi_test_points (x, y)
        VALUES (random() * 5, random() * 7);


SELECT AddGeometryColumn ('chp04','voronoi_test_points','the_
geom',3734,'POINT',2);


 UPDATE chp04.voronoi_test_points
   SET the_geom = ST_SetSRID(ST_MakePoint(x,y), 3734)
     WHERE the_geom IS NULL
   ;
```

## How to do it...

Preparations in place, now we are ostensibly ready to create the Voronoi diagram:

```
CREATE TABLE chp04.voronoi_test AS
  SELECT * FROM voronoi('chp04.voronoi_test_points', 'the_geom') AS (id
integer, the_geom geometry);
```

But, sadly, our input points are a bit degenerate relative to what the function expects—we get an error:

```
RROR:  error fetching next item from iterator DETAIL:  spiexceptions.
InternalError: lwpoly_from_lwlines: shell must have at least 4 points
CONTEXT:  Traceback (most recent call last): PL/Python function "voronoi"
********** Error ********** ERROR: error fetching next item from iterator
SQL state: XX000 Detail: spiexceptions.InternalError: lwpoly_from_
lwlines: shell must have at least 4 points Context: Traceback (most
recent call last): PL/Python function "voronoi"
```

So, we will instead also include the bounding box of our input points.

```sql
DROP TABLE IF EXISTS chp04.voronoi_test_points_u CASCADE;
CREATE TABLE chp04.voronoi_test_points_u AS
   WITH bboxpoints AS (
     SELECT (ST_DumpPoints(ST_SetSRID(ST_Extent(the_geom),3734))).geom AS
the_geom
       FROM chp04.voronoi_test_points
     UNION ALL
     SELECT the_geom FROM chp04.voronoi_test_points
   )
   SELECT (ST_Dump(ST_Union(the_geom))).geom AS the_geom FROM bboxpoints;
```

Now execute the calculation of our diagram:

```sql
CREATE TABLE chp04.voronoi_test AS
   SELECT * FROM voronoi('chp04.voronoi_test_points_u', 'the_geom') AS (id
integer, the_geom geometry);
```

But there is a small bug in our code that returns some polygons that are not Voronoi. We'll patch this by testing to make sure that we have one point per polygon and only return the polygons with one point.

First, we will create an index for our points and our Voronoi using the following function:

```sql
CREATE INDEX chp04_voronoi_test_points_u_the_geom_idx ON chp04.voronoi_
test_points_u USING gist(the_geom);
```

```sql
CREATE INDEX chp04_voronoi_test_the_geom_idx ON chp04.voronoi_test USING
gist(the_geom);
```

Finally, we can return just the Voronoi polygons that intersect with a single point.

```sql
CREATE TABLE chp04.voronoi_test_points_u_clean AS
WITH voronoi AS (
  SELECT COUNT(*), v.the_geom
    FROM chp04.voronoi_test v, chp04.voronoi_test_points_u p
    WHERE ST_Intersects(v.the_geom, p.the_geom)
    GROUP BY v.the_geom
    )
SELECT the_geom FROM voronoi WHERE count = 1;
```

And we will get a nice Voronoi diagram as follows:

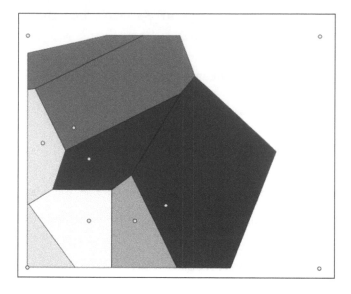

Now, we have the power of Voronoi diagrams built right into our database.

## See also

▶ The *Using external scripts to embed other libraries in order to calculate a Voronoi diagram – advanced* recipe

# Using external scripts to embed other libraries in order to calculate a Voronoi diagram – advanced

While the previous recipe works fine for typical cases, faster approaches are available. Rather than functions built into Python, we can leverage Python libraries that are wrappers for compiled C++ code, resulting in an order-of-magnitude improvement in speed. The price we pay is writing a function to embed the faster functionality. This price is a one-time cost of thought and consideration and well worth the pay off for faster computation that will be, in some cases, orders-of-magnitude faster than our native Python function.

In addition, the pattern we will be using, that is, passing data from PostGIS to an external package and returning information from that package, is useful for doing a variety of processing that is not available in PostGIS or PostgreSQL natively, but may otherwise be available in an external library or program. In other words, once PostGIS has a native Voronoi function, we can reuse this pattern to solve other problems with similar libraries.

This recipe is a good example of how functionality can be imported from external libraries to match the functionality available in PostGIS, even a complicated functionality such as geometry processing.

## Getting ready

The external library we will be using is called pyhull, a Python wrapper to a library called QHull, which allows us to perform a variety of convex geometry calculations. We will take advantage of QHull/pyhull to do Voronoi calculations.

Download the appropriate pyhull for your operating system from `http://pypi.python.org/pypi/pyhull/`.

On Mac OS X, installation is straightforward. On the command line, navigate to the directory where the pyhull egg is downloaded and enter the following command:

```
sudo easy_install pyhull-1.3.5-py2.7-macosx-10.6-intel.egg
```

For Linux and similar systems, simply install `easy_install` and use it to add `pyhull` directly from the repository:

```
sudo easy_install pyhull
```

For Debian-based systems, you may first require to install `python-setuptools`:

```
sudo apt-get install python-dev && sudo apt-get install python-setuptools
```

In order to run pyhull from PostgreSQL, the `postgresql` daemon will need a write access to `/tmp/empty`. Fix it on the command line using:

```
sudo chmod 777 /tmp/empty
```

## How to do it...

The syntax for pyhull to extract a Voronoi diagram is straightforward. To test this, you can follow the directions at `https://github.com/shyuep/pyhull`.

```
python
from pyhull.voronoi import VoronoiTess
pts = [[-0.5, -0.5], [-0.5, 0.5], [0.5, -0.5], [0.5, 0.5], [0,0]]
v = VoronoiTess(pts)
v.vertices
```

The preceding code returns the following output:

```
[[-10.101000000000001, -10.101000000000001], [0.0, -0.5], [-0.5, 0.0],
[0.5, 0.0], [0.0, 0.5]]
v.regions
returns:[[2, 0, 1], [4, 0, 2], [3, 0, 1], [4, 0, 3], [4, 2, 1, 3]]
```

In order to use pyhull, we only need to import the library inside a `plpythonu` function and call the functions available to us. This will require that PostgreSQL's PL / Python - Python Procedural Language be installed. The language also requires addition to our current database. See `http://www.postgresql.org/docs/current/interactive/plpython.html` for more details.

```
CREATE EXTENSION plpythonu;
CREATE OR REPLACE FUNCTION chp04.voronoi_fast (inputtext text)
  RETURNS text
AS $$


from pyhull.voronoi import VoronoiTess
import ast


inputpoints = ast.literal_eval(inputtext)
dummylist = ast.literal_eval('[999999999]')
v = VoronoiTess(inputpoints)


return v.vertices + dummylist + v.regions


$$ LANGUAGE plpythonu;
```

This function will take text from a query, use `ast.literal_eval` to change our text into a list in preparation for pyhull, and then pass that list to the `VoronoiTess` function, returning the vertices-and-regions of our Voronoi calculation. Note the variable `dummylist` as well. This is a quick and dirty delimiter that we will use to determine which portion of the returning list comprises vertices and which comprises regions.

## There's more...

Note the format from the preceding section that the `VoronoiTess` function expects our Voronoi center points in. We will need to write a function to convert from geometry to a string in this list format.

In addition, we should understand what `VoronoiTess` returns for our effort. It does not directly return what we would consider polygons. We will have to construct our polygons from what it returns. It returns points as a list that we will treat as a string that is the values for the points from which we will construct the polygons. It also returns Voronoi regions. These regions are simply a list of which points make up each region or Voronoi polygon. So, to assemble polygons, we require some way to compare the list of regions to the list of points and assemble polygons from the comparison of the two.

This means that what `VoronoiTess` returns is essentially topological. It will give us the regions; for example, ID 196 in the following screenshot; plus the IDs for the vertices associated with the bounds of the regions, in this case numbers 133 through 140; however, these numbers are not necessarily sequential. If we were to look at region 213, also adjacent below, its vertices would include vertex 134 and 135 as shared with region 196.

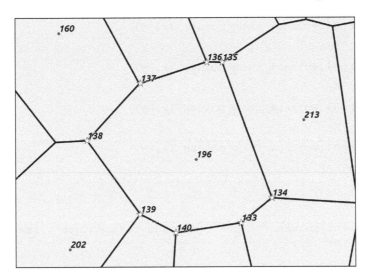

## Step zero – preparing the test table

First, let's prepare a test table. If you don't have a test table in place, from the previous section, let us create it using the following command:

```
DROP TABLE IF EXISTS chp04.voronoi_test_points;
CREATE TABLE chp04.voronoi_test_points
(
 x numeric,
 y numeric
)
WITH (OIDS=FALSE);
```

```
ALTER TABLE chp04.voronoi_test_points ADD COLUMN gid serial;
ALTER TABLE chp04.voronoi_test_points ADD PRIMARY KEY (gid);
-- replace this section with generate_series
INSERT INTO chp04.voronoi_test_points (x, y)
    VALUES (5, 7);
INSERT INTO chp04.voronoi_test_points (x, y)
    VALUES (2, 8);
INSERT INTO chp04.voronoi_test_points (x, y)
    VALUES (10, 4);
INSERT INTO chp04.voronoi_test_points (x, y)
    VALUES (1, 15);
INSERT INTO chp04.voronoi_test_points (x, y)
    VALUES (4, 9);
INSERT INTO chp04.voronoi_test_points (x, y)
    VALUES (8, 3);
INSERT INTO chp04.voronoi_test_points (x, y)
    VALUES (5, 3);
INSERT INTO chp04.voronoi_test_points (x, y)
    VALUES (20, 0)
    ;


SELECT AddGeometryColumn ('chp04','voronoi_test_points','the_
geom',3734,'POINT',2);


 UPDATE chp04.voronoi_test_points
   SET the_geom = ST_SetSRID(ST_MakePoint(x,y), 3734)
     WHERE the_geom IS NULL
   ;
```

## Step one – preparing the input text

Our first step is to prepare the point array to go into our new function. pyhull expects a list of coordinates, so we will construct text that approximates a Python list, knowing that our ast.literal_eval code inside the function will handle the conversion to a Python list.

As we want text, we will use the PostGIS function, `ST_AsText`.

```
SELECT ST_AsText(the_geom) AS pstring
  FROM (
  SELECT (ST_DumpPoints(the_geom)).geom AS the_geom, gid AS gid FROM
chp04.voronoi_test_points
  ) AS point_dump;
```

The preceding function returns the following output:

```
  pstring
- - - - - - - - - - - - -
 POINT(5 7)
 POINT(2 8)
 POINT(10 4)
 POINT(1 15)
 POINT(4 9)
 POINT(8 3)
 POINT(5 3)
 POINT(20 0)
(8 rows)
```

We should review some design considerations in the preceding function. Note the use of `ST_DumpPoints` here. You might ask why, if we are feeding in points, we are calling `ST_DumpPoints`. This is to generalize the function, so that we can feed in polygons or lines if we choose to and thus grab all the points from the polygons or lines for a Voronoi application. This also allows the function to apply to multipoint geometries without modification.

Also note, this is not yet in the format anticipated by pyhull. We will need to do some additional text manipulation. Our string, if you recall, should look more like the following:

```
   [[5, 6], [2, 8], [10, 4]...  [20,0]]
```

In the first step, we will replace all spaces in our points with commas:

```
WITH astext AS (
  SELECT ST_AsText(the_geom) AS pstring
    FROM (
    SELECT (ST_DumpPoints(the_geom)).geom AS the_geom, gid AS gid FROM
chp04.voronoi_test_points
    ) AS point_dump
  ),
```

```
astextcomma AS (
  SELECT replace(pstring, ' ', ',') AS pstring
    FROM astext
  )
```

```
SELECT * FROM astextcomma
```

This will result in the following output:

```
   pstring
-------------
 POINT(5,7)
 POINT(2,8)
 POINT(10,4)
 POINT(1,15)
 POINT(4,9)
 POINT(8,3)
 POINT(5,3)
 POINT(20,0)
(8 rows)
```

Perform a similar set of replacements for the start and end brackets using the following query:

```
WITH astext AS (
  SELECT ST_AsText(the_geom) AS pstring
    FROM (
    SELECT (ST_DumpPoints(the_geom)).geom AS the_geom, gid AS gid FROM
chp04.voronoi_test_points
    ) AS point_dump
  ),
astextcomma AS (
  SELECT replace(pstring, ' ', ',') AS pstring
    FROM astext
  ),
startingbracket AS (
  SELECT replace(pstring, 'POINT(', '[') AS pstring
    FROM astextcomma
  ),
endingbracket AS (
```

```
  SELECT replace(pstring, ')', ']') AS pstring
    FROM startingbracket
  )


SELECT * FROM endingbracket;
```

You will get the following result:

```
 pstring
---------
 [5,7]
 [2,8]
 [10,4]
 [1,15]
 [4,9]
 [8,3]
 [5,3]
 [20,0]
(8 rows)
```

Now, it gets interesting. We want to go from a column of these numbers to a comma-delimited concatenated list of them. PostgreSQL has a very nice function for just this purpose, STRING_AGG. It will require an order by number, so we will leverage our unique id and gid values for this purpose and carry STRING_AGG through as an extra column:

```
WITH astext AS (
  SELECT ST_AsText(the_geom) AS pstring, gid
    FROM (
    SELECT (ST_DumpPoints(the_geom)).geom AS the_geom, gid AS gid FROM
chp04.voronoi_test_points
    ) AS point_dump
  ),
astextcomma AS (
  SELECT replace(pstring, ' ', ',') AS pstring, gid
    FROM astext
  ),
startingbracket AS (
  SELECT replace(pstring, 'POINT(', '[') AS pstring, gid
    FROM astextcomma
```

```
    ),
endingbracket AS (
  SELECT replace(pstring, ')', ']') AS pstring, gid
    FROM startingbracket
  ),
aggstring AS (
  SELECT STRING_AGG(pstring, ',' ORDER BY gid)
    FROM endingbracket
  )
SELECT * FROM aggstring;
```

You will get the following result:

```
                      string_agg
---------------------------------------------------
 [5,7],[2,8],[10,4],[1,15],[4,9],[8,3],[5,3],[20,0]
(1 row)
```

Now, just to wrap this result in brackets use the concatenation operator | | in order to append outside brackets, changing our last WITH statement to the following:

```
aggstring AS (
    SELECT '[' || STRING_AGG(pstring, ',' ORDER BY gid) || ']' AS
inputtext
    FROM endingbracket
  )
SELECT * FROM aggstring;
```

You will get the following result:

```
                      inputtext
-----------------------------------------------------
 [[5,7],[2,8],[10,4],[1,15],[4,9],[8,3],[5,3],[20,0]]
(1 row)
```

## Step two – returning results

Whew! Now, our input text is properly formatted for our function. Let us try feeding it in and getting results, changing our final SELECT statement in the preceding code to feed our input text into our chp04.voronoi_fast function:

```
SELECT chp04.voronoi_fast(inputtext) FROM aggstring;
```

The result is as follows:

```
[[-10.101000000000001, -10.101000000000001], [24.081081081081081,
24.702702702702709], [18.071428571428569, 19.785714285714281],
[6.5, -28.5], [12.66666666666667, -3.833333333333333], [1.5, 11.5],
[10.928571428571431, 11.214285714285721], [7.7727272727272734,
5.954545454545455], [6.5, 5.0], [2.666666666666667, 5.0], [3.5, 7.5],
999999999, [10, 6, 7, 8, 9], [10, 5, 0, 9], [7, 4, 1, 2, 6], [5, 2, 1,
0], [10, 5, 2, 6], [8, 3, 4, 7], [9, 0, 3, 8], [4, 1, 0, 3]]
```

```
(1 row)
```

The complete code that uses the `chp04.voronoi_fast` function is as follows:

```
WITH astext AS (
   SELECT ST_AsText(the_geom) AS pstring, gid
      FROM (
      SELECT (ST_DumpPoints(the_geom)).geom AS the_geom, gid AS gid FROM
chp04.voronoi_test_points
      ) AS point_dump
   ),
astextcomma AS (
   SELECT replace(pstring, ' ', ',') AS pstring, gid
      FROM astext
   ),
startingbracket AS (
   SELECT replace(pstring, 'POINT(', '[') AS pstring, gid
      FROM astextcomma
   ),
endingbracket AS (
   SELECT replace(pstring, ')', ']') AS pstring, gid
      FROM startingbracket
   ),
aggstring AS (
   SELECT '[' || STRING_AGG(pstring, ',' ORDER BY gid) || ']' AS
inputtext
      FROM endingbracket
   )
SELECT chp04.voronoi_fast(inputtext) FROM aggstring;
```

## Step three – bundling as a function

Let's bundle this as a function. To accomplish this, we'll have to return a custom type, which is a row consisting of our output string, and the integer from our temporary ending bracket table:

```
CREATE TYPE vor AS (
  geomstring  text,
  gid     integer
);
```

This type will be the return type for our new function. Now, let's move on to creating a function using this new type. This should look very familiar—it's our previous code up to the step where we run running our `STRING_AGG` function.

```
CREATE OR REPLACE FUNCTION chp04.voronoi_prep (geometry, integer) RETURNS
vor AS $$

WITH astext AS (
  SELECT ST_AsText(the_geom) AS pstring, gid
    FROM (
    SELECT (ST_DumpPoints($1)).geom AS the_geom, $2 AS gid
    ) AS point_dump
  ),
astextcomma AS (
  SELECT replace(pstring, ' ', ',') AS pstring, gid
    FROM astext
  ),
startingbracket AS (
  SELECT replace(pstring, 'POINT(', '[') AS pstring, gid
    FROM astextcomma
  ),
endingbracket AS (
  SELECT replace(pstring, ')', ']') AS pstring, gid
    FROM startingbracket
  )
SELECT ROW(pstring, gid)::vor FROM endingbracket;

$$ LANGUAGE SQL;
```

Now we can use this function to help prepare our data for our fast Voronoi function using the following query:

```
WITH stringprep AS (
  SELECT chp04.voronoi_prep(the_geom, gid) FROM chp04.voronoi_test_points
),
aggstring AS (
    SELECT '[' || STRING_AGG((voronoi_prep).geomstring, ',' ORDER BY
(voronoi_prep).gid) || ']' AS inputtext
    FROM stringprep
  )
SELECT chp04.voronoi_fast(inputtext) FROM aggstring;
```

If you check the output, it looks the same as it did before:

```
[[[-10.101, -10.101], [24.08108108108108, 24.70270270270271],
[18.07142857142857, 19.78571428571428], [6.5, -28.5], [12.66666666666667,
-3.833333333333333], [1.5, 11.5], [10.92857142857143, 11.21428571428572],
[7.772727272727273, 5.954545454545455], [6.5, 5.0], [2.666666666666667,
5.0], [3.5, 7.5], 999999999, [10, 6, 7, 8, 9], [10, 5, 0, 9], [7, 4, 1,
2, 6], [5, 2, 1, 0], [10, 5, 2, 6], [8, 3, 4, 7], [9, 0, 3, 8], [4, 1, 0,
3]]
```

## Step four – translating into geometry

As indicated earlier, what returns from our function is two lists. The first is a list of points making up the boundaries of the Voronoi diagram, and the second is a list of the points associated with each of the polygons. We need to formally convert these to polygons. This is a bit tricky. First, we continue with our query but split the two parts of our returning string into the points that make up the Voronoi regions and the portion that defines the arrays of points that make up these regions. If you recall, when we wrote the original Voronoi function, we slipped a unique delimiter into the text before returning it. As such, we can use this with the SPLIT_PART function of PostgreSQL to return two different strings by searching for the value 999999999 and using this to split the returned string.

```
WITH stringprep AS (
  SELECT chp04.voronoi_prep(the_geom, gid) FROM chp04.voronoi_test_points
),
aggstring AS (
    SELECT '[' || STRING_AGG((voronoi_prep).geomstring, ',' ORDER BY
(voronoi_prep).gid) || ']' AS inputtext
    FROM stringprep
  ),
voronoi_string AS (
```

```
    SELECT chp04.voronoi_fast(inputtext) AS vstring FROM aggstring
    ),
vpoints AS (
    SELECT split_part(vstring, ', 999999999,', 1) || ']' AS points
    FROM voronoi_string
    ),
vids AS (
    SELECT trim(trailing ']' FROM split_part(vstring, ', 999999999,', 2))
|| ']' AS ids
    FROM voronoi_string
    ),
```

Now, we need to convert our points into a floating point, ARRAY (regindex), with a new unique id (gid) generated on-the-fly using ROW_NUMBER() and OVER().

```
arpt(pts) AS (
 SELECT replace(replace((SELECT points FROM vpoints), ']' ,'}'), '[',
'{')::float8[][]
),
reg AS (
    SELECT ROW_NUMBER() OVER() As gid, ('{' || region[1] || '}')::integer[]
as regindex
    FROM regexp_matches((SELECT ids FROM vids), '\[([0-9,\s]+)\]','g')
      AS region
    ),
```

We will seek a normalized list of the relationship between our points and regions using the following function:

```
regptloc AS (
    SELECT gid, ROW_NUMBER() OVER(PARTITION BY gid) AS ptloc,
unnest(regindex) As ptindex
    FROM reg)
```

We require a cross join of the two in order to construct the regions into groups of points making up each Voronoi region:

```
vregions AS (
    SELECT ST_Collect(ST_MakePoint(pts[ptindex + 1][1], pts[ptindex + 1]
[2]) ORDER BY ptloc ) AS vregions
    FROM regptloc CROSS JOIN arpt
    GROUP BY gid
    )
```

Finally, these groups of points can be constructed into polygons. The easiest way to handle this is with convex hulls:

```
SELECT ST_ConvexHull(vregions) AS the_geom FROM vregions
```

The complete code is as follows:

```
CREATE OR REPLACE FUNCTION chp04.voronoi_fast (inputtext text)
  RETURNS text
AS $$

from pyhull.voronoi import VoronoiTess
import ast

inputpoints = ast.literal_eval(inputtext)
dummylist = ast.literal_eval('[999999999]')
v = VoronoiTess(inputpoints)

return v.vertices + dummylist + v.regions

$$ LANGUAGE plpythonu;


DROP TABLE IF EXISTS chp04.voronoi_test_points;
CREATE TABLE chp04.voronoi_test_points
(
 x numeric,
 y numeric
)
WITH (OIDS=FALSE);

ALTER TABLE chp04.voronoi_test_points ADD COLUMN gid serial;
ALTER TABLE chp04.voronoi_test_points ADD PRIMARY KEY (gid);

INSERT INTO chp04.voronoi_test_points (x, y)
    VALUES (5 * random(), 7 * random());
INSERT INTO chp04.voronoi_test_points (x, y)
    VALUES (2 * random(), 8 * random());
```

```
INSERT INTO chp04.voronoi_test_points (x, y)
    VALUES (10 * random(), 4 * random());
INSERT INTO chp04.voronoi_test_points (x, y)
    VALUES (1 * random(), 15 * random());
INSERT INTO chp04.voronoi_test_points (x, y)
    VALUES (4 * random(), 9 * random());
INSERT INTO chp04.voronoi_test_points (x, y)
    VALUES (8 * random(), 3 * random());
INSERT INTO chp04.voronoi_test_points (x, y)
    VALUES (5 * random(), 3 * random());
INSERT INTO chp04.voronoi_test_points (x, y)
    VALUES (20 * random(), 0.1 * random());


SELECT AddGeometryColumn ('chp04','voronoi_test_points','the_
geom',3734,'POINT',2);


 UPDATE chp04.voronoi_test_points
   SET the_geom = ST_SetSRID(ST_MakePoint(x,y), 3734)
     WHERE the_geom IS NULL
   ;


CREATE TYPE vor AS (
  geomstring  text,
  gid     integer
);


CREATE OR REPLACE FUNCTION chp04.voronoi_prep (geometry, integer) RETURNS
vor AS $$


WITH astext AS (
  SELECT ST_AsText(the_geom) AS pstring, gid
    FROM (
    SELECT (ST_DumpPoints($1)).geom AS the_geom, $2 AS gid
    ) AS point_dump
  ),
astextcomma AS (
  SELECT replace(pstring, ' ', ',') AS pstring, gid
    FROM astext
```

```
    ),
startingbracket AS (
    SELECT replace(pstring, 'POINT(', '[') AS pstring, gid
        FROM astextcomma
    ),
endingbracket AS (
    SELECT replace(pstring, ')', ']') AS pstring, gid
        FROM startingbracket
    )
SELECT ROW(pstring, gid)::vor FROM endingbracket;
$$ LANGUAGE SQL;


DROP TABLE IF EXISTS chp04.voronoi_test;


CREATE TABLE chp04.voronoi_test AS (

WITH stringprep AS (
    SELECT chp04.voronoi_prep(the_geom, gid) FROM chp04.voronoi_test_points
),
aggstring AS (
    SELECT '[' || STRING_AGG((voronoi_prep).geomstring, ',' ORDER BY
(voronoi_prep).gid) || ']' AS inputtext
        FROM stringprep
    ),
voronoi_string AS (
    SELECT chp04.voronoi_fast(inputtext) AS vstring FROM aggstring
    ),
vpoints AS (
    SELECT split_part(vstring, ', 999999999,', 1) || ']' AS points
    FROM voronoi_string
    ),
vids AS (
    SELECT trim(trailing ']' FROM split_part(vstring, ', 999999999,', 2))
|| ']' AS ids
    FROM voronoi_string
    ),
arpt(pts) AS (
```

```
  SELECT replace(replace((SELECT points FROM vpoints), ']' ,'}'), '[',
'{')::float8[][]
),
reg AS (
  SELECT ROW_NUMBER() OVER() As gid, ('{' || region[1] || '}')::integer[]
AS regindex
  FROM regexp_matches((SELECT ids FROM vids), '\[([0-9,\s]+)\]','g')
    AS region
  ),
regptloc AS (
  SELECT gid, ROW_NUMBER() OVER(PARTITION BY gid) AS ptloc,
unnest(regindex) As ptindex
  FROM reg),
vregions AS (
  SELECT ST_Collect(ST_MakePoint(pts[ptindex + 1][1], pts[ptindex + 1]
[2]) ORDER BY ptloc ) AS vregions
  FROM regptloc CROSS JOIN arpt
  GROUP BY gid
  )
SELECT ST_ConvexHull(vregions) AS the_geom FROM vregions
  );
```

A thanks is deserved by Regina Obe for helping me to write the preceding query. Now we can process much larger datasets. The following is a Voronoi diagram derived from the address points from the *Improving proximity filtering with KNN – advanced* recipe, with the coloration based on the azimuth to the nearest street, also calculated in that recipe.

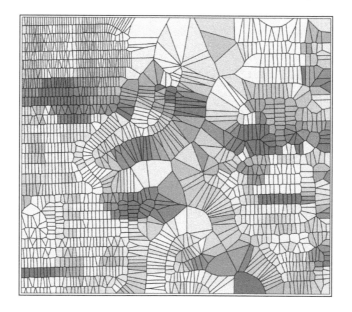

# 5
# Working with Raster Data

In this chapter, we will cover the following:

- ▸ Getting and loading rasters
- ▸ Working with basic raster information and analysis
- ▸ Performing simple map-algebra operations
- ▸ Combining geometries with rasters for analysis
- ▸ Converting between rasters and geometries
- ▸ Processing and loading rasters with GDAL VRT
- ▸ Warping and resampling rasters
- ▸ Performing advanced map-algebra operations
- ▸ Executing DEM operations
- ▸ Sharing and visualizing rasters through SQL

## Introduction

In this chapter, the recipes are presented in a step-by-step workflow that you may apply while working with a raster. This entails loading the raster, getting a basic understanding of the raster, processing and analyzing it, and delivering it to consumers. We intentionally add some detours to the workflow to reflect the reality that the raster, in its original form, may be confusing and not suitable for analysis. At the end of this chapter, you should be able to take the lessons learned from the recipes and confidently apply them to solve your raster problems.

Before going further, we should describe what a raster is and what a raster is used for. At the simplest level, a raster is a photo or image with information describing where to place the raster on the Earth's surface. A photograph typically has three sets of values, one set for each primary color (red, green, and blue). A raster also has sets of values, often more than those found in a photograph. Each set of values is known as a band. So, a photograph typically has three bands while a raster has at least one band. As with digital photographs, rasters come in a variety of file formats. Common raster formats you may come across include **PNG**, **JPEG**, **GeoTIFF**, **HDF5**, and **NetCDF**. Since rasters can have many bands and even more values, they can be used to store large quantities of data in an efficient manner. Due to their efficiency, rasters are used for satellite and aerial sensors and modeled surfaces, such as weather forecasts.

There are a few keywords used in this chapter and in the PostGIS ecosystem that need to be defined:

  ▸  **raster**: This is the PostGIS data type for storing raster files in PostgreSQL.

  ▸  **tile**: This is a small chunk of the original raster file to be stored in one column of a table's row. Each tile has its own set of spatial information and thus is independent of all the other tiles in the same column of the same table, even if the other tiles are from the same original raster file.

  ▸  **coverage**: This consists of all the tiles of a single raster column from one table.

We make heavy use of GDAL in this chapter. GDAL is generally considered the de facto Swiss Army Knife for working with rasters. GDAL is not a single application but is a raster-abstraction library with many useful utilities. Through GDAL, you can get the metadata of a raster, convert that raster to a different format, and warp that raster among many other capabilities. For our needs in this chapter, we will use three GDAL utilities: `gdalinfo`, `gdalbuildvrt`, and `gdal_translate`.

# Getting and loading rasters

In this recipe, we load most of the rasters used in this chapter. These rasters are examples of satellite imagery and model-generated surfaces, two of the most common raster sources.

## Getting ready

If you have not done so already, create a directory and copy the chapter's datasets.

```
> mkdir C:\postgis_cookbook\data\chap05
```

```
> cp -r /path/to/book_dataset/chap05 C:\postgis_cookbook\data\chap05
```

You should also create a new schema for this chapter in the database.

```
> psql -d postgis_cookbook -c "CREATE SCHEMA chap5"
```

## How to do it...

We will start with the PRISM average monthly minimum-temperature raster dataset for 2012 with coverage for the Continental United States. The raster is provided by the PRISM Climate Group at Oregon State University, with additional rasters available at `http://www.prism.oregonstate.edu/mtd/`.

On the command line, navigate to the `PRISM` directory as follows:

```
> cd C:\postgis_cookbook\data\chap05\PRISM
```

Let us spot-check one of the PRISM rasters with the GDAL utility `gdalinfo`. It is always a good practice to inspect at least one raster to get an idea of the metadata and ensure that the raster does not have any issues. This can be done using the following command:

```
> gdalinfo us_tmin_2012.01.asc
```

The `gdalinfo` output is as follows:

```
Driver: AAIGrid/Arc/Info ASCII Grid
Files: us_tmin_2012.01.asc
Size is 1405, 621
Coordinate System is `'
Origin = (-125.020833333333329,49.937500000000206)
Pixel Size = (0.041666666666667,-0.041666666666667)
Corner Coordinates:
Upper Left   (-125.0208333,  49.9375000)
Lower Left   (-125.0208333,  24.0625000)
Upper Right  ( -66.4791667,  49.9375000)
Lower Right  ( -66.4791667,  24.0625000)
Center       ( -95.7500000,  37.0000000)
Band 1 Block=1405x1 Type=Int32, ColorInterp=Undefined NoData
Value=-9999
```

The `gdalinfo` output reveals good and bad news. The good news is that the raster has no issues, as evidenced by the `Corner Coordinates`, `Pixel Size`, and `Band` attributes. The bad news is that the value for `Coordinate System` is empty.

To correct the lack of a coordinate system, we need to check the `PRISM` metadata and see if we can find any spatial reference information at `http://www.prism.oregonstate.edu/docs/meta/temp_realtime_monthly.htm`.

Looking through the metadata, we find spatial information indicating that the PRISM rasters may be unprojected, but in WGS72. We can double-check this by searching for the details of WGS72 in the `spatial_ref_sys` table.

```
SELECT srid, auth_name, auth_srid, srtext, proj4text FROM
spatial_ref_sys WHERE proj4text LIKE '%WGS72%'
```

Comparing the text of `srtext` to the PRISM raster's metadata spatial attributes, we find that the raster is in WGS72 (SRID 4322).

You can load the PRISM rasters into the `chap5.prism` table with `raster2pgsql`.

```
> raster2pgsql -s 4322 -t 100x100 -F -I -C -Y
C:\postgis_cookbook\data\chap5\PRISM\us_tmin_2012.*.asc chap5.prism |
psql -d postgis_cookbook
```

The `raster2pgsql` command is called with the following flags:

- `-s`: This flag assigns SRID `4322` to the imported rasters.
- `-t`: This flag denotes the tile size. It chunks the imported rasters into smaller and more manageable pieces; each record added to the table will be at most 100 x 100 pixels.
- `-F`: This flag adds a column to the table and fills it with the raster's filename.
- `-I`: This flag creates a GIST spatial index on the table's raster column.
- `-C`: This flag applies the standard set of constraints on the table. The standard set of constraints includes checks for dimension, scale, skew, upper-left coordinate, and SRID.
- `-Y`: This flag instructs raster2pgsql to use `COPY` statements instead of `INSERT` statements. `COPY` is typically faster than `INSERT`.

There is a reason why we passed `-F` to `raster2pgsql`. If you look at the filenames of the PRISM rasters, you'll note the year and month. So, let's convert the value in the `filename` column to a date in the table.

```
ALTER TABLE chap5.prism ADD COLUMN month_year DATE;
UPDATE chap5.prism SET month_year = (
    split_part(split_part(filename, ''.'', 1), ''_'', 3) || ''-'' ||
    split_part(filename, ''.'', 2) || ''-01'' )::date;
```

This is all that needs to be done with the PRISM rasters for now.

Now, let's import an SRTM raster. The SRTM raster is from the **Shuttle Radar Topography Mission** (**SRTM**) that was conducted by NASA Jet Propulsion Laboratory in February, 2000. This raster and others like it are available at

```
http://dds.cr.usgs.gov/srtm/version2_1/SRTM1/.
```

Change the current directory to the SRTM directory.

```
> cd C:\postgis_cookbook\data\chap05\SRTM
```

Make sure you spot-check the SRTM raster with gdalinfo to ensure that it is valid and has a value for Coordinate System. Once checked, import the SRTM raster into the chap5. srtm table.

```
> raster2pgsql -s 4326 -t 100x100 -F -I -C -Y
C:\postgis_cookbook\data\chap5\SRTM\N37W123.hgt chap5.srtm | psql -d
postgis_cookbook
```

We use the same raster2pgsql flags for the SRTM raster as those for the PRISM rasters.

We also need to import a shapefile of San Francisco provided by the City and County of San Francisco; it is available at:

```
https://data.sfgov.org/Geography/SF-Shoreline-and-Islands-Zipped-
Shapefile-Format-/feqe-wvxg.
```

We will use San Francisco's boundaries for many of the follow-up recipes.

```
> cd C:\postgis_cookbook\data\chap05\SFPoly
```

```
> shp2pgsql -s 3310 -I
C:\postgis_cookbook\data\chap5\SFPoly\sfpoly.shp chap5.sfpoly | psql
-d postgis_cookbook
```

## How it works...

In this recipe, we imported the required PRISM and SRTM rasters needed for the rest of the recipes. We also imported a shapefile containing San Francisco's boundaries to be used in the various raster analyses. Now, on to the fun!

# Working with basic raster information and analysis

So far, we checked and imported the PRISM and SRTM rasters into the chap5 schema of the postgis_cookbook database. We will now proceed to work with the rasters within the database.

## Getting ready

In this recipe, we explore functions that provide insight into the raster attributes and characteristics found in the postgis_cookbook database. In doing so, we can see whether what is found in the database matches the information provided by gdalinfo.

## How to do it...

PostGIS includes the `raster_columns` view to provide a high-level summary of all the raster columns found in the database. This view is similar to the `geometry_columns` and `geography_columns` views in function and form.

Let's run the following SQL query in the `raster_columns` view to see what information is available in the `prism` table:

```
SELECT
        r_table_name,
        r_raster_column,
        srid,
        scale_x,
        scale_y,
        blocksize_x,
        blocksize_y,
        same_alignment,
        regular_blocking,
        num_bands,
        pixel_types,
        nodata_values,
        out_db,
        ST_AsText(extent) AS extent
FROM raster_columns WHERE r_table_name = 'prism';
```

The SQL query returns a record similar the following:

```
   r_table_name   | r_raster_column | srid  |      scale_x
------------------+-----------------+-------+--------------------
    prism         | rast            | 4322  | 0.041666666666667
```

If you look back at the `gdalinfo` output for one of the PRISM rasters, you'll see that the values for the scales (the pixel size) match. The flags passed to `raster2pgsql`, specifying tile size and `SRID`, worked.

Let's see what the metadata of a single raster tile looks like. We will use the `ST_Metadata()` function.

```
SELECT  rid,  (ST_Metadata(rast)).*
FROM prism
WHERE month_year = '2012-06-01'::date
LIMIT 1;
```

The output will look similar to the following:

```
rid |     upperleftx     |     upperlefty     | width | height
-----+-------------------+-------------------+-------+--------
 550 | -87.520833333333  | 45.7708333333335  |  100  |  100
```

Use `ST_BandMetadata()` to examine the first and only band of raster tile at the record ID 550.

```
SELECT  rid,  (ST_BandMetadata(rast, 1)).*
FROM prism
WHERE rid = 550;
```

The results indicate that the band is of pixel type 32BSI and has a NODATA value of -9999. The NODATA value is the value assigned to an empty pixel.

```
rid | pixeltype | nodatavalue | isoutdb | path
-----+-----------+-------------+---------+------
 550 | 32BSI     |       -9999 | f       |
```

Now, to do something a bit more useful, run some basic statistical functions on this raster tile.

First, let's compute the summary statistics (count, mean, standard deviation, min, and max) with `ST_SummaryStats()`.

```
WITH stats AS (  SELECT    (ST_SummaryStats(rast, 1)).*  FROM prism
WHERE rid = 550
)
SELECT  count,  sum,  round(mean::numeric, 2) AS mean,
round(stddev::numeric, 2) AS stddev,  min,  max
FROM stats;
```

The output of the preceding code will be as follows:

```
count |   sum   |  mean   | stddev | min | max
-------+---------+---------+--------+-----+------
 7081 | 8987349 | 1269.22 | 125.87 | 943 | 1798
```

In the summary statistics, the count indicates that the raster tile is about 30 percent NODATA. But what is really interesting is that the mean, min, and max values do not make sense for minimum temperature values. We'll discuss this issue at the end of this recipe.

Let's see how the values of the raster tile are distributed with `ST_Histogram()`.

```
WITH hist AS (
        SELECT
                (ST_Histogram(rast, 1)).*
        FROM prism
        WHERE rid = 550
)
```

```
SELECT
        round(min::numeric, 2) AS min,
        round(max::numeric, 2) AS max,
        count,
        round(percent::numeric, 2) AS percent
FROM hist
ORDER BY min;
```

The output will look as follows:

```
     min    |    max    | count | percent
  ----------+-----------+-------+---------
     943.00 | 1004.07 |    51 |    0.01
    1004.07 | 1065.14 |   299 |    0.04
    1065.14 | 1126.21 |   884 |    0.12
    1126.21 | 1187.29 |   925 |    0.13
    1187.29 | 1248.36 |   652 |    0.09
    1248.36 | 1309.43 |   997 |    0.14
    1309.43 | 1370.50 |  1785 |    0.25
    1370.50 | 1431.57 |   992 |    0.14
    1431.57 | 1492.64 |   311 |    0.04
    1492.64 | 1553.71 |   130 |    0.02
    1553.71 | 1614.79 |    33 |    0.00
    1614.79 | 1675.86 |    13 |    0.00
    1675.86 | 1736.93 |     6 |    0.00
    1736.93 | 1798.00 |     3 |    0.00
```

It looks as if about 78 percent of all of the values are at or below `1370.50`. Another way to see how the pixel values are distributed is to use `ST_Quantile()`.

```
SELECT
        (ST_Quantile(rast, 1)).*
FROM prism
WHERE rid = 550;
```

The output of the preceding code is as follows:

```
 quantile | value
----------+-------
        0 |   943
     0.25 |  1156
      0.5 |  1296
     0.75 |  1360
        1 |  1798
```

The 75th percentile value of `1360` aligns nicely with the histogram result of about 78 percent of the values that are at or below `1370.50`.

Let's see what the top 10 occurring values are in the raster tile with `ST_ValueCount()`.

```
SELECT
        (ST_ValueCount(rast, 1)).*
FROM prism
WHERE rid = 550
ORDER BY count DESC, value
LIMIT 10;
```

The output of the code is as follows:

```
 value | count
-------+-------
  1341 |    41
  1334 |    40
  1348 |    39
  1352 |    38
  1360 |    37
  1331 |    36
  1344 |    36
  1324 |    35
  1343 |    35
  1314 |    34
```

## How it works...

In the first part of this recipe, we looked at the metadata of the `prism` raster table and a single raster tile. We focused on that single raster tile to run a variety of statistics. The statistics provided some idea of what the data looks like.

We mentioned that the pixel values looked wrong when we looked at the output from `ST_SummaryStats()`. This same issue continued in the output from subsequent statistics functions. We need to look at the `PRISM` raster's metadata available at `http://www.prism.oregonstate.edu/docs/meta/temp_realtime_monthly.htm`.

After looking at the metadata, it appears that the `PRISM` raster values have been scaled by `100` to enable the use of an integer instead of a floating-point pixel type. We also find that the values are in degree Celsius. In the next recipe, we will recompute all the pixel values to their true values with a map algebra operation.

# Performing simple map-algebra operations

In the previous recipe, we saw that the values in the PRISM rasters did not look correct for temperature values. After looking at the PRISM metadata, we learned that the values were scaled by `100`.

In this recipe, we will process the scaled values to get the true values. Doing this will prevent future end user confusion, which is always a good thing.

## Getting ready

PostGIS provides two types of map-algebra functions, both of which return a new raster with one band. The type you use depends on the problem being solved and the number of raster bands involved.

The first map-algebra function (`ST_MapAlgebra()` or `ST_MapAlgebraExpr()`) depends on a valid, user-provided PostgreSQL algebraic expression that is called for every pixel. The expression can be as simple as an equation or as complex as a logic-heavy SQL expression. If the map-algebra operation only requires at most two raster bands, and the expression is not complicated, you should have no problems using the expression-based map-algebra function.

The second map-algebra function (`ST_MapAlgebra()`, `ST_MapAlgebraFct()`, or `ST_MapAlgebraFctNgb()`) requires the user to provide an appropriate PostgreSQL function to be called for each pixel. The function being called can be written in any of the PostgreSQL PL languages (for example, PL/pgSQL, PL/R, PL/Perl) and be as complex as needed. This type is more challenging to use than the expression map-algebra function type, but it has the flexibility to work on any number of raster bands.

For this recipe, we use only the expression-based map-algebra function `ST_MapAlgebra()` to create a new band with the true temperature values and then append this band to the processed raster. If you are not using PostGIS 2.1 or a later version, use the equivalent `ST_MapAlgebraExpr()` function.

## How to do it...

With any operation that is going to take a while and/or modify a stored raster, it is best to test that operation to ensure there are no mistakes and the output looks correct.

Let's run `ST_MapAlgebra()` (or `ST_MapAlgebraExpr()` if you are running PostGIS 2.0) on one raster tile and compare the summary statistics before and after the map-algebra operation.

```
WITH stats AS (
        SELECT
                'before' AS state,
                (ST_SummaryStats(rast, 1)).*
```

```
        FROM prism
        WHERE rid = 550
        UNION ALL
        SELECT
                'after' AS state, (
                        ST_SummaryStats(
                                ST_MapAlgebra(rast, 1, '32BF', '
[rast] / 100.', -9999),
                                1
                        )
                ).*
        FROM prism
        WHERE rid = 550
)
SELECT
        state,
        count,
        round(sum::numeric, 2) AS sum,
        round(mean::numeric, 2) AS mean,
        round(stddev::numeric, 2) AS stddev,
        round(min::numeric, 2) AS min,
        round(max::numeric, 2) AS max
FROM stats
ORDER BY state DESC;
```

The output looks as follows:

```
 state  | count |     sum      |  mean   | stddev |  min
--------+-------+--------------+---------+--------+--------
 before |  7081 |  8987349.00  | 1269.22 | 125.87 | 943.00
 after  |  7081 |    89873.49  |   12.69 |   1.26 |   9.43
```

In the ST_MapAlgebra() function, we indicate that the output raster's band will have a pixel type of 32BF and a NODATA value of -9999. We use the expression ' [rast] / 100.' to convert each pixel value to its true value. Before ST_MapAlgebra() evaluates the expression, the pixel value replaces the placeholder ' [rast] '. There are several other placeholders available; these can be found in the ST_MapAlgebra() documentation.

Looking at the summary statistics and comparing the before and after processing, we see that the map-algebra operation works correctly. So, let's correct the entire table. We will append the band created from ST_MapAlgebra() to the existing raster.

```
UPDATE prism SET  rast = ST_AddBand(   rast,    ST_MapAlgebra(rast,
1, '32BF', '[rast] / 100.', -9999), 1    );
ERROR:  new row for relation "prism" violates check constraint
"enforce_out_db_rast"
```

The SQL query will not work. Why? If you remember, when we loaded the PRISM rasters, we instructed `raster2pgsql` to add the standard constraints with the `-C` flag. It looks as if we violated at least one of those constraints.

When installed, the standard constraints enforce a set of rules on each value of a raster column in the table. These rules guarantee that each raster column value has the same or appropriate attributes. The standard constraints comprise the following rules:

▸ **Width and height**: This rule states that all the rasters must have the same width and height

▸ **Scale X and Y**: This rule states that all the rasters must have the same scale X and Y

▸ **SRID**: This rule states that all rasters must have the same SRID

▸ **Same alignment**: This rule states that all rasters must be aligned to one another

▸ **Maximum extent**: This rule states that all rasters must be within the table's maximum extent

▸ **Number of bands**: This rule states that all rasters must have the same number of bands

▸ **NODATA values**: This rule states that all raster bands at a specific index must have the same NODATA value

▸ **Out-db**: This rule states that all raster bands at a specific index must be `in-db` or `out-db`, not both

▸ **Pixel type**: This rule states that all raster bands at a specific index must be of the same pixel type

The error message indicates that we violated the `out-db` constraint. But we can't accept the error message as is because we are not doing anything related to `out-db`. All we are doing is adding a second band to the raster. Adding the second band violates the `out-db` constraint because the constraint is prepared only for one band in the raster, not a raster with two bands.

We will have to drop the constraints, make our changes, and reapply the constraints.

```
SELECT DropRasterConstraints('prism', 'rast'::name);
UPDATE prism SET
        rast = ST_AddBand(
                rast,
                ST_MapAlgebra(rast, 1, '32BF', '[rast] / 100.', -9
999),
                1
        );
SELECT AddRasterConstraints('prism', 'rast'::name);
```

The UPDATE will take some time and the output will look as follows:

```
droprasterconstraints
----------------------
 t
UPDATE 1260
 addrasterconstraints
----------------------
 t
```

There is not much information provided in the output, so we will inspect the rasters. We will look at one raster tile.

```
SELECT
        (ST_Metadata(rast)).numbands
FROM prism
WHERE rid = 550;
```

The output is as follows:

```
 numbands
----------
        2
```

The raster has two bands. The following are the details of these two bands:

```
SELECT
        1 AS bandnum,
        (ST_BandMetadata(rast, 1)).*
FROM prism
WHERE rid = 550
UNION ALL
SELECT
        2 AS bandnum,
        (ST_BandMetadata(rast, 2)).*
FROM prism
WHERE rid = 550
ORDER BY bandnum;
```

The output looks as follows:

```
 bandnum | pixeltype | nodatavalue | isoutdb | path
---------+-----------+-------------+---------+------
       1 | 32BSI     |       -9999 | f       |
       2 | 32BF      |       -9999 | f       |
```

The first band is the same as before and the new second band has the correct attributes (the `32BF` pixel type and the `NODATA value` of `-9999`) that we specified in the call to `ST_MapAlgebra()`. The real test though is to look at the summary statistics.

```
WITH stats AS (
        SELECT
                1 AS bandnum,
                (ST_SummaryStats(rast, 1)).*
        FROM prism
        WHERE rid = 550
        UNION ALL
        SELECT
                2 AS bandnum,
                (ST_SummaryStats(rast, 2)).*
        FROM prism
        WHERE rid = 550
)
SELECT
        bandnum,
        count,
        round(sum::numeric, 2) AS sum,
        round(mean::numeric, 2) AS mean,
        round(stddev::numeric, 2) AS stddev,
        round(min::numeric, 2) AS min,
        round(max::numeric, 2) AS max
FROM stats
ORDER BY bandnum;
```

The output is as follows:

| bandnum | count | sum | mean | stddev | min |
|--------:|------:|----:|-----:|-------:|----:|
| 1 | 7081 | 8987349.00 | 1269.22 | 125.87 | 943.00 |
| 2 | 7081 | 89873.49 | 12.69 | 1.26 | 9.43 |

The summary statistics show that band 2 is correct (the band 1 value divided by `100.`). The values now make sense for the average monthly minimum temperature.

## How it works...

In this recipe, we applied a simple map-algebra operation with `ST_MapAlgebra()` to correct the pixel values. In a later recipe, we will present an advanced map-algebra operation to demonstrate the power of `ST_MapAlgebra()`.

# Combining geometries with rasters for analysis

In the previous two recipes, we ran basic statistics only on one raster tile. Though running operations on a specific raster is great, it is not very helpful for answering real questions. In this recipe, we will use geometries to filter, clip, and union raster tiles so that we can answer questions for a specific area.

## Getting ready

We will use the San Francisco boundaries geometry previously imported into the `sfpoly` table. If you have not imported the boundaries, refer to the first recipe of this chapter for instructions.

## How to do it...

Since we are to look at rasters in the context of San Francisco, an easy question to ask is: what was the average temperature for January, 2012 in San Francisco?

```
SELECT (
        ST_SummaryStats(
                ST_Union(
                        ST_Clip(prism.rast, 2,
ST_Transform(sf.geom, 4322), TRUE)
                ),
                1
        )
).mean
FROM prism
JOIN sfpoly sf
        ON ST_Intersects(prism.rast, ST_Transform(sf.geom, 4322))
WHERE prism.month_year = '2012-01-01'::date;
```

In the preceding SQL query, there are four items to pay attention to, as follows:

- ▶ `ST_Transform()`: This method converts the geometry's coordinates from one spatial reference system to another. Transforming a geometry is typically faster than transforming a raster. Transforming a raster requires resampling the pixel values, a computationally-intensive process and one that could introduce undesirable results. If possible, always transform a geometry before transforming a raster.

- ▶ `ST_Intersects()`:The `ST_Intersects()` method found in the `JOIN ON` clause tests whether the raster tile and the geometry spatially intersect. It will use any available spatial indexes. Depending on the installed version of PostGIS, `ST_Intersects()` will implicitly convert the input geometry to a raster (PostGIS 2.0) or the input raster to a geometry (PostGIS 2.1) before comparing the two inputs.

- ▶ `ST_Clip()`: This method trims each intersecting raster tile only to the area that intersects the geometry. It eliminates the pixels that are not spatially part of the geometry. As with `ST_Intersects()`, the geometry is implicitly converted to a raster before clipping.

- ▶ `ST_Union()`: This method aggregates and merges the clipped raster tiles into one raster for further processing.

The following output shows the average minimum temperature for San Francisco:

```
      mean
------------------
 7.35125005245209
```

San Francisco was really cold in January, 2012. So, how does the rest of 2012 look? Is San Francisco always cold?

```
SELECT
        prism.month_year, (
                ST_SummaryStats(
                        ST_Union(
                                ST_Clip(prism.rast, 2,
                                ST_Transform(sf.geom, 4322), TRUE)
                        ),
                        1
                )
        ).mean
FROM prism
JOIN sfpoly sf
        ON ST_Intersects(prism.rast, ST_Transform(sf.geom, 4322))
GROUP BY prism.month_year
ORDER BY prism.month_year;
```

The only change from the prior SQL query is the removal of the `WHERE` clause and the addition of a `GROUP BY` clause. Since `ST_Union()` is an aggregate function, we need to group the clipped rasters by `month_year`.

The output is as follows:

```
month_year  |        mean
------------+------------------
 2012-01-01 |  7.35125005245209
 2012-02-01 |  7.96125000715256
 2012-03-01 |  8.04749995470047
 2012-04-01 |   9.4337500333786
 2012-05-01 |  9.71625006198883
 2012-06-01 |  10.6924999952316
 2012-07-01 |  11.5974999666214
 2012-08-01 |          11.71875
 2012-09-01 |  11.1512498855591
 2012-10-01 |  12.5250000953674
 2012-11-01 |  11.0825001001358
 2012-12-01 |  8.63750004768372
```

Based on the results, the late summer months of 2012 were the warmest, though not by a huge margin.

## How it works...

By using a geometry to filter the rasters in the prism table, only a small set of rasters needed clipping with the geometry and unioning to compute the mean. This maximized the query performance and, more importantly, provided the answer to our question.

# Converting between rasters and geometries

In the last recipe, we used the geometries to filter and clip rasters only to the areas of interest. The functions ST_Clip() and ST_Intersects() implicitly converted the geometry before relating it to the raster.

PostGIS provides several functions for converting rasters to geometries. Depending on the function, a pixel can be returned as an area or a point.

PostGIS provides one function for converting geometries to rasters.

## Getting ready

In this recipe, we will convert rasters to geometries and geometries to rasters. We will use the ST_DumpAsPolygons() and ST_PixelsAsPolygons() functions to convert rasters to geometries. We will then convert geometries to rasters using ST_AsRaster().

## How to do it...

Let's adapt part of the query used in the last recipe to find out the average minimum temperature in San Francisco. We replace `ST_SummaryStats()` with `ST_DumpAsPolygons()` and then return the geometries as WKT.

```
WITH geoms AS (
        SELECT
                ST_DumpAsPolygons(
                        ST_Union(
                                ST_Clip(prism.rast, 2,
                                ST_Transform(sf.geom, 4322), TRUE)
                        ),
                        1
                ) AS gv
        FROM prism
        JOIN sfpoly sf
                ON ST_Intersects(prism.rast, ST_Transform(sf.geom,
                4322))
        WHERE prism.month_year = '2012-01-01'::date
)
SELECT
        (gv).val,
        ST_AsText((gv).geom) AS geom
FROM geoms;
```

The output is as follows:

```
        val          |              geom
------------------+---------------------------------
  7.3899998664856 | POLYGON(...)
  7.3600001335144 | POLYGON(...)
...
  7.30000019073486 | POLYGON(...)
(7 rows)
```

For the sake of brevity, the preceding query results have been trimmed. What is most important about the results is that there are seven rows.

Now, replace the `ST_DumpAsPolygons()` function with `ST_PixelsAsPolyons()`.

```
WITH geoms AS (
        SELECT (
                ST_PixelAsPolygons(
                        ST_Union(
                                ST_Clip(prism.rast, 2,
                                ST_Transform(sf.geom, 4322), TRUE)
```

```
                ),
                1
            )
        ) AS gv
        FROM prism
        JOIN sfpoly sf
                ON ST_Intersects(prism.rast, ST_Transform(sf.geom,
                4322))
        WHERE prism.month_year = '2012-01-01'::date
    )
    SELECT
        (gv).val,
        ST_AsText((gv).geom) AS geom
    FROM geoms;
```

The output is as follows:

```
        val         |              geom
--------------------+--------------------------------
                    | POLYGON(...)
  7.3899998664856   | POLYGON(...)
  7.3600001335144   | POLYGON(...)
...
  7.30000019073486  | POLYGON(...)
                    | POLYGON(...)
(140 rows)
```

Again, the query results have been trimmed. What is important is the number of rows returned. ST_PixelsAsPolygons() returns significantly more geometries than ST_DumpAsPolygons(). This is due to the different mechanism used in each function.

The following image shows the difference between ST_DumpAsPolygons() and ST_PixelsAsPolygons(). The ST_DumpAsPolygons() function only dumps pixels with a value and unions these pixels with the same value. The ST_PixelsAsPolygons() function does not merge pixels and dumps all of them, as shown in the following diagrams:

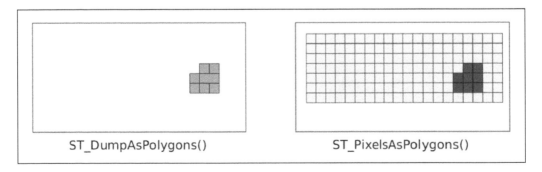

ST_DumpAsPolygons()          ST_PixelsAsPolygons()

The ST_PixelsAsPolygons() function returns one geometry for each pixel. If there are 100 pixels, there will be 100 geometries. Each geometry of ST_DumpAsPolygons() is the union of all of the pixels in an area with the same value. If there are 100 pixels, there may be up to 100 geometries.

There is one other significant difference between ST_PixelAsPolygons() and ST_DumpAsPolygons(). Unlike ST_DumpAsPolygons(), ST_PixelAsPolygons() returns a geometry for pixels with the NODATA value and has an "empty" value for the val column.

Let's convert a geometry to a raster with ST_AsRaster(). We insert ST_AsRaster() to return a raster with a pixel size of 100 by -100 meters and one that contains four bands of the pixel type 8BUI. Each of these bands will have a pixel NODATA value of 0 and a specific pixel value (29, 194, 178, and 255 for each band respectively). The units for pixel size are determined by the geometry's projection, which is also the projection of the created raster.

```
SELECT
        ST_AsRaster(
                sf.geom,
                100., -100.,
                ARRAY['8BUI', '8BUI', '8BUI', '8BUI']::text[],
                ARRAY[29, 194, 178, 255]::double precision[],
                ARRAY[0, 0, 0, 0]::double precision[]
        )
FROM sfpoly sf;
```

If we visualize the generated raster of San Francisco's boundaries and overlay the source geometry, we get the following result, which is a zoomed-in view of the San Francisco boundary's geometry converted to a raster with ST_AsRaster():

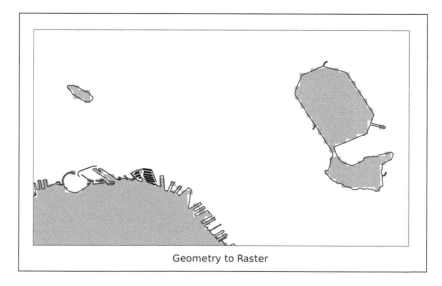

Geometry to Raster

Though it is great that the geometry is now a raster, relating the generated raster to other rasters requires additional processing. This is because the generated raster and the other raster will most likely not be aligned. If the two rasters are not aligned, most PostGIS raster functions do not work. The following screenshot shows two nonaligned rasters (simplified to pixel grids):

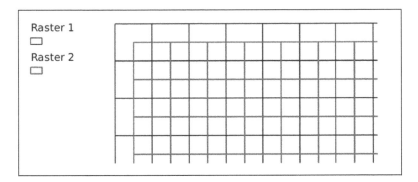

 The pixel grids of **Raster 1** and **Raster 2** are not aligned. If the rasters are aligned, the edges of one grid's cell will be on top of one of the other cell's edges.

When a geometry needs to be converted to a raster so as to relate to an existing raster, use that existing raster as a reference when calling ST_AsRaster().

```
SELECT
        ST_AsRaster(
                sf.geom, prism.rast,
                ARRAY['8BUI', '8BUI', '8BUI', '8BUI']::text[],
                ARRAY[29, 194, 178, 255]::double precision[],
                ARRAY[0, 0, 0, 0]::double precision[]
        )
FROM sfpoly sf
CROSS JOIN prism
WHERE prism.rid = 1;
```

In the preceding query, we use the raster tile at rid = 1 as our reference raster. The ST_AsRaster() function uses the reference raster's metadata to create the geometry's raster. If the geometry and reference raster have different SRIDs, the geometry is transformed to the same SRID before creating the raster.

## How it works...

In this recipe, we converted rasters to geometries. We also created new rasters from geometries. The ability to convert between rasters and geometries allows the use of functions that would otherwise not be possible.

# Processing and loading rasters with GDAL VRT

Though PostGIS has plenty of functions for working with rasters, it is sometimes more convenient and more efficient to work on the source rasters before importing them into the database. One of the times when working with rasters outside the database is more efficient is when the raster contains subdatasets, typically found in HDF4, HDF5, and NetCDF files.

## Getting ready

In this recipe, we will preprocess a MODIS raster with the **GDAL VRT** format to filter and rearrange the subdatasets. Internally, a VRT file is comprised of XML tags. This means we can create a VRT file with any text editor. But, since creating a VRT file manually can be tedious, we will use the gdalbuildvrt utility.

The MODIS raster we use is provided by NASA and available at

http://e4ftl01.cr.usgs.gov/MOLA/MYD09A1.005/2012.06.09/MYD09A1.
A2012161.h08v05.005.2012170065756.hdf.

You will need GDAL built with HDF4 support to continue with this recipe as MODIS rasters are usually in the HDF4-EOS format.

The following screenshot shows the MODIS raster used in this recipe and the next two recipes. In the following image, we see parts of California, Nevada, Arizona, and Baja California:

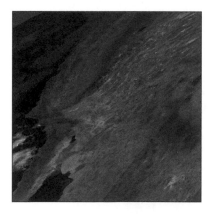

To allow PostGIS to properly support MODIS rasters, we will also need to add the MODIS Sinusoidal projection to the `spatial_ref_sys` table.

## How to do it...

On the command line, navigate to the `MODIS` directory.

```
> cd C:\postgis_cookbook\data\chap05\MODIS
```

In the MODIS directory, there should be several files. One of these files has the name `srs.sql` and contains the `INSERT` statement needed for the MODIS Sinusoidal projection. Run the INSERT statement.

```
> psql -d postgis_cookbook -f srs.sql
```

The main file has the extension HDF. Let's check the metadata of that HDF file.

```
> gdalinfo MYD09A1.A2012161.h08v05.005.2012170065756.hdf
```

When run, `gdalinfo` outputs a lot of information. We are looking for the list of subdatasets found in the `Subdatasets` section.

```
Subdatasets:
  SUBDATASET_1_NAME=HDF4_EOS:EOS_GRID:"MYD09A1.A2012161.h08v05.
005.2012170065756.hdf":MOD_Grid_500m_Surface_Reflectance:sur_refl_b01

  SUBDATASET_1_DESC=[2400x2400] sur_refl_b01
MOD_Grid_500m_Surface_Reflectance (16-bit integer)
  SUBDATASET_2_NAME=HDF4_EOS:EOS_GRID:"MYD09A1.A2012161.
h08v05.005.2012170065756.hdf":MOD_Grid_500m_Surface_Reflectance:sur_
refl_b02
  SUBDATASET_2_DESC=[2400x2400] sur_refl_b02
MOD_Grid_500m_Surface_Reflectance (16-bit integer)
...
  SUBDATASET_12_NAME=HDF4_EOS:EOS_GRID:"MYD09A1.A2012161.
h08v05.005.2012170065756.hdf":MOD_Grid_500m_Surface_Reflectance:sur_
refl_state_500m
  SUBDATASET_12_DESC=[2400x2400] sur_refl_state_500m
MOD_Grid_500m_Surface_Reflectance (16-bit unsigned integer)
```

Each subdataset is one variable of the MODIS raster. For our purposes, we only need the first four subdatasets, as follows:

- ► subdataset 1: 620 - 670 nm (red)
- ► subdataset 2: 841 - 876 nm (near infrared or NIR)
- ► subdataset 3: 459 - 479 nm (blue)
- ► subdataset 4: 545 - 565 nm (green)

Full metadata can be found at the MODIS site for this MODIS product:

```
https://lpdaac.usgs.gov/products/modis_products_table/myd09a1
```

The VRT format allows us to select the subdatasets to be included in the VRT raster as well as change the order of the subdatasets. We want to rearrange the subdatasets so that they are in the RGB order.

Let's call `gdalbuildvrt` to create a VRT file for our MODIS raster. Do not run the following!

```
> gdalbuildvrt -separate  modis.vrt
HDF4_EOS:EOS_GRID:"MYD09A1.A2012161.h08v05.005.2012170065756.hdf":MOD_
Grid_500m_Surface_Reflectance:sur_refl_b01
HDF4_EOS:EOS_GRID:"MYD09A1.A2012161.h08v05.005.2012170065756.hdf":MOD_
Grid_500m_Surface_Reflectance:sur_refl_b04
HDF4_EOS:EOS_GRID:"MYD09A1.A2012161.h08v05.005.2012170065756.hdf":MOD_
Grid_500m_Surface_Reflectance:sur_refl_b03
HDF4_EOS:EOS_GRID:"MYD09A1.A2012161.h08v05.005.2012170065756.hdf":MOD_
Grid_500m_Surface_Reflectance:sur_refl_b02
```

We really hope you did not run the preceding code. The command does work but is too long and cumbersome. It would be better if we can pass a file indicating the subdatasets to include and their order in the VRT. Thankfully, `gdalbuildvrt` provides such an option with the `-input_file_list` flag.

In the MODIS directory, the `modis.txt` file can be passed to `gdalbuildvrt` with the `-input_file_list` flag. Each line of the `modis.txt` file is the name of a subdataset. The order of the subdatasets in the text file dictates the placement of each subdataset in the VRT.

```
HDF4_EOS:EOS_GRID:"MYD09A1.A2012161.h08v05.005.2012170065756.hdf":MOD_
Grid_500m_Surface_Reflectance:sur_refl_b01

HDF4_EOS:EOS_GRID:"MYD09A1.A2012161.h08v05.005.2012170065756.hdf":MOD_
Grid_500m_Surface_Reflectance:sur_refl_b04

HDF4_EOS:EOS_GRID:"MYD09A1.A2012161.h08v05.005.2012170065756.hdf":MOD_
Grid_500m_Surface_Reflectance:sur_refl_b03

HDF4_EOS:EOS_GRID:"MYD09A1.A2012161.h08v05.005.2012170065756.hdf":MOD_
Grid_500m_Surface_Reflectance:sur_refl_b02
```

Now, call `gdalbuildvrt` with `modis.txt` in the following manner:

```
> gdalbuildvrt -separate -input_file_list modis.txt modis.vrt
```

Feel free to inspect the generated `modis.vrt` VRT file in your favorite text editor. Since the contents of the VRT file are just XML tags, it is easy to make additions, changes, and deletions.

We will do one last thing before importing our processed MODIS raster into PostGIS. We will convert the VRT file to a GeoTIFF file with the gdal_translate utility because not all applications have built-in support for HDF4, HDF5, NetCDF, or VRT and the superior portability of GeoTIFF.

```
> gdal_translate -of GTiff modis.vrt modis.tif
```

Finally, import modis.tif with raster2pgsql.

```
> raster2pgsql -s 96974 -F -I -C -Y modis.tif chap5.modis | psql -d
postgis_cookbook
```

## How it works...

This recipe was all about processing a MODIS raster into a form suitable for use in PostGIS. We used the gdalbuildvrt utility to create our VRT. As a bonus, we used gdal_translate to convert between raster formats, in this case from VRT to GeoTIFF.

If you're feeling particularly adventurous, try using gdalbuildvrt to create a VRT of the 12 PRISM rasters with each raster as a separate band.

# Warping and resampling rasters

In the previous recipe, we processed a MODIS raster to extract only those subdatasets that are of interest, in a more suitable order. Once done with the extraction, we imported the MODIS raster into its own table.

Here, we make use of the warping capabilities provided in PostGIS. This ranges from simply transforming the MODIS raster to a more suitable projection to creating an overview by resampling the pixel size.

## Getting ready

We will use several PostGIS warping functions, specifically ST_Transform() and ST_Rescale(). The ST_Transform() function reprojects a raster to a new spatial reference system (for example, from WGS84 to NAD83). The ST_Rescale() function shrinks or grows the pixel size of a raster.

## How to do it...

The first thing we will do is transform our raster since the MODIS rasters have their own unique spatial-reference system. We will convert the raster from **MODIS Sinusoidal projection** to **US National Atlas Equal Area (SRID 2163)**.

Before we transform the raster, we will clip the MODIS raster with our San Francisco boundaries geometry. By clipping our raster before transformation, the operation takes less time than it does to transform and then clip the raster.

```
SELECT  ST_Transform(ST_Clip(m.rast, ST_Transform(sf.geom, 96974)),
2163)
FROM modis m
CROSS JOIN sfpoly sf;
```

The following screenshot shows the clipped MODIS raster with the San Francisco boundaries on top for comparison:

When we call ST_Transform() on the MODIS raster, we only pass the destination SRID 2163. We could specify other parameters, such as the **resampling algorithm** and **error tolerance**. The default resampling algorithm and error tolerance are set to NearestNeighbor and 0.125. Using a different algorithm and/or lowering the error tolerance may improve the quality of the resampled raster at the cost of more processing time.

Let's transform the MODIS raster again, this time specifying the resampling algorithm and error tolerance as Cubic and 0.05 respectively. We also indicate that the transformed raster must be aligned to a reference raster.

```
SELECT  ST_Transform(ST_Clip(m.rast, ST_Transform(sf.geom, 96974)),
prism.rast, 'cubic', 0.05)
FROM modis m
CROSS JOIN prism
CROSS JOIN sfpoly sf
WHERE prism.rid = 1;
```

Unlike the prior queries where we transform the MODIS raster, let's create an overview. An **overview** is a lower resolution version of the source raster. If you are familiar with pyramids, an overview is level one of a pyramid while the source raster is the base level.

```
WITH meta AS (
        SELECT
                (ST_Metadata(rast)).*
        FROM modis
)
SELECT
        ST_Rescale(modis.rast, meta.scalex * 4., meta.scaley * 4., '
cubic') AS rast
FROM modis
CROSS JOIN meta;
```

The overview is 25 percent of the resolution of the original MODIS raster. This means four times the scale and one-quarter the width and height. To prevent hardcoding the desired scale X and scale Y, we use the MODIS raster's scale X and scale Y returned by ST_Metadata(). As you can see in the following screenshot, the overview has a coarser resolution.

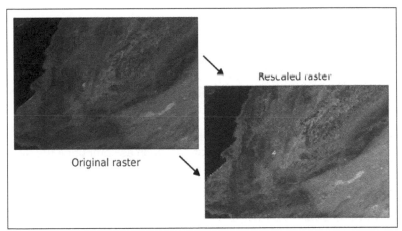

The MODIS raster before and after rescaling with ST_Rescale()

 The rescaled raster is more pixelated due to the reduction of resolution.

## How it works...

Using some of PostGIS's resampling capabilities, we projected the MODIS raster to a different spatial reference with `ST_Transform()` as well as controlled the quality of the projected raster. We also created an overview with `ST_Rescale()`.

Using these functions and other PostGIS resampling functions, you should be able to manipulate all the rasters.

# Performing advanced map-algebra operations

In a prior recipe, we used the expression-based map-algebra function `ST_MapAlgebra()` to convert the PRISM pixel values to their true values. The expression-based `ST_MapAlgebra()` method is easy to use but limited to operating on at most two raster bands. This restricts the `ST_MapAlgebra()` function's usefulness for processes that require more than two input raster bands, such as **Normalized Difference Vegetation Index** (**NDVI**) and **Enhanced Vegetation Index** (**EVI**).

There is a variant of `ST_MapAlgebra()` designed to support an unlimited number of input raster bands. Instead of taking an expression, this `ST_MapAlgebra()` variant requires a callback function. This callback function is run for each set of input pixel values and returns either a new pixel value or `NULL` for the output pixel. Additionally, this variant of `ST_MapAlgebra()` permits operations on neighborhoods (sets of pixels around a center pixel).

PostGIS comes with a set of ready-to-use `ST_MapAlgebra()` callback functions. All of these functions are intended for neighborhood calculations, such as computing the average value of a neighborhood or interpolating empty pixel values.

## Getting ready

We will use the MODIS raster to compute the EVI. **EVI** is a three-band operation consisting of the red, blue, and near-infrared bands. To do a `ST_MapAlgebra()` operation on three bands, PostGIS 2.1 or a higher version is required. If you have PostGIS 2.0, a two-band EVI version is provided after we discuss the three-band variant.

## How to do it...

To use `ST_MapAlgebra()` on more than two bands, we must use the callback function variant. This means we need to create a callback function. Callback functions can be written in any PostgreSQL PL language, such as PL/pgSQL or PL/R. Our callback functions are all written in PL/pgSQL as this language is always included with a base PostgreSQL installation.

Our callback function uses the following equation to compute the three-band EVI:

$$EVI = G \times \frac{(NIR - RED)}{(NIR + C1 \times RED - C2 \times BLUE + L)}$$

```
CREATE OR REPLACE FUNCTION chap5.modis_evi(value double precision[][]
[], position int[][], VARIADIC userargs text[])
RETURNS double precision
AS $$
DECLARE
        L double precision;
        C1 double precision;
        C2 double precision;
        G double precision;
        _value double precision[3];
        _n double precision;
        _d double precision;
BEGIN
        -- userargs provides coefficients
        L := userargs[1]::double precision;
        C1 := userargs[2]::double precision;
        C2 := userargs[3]::double precision;
        G := userargs[4]::double precision;
        -- rescale values, optional
        _value[1] := value[1][1][1] * 0.0001;
        _value[2] := value[2][1][1] * 0.0001;
        _value[3] := value[3][1][1] * 0.0001;
        -- value can't be NULL
        IF
                _value[1] IS NULL OR
                _value[2] IS NULL OR
                _value[3] IS NULL
        THEN
                RETURN NULL;
        END IF;
        -- compute numerator and denominator
        _n := (_value[3] - _value[1]);
        _d := (_value[3] + (C1 * _value[1]) - (C2 * _value[2]) + L
);
        -- prevent division by zero
        IF _d::numeric(16, 10) = 0.::numeric(16, 10) THEN
                RETURN NULL;
        END IF;
        RETURN G * (_n / _d);
END;
$$ LANGUAGE plpgsql IMMUTABLE;
```

If you can't create the function, you probably do not have the necessary privileges in the database.

There are several characteristics required for all of the callback functions. These are as follows:

- All ST_MapAlgebra() callback functions must have three input parameters, namely, double precision[], integer[], and variadic text[]. The value parameter is a 3D array where the first dimension denotes the raster index, the second dimension the Y axis, and the third dimension the X axis. The position parameter is an array of two dimensions with the first dimension indicating the raster index and the second dimension consisting of the X, Y coordinates of the center pixel. The last parameter, userargs, is a 1D array of zero or more elements containing values that a user wants to pass to the callback function. If visualized, the parameters look like the following:

```
value = ARRAY[
        1 => [ -- raster 1
                [pixval, pixval, pixval], -- row of raster 1
                [pixval, pixval, pixval],
                [pixval, pixval, pixval]
        ],
        2 => [ -- raster 2
                [pixval, pixval, pixval], -- row of raster 2
                [pixval, pixval, pixval],
                [pixval, pixval, pixval]
        ],
        ...
        N => [ -- raster N
                [pixval, pixval, pixval], -- row of raster
                [pixval, pixval, pixval],
                [pixval, pixval, pixval]
        ]
];
pos := ARRAY[
        0 => [x-coordinate, y-coordinate], -- center pixel o
f output raster
        1 => [x-coordinate, y-coordinate], -- center pixel o
f raster 1
        2 => [x-coordinate, y-coordinate], -- center pixel o
f raster 2
        ...
        N => [x-coordinate, y-coordinate], -- center pixel o
f raster N
];
userargs := ARRAY[
```

```
                'arg1',
                'arg2',
                ...
                'argN'
        ];
```

▸  All `ST_MapAlgebra()` callback functions must return a double-precision value.

If the callback functions are not correctly structured, the `ST_MapAlgebra()` function will fail or behave incorrectly.

In the function body, we convert the user arguments to their correct datatypes, rescale the pixel values, check that no pixel values are `NULL` (arithmetic operations with `NULL` values always result in `NULL`), compute the numerator and denominator components of `EVI`, check that the denominator is not zero (to prevent division by zero), and then finish the computation of `EVI`.

Now we call our callback function `modis_evi()` with `ST_MapAlgebra()`.

```
SELECT
        ST_MapAlgebra(
                rast,
                ARRAY[1, 3, 4]::int[], -- only use the red, blue a
nd near infrared bands
                'chap5.modis_evi(double precision[], int[], t
ext[])'::regprocedure, -- signature for callback function
                '32BF', -- output pixel type
                'FIRST',
                NULL,
                0, 0,
                '1.', -- L
                '6.', -- C1
                '7.5', -- C2
                '2.5' -- G
        ) AS rast
FROM modis m;
```

In our call to `ST_MapAlgebra()`, there are three criteria to take note of, as follows:

▸  The signature for the `modis_evi()` callback function. When passing the callback function to `ST_MapAlgebra()`, it must be written as a string containing the function name and the input-parameter types.

▸  The last four function parameters (`'1.'`, `'6.'`, `'7.5'`, `'2.5'`) are user-defined arguments that are passed for processing by the `callback` function.

▸  The order of the band numbers affects the order of the pixel values passed to the callback function.

The following screenshot shows the MODIS raster before and after running the EVI operation. The EVI raster has a pale white to dark green colormap applied for highlighting areas of high vegetation.

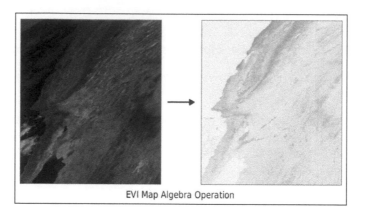

EVI Map Algebra Operation

If you are unable to run the standard EVI operation or want more practice, we will now compute a two-band EVI. We will use the function ST_MapAlgebraFct().

 Please note that ST_MapAlgebraFct() is deprecated in PostGIS 2.1 and may be removed in the future versions.

For the two-band EVI, we will use the following callback function. The two band EVI is computed with this equation:

$$EVI2 = G \times \frac{(NIR - RED)}{(NIR + C1 \times RED + L)}$$

```
CREATE OR REPLACE FUNCTION chap5.modis_evi2(value1 double
precision, value2 double precision, pos int[], VARIADIC userargs
text[])
RETURNS double precision
AS $$
DECLARE
        L double precision;
        C double precision;
        G double precision;
        _value1 double precision;
        _value2 double precision;
        _n double precision;
        _d double precision;
BEGIN
        -- userargs provides coefficients
        L := userargs[1]::double precision;
```

```
        C := userargs[2]::double precision;
        G := userargs[3]::double precision;
        -- value can't be NULL
        IF
                value1 IS NULL OR
                value2 IS NULL
        THEN
                RETURN NULL;
        END IF;
        _value1 := value1 * 0.0001;
        _value2 := value2 * 0.0001;
        -- compute numerator and denominator
        _n := (_value2 - _value1);
        _d := (L + _value2 + (C * _value1));
        -- prevent division by zero
        IF _d::numeric(16, 10) = 0.::numeric(16, 10) THEN
                RETURN NULL;
        END IF;
        RETURN G * (_n / _d);
    END;
    $$ LANGUAGE plpgsql IMMUTABLE;
```

As with `ST_MapAlgebra()` callback functions, `ST_MapAlgebraFct()` requires callback functions to be structured in a specific manner. There is a difference between the callback function for `ST_MapAlgebraFct()` and the prior one for `ST_MapAlgebra()`. This function has two simple pixel-value parameters instead of an array for all pixel values.

```
    SELECT
            ST_MapAlgebraFct(
                    rast, 1, -- red band
                    rast, 4, -- NIR band
                    'modis_evi2(double precision, double precision, int[],
    text[])'::regprocedure, -- signature for callback function
                    '32BF', -- output pixel type
                    'FIRST',
                    '1.', -- L
                    '2.4', -- C
                    '2.5' -- G
            ) AS rast
    FROM modis m;
```

Besides the difference in function names, `ST_MapAlgebraFct()` is called differently from `ST_MapAlgebra()`. The same raster is passed to `ST_MapAlgebraFct()` twice. The other difference is that there is one less user-defined argument being passed to the `callback` function as the two-band EVI has one less coefficient.

## How it works...

We demonstrated some of the advanced uses of PostGIS's map-algebra functions by computing the three-band and two-band EVIs from our MODIS raster. This was achieved using `ST_MapAlgebra()` and `ST_MapAlgebraFct()` respectively. With some planning, PostGIS's map-algebra functions can be applied to other uses, for example, edge detection and contrast stretching.

For additional practice, write your own callback function to generate an NDVI raster from the MODIS raster. The equation for NDVI is:

$$NDVI = \frac{NIR - RED}{NIR + RED}$$

# Executing DEM operations

PostGIS comes with several functions for use on digital elevation model (DEM) rasters to solve terrain-related problems. Though these problems have historically been in the hydrology domain, they can now be found elsewhere, for example, finding the most fuel-efficient route from point A to point B or determining the best location on a roof for a solar panel. PostGIS 2.0 introduced `ST_Slope()`, `ST_Aspect()`, and `ST_HillShade()` while PostGIS 2.1 added the new functions `ST_TRI()`, `ST_TPI()`, and `ST_Roughness()`, and new variants of existing elevation functions.

## Getting ready

We will use the SRTM raster, loaded as 100 x 100 tiles, in this chapter's first recipe. With it, we will generate slope and hillshade rasters using San Francisco as our area of interest.

The two queries below use variants of `ST_Slope()` and `ST_HillShade()` that are only available in PostGIS 2.1 or higher versions. The new variants permit the specification of a custom extent to constrain the processing area of the input raster.

## How to do it...

Let's generate a slope raster from a subset of our SRTM raster tiles using `ST_Slope()`. A slope raster computes the rate of elevation change from one pixel to a neighboring pixel.

```
WITH r AS ( -- union of filtered tiles
    SELECT
            ST_Transform(ST_Union(srtm.rast), 3310) AS rast
    FROM srtm
    JOIN sfpoly sf
```

```
                        ON ST_DWithin(ST_Transform(srtm.rast::geometry, 3
310), ST_Transform(sf.geom, 3310), 1000)
), cx AS ( -- custom extent
        SELECT
                ST_AsRaster(ST_Transform(sf.geom, 3310), r.rast) AS
rast
        FROM sfpoly sf
        CROSS JOIN r
)
SELECT
        ST_Clip(ST_Slope(r.rast, 1, cx.rast), S
T_Transform(sf.geom, 3310)) AS rast
FROM r
CROSS JOIN cx
CROSS JOIN sfpoly sf;
```

All spatial objects in this query are projected to **California Albers** (**SRID 3310**), a projection with units in meters. This projection eases the use of ST_DWithin() to broaden our area of interest to include the tiles within 1000 meters of San Francisco's boundaries, which improves the computed slope values for the pixels at the edges of the San Francisco boundaries. We also use a rasterized version of our San Francisco boundaries as the custom extent for restricting the computed area. After running ST_Slope(), we clip the slope raster just to San Francisco.

We can reuse the ST_Slope() query and substitute ST_HillShade() for ST_Slope() to create a hillshade raster showing how the sun would illuminate the terrain of the SRTM raster.

```
WITH r AS ( -- union of filtered tiles
        SELECT
                ST_Transform(ST_Union(srtm.rast), 3310) AS rast
        FROM srtm
        JOIN sfpoly sf
                ON ST_DWithin(ST_Transform(srtm.rast::geometry, 3
310), ST_Transform(sf.geom, 3310), 1000)
), cx AS ( -- custom extent
        SELECT
                ST_AsRaster(ST_Transform(sf.geom, 3310), r.rast) A
S rast
        FROM sfpoly sf
        CROSS JOIN r
)
SELECT
        ST_Clip(ST_HillShade(r.rast, 1, cx.rast), S
T_Transform(sf.geom, 3310)) AS rast
FROM r
CROSS JOIN cx
CROSS JOIN sfpoly sf;
```

In this case, `ST_HillShade()` is a drop-in replacement for `ST_Slope()` because we do not specify any special input parameters for either function. If we need to specify additional arguments for `ST_Slope()` or `ST_HillShade()`, all changes are confined to just one line.

The following screenshot shows the SRTM raster before and after processing it with `ST_Slope()` and `ST_HillShade()`:

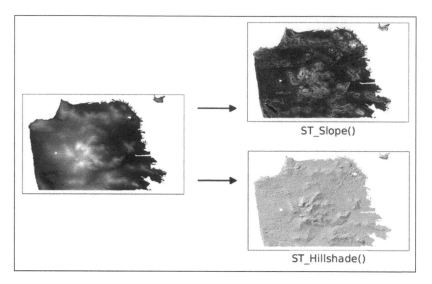

ST_Slope()

ST_Hillshade()

As you can see in the screenshot, the slope and hillshade rasters help us better understand the terrain of San Francisco.

If PostGIS 2.0 is available, we can still use 2.0's `ST_Slope()` and `ST_HillShade()` to create slope and hillshade rasters. But there are several differences you need to be aware of, as follows:

- `ST_Slope()` and `ST_Aspect()` return a raster with values in radians instead of degrees
- Some input parameters of `ST_HillShade()` are expressed in radians instead of degrees
- The computed raster from `ST_Slope()`, `ST_Aspect()`, or `ST_HillShade()` has an empty 1-pixel border on all four sides

We can adapt our `ST_Slope()` query from the beginning of this recipe by removing the creation and application of the custom extent. Since the custom extent constrained the computation to a specific area, the inability to specify such a constraint means PostGIS 2.0's `ST_Slope()` will perform slower.

```
WITH r AS ( -- union of filtered tiles
    SELECT
```

```
                ST_Transform(ST_Union(srtm.rast), 3310) AS rast
        FROM srtm
        JOIN sfpoly sf
                ON ST_DWithin(ST_Transform(srtm.rast::geometry, 3
310), ST_Transform(sf.geom, 3310), 1000)
)
SELECT
        ST_Clip(ST_Slope(r.rast, 1), ST_Transform(sf.geom, 3310)) A
S rast
FROM r
CROSS JOIN sfpoly sf;
```

## How it works...

The DEM functions in PostGIS allowed us to quickly analyze our SRTM raster. In the basic use cases, we were able to swap one function for another without any issues.

What is impressive about these DEM functions is that they are all wrappers around `ST_MapAlgebra()`. The power of `ST_MapAlgebra()` is in its adaptability to different problems.

# Sharing and visualizing rasters through SQL

In a previous chapter, we used `gdal_translate` to export PostGIS rasters to a file. This provides a method for transferring files from one user to another or from one location to another. The only problem with this method is that you may not have access to the `gdal_translate` utility.

A different but equally functional approach is to use the `ST_AsGDALRaster()` family of functions available in PostGIS. In addition to `ST_AsGDALRaster()`, PostGIS provides `ST_AsTIFF()`, `ST_AsPNG()`, and `ST_AsJPEG()` to support the most common raster file formats.

To easily visualize raster files without the need for a GIS application, PostGIS 2.1 and later versions provide `ST_ColorMap()`. This function applies a built-in or user-specified color palette to a raster that, upon exporting with `ST_AsGDALRaster()`, can be viewed with any image viewer, such as a web browser.

## Getting ready

In this recipe, we will use `ST_AsTIFF()` and `ST_AsPNG()` to export rasters to the GeoTIFF and PNG file formats, respectively. We will also apply `ST_ColorMap()` so that we can see them in any image viewer.

The queries below can be run in a standard SQL client such as **psql** or **pgAdminIII**. However, we can't use the returned output because the output has escaped, and these clients do not undo the escaping. Applications with lower level API functions can unescape the query output. Examples of this would be a PHP script passing a record element to `pg_unescape_bytea()` or a Python script using Psycopg2's implicit decoding while fetching a record. A sample PHP script (`save_raster_to_file.php`) can be found in this chapter's `data` directory.

## How to do it...

Let us say that a colleague asks for the monthly minimum temperature data for San Francisco during the summer months as a single raster file. This entails restricting our PRISM rasters to June, July, and August, clipping each monthly raster to San Francisco's boundaries, creating one raster with each monthly raster as a band, and then outputting the combined raster to a portable raster format. We will convert the combined raster to the GeoTIFF format.

```
WITH months AS ( -- extract monthly rasters clipped to San
Francisco
        SELECT
                prism.month_year,
                ST_Union(
                        ST_Clip(prism.rast, 2,
                        ST_Transform(sf.geom, 4322), TRUE)
                ) AS rast
        FROM prism
        JOIN sfpoly sf
                ON ST_Intersects(prism.rast, ST_Transform(sf.geom,
                4322))
        WHERE prism.month_year BETWEEN '2012-06-01'::date AND
'2012-08-01'::date
        GROUP BY prism.month_year
        ORDER BY prism.month_year
), summer AS ( -- new raster with each monthly raster as a band
        SELECT
                ST_AddBand(NULL::raster, array_agg(rast)) AS rast
        FROM months
)
SELECT -- export as GeoTIFF
        ST_AsTIFF(rast) AS content
FROM summer;
```

To filter our PRISM rasters, we use `ST_Intersects()` to keep only those raster tiles that spatially intersect San Francisco's boundaries. We also remove all rasters whose relevant month is not June, July, or August. We then use `ST_AddBand()` to create a new raster with each summer month's new raster band. Finally, we pass the combined raster to `ST_AsTIFF()` to generate a GeoTIFF.

If you output the returned value from ST_AsTIFF() to a file, run gdalinfo on that file. The gdalinfo output shows that the GeoTIFF file has three bands and the coordinate system of SRID 4322.

```
Driver: GTiff/GeoTIFF
Files: surface.tif
Size is 20, 7
Coordinate System is:
GEOGCS["WGS 72",
        DATUM["WGS_1972",
                SPHEROID["WGS 72",6378135,298.2600000000045,
                        AUTHORITY["EPSG","7043"]],
                TOWGS84[0,0,4.5,0,0,0.554,0.2263],
                AUTHORITY["EPSG","6322"]],
        PRIMEM["Greenwich",0],
        UNIT["degree",0.0174532925199433],
        AUTHORITY["EPSG","4322"]]
Origin = (-123.145833333333314,37.937500000000114)
Pixel Size = (0.041666666666667,-0.041666666666667)
Metadata:
        AREA_OR_POINT=Area
Image Structure Metadata:
        INTERLEAVE=PIXEL
Corner Coordinates:
Upper Left  (-123.1458333,  37.9375000) (123d 8'45.00"W, 3
7d56'15.00"N)
Lower Left  (-123.1458333,  37.6458333) (123d 8'45.00"W, 3
7d38'45.00"N)
Upper Right (-122.3125000,  37.9375000) (122d18'45.00"W, 3
7d56'15.00"N)
Lower Right (-122.3125000,  37.6458333) (122d18'45.00"W, 3
7d38'45.00"N)
Center      (-122.7291667,  37.7916667) (122d43'45.00"W, 3
7d47'30.00"N)
Band 1 Block=20x7 Type=Float32, ColorInterp=Gray
        NoData Value=-9999
Band 2 Block=20x7 Type=Float32, ColorInterp=Undefined
        NoData Value=-9999
Band 3 Block=20x7 Type=Float32, ColorInterp=Undefined
        NoData Value=-9999
```

The problem with the GeoTIFF raster is that we generally can't view it in a standard image viewer. If we use ST_AsPNG() or ST_AsJPEG(), the image generated is much more readily viewable. But PNG and JPEG images are limited by the supported pixel types 8BUI and 16BUI (PNG only). Both formats are also limited to at most three bands (four if there is an alpha band).

To help get around various file format limitations, we can use ST_MapAlgebra() or ST_Reclass(), and for this recipe, ST_ColorMap(). The ST_ColorMap() function converts a raster band of any pixel type to a set of up to four 8BUI bands. This facilitates creating a grayscale, RGB or RGBA image that is then passed to ST_AsPNG() or ST_AsJPEG().

Taking our query for computing a slope raster of San Francisco from our SRTM raster in a prior recipe, we can apply one of the ST_ColorMap() function's built-in colormaps and then pass the resulting raster to ST_AsPNG() for creating a PNG image.

```
WITH r AS (
        SELECT
                ST_Transform(ST_Union(srtm.rast), 3310) AS rast
        FROM srtm
        JOIN sfpoly sf
                ON ST_DWithin(ST_Transform(srtm.rast::geometry,
3310), ST_Transform(sf.geom, 3310), 1000)
), cx AS (
        SELECT
                ST_AsRaster(ST_Transform(sf.geom, 3310), r.rast)
AS rast
        FROM sfpoly sf
        CROSS JOIN r
)
SELECT
        ST_AsPNG(
                ST_ColorMap(
                        ST_Clip(
                                ST_Slope(r.rast, 1, cx.rast),
                                ST_Transform(sf.geom, 3310)
                        ),
                        'bluered'
                )
        ) AS rast
FROM r
CROSS JOIN cx
CROSS JOIN sfpoly sf;
```

The "bluered" colormap sets the minimum, median, and maximum pixel values to dark blue, pale white, and bright red respectively. Pixel values between the minimum, median, and maximum values are assigned colors that are linearly interpolated from the minimum to median or median to maximum range. The resulting image readily shows where the steepest slopes in San Francisco are.

The following is a PNG image generated by applying the "bluered" colormap with ST_ColorMap() and ST_AsPNG(). The pixels in red represent the steepest slopes.

In our use of ST_AsTIFF() and ST_AsPNG(), we passed the raster to be converted as the sole argument. Both of these functions have additional parameters to customize the output TIFF or PNG file. These additional parameters include various compression and data organization settings.

## How it works...

Using ST_AsTIFF() and ST_AsPNG(), we exported rasters from PostGIS to GeoTIFF and PNG. The ST_ColorMap() function helped generate images that can be opened in any image viewer. If we needed to export these images to a different format supported by GDAL, we would use ST_AsGDALRaster().

# Working with pgRouting

**6**

In this chapter, we will cover:

- ▸ Startup – Dijkstra routing
- ▸ Loading data from OpenStreetMap and finding the shortest path using A*
- ▸ Driving distance/service area calculation
- ▸ Calculating demographics using driving distance
- ▸ Extracting the centerlines of polygons

## Introduction

So far, we have used PostGIS as a vector and raster tool, using relatively simple relationships between objects and simple structures. In this chapter, we will review an additional PostGIS-related extension: **pgRouting**. pgRouting allows us to interrogate graph structures in order to answer questions, such as "What is the shortest route from where I am to where I am going?" This is a domain heavily occupied by the existing web APIs (such as Google, Bing, MapQuest, and others) and services, but it can be better served by "rolling our own" services for many use cases. Which cases? It might be a good idea to create our own services in situations where we are trying to answer questions that aren't answered by the existing services, such as when the data available to us is better or more applicable, or when we need or want to avoid the Terms of Service conditions for these APIs.

## Startup – Dijkstra routing

pgRouting is a separate extension used in addition to PostGIS. Its download and installation is vastly simplified by DEB, RPM, and OS X packages and Windows binaries available at `http://pgrouting.org/download.html`.

## Getting ready

pgRouting doesn't deal well with non-default schema, so before we begin, we will set the schema in our user preferences using the following command:

```
ALTER ROLE me SET search_path TO chp06,public;
```

Next, we need to add the pgRouting extension to our database. If PostGIS is not already installed on the database, we'll need to add that as an extension, as well:

```
--CREATE EXTENSION postgis;
```

```
CREATE EXTENSION pgrouting;
```

We will start by loading a test dataset. You can get some really basic sample data from `http://docs.pgrouting.org/dev/doc/src/developer/sampledata.html`. This sample data consists of a small grid of streets in which any functions can be run.

Then, run the create table and data insert scripts available at `docs.pgrouting.org/2.0/en/doc/src/developer/sampledata.html`.

Now that the data is loaded, let's build topology on the table (if you haven't already done this during the data-load process):

```
SELECT pgr_createTopology('edge_table',0.001);
```

Building a topology creates a new node table, `chp06.edge_table_vertices_pgr`, which is available for us to view and will aid us in developing queries.

## How to do it...

Now that the data are loaded, we can run a quick test. We'll use a simple algorithm called Dijkstra to calculate the shortest path from node 5 to node 12.

Dijkstra's algorithm is an effective and simple routing algorithm that runs a search of all available paths from point A to point B in a network, also known as the **graph structure**. It is not the most efficient routing algorithm, but will always find the best route. For more information on Dijkstra's algorithm, refer to Wikipedia, which has a good explanation with illustrations, at `http://en.wikipedia.org/wiki/Dijkstra%27s_algorithm`. See especially `http://en.wikipedia.org/wiki/File:Dijkstras_progress_animation.gif`.

An important point to note is that the nodes in pgRouting created during the topology creation process are created non-deterministically for some versions. This has been patched in future versions; but for some versions of pgRouting, this means that your node numbers will not be the same as those we use here in the book. View your data in an application to determine which nodes to use or use a KNN search for the node nearest to a static geographic point. See *Chapter 11*, *Using Desktop Clients*, for more information on viewing PostGIS data, and *Chapter 4*, *Working with Vector Data – Advanced Recipes*, for approaches to finding the nearest node automatically. Dijkstra is run as in the following code:

```
SELECT pgr_dijkstra('SELECT id, source, target,
    cost FROM edge_table',
    16,
    9,
    false,
    false);
```

The preceding query will result in the following:

```
 pgr_dijkstra
--------------
 (0,16,6,1)
 (1,17,7,1)
 (2,5,8,1)
 (3,6,9,1)
 (4,11,15,1)
 (5,9,-1,0)
(6 rows)
```

For new users, this is a surprising result—we ask for a route, we expect a little more than some generic tuples in return. What returns includes a list of segments our route traverses. For Dijkstra and other routing algorithms, this often comes in the following form:

- ▸ `seq`: This returns the sequence number so that we can maintain the order of the output
- ▸ `id1`: This is the node ID
- ▸ `id2`: This is the edge ID
- ▸ `cost`: This is the cost for the route traversal (often, the distance)

For example, to get the geometry back, we need to rejoin the edge IDs with the original table. To make this approach work transparently, we will use the `WITH` common table expression to create a temporary table to which we will join our geometry:

```
WITH dijkstra AS (
SELECT pgr_dijkstra('SELECT id, source, target,
    cost, x1, x2, y1, y2 FROM edge_table',
    16,
    9,
    false,
    false)
    )


SELECT id, ST_AsText(the_geom)
  FROM edge_table et, dijkstra d
  WHERE et.id = (d.pgr_dijkstra).id2;
```

The preceding code will give the following output:

```
 id |       st_astext
----+--------------------
 15 | LINESTRING(4 2,4 3)
  6 | LINESTRING(0 2,1 2)
  7 | LINESTRING(1 2,2 2)
  8 | LINESTRING(2 2,3 2)
  9 | LINESTRING(3 2,4 2)
(5 rows)
 id |       st_astext
----+--------------------
  6 | LINESTRING(0 2,1 2)
  7 | LINESTRING(1 2,2 2)
  8 | LINESTRING(2 2,3 2)
  9 | LINESTRING(3 2,4 2)
 15 | LINESTRING(4 2,4 3)
(5 rows)
```

Congratulations! You have just completed a route in pgRouting. The following diagram illustrates the route:

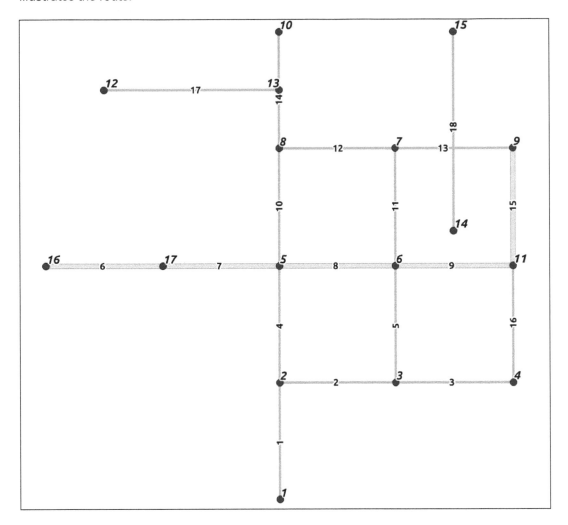

# Loading data from OpenStreetMap and finding the shortest path using A*

Test data are great for understanding how algorithms work, but the real data is often more interesting. A good source for real data worldwide is **OpenStreetMap** (**OSM**), a worldwide, wiki-style geospatial dataset. What is wonderful about using OSM in conjunction with pgRouting is that it is inherently a topological model, meaning that it follows the same kinds of rules in its construction that we do in graph traversal within pgRouting. Because of how editing and community participation works in OSM, it is often an equally good or better data source than commercial ones and, of course, quite compatible with our open source model.

Another great feature is that there is a free and open source software to ingest OSM data and import it into a routing database—osm2pgrouting.

## Getting ready

It is recommended to either get the downloadable files from http://metro.teczno.com, or download the example dataset that we have provided, available at http://www.packtpub. com/support. Either way, you will be using the XML OSM data. You can also get custom extracts directly from the web interface at http://www.openstreetmap.org/, but this could significantly limit the area we would be able to extract.

Once we have the data, we need to unzip it using our favorite compression utility. Double-clicking on the file to unzip it will typically work on Windows and Mac OS machines. Two of the good utilities for unzipping on Linux are bunzip2 and zip. What will remain is an XML extract of the data we want for routing. In our use case, we are downloading the data for the Greater Cleveland area.

Now, we need a utility for placing these data into a routable database. An example of one such tool is osm2pgrouting, which is often a part of binary installs of pgRouting, but it can also be downloaded and compiled using the instructions at http://pgrouting.org/docs/tools/osm2pgrouting.html.

## How to do it...

For my configuration, the binary is located at /usr/share/bin/./osm2pgrouting. To run this binary, type the following command:

```
osm2pgrouting
```

When osm2pgrouting is run without anything set, the output shows us the options to use with osm2pgrouting. Some options are required, others optional:

```
following params are required:
-file <file>  -- name of your osm xml file
-conf <conf>  -- name of your configuration xml file
-dbname <dbname> -- name of your database
-user <user> -- name of the user, which have write access to the database
optional:
-host <host>  -- host of your postgresql database (default: 127.0.0.1)
-port <port> -- port of your database (default: 5432)
-passwd <passwd> --  password for database access
-prefixtables <prefix> --  add at the beginning of table names
-clean -- drop previously created tables
-skipnodes -- don't import the nodes table
```

To run the osm2pgrouting command, we have a small number of required parameters. Double-check the paths pointing to mapconfig.xml and cleveland.osm before running the following command:

```
osm2pgrouting -file cleveland.osm -conf /usr/share/osm2pgrouting/
mapconfig.xml -dbname postgis_cookbook -user me -host localhost
prefixtables cleveland_ -clean
```

Our dataset may be quite large and take some time to process and import. Be patient and the end of the output should say something like the following:

```
Create Topology success
########################
size of streets: 90013
size of splitted ways : 224534
finished
```

Our new vector table, by default, is named cleveland_ways. If no -prefixtables flag were used, the table name would just be ways.

## How it works...

osm2pgrouting is a powerful tool. In this case, it creates eight tables from our input file. Of those eight, we'll address the two primary tables: the ways table and the nodes table.

Our `ways` table is a table of the lines representing all of our streets, roads, trails, and so on that are in OSM. The `nodes` table contains all of the intersections. This helps us identify the beginning and end points for routing.

Let's apply an A* (A star) routing approach to this problem.

 A* is an extension of Dijkstra's algorithm, which uses a heuristic to speed up the search for the shortest path, at the cost of occasionally not finding the optimum route. See `http://en.wikipedia.org/wiki/A*` and `http://en.wikipedia.org/wiki/File:Astar_progress_ animation.gif` for more information.

You will recognize the following syntax from Dijkstra. The code is executed as follows:

```
WITH astar AS (
SELECT pgr_astar('SELECT gid AS id, source, target,
    length AS cost FROM ways',
    89475,
    14584,
    false,
    false)
    )
SELECT gid, the_geom
  FROM ways w, astar a
  WHERE w.gid = (a.pgr_astar).id2;WITH astar AS (
SELECT pgr_astar('SELECT gid AS id, source, target,
length AS cost, x1, x2, y1, y2 FROM cleveland_ways',
89475,
14584,
false,
false)
)
SELECT gid, the_geom
FROM cleveland_ways w, astar a
WHERE w.gid = (a.pgr_astar).id2;
```

The following screenshot shows the results shown on a map (Map tiles by *Stamen Design, under CC BY 3.0*, Data by *OpenStreetMap, under CC BY SA.*):

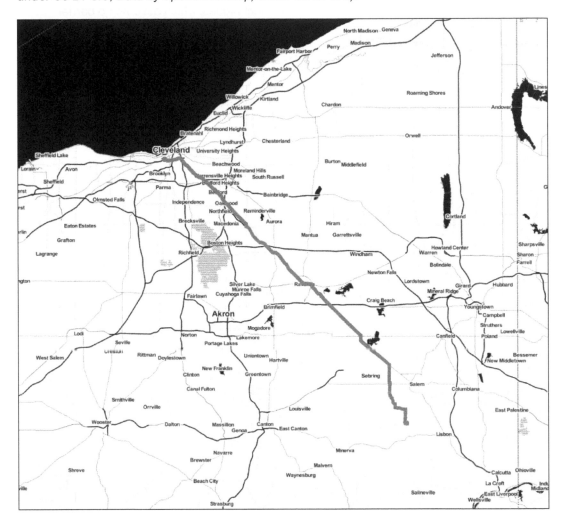

# Driving distance/service area calculation

Driving distance (`pgr_drivingDistance`) is a query that calculates all nodes within the specified driving distance of a starting node. This is an optional feature compiled with pgRouting; so if you compile pgRouting yourself, make sure that you enable it and include the CGAL library, a required dependency for `pgr_drivingDistance`.

Driving distance is useful when "user sheds" are needed that give realistic driving distance estimates, for example, for all customers within 5 miles of driving, biking, or walking distance. These estimates can be contrasted with buffering techniques, which assume no barrier to travelling and are useful for revealing the underlying structures of our transportation networks relative to individual locations.

## Getting ready

We will load the same dataset that we used in the *Startup – Dijkstra routing* recipe. Refer to this recipe to import data.

## How to do it...

In the following example, we will look at all users within the distance of 1.5 units from our starting point, that is, a proposed bike shop at node 7:

```
SELECT seq, id1 AS node, cost
        FROM pgr_drivingDistance(                    'SELECT id, source,
target, cost FROM edge_table',
                67, 1.5, false, false
        );
```

The preceding command gives the following output:

```
 seq | node | cost
-----+------+------
   0 |    3 |    1
   1 |    5 |    1
   2 |    6 |    0
   3 |    7 |    1
   4 |   11 |    1
(5 rows)
```

As usual, we just get a list from the `pgr_drivingDistance` table that, in this case, comprises sequence, node, and cost. pPgRouting, like PostGIS, gives us low-level functionality; we need to reconstruct what geometries we need from that low-level functionality. We can use that node ID to extract the geometries of all of our nodes, by executing the following script:

```
WITH DD AS (

SELECT seq, id1 AS node, cost
        FROM pgr_drivingDistance(
                'SELECT id, source, target, cost FROM edge_table',
```

```
          6, 1.5, false, false
      )
      )
```

```
SELECT ST_AsText(the_geom)
  FROM vertex_table w, DD d
  WHERE w.id = d.node
  ;
```

The preceding command gives the following output:

```
st_astext
------------
 POINT(3 1)
 POINT(0 2)
 POINT(1 2)
 POINT(2 2)
 POINT(3 3)
(5 rows)
```

But, the output seen is just a cluster of points. Normally, when we think of driving distance, we visualize a polygon. Fortunately, we have with the pgr_alphaShapefunction the capacity to create a polygon from a set of points. pgr_alphaShape expects id, x, and y values for input, so we will first change our preceding query a bit:

```
WITH DD AS (
SELECT seq, id1 AS node, cost
        FROM pgr_drivingDistance(
                'SELECT id, source, target, cost FROM edge_table',
                6, 1.5, false, false
        )
        )
SELECT id, x, y
  FROM vertex_table w, DD d
  WHERE w.id = d.node
  ;
```

The output is as follows:

```
id | x | y
---+---+---
 3 | 3 | 1
 5 | 0 | 2
 6 | 1 | 2
 7 | 2 | 2
11 | 3 | 3
(5 rows)
```

Now, we can wrap the preceding script in the alphashape function:

```
WITH alphashape AS (
SELECT pgr_alphaShape('
  WITH DD AS (
  SELECT seq, id1 AS node, cost
    FROM pgr_drivingDistance(
      ''SELECT id, source, target, cost FROM edge_table'',
      6, 1.5, false, false
    )
        ),
  dd_points AS(
  SELECT id, x, y
    FROM vertex_table w, DD d
    WHERE w.id = d.node
    )
    SELECT * FROM dd_points
  ')
  ),
```

First, we will get our cluster of points. As done earlier, we will explicitly convert the text to geometric points:

```
alphapoints AS (
  SELECT ST_MakePoint((pgr_alphashape).x, (pgr_alphashape).y) FROM
alphashape
  ),
```

Now that we have points, we can create a line by connecting them:

```
alphaline AS (
  SELECT ST_Makeline(ST_MakePoint) FROM alphapoints
  )
SELECT ST_MakePolygon(ST_AddPoint(ST_Makeline, ST_StartPoint(ST_
Makeline))) FROM alphaline;
```

Finally, we construct the line as a polygon using `ST_MakePolygon`. This requires adding the starting point by executing `ST_StartPoint` in order to properly close the polygon. The complete code is as follows:

```
WITH alphashape AS (
SELECT pgr_alphaShape('
  WITH DD AS (
  SELECT seq, id1 AS node, cost
    FROM pgr_drivingDistance(
      ''SELECT id, source, target, cost FROM edge_table'',
      6, 1.5, false, false
    )
      ),
  dd_points AS(
  SELECT id, x, y
    FROM vertex_table w, DD d
    WHERE w.id = d.node
    )
    SELECT * FROM dd_points
  ')
  ),
alphapoints AS (
  SELECT ST_MakePoint((pgr_alphashape).x, (pgr_alphashape).y) FROM
alphashape
  ),
alphaline AS (
  SELECT ST_Makeline(ST_MakePoint) FROM alphapoints
  )
SELECT ST_MakePolygon(ST_AddPoint(ST_Makeline, ST_StartPoint(ST_
Makeline))) FROM alphaline;
```

Our first driving distance value is not too interesting, but it can be with real data as in the *Calculating demographics using driving distance* recipe. See the following screenshot:

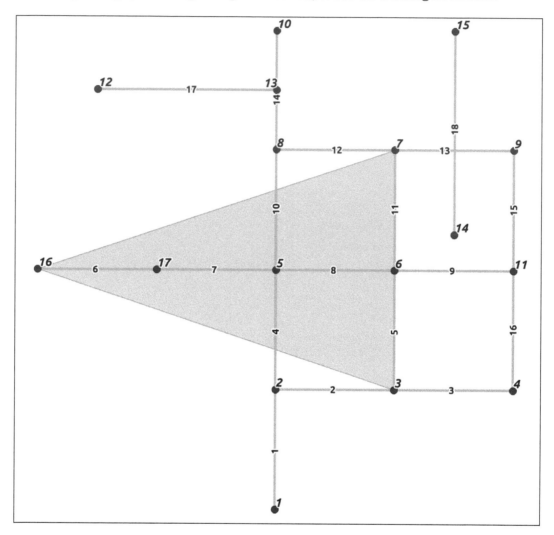

## See also

▶   The *Calculating demographics using driving distance* recipe

# Calculating demographics using driving distance

In the *Using polygon overlays for proportional census estimates* recipe in *Chapter 2, Structures that Work*, we employed a simple buffer around a trail alignment in conjunction with the census data to get estimates of what the demographics were of the people within walking distance of the trail, estimated as a distance of 1 mile. The problem with this approach, of course, is that it assumes that it is an "as the crow flies" estimate. In reality, rivers, large roads, and roadless stretches serve as real barriers to people's movement through space. Using pgRouting's `pgr_drivingDistance` function, we can realistically simulate people's movement on routable networks and get better estimates. For our use case, we'll keep the simulation a bit simpler than a trail alignment—we'll consider the demographics of a park facility, say, the Cleveland Metroparks Zoo, and potential bike users within 4 miles of it, which we estimate as approximately a 15 minute bike ride.

## Getting ready

For our analysis, we will use the `proportionalsum` function from *Chapter 2, Structures that Work*; so if you have not added this to your PostGIS tool belt, run the following commands:

```
CREATE OR REPLACE FUNCTION chp02.proportional_sum(geometry, geometry,
numeric)
    RETURNS numeric AS
$BODY$
    SELECT $3 * areacalc FROM
        (
        SELECT (ST_Area(ST_Intersection($1, $2))/ST_Area($2))::numeric
AS areacalc
        ) AS areac
;
$BODY$
    LANGUAGE sql VOLATILE;
```

The `proportional_sum` function will take into account our input geometry and the `count` value of the population and return an estimate of the proportional population.

Now, we need to load our census data and zoo location. Use the following command:

```
shp2pgsql -s 3734 -d -i -I -W LATIN1 -g the_geom census chp06.census |
psql -U me -d postgis_cookbook -h localhost
```

Also, if you have not yet loaded the data mentioned in the *Loading data from OpenStreetMap and finding the shortest path using A** recipe, take the time to do so now.

Once all of the data is entered, we can proceed with the analysis.

## How to do it...

The `pgr_drivingdistance` polygon we created is the first step in the demographic analysis. Refer to the *Driving distance/service area calculation* recipe if you need to familiarize yourself with its use. In this case, we'll consider bicycling distance. Cleveland Metroparks Zoo is nearest the node, 164495; so we'll use that as the center point for our `pgr_drivingdistance` calculation, and 6.437376 kilometers as our distance, as we want to know the number of zoo visitors within 4 miles of the Cleveland Metroparks Zoo:

```
CREATE TABLE zoo_bikezone AS (
WITH alphashape AS (
SELECT pgr_alphaShape('
  WITH DD AS (
  SELECT seq, id1 AS node, cost
    FROM pgr_drivingDistance(
      ''SELECT gid AS id, source, target, reverse_cost AS cost FROM
cleveland_ways'',
      165232, 6.437376, false, false
    )
      ),
  dd_points AS(
  SELECT id::int4, ST_X(the_geom)::float8 as x, ST_Y(the_geom)::float8 AS
y
    FROM cleveland_ways_vertices_pgr w, DD d
    WHERE w.id = d.node
    )
    SELECT * FROM dd_points
  ')
  ),
alphapoints AS (
  SELECT ST_MakePoint((pgr_alphashape).x, (pgr_alphashape).y) FROM
alphashape
  ),
alphaline AS (
  SELECT ST_Makeline(ST_MakePoint) FROM alphapoints
  )
SELECT 1 as id,  ST_SetSRID(ST_MakePolygon(ST_AddPoint(ST_Makeline, ST_
StartPoint(ST_Makeline))), 4326) AS the_geom FROM alphaline
);
```

The preceding script gives us a very interesting shape (Map tiles by *Stamen Design, under CC BY 3.0,* Data by *OpenStreetMap, under CC BY SA*). See the following screenshot:

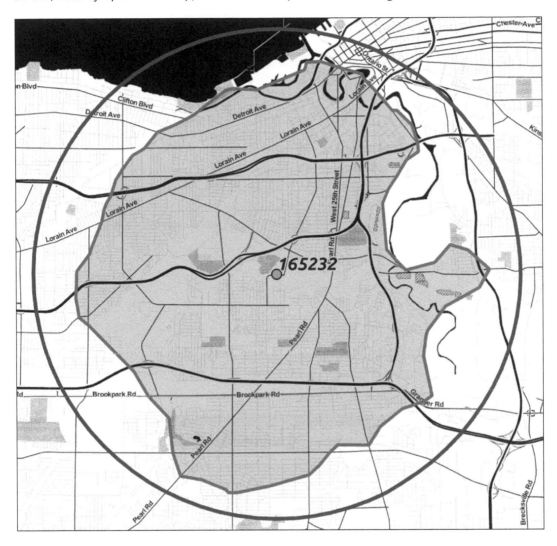

In the previous screenshot, we can see the difference between the bicycling distance across the real road network, shaded in blue, and the equivalent 4 mile buffer, or "as the crow flies" distance. Let's apply this to our demographic analysis, using the following script:

```
SELECT ROUND(SUM(chp02.proportional_sum(ST_Transform(a.geom,3734),
b.geom, b.pop))) AS population FROM
     zoo_bikezone AS a, census as b
   WHERE ST_Intersects(ST_Transform(a.the_geom, 3734), b.the_geom)
   GROUP BY a.id;
```

The output is as follows:

```
 population
------------
     167714
(1 row)
```

So, how does the preceding output compare to what we would get if we look at the buffered distance?

```
SELECT ROUND(SUM(chp02.proportional_sum(ST_Transform(a.the_geom,3734),
b.the_geom, b.pop))) AS population FROM
    (SELECT 1 AS id, ST_Buffer(ST_Transform(the_geom, 3734), 21120) AS
the_geom FROM cleveland_ways_vertices_pgr WHERE id = 165232) AS a,
    census as b
    WHERE ST_Intersects(ST_Transform(a.the_geom, 3734), b.the_geom)
    GROUP BY a.id;
```

```
 population
------------
    2341662
(1 row)
```

The preceding output shows a difference of more than 60,000 people. In other words, using a buffer overestimates population by more than 28 percent compared to using `pgr_drivingdistance`.

# Extracting the centerlines of polygons

In several recipes in *Chapter 4, Working with Vector Data – Advanced Recipes*, we explored extracting Voronoi polygons from sets of points. In this recipe, we'll use the Voronoi function employed in the *Using external scripts to embed new functionality in order to calculate a Voronoi diagram* recipe, in *Chapter 4, Working with Vector Data – Advanced Recipes*, to serve as the first step in extracting the centerline of a polygon. One could also use the *Using external scripts to embed other libraries in order to calculate a Voronoi diagram – advanced* recipe, in *Chapter 4, Working with Vector Data – Advanced Recipes*, which would run faster on large datasets. For this recipe, we will use the simpler but slower approach.

One additional dependency is that we will be using the `chp02.polygon_to_line(geometry)` function from the *Normalizing internal overlays* recipe in *Chapter 2, Structures that Work*.

What do we mean by the centerline of a polygon? Imagine a digitized stream between its pair of banks as shown in the following screenshot:

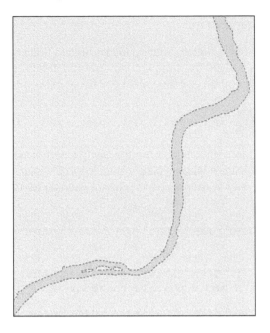

If we wanted to find the center of this, in order to model water flow, we could extract this using a skeletonization approach, as shown in the following screenshot:

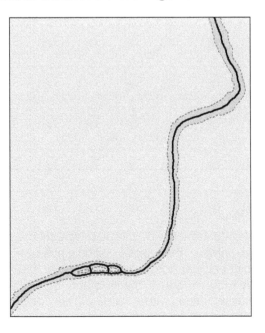

The difficulty with skeletonization approaches, as we'll soon see, is that they are often subject to noise, which is something that natural features like our stream have plenty of. This means that typical skeletonization, which could be done simply with a Voronoi approach, is therefore inherently inadequate for our purposes.

This brings us to the reason why skeletonization is included in this chapter. Routing is a way for us to simplify skeletons derived from the Voronoi method. It allows us to trace from one end of a major feature to the other, and skip all of the noise in between.

## Getting ready

As we will be using the Voronoi calculations from the *Using external scripts to embed new functionality in order to calculate a Voronoi diagram* recipe in *Chapter 4, Working with Vector Data – Advanced Recipes*, refer to that recipe to prepare yourself for using the functions in this recipe.

Once the Voronoi function is in place, we can begin with our problem dataset—a stream—using the following command:

```
shp2pgsql -s 3734 -d -i -I -W LATIN1 -g the_geom ebrr_polygon public.
voronoi_hydro | psql -U me -d postgis_cookbook
```

The streams we create will look as shown in the following screenshot:

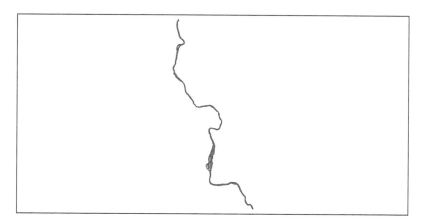

## How to do it...

In order to perform basic skeletonization, we'll calculate Voronoi polygons on the nodes that make up the original stream polygon. The edges of Voronoi polygons, by nature, find the line that demarcates the midpoint between points. We will leverage this tendency by treating our lines like points—adding extra vertexes to the lines and then converting the lines to a point set. This approach, in combination with Voronoi, will provide an initial estimate of the polygon's centerline.

We will add extra points to our input geometries using the `ST_Segmentize` function, and then convert the geometries to points using `ST_DumpPoints`:

```
CREATE TABLE voronoi_points AS
  WITH rawpoints AS (
    SELECT (ST_DumpPoints(ST_Segmentize(the_geom, 5))).geom AS the_geom
FROM voronoi_hydro
      UNION ALL
    SELECT (ST_DumpPoints(ST_Extent(the_geom))).geom AS the_geom FROM
voronoi_hydro
    )

  SELECT (ST_Dump(ST_Union(the_geom))).geom AS the_geom FROM
    rawpoints;
```

The following screenshot shows our polygons as a set of points:

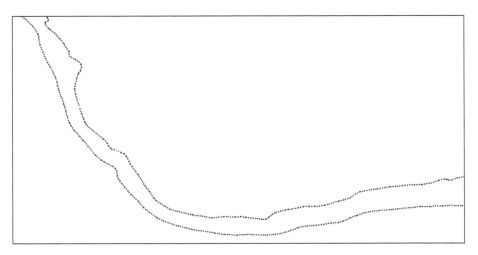

The set of points in the preceding screenshot is what we feed into our Voronoi calculation:

```
CREATE TABLE voronoi AS
  SELECT * FROM voronoi('voronoi_points', 'the_geom') AS (id integer,
the_geom geometry);
```

The following screenshot shows a Voronoi diagram derived from our points:

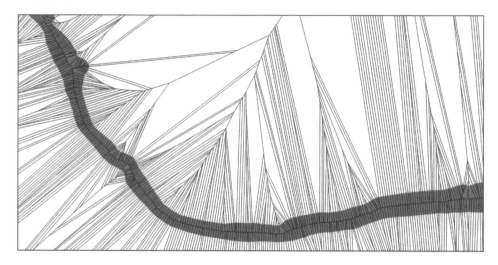

If you look closely at the preceding screenshot, you will see the basic centerline extant in our new data. Now, we take step one toward extracting it. We should index our inputs and then intersect the Voronoi output with the original stream polygon in order to clean the data back to something reasonable. In the extraction process, we'll also extract the edges from the polygons and remove the edges along the original polygon in order to remove any excess lines before our routing step. This is implemented in the following script:

```
CREATE INDEX chp04_voronoi_geom_gist
    ON public.voronoi
    USING gist(the_geom);


DROP TABLE IF EXISTS voronoi_intersect;


CREATE TABLE voronoi_intersect AS
  WITH vintersect AS (
  SELECT ST_Intersection(ST_SetSRID(ST_MakeValid(a.the_geom), 3734), ST_
MakeValid(b.the_geom)) AS the_geom FROM
    voronoi a, voronoi_hydro b
    WHERE ST_Intersects(ST_SetSRID(a.the_geom, 3734), b.the_geom)
    ),
  linework AS (
    SELECT chp02.polygon_to_line(the_geom) AS the_geom FROM
    vintersect
```

```
    ),
polylines AS (
        SELECT ((ST_Dump(ST_Union(lw.the_geom))).
geom)::geometry(linestring, 3734) AS the_geom FROM
    linework AS lw
),
externalbounds AS (
    SELECT chp02.polygon_to_line(the_geom) AS the_geom FROM
        voronoi_hydro
)


SELECT (ST_Dump(ST_Union(p.the_geom))).geom FROM
    polylines p, externalbounds b
    WHERE NOT ST_DWithin(p.the_geom, b.the_geom, 5)
    ;
```

Now, we have a second-level approximation of the skeleton (shown in the following screenshot). It is messy, but starts to highlight that centerline that we seek:

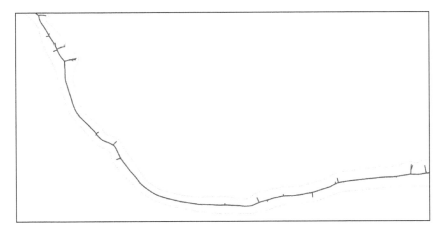

## There's more...

Now, we are nearly ready for routing. The centerline calculation we have is a good approximation of a straight skeleton, but still subject to the noisiness of the natural world. We'd like to eliminate that noisiness by choosing our features and emphasizing them through routing. First, we need to prepare the table to allow for routing calculations, as shown in the following commands:

```
ALTER TABLE voronoi_intersect ADD COLUMN gid serial;
ALTER TABLE voronoi_intersect ADD PRIMARY KEY (gid);


ALTER TABLE voronoi_intersect ADD COLUMN source integer;
ALTER TABLE voronoi_intersect ADD COLUMN target integer;
```

Then, to create a routable network from our skeleton, enter the following commands:

```
SELECT pgr_createTopology('voronoi_intersect', 0.001, 'the_geom', 'gid',
'source', 'target', 'true');


CREATE INDEX source_idx ON voronoi_intersect("source");
CREATE INDEX target_idx ON voronoi_intersect("target");


ALTER TABLE voronoi_intersect ADD COLUMN length double precision;
UPDATE voronoi_intersect SET length = ST_Length(the_geom);


ALTER TABLE voronoi_intersect ADD COLUMN reverse_cost double precision;
UPDATE voronoi_intersect SET reverse_cost = length;
```

Now, we can route along the primary centerline of our polygon, using the following commands:

```
CREATE TABLE voronoi_route AS
WITH dijkstra AS (
SELECT pgr_dijkstra('SELECT gid AS id, source, target,
    length AS cost FROM voronoi_intersect',
    10851, 3,
    false,
    false)
    )

SELECT gid, the_geom
  FROM voronoi_intersect et, dijkstra d
  WHERE et.gid = (d.pgr_dijkstra).id2;
```

Finally, we can compare the original polygon with the trace of its centerline:

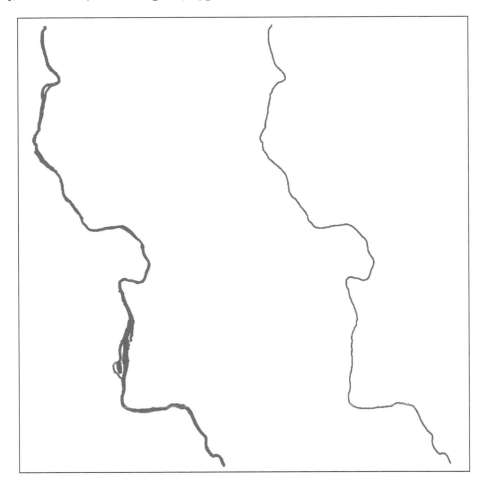

The preceding figure shows the original geometry of the stream in contrast to our centerline, or skeleton. It is an excellent output that vastly simplifies our input geometry while retaining its relevant features.

# 7

# Into the Nth Dimension

In this chapter, we will cover:

- Importing LiDAR data
- Performing 3D queries on a LiDAR point cloud
- Constructing and serving buildings 2.5 D
- Using `ST_Extrude` to extrude building footprints
- Creating arbitrary 3D objects for PostGIS
- Exporting models as X3D for the Web
- Reconstructing **Unmanned Aerial Vehicle** (**UAV**) image footprints with PostGIS 3D
- UAV photogrammetry in PostGIS – point cloud
- UAV photogrammetry in PostGIS – orthorectification
- UAV photogrammetry in PostGIS – DSM creation

# Introduction

In this chapter, we will delve into the 3D capabilities of PostGIS, focusing on three basic categories: how to get 3D data into PostGIS, 3D analyses within PostGIS, and ways of serving 3D data out of PostGIS. The chapter will focus on 3D point clouds, including LiDAR point clouds and point clouds derived from **Structure from Motion** (**SfM**) techniques. In addition, we will build a function that extrudes building footprints to 3D. Finally, we will explore ways of distributing the 3D models through the Web as exported from PostGIS using the X3D standard.

We will not be addressing the pointcloud extension in this chapter, which enables the use of larger LiDAR and other point cloud data in PostgreSQL with optional capacity to tie into PostGIS. For information on pointcloud PostgreSQL/PostGIS development, see Paul Ramsey's tutorial at `http://workshops.boundlessgeo.com/tutorial-lidar/` and other forthcoming resources at `http://boundlessgeo.com`.

Download the example datasets we have for your use available at `http://www.packtpub.com/support`.

# Importing LiDAR data

**Light Detection And Ranging** (**LiDAR**) are data collected that measure the 3D location and other properties of objects in space. LiDAR is similar in many respects to radar in that it uses electromagnetic waves to measure distance, brightness, and other properties. It is distinct from radar in that it uses laser and, thus, optical techniques, instead of microwaves or radio waves. An additional distinction is that LiDAR typically sends out a single focused pulse at any given time, awaits a return pulse, and records it. Radar, by contrast, will send out multiple pulses before receiving return pulses and, therefore, requires additional processing to determine the source of each pulse.

LiDAR data has become quite common in conjunction with both ground and airborne applications, aiding in ground surveys and enhancing and substantially automating aspects of photogrammetric engineering. As such, data sources for LiDAR data abound.

LiDAR data is typically distributed in an interchange format called **LAS** or **LASer**. The **American Society for Photogrammetry and Remote Sensing** (**ASPRS**) establishes the LAS standard. LAS is a binary format, so reading it to push into a PostGIS database is non-trivial. Fortunately, several open-source and partially open-source tools exist to convert and process LAS files, including LASTools and libLAS.

## Getting ready

Our source data will be in the LAS format, which we will convert with either LASTools, available from Martin Isenburg at `http://www.cs.unc.edu/~isenburg/` or utilities built around libLAS at `http://www.liblas.org/`. For Windows users, we recommend Martin Isenburg's tools as they tend to trend toward more advanced functionality but pay close attention to license terms or use libLAS instead, as the licensing is much more permissive for libLAS. For Linux/UNIX and Mac users, we recommend libLAS as it is easier to install and maintain.

LAS data can contain a lot of interesting data, not just X, Y, and Z values. It can include the intensity of the return from the object sensed and the classification of the object (ground vs. vegetation vs. buildings). When we convert a LAS file to text and then place it in our PostGIS dataset, we can optionally collect any of this information. In preparation for this, we will create a table with appropriate rows to collect some of the information from our pending LAS file.

```
CREATE TABLE chp07.lidar
(
  x numeric,
  y numeric,
  z numeric,
  intensity integer,
  tnumber integer,
  number integer,
  class integer,
  id integer,
  vnum integer
)
WITH (OIDS=FALSE);
ALTER TABLE chp07.lidar OWNER TO me;
```

Now, we can download our data. We recommend either getting it downloaded from `http://gis5.oit.ohio.gov/geodatadownload/` or downloading the example dataset we have for your use available at `http://www.packtpub.com/support`.

## How to do it...

We need to convert our LAS file to a format that can be read by PostgreSQL. To this end, we will use las2txt, either from LAStools or libLAS, to convert our LAS file to text.

```
las2txt --parse xyzinrcpM -sep komma input output.csv
```

If we have a large directory of LAS files, we can automate their conversion to text. In BASH on Linux, Unix, and Mac OS X systems, we can do that with the following:

```
#!/bin/bash
x=0
total=`ls *.las | wc | awk '{print $1}'`
for f in $( ls *.las); do
 x=`expr $x + 1`
 echo $x of $total started. $f processing.
 las2txt --parse xyzinrcpM -sep komma $f $f.csv
done
```

For Windows, we can accomplish this with PowerShell (a special thanks to Leland Barnes for providing this approach), as follows:

```
$las = dir *.las
$x = 0

$las |foreach {
  write-host ($x++) "of $($las.count) is started. $($_.Name) is
    processing"
  write-host "las2txt --parse xyzinrcpM -sep komma $($_.name)
    $($_.basename).csv"
}
```

 Additional options for las2txt can be accessed by simply running the previous command without any options.

Now that the data are in text format, available as **Comma Separated Values** (**CSVs**), loading them into PostgreSQL is easy. From within psql, we can use the \copy command to accomplish this, as follows:

```
\copy chp07.lidar from 'N2210595.las.csv' with csv
\copy chp07.lidar from 'N2215595.las.csv' with csv
\copy chp07.lidar from 'N2220595.las.csv' with csv
```

Now, the data are in our database, but they are only implicitly spatial data. Let's make this explicit by executing the following commands:

```
SELECT AddGeometryColumn('chp07','lidar','the_geom',3734,'POINT', 3);
UPDATE chp07.lidar SET the_geom =
  ST_SetSRID(ST_MakePoint(x,y,z),3734);We add a primary key:
ALTER TABLE chp07.lidar ADD COLUMN gid serial;
ALTER TABLE chp07.lidar ADD PRIMARY KEY (gid);
```

Now, we can view our data as shown in the following image:

▸ The *Performing 3D queries on a LiDAR point cloud* recipe

# Performing 3D queries on a LiDAR point cloud

In the previous recipe, *Importing LiDAR data*, we brought a LiDAR 3D point cloud into PostGIS, creating an explicit 3D dataset from the input. With the data in 3D form, we have the ability to perform spatial queries against it. In this recipe, we will leverage 3D indexes such that our query works in all the dimensions our data are in.

## How to do it...

We will use the LiDAR data imported in the previous recipe as our dataset of choice. We named that table `chp07.lidar`. To perform our query, we will require an index created on the dataset. Spatial indexes, much like ordinary database table indexes, are similar to book indexes insofar as they help us find what we are looking for faster. Ordinarily, such an index-creation step would look like the following (which we won't run this time):

```
CREATE INDEX chp07_lidar_the_geom_idx ON chp07.lidar USING
  gist(the_geom);
```

A 3D index does not perform as quickly as a 2D index for 2D queries, so a `CREATE INDEX` query defaults to creating a 2D index. In our case, we want to force the index to apply to all three dimensions, so we will explicitly tell PostgreSQL to use the n-dimensional version of the index, as follows:

```
CREATE INDEX chp07_lidar_the_geom_3dx ON chp07.lidar USING
  gist(the_geom gist_geometry_ops_nd);
```

Note that the approach depicted in the previous code would also work if we had a time dimension or a 3D plus time. Let's load a second 3D dataset and stream centerlines that we will use in our query, as follows:

```
shp2pgsql -s 3734 -d -i -I -W LATIN1 -t 3DZ -g the_geom hydro_line
  chp07.hydro | psql -U me -d postgis_cookbook -h localhost
```

These data, as shown in the following image, overlay nicely with our LiDAR point cloud:

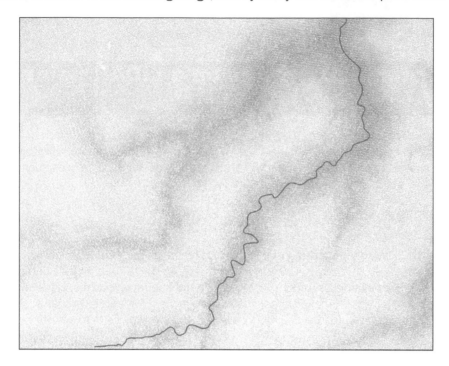

Now, we can build a simple query to retrieve all the LiDAR points within one foot of our stream centerline as in the following query:

```
SELECT l.gid, l.the_geom FROM
   chp07.hydro h, chp07.lidar l
   WHERE ST_3DDWithin(h.the_geom, l.the_geom, 5);
```

But, this is a little bit of a sloppy approach—we could end up with duplicate LiDAR points, so we will refine our query with LEFT JOIN and SELECT DISTINCT instead, but continue using ST_3DWithin as our limiting condition, as follows:

```
SELECT DISTINCT ON (l.gid) l.gid, l.the_geom
FROM chp07.hydro h
LEFT JOIN chp07.lidar l ON ST_3DDWithin(h.the_geom, l.the_geom, 5);
```

Now, we can visualize our returned points, as shown in the following image:

Try this query using ST_DWithin instead of ST_3DDWithin. You'll find an interesting difference in the number of points returned, since ST_DWithin will collect LiDAR points that may be close to our streamline in the XY plane, but not as close when looking at a 3D distance.

You can imagine ST_3DWithin querying within a tunnel around our line. ST_DWithin, by contrast, is going to query a vertical wall of LiDAR points, as it is only searching for adjacent points based on XY distance, ignoring height altogether, and, thus, gathering up all the points within a narrow wall above and below our stream centerline.

# Constructing and serving buildings 2.5 D

In the *Generating detailed building footprints from LiDAR* recipe in *Chapter 4, Working with Vector Data – Advanced Recipes*, we explored the automatic generation of building footprints using LiDAR data. What we were attempting to do was create 2D data from 3D data. In this recipe, we attempt the opposite, in a sense. We start with 2D polygons of building footprints and feed them into a function that extrudes them as 3D polygons.

## Getting ready

For use in this project, we will extrude a building footprint of our own making. Let us quickly create a table with a single building footprint, for testing purposes, as follows:

```
CREATE TABLE chp07.simple_building AS
   SELECT 1 AS gid, ST_MakePolygon(ST_GeomFromText('LINESTRING(0 0,2
     0,2 1, 1 1, 1 2, 0 2, 0 0)')) AS the_geom;
```

Let us add a function from the *Improving ST_Polygonize* recipe in *Chapter 4, Working with Vector Data – Advanced Recipes*, that converts geometry collections to multipolygons and add it to this schema. The converted function is as shown below:

```
CREATE OR REPLACE FUNCTION chp07.polygonize_to_multi (geometry)
   RETURNS geometry AS $$

   WITH polygonized AS (
     SELECT ST_Polygonize($1) AS the_geom
   ),
   dumped AS (
     SELECT (ST_Dump(the_geom)).geom AS the_geom FROM
       polygonized
   )
   SELECT ST_Multi(ST_Collect(the_geom)) FROM
     dumped
;
$$ LANGUAGE SQL;
```

It would be beneficial to keep the creation of 3D buildings encapsulated as simply as possible in a function with the following properties:

```
CREATE OR REPLACE FUNCTION chp07.threeDbuilding(footprint geometry,
  height numeric)
   RETURNS geometry AS
$BODY$
```

Our function takes two inputs: the building footprint and a height to extrude to. We can also imagine a function that takes in a third parameter: the height of the base of the building.

To construct the building walls, we will need to first convert our polygons into linestrings and then further separate the linestrings into their individual, two-point segments:

```
WITH simple_lines AS
(
  SELECT 1 AS gid, ST_MakeLine(ST_PointN(the_geom,pointn),
    ST_PointN(the_geom,pointn+1)) AS the_geom
  FROM (SELECT 1 AS gid, chp02.polygon_to_line($1) AS the_geom ) AS a
  LEFT JOIN
  (SELECT 1 AS gid, generate_series(1,
    ST_NumPoints(chp02.polygon_to_line($1))-1) AS pointn
  ) AS b
  ON a.gid = b.gid
),
```

The preceding code returns each of the two-point segments of our original shape, for example, for our `simple_building`:

```
                              st_astext
--------------------------------------------------------------------------
-----
MULTILINESTRING((2 0,2 1),(1 2,0 2),(2 1,1 1),(0 0,2 0),(1 1,1 2),(0
  2,0 0))
(1 row)
```

Now that we have a series of individual lines, we can use those to construct the walls of the building. First, we need to recast our 2D lines as 3D using `ST_Force3DZ`, as follows:

```
threeDlines AS
(
  SELECT ST_Force3DZ(the_geom) AS the_geom FROM simple_lines
)
```

Returning:

```
Returning:
MULTILINESTRING Z ((2 0 0,2 1 0),(1 2 0,0 2 0),(2 1 0,1 1 0),(0 0 0,2
  0 0),(1 1 0,1 2 0),(0 2 0,0 0 0))
```

The next step is to break each of those lines from the multilinestring into linestrings. For those paying attention, you'll note that these are effectively lines masquerading as linestrings:

```
splodedLine AS
(
   SELECT (ST_Dump(the_geom)).geom AS the_geom FROM threeDLines
),
```

Thus returning:

```
LINESTRING Z (2 0 0,2 1 0)
LINESTRING Z (1 2 0,0 2 0)
LINESTRING Z (2 1 0,1 1 0)
LINESTRING Z (0 0 0,2 0 0)
LINESTRING Z (1 1 0,1 2 0)
LINESTRING Z (0 2 0,0 0 0)
```

The next step is to construct a line representing the boundary of the extruded **wall**, as follows:

```
threeDline AS
(
   SELECT ST_MakeLine(
     ARRAY[
     ST_StartPoint(the_geom),
     ST_EndPoint(the_geom),
     ST_Translate(ST_EndPoint(the_geom), 0, 0, $2),
     ST_Translate(ST_StartPoint(the_geom), 0, 0, $2),
     ST_StartPoint(the_geom)
     ]
   )
   AS the_geom FROM splodedLine
),
```

Now, we need to convert each linestring to a polygon.

```
threeDwall AS
(
   SELECT ST_MakePolygon(the_geom) as the_geom FROM threeDline
),
```

Finally, put the roof and floor on our building, using the original geometry for the floor (forced to 3D) and a copy of the original geometry translated to our input height, as follows:

```
buildingTop AS
(
  SELECT ST_Translate(ST_Force3DZ($1), 0, 0, $2) AS the_geom
),
buildingBottom AS
(
  SELECT ST_Translate(ST_Force3DZ($1), 0, 0, 0) AS the_geom
),
```

We put the walls, roof, and floor together and, during the process, convert this to a 3D multipolygon:

```
wholeBuilding AS
(
  SELECT the_geom FROM buildingBottom
    UNION ALL
  SELECT the_geom FROM threeDwall
    UNION ALL
  SELECT the_geom FROM buildingTop
),
multiBuilding AS
(
  SELECT ST_Multi(ST_Collect(the_geom)) AS the_geom FROM
    wholeBuilding
),
```

While we could leave our geometry as a multipolygon, we'll do things properly and munge an informal cast to polyhedralsurface. In our case, we are already effectively formatted as a polyhedralsurface, so we'll just convert our geometry to text with ST_AsText, replace the word MULTIPOLYGON with POLYHEDRALSURFACE, and then convert our text back to geometry with ST_GeomFromText:

```
textBuilding AS
(
  SELECT ST_AsText(the_geom) textbuilding FROM multiBuilding
),
textBuildSurface AS
(
```

```
  SELECT ST_GeomFromText(replace(textbuilding, 'MULTIPOLYGON',
    'POLYHEDRALSURFACE')) AS the_geom FROM textBuilding
)

SELECT the_geom FROM textBuildSurface;
```

Finally, the entire function is as follows:

```
CREATE OR REPLACE FUNCTION chp07.threedbuilding(footprint geometry,
  height numeric)

RETURNS geometry AS

$BODY$


-- make our polygons into lines, and then chop up into individual
  line segments
WITH simple_lines AS
(
  SELECT 1 AS gid, ST_MakeLine(ST_PointN(the_geom,pointn),
    ST_PointN(the_geom,pointn+1)) AS the_geom
  FROM (SELECT 1 AS gid, chp02.polygon_to_line($1) AS the_geom ) AS a
  LEFT JOIN
  (SELECT 1 AS gid, generate_series(1,
    ST_NumPoints(chp02.polygon_to_line($1))-1) AS pointn
  ) AS b
  ON a.gid = b.gid
),
-- convert our lines into 3D lines, which will set our third
  coordinate to 0 by default
threeDlines AS
(
  SELECT ST_Force3DZ(the_geom) AS the_geom FROM simple_lines
),
-- now we need our lines as individual records, so we dump them out using
ST_Dump, and then just grab the geometry portion of the dump
splodedLine AS
(
  SELECT (ST_Dump(the_geom)).geom AS the_geom FROM threeDLines
),
-- Next step is to construct a line representing the boundary of the
  extruded "wall"
```

```
threeDline AS
(
  SELECT ST_MakeLine(
    ARRAY[
    ST_StartPoint(the_geom),
    ST_EndPoint(the_geom),
    ST_Translate(ST_EndPoint(the_geom), 0, 0, $2),
    ST_Translate(ST_StartPoint(the_geom), 0, 0, $2),
    ST_StartPoint(the_geom)
    ]
  )
AS the_geom FROM splodedLine
),
-- we convert this line into a polygon
threeDwall AS
(
  SELECT ST_MakePolygon(the_geom) as the_geom FROM threeDline
),
-- add a top to the building
buildingTop AS
(
  SELECT ST_Translate(ST_Force3DZ($1), 0, 0, $2) AS the_geom
),
-- and a floor
buildingBottom AS
(
  SELECT ST_Translate(ST_Force3DZ($1), 0, 0, 0) AS the_geom
),
-- now we put the walls, roof, and floor together
wholeBuilding AS
(
  SELECT the_geom FROM buildingBottom
    UNION ALL
  SELECT the_geom FROM threeDwall
    UNION ALL
```

```
    SELECT the_geom FROM buildingTop
),
-- then convert this collecion to a multipolygon
multiBuilding AS
(
   SELECT ST_Multi(ST_Collect(the_geom)) AS the_geom FROM
      wholeBuilding
),
-- While we could leave this as a multipolygon, we'll do things
   properly and munge an informal cast
-- to polyhedralsurfacem which is more widely recognized as the
   appropriate format for a geometry like
-- this. In our case, we are already formatted as a
   polyhedralsurface, minus the official designation,
-- so we'll just convert to text, replace the word MULTIPOLYGON with
POLYHEDRALSURFACE and then convert
-- back to geometry with ST_GeomFromText


textBuilding AS
(
   SELECT ST_AsText(the_geom) textbuilding FROM multiBuilding
),
textBuildSurface AS
(
   SELECT ST_GeomFromText(replace(textbuilding, 'MULTIPOLYGON',
      'POLYHEDRALSURFACE')) AS the_geom FROM textBuilding
)
SELECT the_geom FROM textBuildSurface
;
$BODY$
   LANGUAGE sql VOLATILE
   COST 100;
ALTER FUNCTION chp07.threedbuilding(geometry, numeric)
   OWNER TO me;
```

## How to do it...

Now that we have a 3D-building extrusion function, we can easily extrude our building footprint with our nicely encapsulated function, as follows:

```
CREATE TABLE chp07.threed_building AS

    SELECT chp07.threeDbuilding(the_geom, 10) AS the_geom FROM
        chp07.simple_building;
```

We can apply this function to a real building footprint dataset, in which case, if we have a height field, we can extrude according to that:

```
shp2pgsql -s 3734 -d -i -I -W LATIN1 -g the_geom building_footprints
    chp07.building_footprints | psql -U me -d postgis_cookbook

CREATE TABLE chp07.build_footprints_threed AS

    SELECT gid, height, chp07.threeDbuilding(the_geom, height) AS
        the_geom FROM chp07.building_footprints;
```

The resultant output gives us a nice, extruded set of building footprints, as shown in the following image:

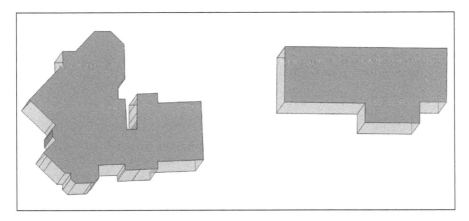

The *Generating detailed building footprints from LiDAR* recipe in *Chapter 4, Working with Vector Data – Advanced Recipes*, explores the extraction of building footprints from LiDAR. A complete workflow could be envisioned, which extracts building footprints from LiDAR and then reconstructs polygon geometries using the current recipe, thus converting point clouds to surfaces, combining the current recipe with the one referenced above.

# Using ST_Extrude to extrude building footprints

PostGIS 2.1 brought a lot of really cool additional functionality to PostGIS. Operation on PostGIS raster types are among the more important improvements that come with PostGIS 2.1. A quieter and equally potent game changer was the addition of the SFCGAL library as an optional extension to PostGIS. According to the website `http://sfcgal.org/`, SFCGAL is a C++ wrapper library around CGAL with the aim of supporting ISO 19107:2013 and OGC Simple Features Access 1.2 for 3D operations.

From a practical standpoint, what does this mean? It means that PostGIS is moving toward a fully functional 3D environment, with representation of the geometries themselves and the operations on those 3D geometries. More information is available at `http://postgis.net/docs/reference.html#reference_sfcgal`.

This and several other recipes will assume that you have a version of PostGIS installed with SFCGAL compiled and enabled. To do so enables the following functions:

- `ST_Extrude`: It extrudes a surface to a related volume
- `ST_StraightSkeleton`: It computes a straight skeleton from a geometry
- `ST_IsPlanar`: It checks whether a surface is a planar or not
- `ST_Orientation`: It determines the surface orientation
- `ST_ForceLHR`: It forces LHR orientation
- `ST_MinkowskiSum`: It computes the Minkowski sum
- `ST_Tesselate`: It performs surface tesselation

For this recipe, we'll use `ST_Extrude` in much the same way we used our own custom-built function in the previous recipe, *Constructing and serving buildings 2.5 D*. The advantage to the previous recipe is that we are not required to have the SFCGAL library compiled in PostGIS. The advantage to this recipe is that we have more control over the extrusion process, that is, we can extrude in all three dimensions.

`ST_Extrude` returns a geometry, specifically, a polyhedralsurface. It requires four parameters—an input geometry and the extrusion amount along the X, Y, and Z axes:

```
CREATE TABLE chp07.buildings_extruded AS
SELECT gid, ST_Extrude(the_geom, 0,0, height) as the_geom
  FROM chp07.building_footprints
```

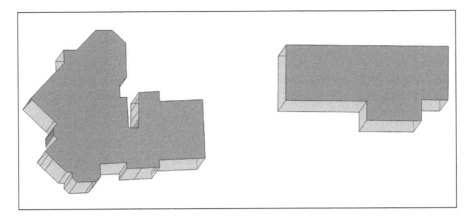

And so, much with the help of the *Constructing and serving buildings 2.5 D* recipe, we get our extruded buildings, but with some additional flexibility.

# Creating arbitrary 3D objects for PostGIS

3D information need not only come from things such as LiDAR, nor be purely synthesized from 2D geometries and associated attributes as in the *Constructing and serving buildings 2.5 D* and *Using ST_Extrude to extrude building footprints* recipes, but can also be derived from the principles of computer vision. The process of calculating 3D information from motion between images is known as **Structure from Motion (SfM)**. As a computer vision concept, we can leverage SfM to generate 3D information in ways similar to how the human mind perceives the world in 3D and further store and process that information in a PostGIS database.

 Computer vision is a discipline within computer science focused on the automated analysis, such as using images to extract information from the world in a way that can be interpreted by computers in ways similar to human vision. An excellent summary can be found at http://en.wikipedia.org/wiki/Computer_vision.

A number of open-source projects have matured to deal with solving SfM problems. Popular among these are Bundler, which can be found at http://phototour.cs.washington.edu/bundler/, and PMVS at http://grail.cs.washington.edu/software/pmvs/. Binaries exist for multiple platforms for these tools, including versions, which can be found at http://homes.cs.washington.edu/~ccwu/vsfm/ and http://www.lancaster.ac.uk/staff/jamesm/software/sfm_georef.htm.

The nice thing about such projects is that a simple set of photos can be used to reconstruct 3D scenes.

For our purposes, we will use a hosted service as a starting place, thus skipping the installation and configuration steps. For our tests, we will use My3DScanner, which is available at `http://My3Dscanner.com/`. My3DScanner is built upon Bundler and PMVS. Another source for a similar service is `http://www.cubify.com/`. We will skip the installation of Bundler and PMVS for two reasons. The first reason is that SfM is beyond the scope of a PostGIS book to cover in detail, so using a service allows us to abstract away the complications of this, while focusing on how we can use the data in PostGIS. The second reason is that depending on the specifics of the implementation of the Bundler/PMVS solution, the solution may not be without intellectual property limitations in the form of patents. If you use this combination commercially, make sure you pay attention to the licensing and intellectual property rights associated with the underlying SIFT algorithm. Some versions of SIFT are protected in certain locales by software patents.

## Getting ready

It is important to understand that SfM techniques, while highly effective, have certain limitations in the kinds of imagery that can be effectively processed into point clouds. The techniques are dependent upon finding **matches** between subsequent images and thus, can have trouble processing images that are smooth, are missing the camera's embedded **Exchangeable Image File format** (**EXIF**) information, or are from cell phone cameras.

 EXIF tags are a metadata format for images. Stored in these tags are often the camera settings, camera type, lense type, and other information relevant to SfM extraction.

We will start processing an image series into a point cloud with a photo series that we know largely works, but as you experiment with SfM, you can feed in your own photo series. Good tips on how to create a photo series that will result in a 3D model can be found at `http://my3dscanner.com/index.php?option=com_k2&view=item&id=5:general-scanning-guide&Itemid=59` and `http://www.cubify.com/products/capture/photography_tips.aspx`.

## How to do it...

Set up an account at `my3Dscanner.com`, log in to the service, and choose **Create New Project**. Give your project a name and upload the images either zipped or in a RAR archive.

Once our image series is loaded, you need to wait anywhere from a few hours to a couple of days for it to process. If you want your data processed faster, see the preceding binary installation of SfM software and run it on your own hardware or virtual machine.

My3DScanner will return a point cloud and a triangular mesh representing the data for download. These can also be viewed in a browser. Download the point cloud and unzip it.

We can view these data in a program such as MeshLab at `http://meshlab.
sourceforge.net/`. A good tutorial on using MeshLab to view point clouds
can be found at `http://my3dscanner.com/index.php?option=com_
k2&view=item&id=61:tutorial-1-understanding-your-3d-model&Itemid=72`.
Also, other recommended viewers can be found at `http://my3dscanner.com/index.
php?option=com_k2&view=item&id=3:free-point-cloud-viewers&Itemid=73`.

The following image shows what our point cloud looks like when viewed in MeshLab:

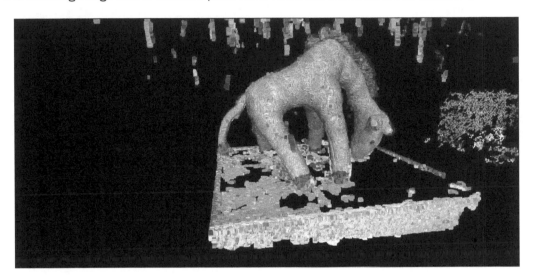

We will unzip the file with the extension `.ply`, for example, `giraffe.ply`. If you open this file
in a text editor, it will look something like the following:

```
ply
format ascii 1.0
element vertex 153781
property float x
property float y
property float z
property float nx
property float ny
property float nz
property uchar red
property uchar green
property uchar blue
end_header
-1.32668 1.00806 -1.89154 0.261367 -0.869846 0.418395 81 110 63
-1.32696 1.00782 -1.89235 0.0799267 -0.788881 0.609326 81 111 64
-1.32637 1.01745 -1.91275 0.788484 0.435774 0.434043 58 69 51
-1.31129 1.02467 -1.92708 0.522892 -0.825308 0.213189 45 67 42
...
```

This is the header portion of our file. It specifies the format, `ply`, the encoding `format ascii 1.0`, the number of vertices, and then the column names for each of the data returned, `x`, `y`, `z`, `nx`, `ny`, `nz`, `red`, `green`, and `blue`.

For import into PostGIS, we will import all fields, but will focus on `x`, `y`, and `z` for our point cloud, as well as look to color. For our interests, this file specifies relative x, y, and z coordinates and the color of each of those points in channels `red`, `green`, and `blue`. These colors are 24-bit colors—8 bits for each channel—and thus, they can have integer values between 0 and 255.

For the remainder of the recipe, let us create a table into which we will enter the point cloud data and get some SfM point cloud data into our database.

```
CREATE TABLE chp07.point_cloud (
  x double precision,
  y double precision,
  z double precision,
  nx double precision,
  ny double precision,
  nz double precision,
  red integer,
  green integer,
  blue integer
);
```

In order to load the data into PostGIS, we need to remove the header information. The simplest way to do that for our example is to trim the first 14 lines of the file. Once this is done, we can copy the data into our table directly, specifying spaces as our delimiter. From `psql`:

```
\copy chp07.point_cloud from
  '/path/to/data/headerless_giraffe.ply' DELIMITER ' ';
```

Now, we make the data spatial.

```
ALTER TABLE chp07.point_cloud ADD COLUMN the_geom GEOMETRY(PointZ,
  0);
UPDATE chp07.point_cloud SET the_geom =
  ST_SetSRID(ST_MakePoint(x,y,z),0);
```

# Exporting models as X3D for the Web

Entering 3D data in a PostGIS database is not nearly as interesting if we have no capacity for extracting the data back out in some usable form. One way to approach this problem is to leverage the PostGIS ability to write 3D tables to the X3D format.

X3D is an XML standard for displaying 3D data and works well via the Web. For those familiar with **Virtual Reality Modeling Language** (**VRML**), X3D is the next generation of that.

To view X3D in the browser, a user has the choice of a variety of plugins or they can leverage JavaScript APIs to enable viewing. We will perform the latter, as it requires no user configuration to work. We will use X3DOM's framework to accomplish this. X3DOM is a demonstration of the integration of HTML5 and 3D and uses WebGL (https://www.khronos.org/webgl/) to allow for the rendering and interaction with 3D content in the browser. This means that our data will not get displayed in browsers that are not WebGL compatible. So, we trade off convenience here for some amount of universality available to us with X3D plugins.

## Getting ready

We will be using the point cloud from the previous example to serve in X3D format. PostGIS documentation on X3D includes an example of using the ST_AsX3D function to output the formatted X3D code. That is similar to the this:

```sql
SELECT '
<X3D xmlns="http://www.web3d.org/specifications/x3d-namespace"
  showStat="false" showLog="false" x="0px" y="0px" width="800px"
  height="600px">
  <Scene>
    <Transform>
      <Shape>' ||    ST_AsX3D(ST_Union(the_geom))    ||
      '</Shape>
    </Transform>
  </Scene>
</X3D>' As x3dXML
  FROM chp07.point_cloud;
```

## How to do it...

This example, while complete in serving the pure X3D, needs additional code to allow for in-browser viewing. We do so by including style sheets and the appropriate X3DOM includes the headers of an XHTML document:

```
<link rel="stylesheet" type="text/css"
  href="http://x3dom.org/x3dom/example/x3dom.css" />
<script type="text/javascript"
  src="http://x3dom.org/x3dom/example/x3dom.js"></script>
```

The full query to generate the XHTML of X3D data is as follows:

```
SELECT '
<!DOCTYPE html PUBLIC "-//W3C//DTD XHTML 1.0 Strict//EN"
  "http://www.w3.org/TR/xhtml1/DTD/xhtml1-strict.dtd">
<html xmlns="http://www.w3.org/1999/xhtml">
  <head>
    <meta http-equiv="X-UA-Compatible" content="chrome=1" />
    <meta http-equiv="Content-Type" content="text/html;charset=utf-8"
      />
    <title>Point Cloud in a Browser</title>
    <link rel="stylesheet" type="text/css"
        href="http://x3dom.org/x3dom/example/x3dom.css" />
    <script type="text/javascript"
      src="http://x3dom.org/x3dom/example/x3dom.js"></script>
  </head>
  <body>
    <h1>Point Cloud in the Browser</h1>
    <p>
      Use mouse to rotate, scroll wheel to zoom, and control (or
        command) click to pan.
    </p>
    <X3D xmlns="http://www.web3d.org/specifications/x3d-namespace"
      showStat="false" showLog="false" x="0px" y="0px" width="800px"
      height="600px">
      <Scene>
        <Transform>
          <Shape>' ||   ST_AsX3D(ST_Union(the_geom))   ||
          '</Shape>
        </Transform>
```

```
    </Scene>
  </X3D>
 </body>
</html>' As x3dXHTML
  FROM chp07.point_cloud;
```

x3dxhtml ----

## Point Cloud in the Browser

Use mouse to rotate, scroll wheel to zoom, and control (or command) click to pan.

(1 row)

## There's more...

One might want to use this X3D conversion as a function, feeding geometry into a function and getting a page in return. This way, we can reuse the code easily for other tables. Embodied in a function, X3D conversion is as follows:

```
CREATE OR REPLACE FUNCTION chp07.AsX3D_XHTML(geometry)
  RETURNS character varying AS
$BODY$
```

```
SELECT '
<!DOCTYPE html PUBLIC "-//W3C//DTD XHTML 1.0 Strict//EN"
  "http://www.w3.org/TR/xhtml1/DTD/xhtml1-strict.dtd">
<html xmlns="http://www.w3.org/1999/xhtml">
  <head>
    <meta http-equiv="X-UA-Compatible" content="chrome=1" />
    <meta http-equiv="Content-Type" content="text/html;charset=utf-8"
      />
    <title>Point Cloud in a Browser</title>
    <link rel="stylesheet" type="text/css"
      href="http://x3dom.org/x3dom/example/x3dom.css" />
    <script type="text/javascript"
      src="http://x3dom.org/x3dom/example/x3dom.js"></script>
  </head>
  <body>
    <h1>Point Cloud in the Browser</h1>
    <p>
      Use mouse to rotate, scroll wheel to zoom, and control (or
        command) click to pan.
    </p>
    <X3D xmlns="http://www.web3d.org/specifications/x3d-namespace"
      showStat="false" showLog="false" x="0px" y="0px" width="800px"
      height="600px">
      <Scene>
        <Transform>
          <Shape>' ||  ST_AsX3D($1)  ||
          '</Shape>
        </Transform>
      </Scene>
    </X3D>
  </body>
</html>' As x3dXHTML
```

```
;
$BODY$
    LANGUAGE sql VOLATILE
    COST 100;
ALTER FUNCTION chp07.AsX3D_XHTML(geometry)
    OWNER TO me;
```

Usage would require that we pass such a function a geometry that has been unioned.

```
SELECT chp07.AsX3D_XHTML(ST_UNION(the_geom)) FROM
    chp07.point_cloud;
```

We can now very simply generate the appropriate XHTML directly from the command line or a web framework.

# Reconstructing Unmanned Aerial Vehicle (UAV) image footprints with PostGIS 3D

The rapid development of **Unmanned Aerial Systems** (**UAS**, also known as **Unmanned Aerial Vehicles**, or **UAVs**) as data collectors is revolutionizing remote data collection in all sectors. Barriers to wider adoption outside military sectors include regulatory frameworks preventing their flight in some nations, for example, the United States, and the lack of open-source implementations of post processing software. In the next four recipes, we'll attempt preliminary solutions to the latter of these two barriers.

For this recipe, we will be using the metadata from a UAV flight in Seneca County, Ohio, to map the coverage of the flight. More information about this flight, which was piloted by the Ohio Department of Transportation, can be found at `http://www.13abc.com/ story/22186538/o-dot-using-tiny-technology-on-big-projects`.

The basic idea for this recipe is to estimate the field of view of the UAV camera, generate a 3D pyramid that represents that field of view, and use the flight ephemeris (bearing, pitch, and roll) to estimate ground coverage.

## Getting ready

The metadata or ephemeris we have for the flight includes the bearing, pitch, and roll of the UAS, in addition to its elevation and location.

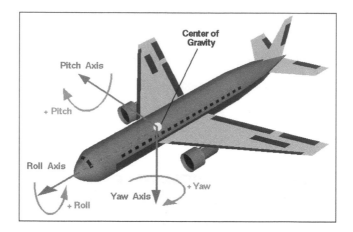

To translate these ephemeris into PostGIS terms, we'll assume the following:

- 90-degrees minus the pitch is equivalent to `ST_RotateX`
- The negative roll is equivalent to `ST_RotateY`
- 90-degrees minus the bearing is equivalent to `ST_RotateZ`

In order to perform our analysis, we require functions that are not yet part of the PostGIS core. These functions can be downloaded from `https://github.com/smathermather/postgis-etc/tree/master/3D`.

We will use patched versions of `ST_RotateX` and `ST_RotateY` (`ST_RotateX.sql` and `ST_RotateY.sql`), which allow us to rotate geometries around an input point, as well as a function for calculating our field of view—`pyramidMaker.sql`. Future versions of PostGIS will include these versions of `ST_RotateX` and `ST_RotateY` built in. We have another function, `ST_RotateXYZ`, which is built upon these and will also simplify our code by allowing us to specify three axes at the same time for rotation.

For the final step, we'll need the capacity to perform volumetric intersection (the 3D equivalent of intersection). For this, we'll use `volumetricIntersection.sql`, which allows us to just return the volumetric portion of the intersection as a **Triangular Irregular Network** (**TIN**).

 A TIN is a 3D surface model for representing surfaces and volumes as a mesh of triangles.

We will install the functions as follows:

```
psql -U me -d postgis_cookbook -f ST_RotateX.sql
psql -U me -d postgis_cookbook -f ST_RotateY.sql
psql -U me -d postgis_cookbook -f ST_RotateXYZ.sql
psql -U me -d postgis_cookbook -f pyramidMaker.sql
psql -U me -d postgis_cookbook -f volumetricIntersection.sql
```

## How to do it...

In order to calculate the viewing footprint, we will calculate a rectangular pyramid descending from the viewpoint to the ground. This pyramid will need to point to the left and right of nadir according to the UAS' roll; forward or backward from the craft according to its pitch, and be oriented relative to the direction of movement of the craft according to its bearing.

The `pyramidMaker` function will construct our pyramid for us and `ST_RotateXYZ` will rotate the pyramid in the direction we need to compensate for roll, pitch, and bearing.

The following image is an example map of such a calculated footprint for a single image. Note the slight roll to the left for this example, resulting in an asymmetric-looking pyramid, when viewed from above.

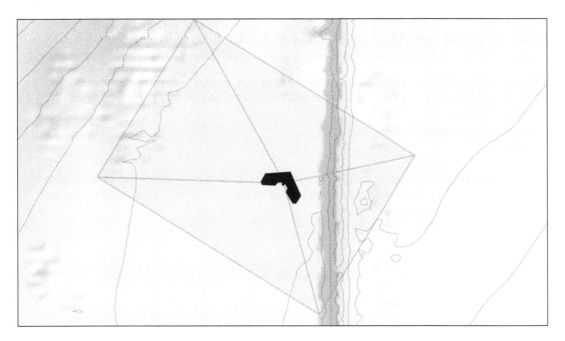

The total track for the UAS flight overlayed on a contour map is shown below, as well:

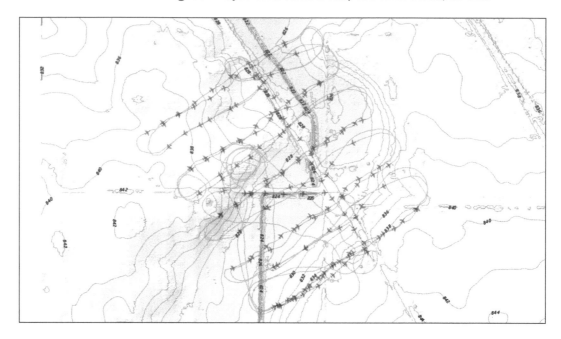

We will write a function to calculate our footprint pyramid. Input to the function, we'll need the position of the UAS as geometry (origin), the pitch, bearing, and roll, as well as the field of view angle in x and y for the camera. Finally, we'll need the relative height of the craft above ground.

```
CREATE OR REPLACE FUNCTION chp07.pbr(origin geometry, pitch numeric,
    bearing numeric, roll numeric, anglex numeric, angley numeric,
    height numeric)
    RETURNS geometry AS
$BODY$
```

Our pyramid function assumes that we know what the base size of our pyramid is. We don't know this initially, so we'll calculate its size based on the field of view angle of the camera and the height of the craft:

```
WITH widthx AS
(
    SELECT height / tan(anglex) AS basex
),
widthy AS
(
    SELECT height / tan(angley) AS basey
),
```

Now we have enough information to construct our pyramid:

```
iViewCone AS (

  SELECT pyramidMaker(origin, basex::numeric, basey::numeric, height)
    AS the_geom

    FROM widthx, widthy

),
```

We will require the following code to rotate our code relative to pitch, roll, and bearing:

```
iViewRotated AS (

  SELECT ST_RotateXYZ(the_geom, pi() - pitch, 0 - roll, pi() -
    bearing, origin) AS the_geom FROM iViewCone

)
```

```
SELECT the_geom FROM iViewRotated;
```

The whole function is as follows:

```
CREATE OR REPLACE FUNCTION chp07.pbr(origin geometry, pitch numeric,
  bearing numeric, roll numeric, anglex numeric, angley numeric,
  height numeric)

  RETURNS geometry AS

$BODY$


WITH widthx AS

(

  SELECT height / tan(anglex) AS basex

),

widthy AS

(

  SELECT height / tan(angley) AS basey

),

iViewCone AS (

  SELECT pyramidMaker(origin, basex::numeric, basey::numeric, height)
    AS the_geom

    FROM widthx, widthy

),

iViewRotated AS (

  SELECT ST_RotateXYZ(the_geom, pi() - pitch, 0 - roll, pi() -
    bearing, origin) AS the_geom FROM iViewCone

)
```

```
SELECT the_geom FROM iViewRotated

;

$BODY$

  LANGUAGE sql VOLATILE

  COST 100;
```

Now, to use our function, let us bring in the UAS positions.

```
shp2pgsql -s 3734 -W LATIN1 uas_locations_altitude_hpr_3734
  uas_locations | psql -U postgres -d postgis_cookbook
```

Now, it is possible to calculate an estimated footprint for each UAS position.

```
CREATE TABLE chp07.viewshed AS

  SELECT 1 AS gid, roll, pitch, heading, fileName,
    chp07.pbr(the_geom, radians(0)::numeric,
    radians(heading)::numeric, radians(roll)::numeric,
    radians(40)::numeric, radians(50)::numeric, ( (3.2808399 *
    altitude_a) - 838)::numeric) AS the_geom

    FROM chp07.uas_locations;
```

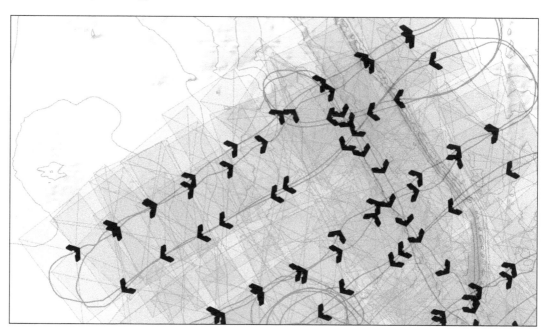

With a terrain model, we can go a step deeper in this analysis. Since our UAS footprints are volumetric, we will first load the terrain model. We will load this from a `.backup` file.

```
pg_restore --host localhost --port 5432 --username "me" --dbname
  "postgis_cookbook" --no-password  --schema chp07 --verbose

  "lidar_tin.backup"
```

Next, we will create a smaller version of our viewshed table.

```
DROP TABLE IF EXISTS chp07.viewshed;

CREATE TABLE chp07.viewshed AS

  SELECT 1 AS gid, roll, pitch, heading, fileName,
    chp07.pbr(the_geom, radians(0)::numeric,
    radians(heading)::numeric, radians(roll)
    ::numeric,radians(40)::numeric, radians(50)::numeric,
    1000::numeric) AS the_geom

  FROM chp07.uas_locations

  WHERE fileName = 'IMG_0512.JPG';
```

To intersect this with our footprints, our terrain model will need to be a volumetric. We can make it so using `ST_Extrude`.

```
CREATE TABLE chp07.lidar_tin_extruded AS

  SELECT ST_Extrude(the_geom, 0,0,1) AS the_geom FROM

    chp07.lidar_tin;

CREATE INDEX chp07_lidar_tin_extruded_the_geom_3dx ON
  chp07.lidar_tin_extruded USING gist(the_geom gist_geometry_ops_nd);
```

We complete the operation by calculating the intersection with our footprints.

```
DROP TABLE IF EXISTS chp07.viewshed_true;

CREATE TABLE chp07.viewshed_true AS

  SELECT ST_3DIntersection(ST_SetSRID(v.the_geom, 3734),
    ST_SetSRID(t.the_geom, 3734))

  FROM chp07.viewshed v, chp07.lidar_tin_extruded t

  WHERE ST_3DIntersects(ST_SetSRID(v.the_geom, 3734),
    ST_SetSRID(t.the_geom, 3734));
```

When compared with a naïve un-intersected estimate of a footprint (a newly calculated footprint in blue and an old one in green), we find a large improvement in the intersection.

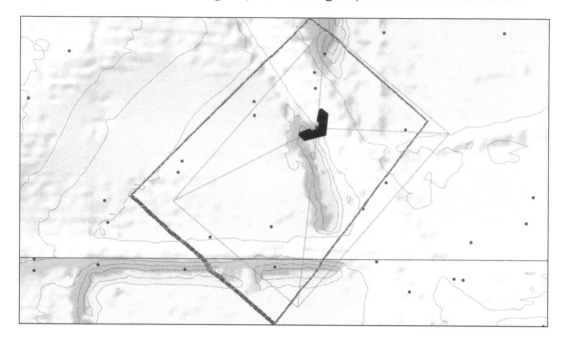

# UAV photogrammetry in PostGIS – point cloud

We will use the techniques we've used in a previous recipe, *Creating arbitrary 3D objects for PostGIS*, of this chapter, to learn how to create and import a UAV-derived point cloud in PostGIS.

One caveat before we begin is that while we will be working with geospatial data, we will be doing so in relative space, rather than a known coordinate system. In other words, this approach will calculate our dataset in an arbitrary coordinate system. ST_Affine could be used in combination with the field measurements of locations to transform our data into a known coordinate system, but is beyond the scope of this book.

## Getting ready

Much like with the recipe, *Creating arbitrary 3D objects for PostGIS*, we will be taking an image series and converting it into a point cloud. In this case, however, our image series will be from UAV imagery. Download the image series from http://www.packtpub.com/ support and feed it into http://my3dscanner.com or a local Bundler/PMVS solution, returning a point cloud, uas_points.ply.

The input to PostGIS is the same as before. Delete the first 14 lines (header) of the `ply` file and create a PostGIS table to accept the point cloud.

```
CREATE TABLE chp07.uas (
  x double precision,
  y double precision,
  z double precision,
  red integer,
  green integer,
  blue integer
);
```

Depending on what software constructed your point cloud, your specific columns may vary.

## How to do it...

Now, we copy data from the point cloud into our table.

```
\copy chp07.uas from '/path/to/data/headless_uas_points.ply'
  DELIMITER ' ';
```

We will convert our implicit spatial data to explicit spatial data with the following code:

```
ALTER TABLE chp07.uas ADD COLUMN the_geom GEOMETRY(PointZ, 0);
UPDATE chp07.uas SET the_geom = ST_SetSRID(ST_MakePoint(x,y,z),0);
```

These data, as viewed in MeshLab from the `ply` file, are pretty interesting:

The original data is color infrared imagery, so vegetation shows up red; and farm fields and roads as gray. Note the bright colors in the sky—those are camera position points that we'll need to filter out.

The next step is to generate orthographic imagery from these data.

# UAV photogrammetry in PostGIS – orthorectification

In the previous recipe, we explored the initial steps in photogrammetric processing, with PostGIS as our storage endpoint for the point cloud derived from aerial imagery. The next step is to create imagery from this point cloud in the plan view, that is, in 2D map coordinates.

To derive the plan view orthophotography from the point cloud, we need to do several things. First, we need a method to convert the point cloud to a 2D areal representation. We could use formal interpolation; but, for the sake of simplicity, we will do this using Voronoi polygons, a space-filling approach that allows us to convert our points to polygons. Next, we need to attribute those polygons with the colors derived from the original imagery. Finally, we need to render those polygons to raster.

This is not a complete orthorectification approach and fails badly where our point cloud is least dense; but, in the absence of a drape function with a PostGIS raster for draping our imagery over a digital surface model, this is a good first approximation.

## Getting ready

We will use the point cloud from the previous recipe for this exercise. Recall that we have a point cloud with x, y, and z values, normal values nx, ny, and nz, and 24-bit color values separated into three integer columns: red, green, and blue.

The processing we will do with this point cloud will be relatively compute-time intensive, so let us start off with a subset of our data while we work our way through the steps.

```
CREATE TABLE chp07.uas_subset AS
  SELECT * FROM chp07.uas
    ORDER BY RANDOM()
    LIMIT 5000;
```

Moving temporarily from more than 240,000 records to 500.

## How to do it...

Now that we have our data paired down, we will revisit our short outline of tasks.

1. Convert the point cloud to Voronoi polygons.
2. Attribute polygons with the color.
3. Render polygons to raster.

### Converting the point cloud to Voronoi polygons

Converting our points to Voronoi polygons is well covered in *Chapter 4, Working with Vector Data – Advanced Recipes*, in the *Using external scripts to embed new functionality in order to calculate a Voronoi diagram* recipe. In this recipe, we will use that function as a simple interpolator for between the points of our point cloud.

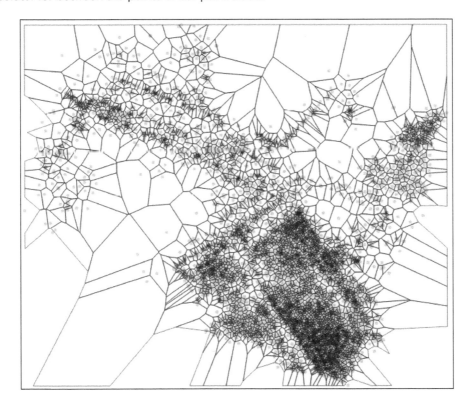

Our code is simple.

```
DROP TABLE IF EXISTS chp07.uas_voronoi CASCADE;
CREATE TABLE chp07.uas_voronoi AS
   SELECT * FROM voronoi('chp07.uas_subset', 'the_geom') AS (id
      integer, the_geom geometry);
   ALTER TABLE chp07.uas_voronoi ADD COLUMN gid serial NOT NULL
      PRIMARY KEY;
```

## Attributing polygons with the color

Our next step is to attribute our new polygons with the color information associated with the original points. This can be accomplished with a simple ST_Intersects query, but first indexes in order to be efficient.

```
CREATE INDEX uas_the_geom_gist
   ON chp07.uas
   USING gist
   (the_geom );
CREATE INDEX uas_voronoi_the_geom_gist
   ON chp07.uas_voronoi
   USING gist
   (the_geom );
```

Next, we will perform the join itself. Due to some issues with non-voronoi polygons returning, we will first count how many points are present in each polygon and only return those polygons that have a single point.

```
DROP TABLE IF EXISTS chp07.uas_voronoi_count CASCADE;
CREATE TABLE chp07.uas_voronoi_count AS
   WITH distinction AS (
   SELECT DISTINCT ON (uv.gid) uv.gid, uv.the_geom, COUNT(uas.*)
      FROM chp07.uas_voronoi uv
      LEFT JOIN chp07.uas_subset uas
      ON ST_Intersects(uv.the_geom, uas.the_geom)
      GROUP BY uv.gid, uv.the_geom
   )
   SELECT gid, the_geom, count FROM distinction
      WHERE count = 1
         AND
```

```
    ST_Covers(ST_Envelope( ((SELECT ST_Union(the_geom) FROM
      chp07.uas_subset)) ), the_geom)
  ;
CREATE INDEX uas_voronoi_count_the_geom_gist
  ON chp07.uas_voronoi_count
  USING gist
  (the_geom );
```

Now, we can construct our Voronoi polygons with the colors from the point cloud joined to the polygons themselves.

```
DROP TABLE IF EXISTS chp07.uas_voronoi_join;
CREATE TABLE chp07.uas_voronoi_join AS
  SELECT uv.gid, uv.the_geom, red, green, blue
    FROM chp07.uas_voronoi_count uv
    LEFT JOIN chp07.uas_subset uas
    ON ST_Intersects(uv.the_geom, uas.the_geom);
```

## Rendering polygons to raster

The final step in our processing chain is to convert our Voronoi polygons to raster. ST_AsRaster will convert our geometry to raster. To do so, we first need to create a dummy raster with the size and type of our final raster. ST_AsRaster takes a few inputs, depending on the use case. In our case:

```
ST_AsRaster(ST_Union(the_geom), 100, 100, ARRAY['8BUI', '8BUI',
  '8BUI'], ARRAY[0,0,0], ARRAY[0,0,0])
```

So, for our inputs, we have our geometry, width, height, and three arrays specifying pixel type, input pixel value, and background pixel value. For our remaining arrays, we populate them with zeros for background values. But, first, we should modify our function a bit to ensure that we maintain square pixels in our output raster. To do so, we will calculate the ratio of width to height in the input geometry envelope. For a 100-pixel image, this would look something like this:

```
SELECT round(100 * ( (ST_XMax(ST_Collect(the_geom)) -
  ST_XMin(ST_Collect(the_geom))) / (ST_YMax(ST_Collect(the_geom)) -
  ST_YMin(ST_Collect(the_geom))) ))::integer;
```

Resulting in an on-the-fly raster creation using the following code and we want to write this to file as an image external to the database, we can. We'll use the `write_file` script available at `http://postgis.net/docs/manual-2.0/using_raster.xml.html#RT_PLPython`.

```
WITH tempraster AS (
  SELECT ST_AsRaster(
    ST_Union(the_geom),
    round(500 * ( (ST_XMax(ST_Collect(the_geom)) -
      ST_XMin(ST_Collect(the_geom))) / (ST_YMax(ST_Collect(the_geom))
      - ST_YMin(ST_Collect(the_geom))) ))::integer,
  500,
  ARRAY['8BUI', '8BUI', '8BUI'],
  ARRAY[0,0,0],
  ARRAY[0,0,0]) AS rast
  FROM
  (SELECT *
  FROM chp07.uas_voronoi_join) AS uv
  ),
  rasterized AS (
    SELECT ST_Union(ST_AsRaster(
    the_geom,
    rast,
    ARRAY['8BUI', '8BUI', '8BUI'],
    ARRAY[red, green, blue],
    ARRAY[0,0,0]
    )
  ) AS raster
  FROM
  (
    SELECT * FROM
    chp07.uas_voronoi_join
    CROSS JOIN
    tempraster
  ) AS pcr
)
SELECT write_file(ST_AsPNG(raster), '/tmp/test.png'::text) FROM
  rasterized;
```

```
-- write to file in windows -- comment previous line and uncomment
   following line:
-- SELECT write_file(ST_AsPNG(raster), 'c:\temp\test.png'::text) FROM
   rasterized  ;
```

If we choose to and are patient, we may now rerun our code with the entire dataset and get a first level approximation of an orthophoto. A formal orthophoto is on the left for comparison and our first level approximation from UAS imagery on the right:

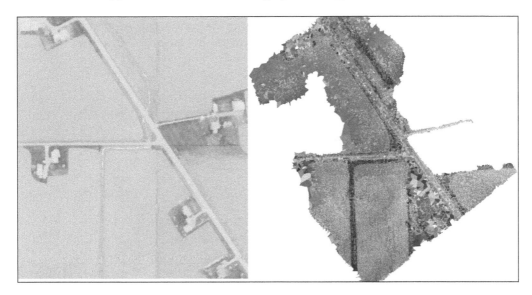

As a proof of concept, this process is promising. With forthcoming functions being added to PostGIS, especially to the raster functionality, we should be able to refine these results substantially, for example, by draping the original imagery back to its appropriate location and rendering it to a high-resolution, photogrammetrically-correct aerial photograph.

# UAV photogrammetry in PostGIS – DSM creation

The photogrammetry example would be incomplete if we did not produce a digital terrain model from our inputs. A fully rigorous solution where the input point cloud would be classified into ground points, building points, and vegetation points is not feasible here, but this recipe will provide the basic framework for accomplishing such a solution.

In this recipe, we will create a 3D TIN, which will represent the surface of the point cloud.

## Getting ready

Before we start, `ST_DelaunayTriangles` is available only in PostGIS 2.1 using GEOS 3.4. This is one of the few recipes in this book to require such advanced versions of PostGIS and GEOS.

## How it works...

`ST_DelaunayTriangles` will calculate a 3D TIN with the correct flag: geometry `ST_DelaunayTriangles` (geometry g1, float tolerance, int4 flags).

CREATE TABLE chp07.uas_tin AS

```
WITH tin AS
(
   SELECT ST_DelaunayTriangles(ST_Union(the_geom), 0.0, 2) AS the_geom
      FROM

   chp07.uas
)
SELECT the_geom FROM tin;
```

Now, we have a full TIN of a digital surface model at our disposal.

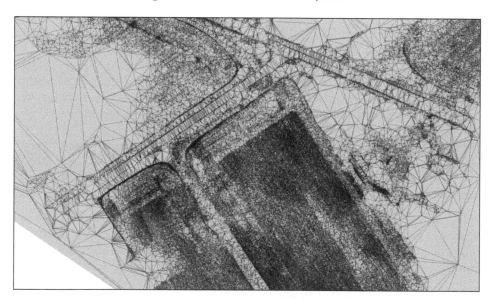

# 8

# PostGIS Programming

In this chapter, we will cover the following topics:

- ▶ Writing PostGIS vector data with Psycopg
- ▶ Writing PostGIS vector data with OGR Python bindings
- ▶ Writing PostGIS functions with PL/Python
- ▶ Geocoding and reverse-geocoding using the GeoNames datasets
- ▶ Geocoding using the OSM datasets with trigrams
- ▶ Geocoding with geopy and PL/Python
- ▶ Importing netCDF datasets with Python and GDAL

## Introduction

There are several ways to write PostGIS programs; in this chapter, we will see a few of them. You will mainly use the Python language throughout this chapter. Python is a fantastic language with a plethora of GIS and a scientific library that can be combined with PostGIS to write awesome geospatial applications.

In case you are new to Python, you can quickly get productive with these excellent web resources:

- ▶ The official Python tutorial at `http://docs.python.org/2/tutorial/`
- ▶ The popular *Dive into Python* book at `http://www.diveintopython.net/`
- ▶ The *Learn Python in the hard way* class for a task-oriented training at `http://learnpythonthehardway.org/`

You can combine Python with some excellent and popular libraries such as:

- **Psycopg**: This is the most complete and popular Python DB API implementation for PostgreSQL; see `http://initd.org/psycopg/`
- **GDAL Python bindings**: These are used to unchain the powerful GDAL library in your Python scripts; see `http://www.gdal.org/gdal_tutorial.html`
- **urllib2**: This is a handy Python standard library to manage HTTP stuff such as opening URLs
- **simplejson**: This is a simple and fast JSON encoder/decoder

The recipes of this chapter will not cover some other useful geospatial Python libraries that are worthy of being looked at if you are developing a geospatial application. Under these Python libraries, the following libraries are included:

- **Shapely**: This is a Python interface to the GEOS library for the manipulation and analysis of planar geometric objects: `http://toblerity.github.io/shapely/`
- **Fiona**: This is a very light OGR Python API that can be used as an alternative to the OGR bindings used in this chapter to manage vector datasets: `https://github.com/Toblerity/Fiona`
- **Rasterio**: This is the new kid on the block, a pythonic GDAL Python API that can be used as an alternative to the GDAL bindings used in this chapter in order to manage raster datasets: `https://github.com/sgillies/rasterio`
- **pyproj**: This is the Python interface to the PROJ.4 library: `https://code.google.com/p/pyproj/`
- **Rtree**: This is a `ctype` Python wrapper to the `libspatialindex` library, providing several spatial indexing features that can be extremely useful for some kind of geospatial development: `http://toblerity.github.io/rtree/`

In the first recipe, you will write a program that uses Python and the `psycopg`, `urllib2`, and `simplejson` libraries to fetch weather data from the Web and import them into PostGIS.

In the second recipe, we will drive you to use Python and the GDAL OGR Python bindings library to create a script for geocoding a list of place names using one of the GeoNames Web services.

You will then write a Python function for PostGIS using the PL/Python language to query the `openweathermap.org` Web services, already used in the first recipe, to calculate the weather for a PostGIS geometry from within a PostgreSQL function.

In the fourth recipe, you will create two PL/pgSQL PostGIS functions that will let you perform geocoding and reverse geocoding using the GeoNames datasets.

After this, there is a recipe in which you will use the `OpenStreetMap` street datasets imported in PostGIS to implement a very basic Python class in order to provide a geocode implementation to the class's consumer using the PostGIS trigrams support.

The sixth recipe will show you how to create a PL/Python function using the `geopy` library to geocode addresses using web geocoding API such as Google Maps, Yahoo! Maps, Geocoder. us, GeoNames, and other ones.

In the last recipe of this chapter, you will create a Python script to import data from the `netCDF` format to PostGIS using the GDAL Python bindings.

Let's see some notes before starting with the recipes in this chapter.

If you are using Linux, follow these steps:

1. Create a Python `virtualenv` (http://www.virtualenv.org/en/latest/) to set up a Python-isolated environment to be used for all the Python recipes in this book and activate it. Create it in a central directory, as you will need to use it for most of the Python recipes of this book.

   ```
   $ cd ~/virtualenvs
   $ virtualenv --no-site-packages postgis-cb-env
   $ source postgis-cb-env/bin/activate
   ```

2. Once activated, you can install the Python libraries you will need for the recipes in this chapter:

   ```
   $ pip install simplejson
   $ pip install psycopg2
   $ pip install numpy
   $ pip install gdal
   $ pip install geopy
   ```

3. In case you are new to the virtual environment and you are wondering where the libraries have been installed, you should find everything in the `virtualenv` directory in our development box. You can find the libraries using the following command:

   ```
   $ ls /home/capooti/virtualenv/postgis-cb-env/lib/python2.7/site-packages
   ```

   In case you are wondering what is going on with the previous command lines: then `virtualenv` is a tool that will be used to create isolated Python environments, and you can find more information about this tool at http://www.virtualenv.org, while pip (http://www.pip-installer.org) is a package-management system used to install and manage software packages written in Python.

If you are using Windows, follow these steps:

1. The easiest way to have Python and all the libraries needed for the recipes of this chapter is to use **OSGeo4W**, a popular binary distribution of open source geospatial software for Windows. You can download it from `http://trac.osgeo.org/osgeo4w/`.

2. On my Windows box, the OSGeo4W shell, at the time of writing this book, comes with Python 2.7.4, GDAL 1.10.1 Python bindings, simplejson, psycopg2, and numpy. You will only need to install geopy.

3. The easiest way to install geopy and to eventually add more Python libraries to the OSGeo4W shell is to install `setuptools` and `pip` by following the instructions found at `http://www.pip-installer.org/en/latest/installing.html`. Open the OSGeo4W shell and just enter the following commands:

```
> python ez_setup.py
> python get-pip.py
> pip install geopy
```

# Writing PostGIS vector data with Psycopg

In this recipe, you will use Python combined with Psycopg, the most popular PostgreSQL database library for Python, in order to write some data to PostGIS using the SQL language.

You will write a procedure to import weather data for the most populated US cities. You will import such weather data from `OpenWeatherData.org`, which is a web service that provides free weather data and forecast API. The procedure you are going to write will iterate each major USA city and get the actual temperature for it from the closest weather stations using the `OpenWeatherData.org` Web service API, getting the output in the JSON format. (In case you are new to the JSON format, you can find details about it at `http://www.json.org/`.)

You will also generate a new PostGIS layer with the 10 closest weather stations to each city.

## Getting ready

1. Create a database schema for the recipes in this chapter using the following command:
```
postgis_cookbook=# CREATE SCHEMA chp08;
```

2.  Download the USA cities' shapefile from the `nationalatlas.gov` website at `http://dds.cr.usgs.gov/pub/data/nationalatlas/citiesx020_nt00007.tar.gz` (this archive is anyway included in the dataset that is available with the code bundle), extract it to `working/chp08`, and import it in PostGIS, filtering out cities with less than 100,000 inhabitants:

```
$ ogr2ogr -f PostgreSQL -s_srs EPSG:4269 -t_srs EPSG:4326 -lco
GEOMETRY_NAME=the_geom -nln chp08.cities PG:"dbname='postgis_
cookbook' user='me' password='mypassword'" -where "POP_2000 >
100000" citiesx020.shp
```

3.  Add a `real` field to store the temperature for each city using the following command:

```
postgis_cookbook=# ALTER TABLE chp08.cities ADD COLUMN temperature
real;
```

4.  If you are on Linux, ensure that you follow the initial instructions of this chapter and create a Python virtual environment in order to create a Python-isolated environment, to be used for all the Python recipes of this book, and activate it:

```
$ source postgis-cb-env/bin/activate
```

5.  Once activated, if you still haven't done it, you can install the Python psycopg2 and simplejson packages needed for this recipe:

```
(postgis-cb-env)$ pip install psycopg2
(postgis-cb-env)$ pip install simplejson
```

## How to do it...

Carry out the following steps:

1.  Create the following table to host weather station data:

```
postgis_cookbook=# CREATE TABLE chp08.wstations
postgis_cookbook-#     (
postgis_cookbook(#         id bigint NOT NULL,
postgis_cookbook(#         the_geom geometry(Point,4326),
postgis_cookbook(#         name character varying(48),
postgis_cookbook(#         temperature real,
postgis_cookbook(#         CONSTRAINT wstations_pk PRIMARY KEY (id )
postgis_cookbook(#     );
```

2.  Check the JSON response for the web service you are going to use. If you want the 10 closest weather stations from a point (the city centroid), the request you need to run is as follows (test it in a browser):

```
http://api.openweathermap.org/data/2.1/find/
station?lat=55&lon=37&cnt=10
```

3. You should get the following JSON response (the closest 10 stations and their relative data are ordered by their distance from the point coordinates that for this case are `lon=37` and `lat=55`):

```
{
"calctime": "",
"cnt": 10,
"cod": "200",
"list": [
    {
        "clouds": [
            {
                "condition": "OVC",
                "distance": 610
            }
        ],
        "coord": {
            "lat": 55.5,
            "lon": 37.5
        },
        "distance": 63.995,
        "dt": 1362061800,
        "id": 7325,
        "main": {
            "pressure": 1001,
            "temp": 275.15
        },
        "name": "UUMO",
        "rang": 50,
        "type": 1,
        "wind": {
            "deg": 280,
            "speed": 4
        }
    }, ...
```

4. Now, create the Python program that will perform the desired output and name it `get_weather_data.py`:

```python
import urllib2
import simplejson as json
import psycopg2

def GetWeatherData(lon, lat):
    """
```

```
    Get the 10 closest weather stations data for a given point.
    """
    # uri to access the JSON openweathermap web service
    uri = (
      'http://api.openweathermap.org/data/2.1/find/
station?lat=%s&lon=%s&cnt=10'
        % (lat, lon))
    print 'Fetching weather data: %s' % uri
    try:
        data = urllib2.urlopen(uri)
        js_data = json.load(data)
        return js_data['list']
    except:
        print 'There was an error getting the weather data.'
        return []


def AddWeatherStation(station_id, lon, lat, name, temperature):
    """
    Add a weather station to the database, but only if it does not
already exists.
    """
    curws = conn.cursor()
    curws.execute('SELECT * FROM chp08.wstations WHERE id=%s',
(station id,))
    count = curws.rowcount
    if count==0: # we need to add the weather station
        curws.execute(
            """INSERT INTO chp08.wstations (id, the_geom, name,
temperature)
            VALUES (%s, ST_GeomFromText('POINT(%s %s)', 4326), %s,
%s)""",
            (station_id, lon, lat, name, temperature)
        )
        curws.close()
        print 'Added the %s weather station to the database.' %
name
        return True
    else: # weather station already in database
        print 'The %s weather station is already in the database.'
% name
        return False


# program starts here
# get a connection to the database
```

```
conn = psycopg2.connect('dbname=postgis_cookbook user=me
password=mypassword')
# we do not need transaction here, so set the connection to
autocommit mode
conn.set_isolation_level(0)

# open a cursor to update the table with weather data
cur = conn.cursor()

# iterate all of the cities in the cities PostGIS layer, and for
each of them
# grap the actual temperature from the closest weather station,
and add the 10
# closest stations to the city to the wstation PostGIS layer
cur.execute("""SELECT ogc_fid, name,
    ST_X(the_geom) AS long, ST_Y(the_geom) AS lat FROM chp08.
cities;""")
for record in cur:
    ogc_fid = record[0]
    city_name = record[1]
    lon = record[2]
    lat = record[3]
    stations = GetWeatherData(lon, lat)
    print stations
    for station in stations:
        print station
        station_id = station['id']
        name = station['name']
        # for weather data we need to access the 'main' section in
the json
        # 'main': {'pressure': 990, 'temp': 272.15, 'humidity':
54}
        if 'main' in station:
            if 'temp' in station['main']:
                temperature = station['main']['temp']
        else:
            temperature = -9999 # in some case the temperature is
not available
        # "coord":{"lat":55.8622,"lon":37.395}
        station_lat = station['coord']['lat']
        station_lon = station['coord']['lon']
```

```
            # add the weather station to the database
            AddWeatherStation(station_id, station_lon, station_lat,
                name, temperature)
            # first weather station from the json API response is
    always the closest
            # to the city, so we are grabbing this temperature and
    store in the
            # temperature field in the cities PostGIS layer
            if station_id == stations[0]['id']:
                print 'Setting temperature to %s for city %s' % (
                    temperature, city_name)
                cur2 = conn.cursor()
                cur2.execute(
                    'UPDATE chp08.cities SET temperature=%s WHERE ogc_
    fid=%s',
                    (temperature, ogc_fid))
                cur2.close()

    # close cursor and close connection to database
        cur.close()
        conn.close()
```

5.  Run the Python program:

    ```
    (postgis-cb-env)$ python get_weather_data.py
    Added the PAMR weather station to the database.
    Setting temperature to 268.15 for city Anchorage
    Added the PAED weather station to the database.
    Added the PANC weather station to the database.
    ...
    The KMFE weather station is already in the database.
    Added the KOPM weather station to the database.
    The KBKS weather station is already in the database.
    ```

6. Check the output of the Python program you just wrote. Open the two PostGIS layers, `cities` and `wstations`, with your favorite GIS desktop tool and investigate the results. The following screenshot shows how it looks in QGIS:

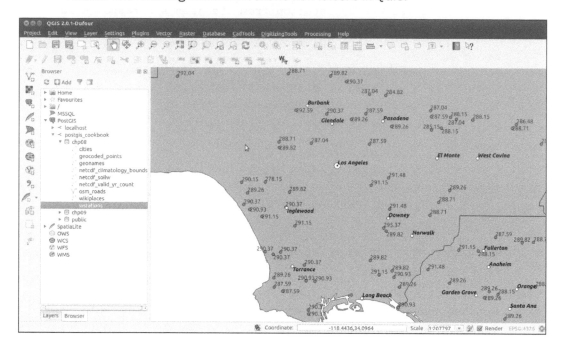

## How it works...

**Psycopg** is the most popular PostgreSQL adapter for Python, and it can be used to create Python scripts that send SQL commands to PostGIS. In this recipe, you created a Python script that queries weather data from the `OpenWeatherData.org` web server using the popular **JSON** format to get the output data and then used that data to update two PostGIS layers.

For one of the layers, `cities`, the weather data is used to update the `temperature` field using the temperature data of the weather station closest to the city. For this purpose, you used an `UPDATE SQL` command. The other layer, `wstations`, is updated every time a new weather station is identified from the weather data and inserted in the layer. In this case, you used an `INSERT SQL` statement.

This is a quick overview of the script's behavior (you can find more details in the comments within the Python code): in the beginning, a PostgreSQL connection is created using the Psycopg `connection` object. The `connection` object is created using the main connection parameters (dbname, user, and password, while default values for server name and port are not specified, as the default values, `localhost` and `5432` are used). The connection behavior is set to `auto commit` so that any SQL performed by psycopg will be run immediately and will not be embedded in a transaction.

Using a cursor, you first iterate all of the records in the `cities` PostGIS layer: for each of the cities, you need to get the temperature from the `OpenWeatherData.org` web server. For this purpose, for each city, you make a call to the `GetWeatherData` method, passing the coordinates of the city to it. The method queries the server using the `urllib2` library and parses the JSON response using the `simplejson` Python library.

You should send the URL request to a `try...catch` block. This way, if there is any issue with the web service (internet connection not available, any HTTP status codes different from 200, or whatever else), the process can safely continue with the data of the next city (iteration).

The JSON response contains, as per the request, the information about the 10 weather stations closest to the city. You will use the information of the first weather station, the closest one to the city, to set the `temperature` field for the city.

You then iterate all of the `station` JSON objects and by using the `AddWeatherStation` method, you create a weather station in the `wstation` PostGIS layer, but only if a weather station with the same `id` does not exist.

# Writing PostGIS vector data with OGR Python bindings

In this recipe, you will use Python and the Python bindings of the GDAL/OGR library to create a script for geocoding a list of the names of places using one of the GeoNames Web services (`http://www.geonames.org/export/ws-overview.html`). You will use the Wikipedia Full Text Search Web service (`http://www.geonames.org/export/wikipedia-webservice.html#wikipediaSearch`), which for a given search string returns the coordinates of the places matching that search string as the output and some other useful attributes from Wikipedia, including the Wikipedia `page title` and `url`.

The script should first create a PostGIS point layer named `wikiplaces` in which all of the locations and their attributes returned by the web service will be stored.

This recipe should give you the basis to use other similar web services, such as Google Maps, Yahoo! BOSS Geo Services, and so on, to get results in a similar way.

Before you start, please note the terms of use of GeoNames: `http://www.geonames.org/export/`. In a few words, on the date of writing, you have 30,000 credits' daily limit per application (identified by the `username` parameter); the hourly limit is 2000 credits. A credit is a web service request hit for most services.

You will generate the PostGIS table containing the geocoded place names using the GDAL/OGR Python bindings (`http://trac.osgeo.org/gdal/wiki/GdalOgrInPython`).

## Getting ready

1. To access GeoNames Web services, you need to create a user at
   `http://www.geonames.org/login`. The user being used in this recipe
   is `postgis`; you will need to change it with your username whenever you
   query the GeoNames Web services URL.

2. If you are using Windows, be sure to have OSGeo4W installed as suggested in the
   initial instructions of this chapter.

3. If you are using Linux, follow the initial instructions for this chapter and create a
   Python `virtualenv`, in order to keep a Python-isolated environment to be used
   for all the Python recipes of this book, and activate it:

   ```
   $ source postgis-cb-env/bin/activate
   ```

4. Once activated, if you still haven't done it, you have to install the Python GDAL and
   simplejson packages needed for this recipe:

   ```
   (postgis-cb-env)$ pip install gdal

   (postgis-cb-env)$ pip install simplejson
   ```

## How to do it...

Carry out the following steps:

1. First test the web service and its JSON output yourself with the following request
   (change the `q` and `username` parameters as you wish):

   ```
   http://api.geonames.org/wikipediaSearchJSON?formatted=true&q=lo
   ndon&maxRows=10&username=postgis&style=full
   ```

   You should get the following JSON output:

   ```
   {"geonames": [
     {
       "summary": "London Bridge railway station is a central London
   railway terminus and London Underground complex in the London
   Borough of Southwark, occupying a large area on two levels
   immediately south-east of London Bridge and 1.6 miles (2.6 km)
   east of Charing Cross (...)",
       "rank": 100,
       "title": "London Bridge station",
       "wikipediaUrl": "en.wikipedia.org/wiki/London_Bridge_station",
       "elevation": 18,
       "countryCode": "GB",
       "lng": -0.0866,
       "feature": "railwaystation",
       "thumbnailImg": "http://www.geonames.org/img/wikipedia/115000/
   thumb-114758-100.jpg",
   ```

```
    "lang": "en",
    "lat": 51.5055
  },
  {
    "summary": "London is a city in Southwestern Ontario, Canada,
  situated along the Quebec City-Windsor Corridor. The city has
  a population of 366,151 according to the 2011 Canadian census.
  London is the seat of Middlesex County, at the forks of the non-
  navigable Thames River, approximately halfway between (...)",
    "rank": 100,
    "title": "London, Ontario",...
```

2. As you can see from the JSON output for the GeoNames Web service, for a given query string (a location name), you get a list of Wikipedia pages related to that location in a JSON format. For each JSON object representing a Wikipedia page, you can get access to the attributes such as the page `title`, `summary`, `url`, and the `coordinates` of the location.

3. Now, create a text file named `working/chp08/names.txt` with the names of places you would like to geocode from the Wikipedia Full Text Search Web services. Add some place names, for example (in Windows, use a text editor such as Notepad):

```
$ vi names.txt


London

Rome

Boston

Chicago

Madrid

Paris

...
```

4. Now create a file named `import_places.py` under `working/chp08/` and add to it the Python script of this recipe. The following is how the script should look (you should be able to follow it by reading the in-line comments and the *How it works...* section):

```python
import sys
import urllib2
import simplejson as json
from osgeo import ogr, osr

MAXROWS = 10
USERNAME = 'postgis' #enter your username here

def CreatePGLayer():
    """
```

```
    Create the PostGIS table.
    """
    driver = ogr.GetDriverByName('PostgreSQL')
    srs = osr.SpatialReference()
    srs.ImportFromEPSG(4326)
    pg_ds = ogr.Open(
        "PG:dbname='postgis_cookbook' host='localhost' port='5432'
user='me' password='mypassword'",
        update = 1 )
    pg_layer = pg_ds.CreateLayer('wikiplaces', srs = srs, geom_
type=ogr.wkbPoint,
        options = [
            'DIM=3', # we want to store the elevation value in
point z coordinate
            'GEOMETRY_NAME=the_geom',
            'OVERWRITE=YES', # this will drop and recreate the
table every time
            'SCHEMA=chp08',
        ])
    # add the fields
    fd_title = ogr.FieldDefn('title', ogr.OFTString)
    pg_layer.CreateField(fd_title)
    fd_countrycode = ogr.FieldDefn('countrycode', ogr.OFTString)
    pg_layer.CreateField(fd_countrycode)
    fd_feature = ogr.FieldDefn('feature', ogr.OFTString)
    pg_layer.CreateField(fd_feature)
    fd_thumbnail = ogr.FieldDefn('thumbnail', ogr.OFTString)
    pg_layer.CreateField(fd_thumbnail)
    fd_wikipediaurl = ogr.FieldDefn('wikipediaurl', ogr.OFTString)
    pg_layer.CreateField(fd_wikipediaurl)
    return pg_ds, pg_layer


def AddPlacesToLayer(places):
    """
    Read the places dictionary list and add features in the
PostGIS table for each place.
    """
    # iterate every place dictionary in the list
    for place in places:
        lng = place['lng']
        lat = place['lat']
        z = place['elevation'] if 'elevation' in place else 0
        # we generate a point representation in wkt, and create an
ogr geometry
        point_wkt = 'POINT(%s %s %s)' % (lng, lat, z)
        point = ogr.CreateGeometryFromWkt(point_wkt)
        # we create a LayerDefn for the feature using the one from
the layer
        featureDefn = pg_layer.GetLayerDefn()
        feature = ogr.Feature(featureDefn)
```

```
        # now time to assign the geometry and all the other
feature's fields,
        # if the keys are contained in the dictionary (not always
the GeoNames
        # Wikipedia Fulltext Search contains all of the
information)
        feature.SetGeometry(point)
        feature.SetField('title',
            place['title'].encode("utf-8") if 'title' in place
else '')
        feature.SetField('countrycode',
            place['countryCode'] if 'countryCode' in place else
'')
        feature.SetField('feature',
            place['feature'] if 'feature' in place else '')
        feature.SetField('thumbnail',
            place['thumbnailImg'] if 'thumbnailImg' in place else
'')
        feature.SetField('wikipediaurl',
            place['wikipediaUrl'] if 'wikipediaUrl' in place else
'')
        # here we create the feature (the INSERT SQL is issued
here)
        pg_layer.CreateFeature(feature)
        print 'Created a places titled %s.' % place['title']


def GetPlaces(placename):
    """
    Get the places list for a given placename.
    """
    # uri to access the JSON GeoNames Wikipedia Fulltext Search
web service
    uri = ('http://api.geonames.org/wikipediaSearchJSON?formatted=
true&q=%s&maxRows=%s&username=%s&style=full'
            % (placename, MAXROWS, USERNAME))
    data = urllib2.urlopen(uri)
    js_data = json.load(data)
    return js_data['geonames']

def GetNamesList(filepath):
    """
    Open a file with a given filepath containing place names and
return a list.
    """
    f = open(filepath)
    return f.read().splitlines()


# first we need to create a PostGIS table to contains the places
# we must keep the PostGIS OGR dataset and layer global, for the
reasons
```

```
        # described here: http://trac.osgeo.org/gdal/wiki/PythonGotchas
        from osgeo import gdal
        gdal.UseExceptions()
        pg_ds, pg_layer = CreatePGLayer()

        # query geonames for each name and store found places in the table
        names = GetNamesList('names.txt')
        for name in names:
            AddPlacesToLayer(GetPlaces(name))
```

5. Now, execute the Python script:

```
(postgis-cb-env)$ python import_places.py
Created a places titled London Bridge station.
Created a places titled London.
Created a places titled London, Ontario.

...
```

6. Test whether the table was correctly created and populated using SQL and eventually use your favorite Desktop GIS tool to display the layer:

```
postgis_cookbook=# select ST_AsText(the_geom), title, countrycode,
feature from chp08.wikiplaces;

st_astext                              |                 title
 | countrycode |      feature
-------------------------------------------------+--------------------
------------------+-------------+----------------
POINT Z (-0.0866 51.5055 18) | London Bridge station | GB |
railwaystation
 POINT Z (-81.2497 42.9837 262)                  | London, Ontario
 | CA         | city
 POINT Z (-72.1008333333 41.3555555556 27)  | New London,
Connecticut                    | US          | city
 POINT Z (-0.07857 51.504872 2)            | London
 | GB         | city
 ...
 POINT Z (2.33305556 48.90694444 36)             | Saint-Ouen, Seine-
Saint-Denis           | FR          |
 POINT Z (2.343333 48.848611 61)           | Sorbonne
 |          |
 POINT Z (2.30472222222 48.9325 28)              | Gennevilliers
 | FR         | city

(60 rows)
```

## How it works...

This Python script uses the `urllib2` (part of the standard Python library) and `simplejson` libraries to fetch data from the GeoNames `wikipediaSearchJSON` web service and the GDAL/OGR library to store geographic information inside the PostGIS database.

First, you create a PostGIS point table to store the geographic data. This is made using the GDAL/OGR bindings. You need to instantiate a OGR PostGIS driver (`http://www.gdal.org/ogr/drv_pg.html`) from where it is possible to instantiate a dataset to connect to your `postgis_cookbook` database using a specified connection string.

The `update` parameter in the connection string specifies to the GDAL driver that will open the dataset for updating.

From the PostGIS dataset, we created a PostGIS layer named `wikiplaces` that will store points (`geom_type=ogr.wkbPoint`) using the *WGS 84* spatial reference system (`srs.ImportFromEPSG(4326)`). When creating the layer, we specified other parameters as well such as `dimension` (3, as you want to store the z values), `GEOMETRY_NAME` (the name of the geometric field) and `schema`. After creating the layer, you can use the `CreateField` layer method to create all the fields that are needed to store the information. Each field will have a specific `name` and `datatype` (all of them are `ogr.OFTString` for this case).

After the layer has been created (note that we need to have the `pg_ds` and `pg_layer` objects always in context for the whole script, as noticed at `http://trac.osgeo.org/gdal/wiki/PythonGotchas`), you can query the GeoNames Web services for each place name in the `names.txt` file using the `urllib2` library.

We parsed the JSON response using the `simplejson` library, then iterated the JSON objects list, and added a feature to the PostGIS layer for each of the objects in the JSON output. For each element, we created a feature with a point `wkt` geometry (using the `lng`, `lat`, and `elevation` object attributes) using the `ogr.CreateGeometryFromWkt` method, and updated the other fields using the other object attributes returned by GeoNames using the feature `setField` method (`title`, `countryCode`, and so on).

You can get more information on programming with GDAL Python bindings using the following great resource by Chris Garrard:

`http://www.gis.usu.edu/~chrisg/python/2009/`

## Writing PostGIS functions with PL/Python

In this recipe, you will write a Python function for PostGIS using the PL/Python language. The PL/Python procedural language allows you to write PostgreSQL functions with the Python language.

You will use Python for querying the `openweathermap.org` web services, already used in a previous recipe, to get the weather for a PostGIS geometry from within a PostgreSQL function.

## Getting ready

1.  Verify whether your PostgreSQL server installation has PL/Python support. On Windows, this should be already included, but this is not the default if you are using, for example, Ubuntu 12.4 LTS, so you will most likely need to install it:

    ```
    $ sudo apt-get install postgresql-plpython-9.1
    ```

2.  Install PL/Python on the database (you could consider installing it in your `template1` database; in this way, every newly created database will have PL/Python support by default):

>  You could alternatively add PL/Python support to your database using the `createlang` shell command (this is the only way if you are using a PostgreSQL Version 9.1 or lower):
>
> ```
> $ createlang plpythonu postgis_cookbook
> ```

```
$ psql -U me postgis_cookbook
psql (9.1.6, server 9.1.8)
Type "help" for help.

postgis_cookbook=# CREATE EXTENSION plpythonu;
```

## How to do it...

Carry out the following steps:

1.  In this recipe, as with a previous one, you will use an `openweathermap.org` Web service to get the temperature for a point from the closest weather station. The request you need to run (test it in a browser) is `http://api.openweathermap.org/data/2.1/find/station?long=100.49&lat=13.74&cnt=1`. You should get the following JSON output (the closest weather station's data from which you will read the temperature to the point, with the coordinates of the given longitude and latitude):

    ```
    {
        message: "",
        cod: "200",
        calctime: "",
        cnt: 1,
        list: [
            {
                id: 9191,
                dt: 1369343192,
                name: "100704-1",
                type: 2,
                coord: {
                    lat: 13.7408,
    ```

```
                    lon: 100.5478
                },
                distance: 6.244,
                main: {
                    temp: 300.37
                },
                wind: {
                    speed: 0,
                    deg: 141
                },
                rang: 30,
                rain: {
                    1h: 0,
                    24h: 3.302,
                    today: 0
                }
            }
        }
    ]
}
```

2.  Create the following PostgreSQL function in Python using the PL/Python language:

```
CREATE OR REPLACE FUNCTION chp08.GetWeather(lon float, lat float)
    RETURNS float
AS $$
    import urllib2
    import simplejson as json
    data = urllib2.urlopen(
        'http://api.openweathermap.org/data/2.1/find/
station?lat=%s&lon=%s&cnt=1'
        % (lat, lon))
    js_data = json.load(data)
    if js_data['cod'] == '200': # only if cod is 200 we got some
effective results
                if int(js_data['cnt'])>0: # check if we have at
least a weather station
                    station = js_data['list'][0]
                    print 'Data from weather station %s' %
station['name']
                    if 'main' in station:
                        if 'temp' in station['main']:
                            temperature = station['main']['temp']
- 273.15 # we want the temperature in Celsius
                        else:
                            temperature = None
    else:
            temperature = None
    return temperature
$$ LANGUAGE plpythonu;
```

3. Now, test your function; for example, get the temperature from the closest weather station to Wat Pho Templum in Bangkok:

```
postgis_cookbook=# SELECT chp08.GetWeather(100.49, 13.74);
 getweather
------------
      27.22
(1 row)
```

4. In case you want to get the temperature for the point features in a PostGIS table, you can use the coordinates of each feature's geometry:

```
postgis_cookbook=# SELECT name, temperature, chp08.
GetWeather(ST_X(the_geom), ST_Y(the_geom)) AS temperature2 FROM
chp08.cities LIMIT 5;
```

| name | temperature | temperature2 |
|------|-------------|--------------|
| Minneapolis | 275.15 | 15 |
| Saint Paul | 274.15 | 16 |
| Buffalo | 274.15 | 19.44 |
| New York | 280.93 | 19.44 |
| Jersey City | 282.15 | 21.67 |

```
(5 rows)
```

5. Now it would be nice if our function could accept not only the coordinates of a point but also a true PostGIS geometry as well as an input parameter. For the temperature of a feature, you could return the temperature of the weather station closest to the centroid of the feature geometry. You can easily get this behavior using function overloading. Add a new function, with the same name, supporting a PostGIS geometry directly as an input parameter. In the body of the function, call the previous function, passing the coordinates of the centroid of the geometry. Note that in this case you can write the function without using Python, with the PL/PostgreSQL language:

```
CREATE OR REPLACE FUNCTION chp08.GetWeather(geom geometry)
    RETURNS float
AS $$
    BEGIN
        RETURN chp08.GetWeather(ST_X(ST_Centroid(geom)),
            ST_Y(ST_Centroid(geom)));
    END;
$$ LANGUAGE plpgsql;
```

6. Now test the function, passing a PostGIS geometry to the function:

```
postgis_cookbook=# SELECT chp08.GetWeather(ST_
GeomFromText('POINT(-71.064544 42.28787)'));

 getweather
------------
      23.89
(1 row)
```

7. If you use the function on a PostGIS layer, you can pass the feature's geometries to the function directly, using the overloaded function written in the PL/pgSQL language:

```
postgis_cookbook=# SELECT name, temperature, chp08.GetWeather(the_
geom) AS temperature2 FROM chp08.cities LIMIT 5;
     name     | temperature | temperature2
--------------+-------------+--------------
 Minneapolis  |      275.15 |        17.22
 Saint Paul   |      274.15 |           16
 Buffalo      |      274.15 |        18.89
 New York     |      280.93 |        19.44
 Jersey City  |      282.15 |        21.67
(5 rows)
```

## How it works...

In this recipe, you wrote a Python function in PostGIS using the PL/Python language. Using Python inside PostgreSQL and PostGIS functions gives you the great advantage of using any Python library you wish. Therefore, you will be able to write much more powerful functions compared to those written using the standard PL/PostgreSQL language.

In fact, in this case, you used the urllib2 and simplejson Python libraries to query a web service from within a PostgreSQL function—this would be an impossible operation to do using plain PL/PostgreSQL. You have also seen how to overload functions in order to provide the function's user with a different way to access the function, using input parameters in a different way.

# Geocoding and reverse-geocoding using the GeoNames datasets

In this recipe, you will write two PL/PostgreSQL PostGIS functions that will let you perform geocoding and reverse-geocoding using the GeoNames datasets.

GeoNames is a database of the place names of the world, containing over eight million records that are available for download free of charge. For the purpose of this recipe, you will download a part of the database, load it in PostGIS, and then use it within two functions to perform geocoding and reverse-geocoding. Geocoding is the process of finding coordinates from geographical data such as an address or a place name, while reverse-geocoding is the process of finding geographical data such as an address or place name from its coordinates.

You are going to write the two functions using PL/pgSQL, which adds on top of the PostgreSQL SQL commands the ability to tie more commands and queries together, a bunch of control structures, cursors, error management, and other goodness.

## Getting ready

Download a GeoNames dataset. At the time of downloading, you can find some of the datasets ready to be downloaded from `http://download.geonames.org/export/dump/`. You may decide which dataset you want to use; if you want to follow this recipe, it will be enough to download the Italian dataset, `IT.zip` file (included in the book's dataset, in the `chp08` directory).

In case you want to download the full GeoNames dataset, you need to download the `allCountries.zip` file; it will take a long time as it is about 250 MB.

## How to do it...

Carry out the following steps:

1.  Unzip the `IT.zip` file to the `working/chp08` directory. Two files will be extracted: the `readme.txt` file that contains information on the GeoNames database structure—you can read it to get some more information—and the `IT.txt` file, which is a `.csv` file containing all the GeoNames entities for Italy. As suggested from the `readme.txt` file, the content of the CSV file is composed of records with the following attributes:

    ```
    geonameid        : integer id of record in geonames database
    name             : name of geographical point (utf8) varchar(200)
    asciiname        : name of geographical point in plain ascii
    characters, varchar(200)
    alternatenames   : alternatenames, comma separated varchar(5000)
    ```

```
latitude            : latitude in decimal degrees (wgs84)
longitude           : longitude in decimal degrees (wgs84)
...
```

2. Get an overview of this CSV dataset using `ogrinfo`:

```
$ ogrinfo CSV:IT.txt IT -al -so
INFO: Open of `CSV:IT.txt'
      using driver `CSV' successful.

Layer name: IT
Geometry: Point
Feature Count: 8535
Extent: (1.200000, 35.483330) - (20.750000, 47.083330)
Layer SRS WKT:
(unknown)
GEONAMEID: String (0.0)
NAME: String (0.0)
...
GTOPO30: Integer (0.0)
TIMEZONE: String (0.0)
MODDATE: String (0.0)
```

3. You could query the `IT.txt` file as an OGR entity. For example, analyze one of the dataset features as shown in the following code:

```
$ ogrinfo CSV:IT.txt IT -where "NAME = 'San Gimignano'"
INFO: Open of `IT.vrt'
      using driver `VRT' successful.

    Layer name: IT
    Geometry: Point
    Feature Count: 1
    Extent: (11.042720, 43.469240) - (11.042720, 43.469240)
    Layer SRS WKT:
    GEOGCS["WGS 84",
    ...
    GEONAMEID: String (0.0)
    NAME: String (0.0)
    ASCIINAME: String (0.0)
    ...
    MODDATE: String (0.0)
    OGRFeature(IT):7791
      GEONAMEID (String) = 3168320
      NAME (String) = San Gimignano
      ASCIINAME (String) = San Gimignano
      ...
      MODDATE (String) = 2012-02-15
      POINT (11.04272 43.46924)
```

4. For your purpose, you just need the `name`, `asciiname`, `latitude`, and `longitude` attributes. You will import the file to PostGIS using the CSV OGR driver (`http://www.gdal.org/ogr/drv_csv.html`). Use `ogr2ogr` command to import this GeoNames dataset in PostGIS:

```
$ ogr2ogr -f PostgreSQL -s_srs EPSG:4326 -lco GEOMETRY_NAME=the_
geom -nln chp08.geonames PG:"dbname='postgis_cookbook' user='me'
password='mypassword'" CSV:IT.txt -sql "SELECT NAME, ASCIINAME
FROM IT"
```

5. Try to query the new `geonames` table in PostGIS to see if the process completed correctly:

```
postgis_cookbook=# SELECT ST_AsText(the_geom), name FROM chp08.
geonames ORDER BY name LIMIT 5;

        st_astext           |         name
----------------------------+----------------------
 POINT(6.83333 45.03333)    | Abbazia
 POINT(12.76667 42.95)      | Abbazia di Sassovivo
 POINT(14.49298 37.02504)   | Acate
 POINT(15.10789 37.59765)   | Aci Bonaccorsi
 POINT(15.13459 37.55825)   | Aci Castello

(5 rows)
```

6. Now, create a PL/PostgreSQL function that will return the five closer place names to the given point and their coordinates (the reverse-geocoding process):

```
CREATE OR REPLACE FUNCTION chp08.Get_Closest_PlaceNames(in_geom
geometry, num_results int DEFAULT 5, OUT geom geometry, OUT place_
name character varying)
    RETURNS SETOF RECORD
AS $$
    BEGIN
        RETURN QUERY
        SELECT the_geom as geom, name as place_name
        FROM chp08.geonames
        ORDER BY the_geom <-> ST_Centroid(in_geom) LIMIT num_
results;
    END;
$$ LANGUAGE plpgsql;
```

7. Query the new function. You can specify the number of results you want by passing the optional `num_results` input parameter:

```
postgis_cookbook=# SELECT * FROM chp08.Get_Closest_PlaceNames(ST_
PointFromText('POINT(13.5 42.19)', 4326), 10);
```

8. If you don't specify the `num_results` optional parameter, it will default to five results:

```
postgis_cookbook=# SELECT * FROM chp08.Get_Closest_PlaceNames(ST_
PointFromText('POINT(13.5 42.19)', 4326));
```

9. Now create a PL/pgSQL function that will return a list of place names and geometries containing a text search in their name field (geocoding process):

```
CREATE OR REPLACE FUNCTION chp08.Find_PlaceNames(search_string
text,
        num_results int DEFAULT 5,
        OUT geom geometry,
        OUT place_name character varying)
    RETURNS SETOF RECORD
AS $$
    BEGIN
        RETURN QUERY
        SELECT the_geom as geom, name as place_name
        FROM chp08.geonames
        WHERE name @@ to_tsquery(search_string)
        LIMIT num_results;
    END;
$$ LANGUAGE plpgsql;
```

10. Query this second function to check if it is working properly:

```
postgis_cookbook=# SELECT * FROM chp08.Find_PlaceNames('Rocca',
10);
```

## How it works...

In this recipe, you wrote two PostgreSQL functions to perform geocoding and reverse-geocoding. For both the functions, you defined a set of input and output parameters; after some PL/PostgreSQL processing, you returned a set of records to the function client, given by executing a query.

As the input parameters, the `Get_Closest_PlaceNames` function accepts a PostGIS geometry and an optional `num_results` parameter that is set to a default of five in case the function caller does not provide it. The output of this function is `SETOF RECORD`, which is returned after running a query in the function body (defined by the $$ notation). Here, the query finds the closer places to the centroid of the input geometry. This is done using an indexed nearest neighbor search (KNN index), a new feature available in PostGIS 2.

The `Find_PlaceNames` function accepts as the input parameters a search string to look for and an optional `num_results` parameter, which in this case also is set to a default of 5 if not provided by the function caller. The output is a `SETOF RECORD`, which is returned after running a query that uses the `to_tsquery` PostgreSQL text search function. The results of the query are the places from the database that contain the `search_string` value in the name field.

# Geocoding using the OSM datasets with trigrams

In this recipe, you will use **OpenStreetMap** streets' datasets imported in PostGIS to implement a very basic Python class in order to provide geocoding features to the class consumer. The geocode engine will be based on the implementation of the PostgreSQL trigrams provided by the `contrib` module of PostgreSQL: `pg_trgm`.

A trigram is a group of three consecutive characters contained in a string; it looks very effective to measure the similarity of two strings by counting the number of trigrams they have in common.

This recipe aims to be a very basic sample to implement some kind of geocoding functionalities (it will just return one or more points from a street name), but it could be extended to support more advanced features.

## Getting ready

1. For this recipe, make sure you have the latest GDAL, at least Version 1.10, as you will use it with `ogr2ogr` the new OGR OSM driver (http://www.gdal.org/ogr/drv_osm.html):

   ```
   $ ogrinfo --version
   GDAL 1.10dev, released 2011/12/29
   $ ogrinfo --formats | grep -i osm
     -> "OSM" (readonly)
   ```

2. As you will use PostgreSQL trigrams, install the PostgreSQL `contrib` package (that includes `pg_trgm`). Windows EDB installer should already include this. In a Ubuntu 12.4 box, the following command will help you to do it:

   ```
   $ sudo apt-get install postgresql-contrib-9.1
   ```

3. Make sure to add the `pg_trgm` extension to the database:

   ```
   postgis_cookbook=# CREATE EXTENSION pg_trgm;
   CREATE EXTENSION
   ```

4. You will need to download some OSM datasets to use. Download the area of your city/place or download the `lazio.pbf` OSM file from http://download.gfoss.it/osm/osm/regioni/ if you want to go with the recipe and get similar results (you can find a copy of this file in the `data/chp08` book's dataset directory).

5. If you are using Windows, be sure to have installed the OSGeo4W suite as suggested in the initial instructions of this chapter.

6. If you are using Linux, follow the initial instructions of this chapter and create a Python virtual environment in order to keep a Python-isolated environment to be used for all the Python recipes of this book. Then activate it as follows:

```
$ source postgis-cb-env/bin/activate
```

7. Once the environment has been activated, if you still haven't done it, you can install the Python packages needed for this recipe:

```
(postgis-cb-env)$ pip install gdal
(postgis-cb-env)$ pip install psycopg2
```

## How to do it...

Carry out the following steps:

1. First, check out how the OSM .pbf file is built using ogrinfo. PBF is a binary format intended as an alternative to the OSM XML format, mainly because it is much smaller. As you must have noticed, it is composed of several layers—you will export the lines layer to PostGIS as that layer contains the street names that you will use for the overall geocoding process:

```
$ ogrinfo lazio.pbf
Had to open data source read-only.
INFO: Open of `lazio.pbf'
      using driver `OSM' successful.
1: points (Point)
2: lines (Line String)
3: multilinestrings (Multi Line String)
4: multipolygons (Multi Polygon)

5: other_relations (Geometry Collection)
```

2. Export the lines' OSM features to a PostGIS table using ogr2ogr (ogr2ogr, as always, will implicitly create the GiST index that is needed by the pg_trgm module to run):

```
$ ogr2ogr -f PostgreSQL -lco GEOMETRY_NAME=the_geom -nln
chp08.osm_roads PG:"dbname='postgis_cookbook' user='me'
password='mypassword'" lazio.pbf lines
```

3. Now try a trigram matching to identify the road names similar to a given search text string) using a query like the following. Note that the similarity function returns a value that decreases from 1 to 0 as the similarity of the word decreases (with 1, the strings are identical; with 0, they are totally different):

```
postgis_cookbook=# SELECT name, similarity(name, 'via benedetto
croce') AS sml, ST_AsText(ST_Centroid(the_geom)) AS the_geom
 FROM chp08.osm_roads
 WHERE name % 'via benedetto croce'
 ORDER BY sml DESC, name;
```

```
name                          | sml | the_geom
------------------------------+---------+----------------------
---------------------
 Via Benedetto Croce | 1    | POINT(13.4323581 41.3558496)
 Via Benedetto Croce |      |       1 | POINT(12.067122592122
41.9587406015601)
 Via Benedetto Croce |      |       1 | POINT(14.0540279250186
41.4805402269014)

 . . .
```

4. As a variant, you will use the following query for completing the recipe (in this case, when the weight is 0, the strings are identical):

```
postgis_cookbook=# SELECT name, name <-> 'via benedetto croce' AS
weight
 FROM chp08.osm_roads
 ORDER BY weight LIMIT 10;
          name           | weight
-------------------------+----------
 Via Benedetto Croce     |     0
 Via Benedetto Croce     |     0

 . . .
 Via Benedetto XIV       | 0.416667
 Via Benedetto XIV       | 0.416667

(10 rows)
```

5. We will use the last query as the SQL core of a Python class, which will provide geocoding features to the consumer, using the layer we just imported in PostGIS (chp08.osm_roads). First, create a file named osmgeocoder.py and add the following class to it:

```python
import sys
import psycopg2

class OSMGeocoder(object):
    """
    A class to provide geocoding features using an OSM dataset in
PostGIS.
    """

    def __init__(self, db_connectionstring):
        # initialize db connection parameters
        self.db_connectionstring = db_connectionstring

    def geocode(self, placename):
        """
        Geocode a given place name.
        """
```

```
# here we create the connection object
conn = psycopg2.connect(self.db_connectionstring)
cur = conn.cursor()
# this is the core sql query, using trigrams to detect
streets similiar
# to a given placename
sql = """
    SELECT name, name <-> '%s' AS weight,
    ST_AsText(ST_Centroid(the_geom)) as  point
    FROM chp08.osm_roads
    ORDER BY weight LIMIT 10;
""" % placename
# here we execute the sql and return all of the results
cur.execute(sql)
rows = cur.fetchall()
cur.close()
conn.close()
return rows
```

6.  Now, add the __main__ check to provide the class user with a method to directly use the geocoder from the command line:

```
if __name__ == '__main__':
    # the user must provide at least two parameters, the place
name
    # and the connection string to PostGIS
    if len(sys.argv) < 3 or len(sys.argv) > 3:
        print "usage: <placename> <connection string>"
        raise SystemExit
    placename = sys.argv[1]
    db_connectionstring = sys.argv[2]
    # here we instantiate the geocoder, providing the needed
PostGIS connection
    # parameters
    geocoder = OSMGeocoder(db_connectionstring)
    # here we query the geocode method, for getting the geocoded
points for the
    # given placename
    results = geocoder.geocode(placename)
    print results
```

7.  Now you can test the class by calling the script as shown:

```
(postgis-cb-env)$ python osmgeocoder.py "Via Benedetto Croce"
"dbname=postgis_cookbook user=me password=mypassword"
[('Via Benedetto Croce', 0.0, 'POINT(12.6999095325807
42.058016054317)'),...
```

8. So, now that you wrote a class that can be used to geocode street names, let's suppose that another user wants to use it to geocode a file with a list of street names in order to import it in a new PostGIS layer. Here is how the user could do this (try this as well). First, create a `streets.txt` file with a list of street names, for example:

```
Via Delle Sette Chiese
Via Benedetto Croce
Lungotevere Degli Inventori
Viale Marco Polo

Via Cavour
```

9. Now create a file named `geocode_streets.py`, and add this Python code in it (you are going to use the OSMGeocoder class to geocode the street name list, and GDAL/OGR to create a new PostGIS layer for storing the geocoded points for the street names):

```python
from osmgeocoder import OSMGeocoder
from osgeo import ogr, osr

# here we read the file
f = open('streets.txt')
streets = f.read().splitlines()
f.close()

# here we create the PostGIS layer using gdal/ogr
driver = ogr.GetDriverByName('PostgreSQL')
srs = osr.SpatialReference()
srs.ImportFromEPSG(4326)
pg_ds = ogr.Open(
    "PG:dbname='postgis_cookbook' host='localhost' port='5432'
user='me' password='mypassword'", update = 1 )
pg_layer = pg_ds.CreateLayer('geocoded_points', srs = srs, geom_
type=ogr.wkbPoint,
    options = [
        'GEOMETRY_NAME=the_geom',
        'OVERWRITE=YES', # this will drop and recreate the table
every time
        'SCHEMA=chp08',
    ])
# here we add the field to the PostGIS layer
fd_name = ogr.FieldDefn('name', ogr.OFTString)
pg_layer.CreateField(fd_name)
print 'Table created.'

# now we geocode all of the streets in the file using the
osmgeocoder class
```

```
geocoder = OSMGeocoder('dbname=postgis_cookbook user=me
password=mypassword')
for street in streets:
    print street
    geocoded_street = geocoder.geocode(street)[0]
    print geocoded_street
    # format is
    # ('Via delle Sette Chiese', 0.0, 'POINT(12.5002166330412
41.859774874774)')
    point_wkt = geocoded_street[2]
    point = ogr.CreateGeometryFromWkt(point_wkt)
    # we create a LayerDefn for the feature using the one from the
layer
    featureDefn = pg_layer.GetLayerDefn()
    feature = ogr.Feature(featureDefn)
    # now we store the feature geometry and the value for the name
field
    feature.SetGeometry(point)
    feature.SetField('name', geocoded_street[0])
    # finally we create the feature (an INSERT command is issued
only here)
    pg_layer.CreateFeature(feature)
```

10. Run the preceding script and then check with your favorite PostgreSQL client or with a GIS Desktop tool whether the points for the street names were correctly geocoded:

```
(postgis-cb-env)capooti@ubuntu:~/postgis_cookbook/working/chp08$
python geocode_streets.py
Table created.
Via Delle Sette Chiese
('Via delle Sette Chiese', 0.0, 'POINT(12.5002166330412
41.859774874774)')
...
Via Cavour
('Via Cavour', 0.0, 'POINT(12.7519263341222 41.9631244835521)')
```

## How it works...

For this recipe, you first downloaded and imported an OSM dataset to PostGIS with ogr2ogr using the GDAL OSM driver.

Then, you created a Python class, OSMGeocoder, to provide a very basic support to the class consumer for geocoding streets names using the OSM data imported in PostGIS. For this purpose, you have used the trigrams support included in PostgreSQL with the pg_trgm contrib module.

The class that you have written is mainly composed of two methods: the `__init__` method, where the connection parameters must be passed in order to instantiate an `OSMGeocoder` object, and the `geocode` method. The `geocode` method accepts an input parameter, `placename`, and creates a connection to the PostGIS database using the Psycopg2 library in order to execute a query to find the streets in the database with a name similar to the `placename` parameter.

The class can be consumed both from the command line, using the `__name__ == '__main__'` code block, or from an external Python code. You tried both the approaches. In the latter, you created another Python script, where you imported the `OSMGeocoder` class combined with the GDAL/OGR Python bindings to generate a new PostGIS point layer with features resulting from a list of geocoded street names.

# Geocoding with geopy and PL/Python

In this recipe, you will geocode addresses using a web geocoding API such as Google Maps, Yahoo! Maps, geocoder.us, GeoNames, and so on. Be sure to read the Terms of Services of these APIs carefully before using them in production.

The `geopy` Python library (`http://code.google.com/p/geopy/`) offers a convenient, uniform access to all of these web services. Therefore, you will use it to create a PL/Python PostgreSQL function that can be used in your SQL commands to query all of these engines.

## Getting ready

1.  Install `geopy` globally. (You cannot use a virtual environment in this case, as the user running the PostgreSQL service needs to access it on its Python path.)

    In a Debian/Ubuntu box, it is as easy as typing the following:

    ```
    $ sudo pip install geopy
    ```

    In Windows, you can use the following command:

    ```
    > pip install geopy
    ```

2.  If you still did not use PL/Python, verify whether your PostgreSQL server installation supports it. The Windows EDB installer should already include this support, but this is not the default if you are using, for example, Ubuntu 12.4 LTS, so you most likely need to install it:

    ```
    $ sudo apt-get install postgresql-plpython-9.1
    ```

3. Install PL/Python on the database (you could consider installing it in the `template1` database; this way, every newly created database will have PL/Python support by default):

```
$ psql -U me postgis_cookbook
psql (9.1.6, server 9.1.8)
Type "help" for help.

postgis_cookbook=# CREATE EXTENSION plpythonu;
```

> Alternatively, you could add PL/Python support to your database using the `createlang` shell command (this is the only way if you are using a PostgreSQL Version 9.0 and lower):
>
> ```
> $ createlang plpythonu postgis_cookbook
> ```

## How to do it...

Carry out the following steps:

1. As the first test, open your favorite SQL client (`psql` or `pgAdmin`), and write a very basic PL/Python function just using the GoogleV3 geocoding API with `geopy`. The function will accept the address string as an input parameter and, after importing `geopy`, it will instantiate a `geopy` Google Geocoder, run the geocode process, and then return the point geometry using the `ST_GeomFromText` function and the `geopy` output:

```
CREATE OR REPLACE FUNCTION chp08.Geocode(address text)
        RETURNS geometry(Point,4326)
    AS $$
        from geopy import geocoders
        g = geocoders.GoogleV3()
        place, (lat, lng) = g.geocode(address)
        plpy.info('Geocoded %s for the address: %s' % (place,
address))
        plpy.info('Longitude is %s, Latitude is %s.' % (lng, lat))
        plpy.info("SELECT ST_GeomFromText('POINT(%s %s)', 4326)" %
(lng, lat))
        result = plpy.execute("SELECT ST_GeomFromText('POINT(%s
%s)', 4326) AS point_geocoded" % (lng, lat))
        geometry = result[0]["point_geocoded"]
        return geometry
    $$ LANGUAGE plpythonu;
```

2. After creating the function, try to test it:

```
postgis_cookbook=# SELECT chp08.Geocode('Viale Ostiense 36,
Rome');
INFO:  Geocoded Via Ostiense, 36, 00154 Rome, Italy for the
address: Viale Ostiense 36, Rome
CONTEXT:  PL/Python function "geocode"
INFO:  Longitude is 12.480457, Latitude is 41.874345.
CONTEXT:  PL/Python function "geocode"
INFO:  SELECT ST_GeomFromText('POINT(12.480457 41.874345)', 4326)
CONTEXT:  PL/Python function "geocode"
                        geocode
--------------------------------------------------
 0101000020E6100000BF44BC75FEF52840E7357689EAEF4440
(1 row)
```

3. Now, you will make the function a little bit more sophisticated. First, you will add another input parameter to let the user specify the geoocode API engine (defaulting to GoogleV3). Then, using the Python `try...except` block, you will try to set up some kind of error management in case the geopy Geocoder cannot manage to return valid results for any reason:

```
CREATE OR REPLACE FUNCTION chp08.Geocode(address text, api text
DEFAULT 'google')
    RETURNS geometry(Point,4326)
AS $$
    from geopy import geocoders
    plpy.info('Geocoing the given address using the %s api' %
(api))
    if api.lower() == 'geonames':
        g = geocoders.GeoNames()
    elif api.lower() == 'geocoderdotus':
        g = geocoders.GeocoderDotUS()
    else: # if the user give a wrong api name we use google
        g = geocoders.GoogleV3()
    try:
        place, (lat, lng) = g.geocode(address)
        plpy.info('Geocoded %s for the address: %s' % (place,
address))
        plpy.info('Longitude is %s, Latitude is %s.' % (lng, lat))
        result = plpy.execute("SELECT ST_GeomFromText('POINT(%s
%s)', 4326) AS point_geocoded" % (lng, lat))
        geometry = result[0]["point_geocoded"]
```

```
        return geometry

    except:

        plpy.warning('There was an error in the geocoding process,
setting geometry to Null.')

        return None

$$ LANGUAGE plpythonu;
```

4. Test the new version of your function without specifying the parameter for the API. In such a case, it should default to the Google API:

```
postgis_cookbook=# SELECT chp08.Geocode('161 Court Street,
Brooklyn, NY');
INFO:  Geocoing the given address using the google api
CONTEXT:   PL/Python function "geocode2"
INFO:  Geocoded 161 Court Street, Brooklyn, NY 11201, USA for the
address: 161 Court Street, Brooklyn, NY
CONTEXT:   PL/Python function "geocode2"
INFO:  Longitude is -73.9924659, Latitude is 40.688665.
CONTEXT:   PL/Python function "geocode2"
INFO:  SELECT ST_GeomFromText('POINT(-73.9924659 40.688665)', 4326)
CONTEXT:   PL/Python function "geocode2"
                          geocode2
--------------------------------------------------
 0101000020E61000004BB9B18F847F52C02E73BA2C26584440
(1 row)
```

5. If you test it by specifying a different API, it should return the result processed for the given API. For example:

```
postgis_cookbook=# SELECT chp08.Geocode('161 Court Street,
Brooklyn, NY', 'GeocoderDotUS');
INFO:  Geocoing the given address using the GeocoderDotUS api
CONTEXT:   PL/Python function "geocode2"
INFO:  Geocoded 161 Court St, New York, NY 11201 for the address:
161 Court Street, Brooklyn, NY
CONTEXT:   PL/Python function "geocode2"
INFO:  Longitude is -73.992809, Latitude is 40.688774.
CONTEXT:   PL/Python function "geocode2"
INFO:  SELECT ST_GeomFromText('POINT(-73.992809 40.688774)', 4326)
CONTEXT:   PL/Python function "geocode2"
                          geocode2
--------------------------------------------------
 0101000020E61000002A8BC22E8A7F52C0E52A16BF29584440
(1 row)
```

6. As a bonus step, create a table in PostgreSQL with street addresses, and generate a new point PostGIS layer storing the geocoded points returned by the Geocode function.

## How it works...

You wrote a PL/Python function to geocode an address. For this purpose, you used the `geopy` Python library that let you query several geocoding APIs in the same manner.

Using geopy, you need to instantiate a `geocoder` object with a given API and query it to get the results such as a place name and a couple of coordinates. You can use the `plpy` module utilities to run a query to the database using the PostGIS `ST_GeomFromText` function and to log informative messages and warnings to the user.

In case the geocoding process fails, you return a `NULL` geometry to the user with a warning message, using a `try..except` Python block.

# Importing netCDF datasets with Python and GDAL

In this recipe, you will write a Python script to import data from the netCDF format to PostGIS.

netCDF is an open standard format, widely used for scientific applications, that can contain multiple raster datasets, each composed of a spectrum of bands. For this purpose, you will use the GDAL Python bindings and the popular Numpy scientific library.

## Getting ready

1. If you are using Windows, be sure to install OSGeo4W, as suggested in the initial instructions of this chapter, that will include Python and GDAL Python bindings with Numpy support.

   For Linux users, if you did not do it, follow the initial instructions of this chapter and create a Python virtual environment, in order to keep a Python-isolated environment to be used for all the Python recipes of this book, and activate it:

   ```
   $ source postgis-cb-env/bin/activate
   ```

2. For this recipe, you need the GDAL Python bindings and Numpy, the latest being needed by some GDAL methods (`ReadAsArray`) for arrays. In the most likely scenario, you have already installed GDAL in your virtual environment as you have been using it for other recipes; so be sure to remove it and reinstall it after installing Numpy. In fact, GDAL needs to be compiled with Numpy support if you want to use its array's features:

```
(postgis-cb-env)$ pip uninstall gdal
(postgis-cb-env)$ pip install numpy
(postgis-cb-env)$ pip install gdal
```

3. For the purpose of this recipe, you will use a sample dataset from the NOAA Earth System Research Laboratory (ESRL). The excellent ESRL web portal offers a plethora of data in the netCDF format to be freely downloaded. For example, download the following dataset from the ESRL CPC Soil Moisture data repository (you can find, as usual, a copy of this dataset in the book's dataset directory for this chapter):

```
http://www.esrl.noaa.gov/psd/thredds/fileServer/Datasets/
cpcsoil/soilw.mon.ltm.v2.nc
```

## How to do it...

Carry out the following steps:

1. As the first step, investigate the netCDF format of the dataset you downloaded using `gdalinfo`. This kind of dataset is composed of several subdatasets, as you must have realized looking at the `gdalinfo` output:

```
$ gdalinfo NETCDF:"soilw.mon.ltm.v2.nc"
Driver: netCDF/Network Common Data Format
Files: none associated
Size is 512, 512
Coordinate System is `'
Metadata:
  NC_GLOBAL#Conventions=CF-1.0
  NC_GLOBAL#history=Created 2011/08/31 by doMonthLTM
  NC_GLOBAL#institution=NOAA/ESRL PSD
  NC_GLOBAL#not_missing_threshold_percent=minimum 3% values input
to have non-missing output value
  NC_GLOBAL#references=http://www.cpc.ncep.noaa.gov/soilmst/index.
htm
http://www.esrl.noaa.gov/psd/data/gridded/data.cpcsoil.html
  NC_GLOBAL#title=CPC Soil Moisture
```

```
Subdatasets:
  SUBDATASET_1_NAME=NETCDF:"soilw.mon.ltm.v2.nc":climatology_
bounds
  SUBDATASET_1_DESC=[12x2] climatology_bounds (64-bit floating-
point)
  SUBDATASET_2_NAME=NETCDF:"soilw.mon.ltm.v2.nc":soilw
  SUBDATASET_2_DESC=[12x360x720] lwe_thickness_of_soil_moisture_
content (32-bit floating-point)
  SUBDATASET_3_NAME=NETCDF:"soilw.mon.ltm.v2.nc":valid_yr_count
  SUBDATASET_3_DESC=[12x360x720] valid_yr_count (16-bit integer)
Corner Coordinates:
Upper Left  (     0.0,     0.0)
Lower Left  (     0.0,   512.0)
Upper Right (   512.0,     0.0)
Lower Right (   512.0,   512.0)
Center      (   256.0,   256.0)
```

2.  Use `gdalinfo` to investigate one of the file's subdatasets. The syntax that the netCDF GDAL driver (`http://www.gdal.org/frmt_netcdf.html`) uses is to append a colon followed by the variable name at the end of the filename. For example, try to figure out how many bands make up the `soilw` subdataset. This subdataset, representing the `lwe_thickness_of_soil_moisture_content`, is composed of 12 bands. Each band, according to the information derived by its metadata, represents the CPC Monthly Soil Moisture for a given month. The month is identified by the `NETCDF_DIM_time` metadata value, which is the number of days from the beginning of the year (`0` for January, `31` for February, `59` for March, and so on):

```
$ gdalinfo NETCDF:"soilw.mon.ltm.v2.nc":soilw
Driver: netCDF/Network Common Data Format
Files: none associated
Size is 512, 512
Coordinate System is `'
Metadata:
  NC_GLOBAL#Conventions=CF-1.0
  ...(other metadata)...
Band 1 Block=720x1 Type=Float32, ColorInterp=Undefined
  NoData Value=-9.96920996838686905e+36
  Metadata:
    actual_range={1.8626451e-06,743.505}
    add_offset=0
    cell_methods=time: mean (monthly from values)
    dataset=CPC Monthly Soil Moisture
    level_desc=Surface
    long_name=Model-Calculated Long Term Monthly Mean Soil
Moisture
```

```
missing_value=-9.96921e+36
NETCDF_DIM_time=0
NETCDF_VARNAME=soilw
parent_stat=Other
scale_factor=1
standard_name=lwe_thickness_of_soil_moisture_content
statistic=Long Term Mean
units=mm
valid_range={0,1000}
var_desc=Soil Moisture
...(other 11 bands)...
```

3. What you are going to do is create a Python script using GDAL and Numpy. You will read a given netCDF dataset, iterate its subdatasets, and then iterate each subdataset's bands. For each subdataset, you will create a point PostGIS layer, and you will add a field for each band in order to store the band values in the layer table. Then, you will iterate the band's cells; for each cell, you will add a point in the layer with the corresponding band's values. Therefore, create a `netcdf2postgis.py` file and add the following Python code to it:

```python
import sys
from osgeo import gdal, ogr, osr
from osgeo.gdalconst import GA_ReadOnly, GA_Update


def netcdf2postgis(file_nc, pg_connection_string, postgis_table_
prefix):
    # register gdal drivers
    gdal.AllRegister()
    # postgis driver, needed to create the tables
    driver = ogr.GetDriverByName('PostgreSQL')
    srs = osr.SpatialReference()
    # for simplicity we will assume all of the bands in the
datasets are in the
    # same spatial reference, wgs 84
    srs.ImportFromEPSG(4326)

    # first, check if dataset exists
    ds = gdal.Open(file_nc, GA_ReadOnly)
    if ds is None:
        print 'Cannot open ' + file_nc
        sys.exit(1)

    # 1. iterate subdatasets
    for sds in ds.GetSubDatasets():
        dataset_name = sds[0]
        variable = sds[0].split(':')[-1]
```

```
            print 'Importing from %s the variable %s...' % (dataset_
name, variable)
            # open subdataset and read its properties
            sds = gdal.Open(dataset_name, GA_ReadOnly)
            cols = sds.RasterXSize
            rows = sds.RasterYSize
            bands = sds.RasterCount

            # create a PostGIS table for the subdataset variable
            table_name = '%s_%s' % (postgis_table_prefix, variable)
            pg_ds = ogr.Open(pg_connection_string, GA_Update )
            pg_layer = pg_ds.CreateLayer(table_name, srs = srs, geom_
type=ogr.wkbPoint,
                options = [
                    'GEOMETRY_NAME=the_geom',
                    'OVERWRITE=YES', # this will drop and recreate the
table every time
                    'SCHEMA=chp08',
                ])
            print 'Table %s created.' % table_name

            # get georeference transformation information
            transform = sds.GetGeoTransform()
            pixelWidth = transform[1]
            pixelHeight = transform[5]
            xOrigin = transform[0] + (pixelWidth/2)
            yOrigin = transform[3] - (pixelWidth/2)

            # 2. iterate subdataset bands and append them to data
            data = []
            for b in range(1, bands+1):
                band = sds.GetRasterBand(b)
                band_data = band.ReadAsArray(0, 0, cols, rows)
                data.append(band_data)
                # here we add the fields to the table, a field for
each band
                # check datatype (Float32, 'Float64', ...)
                datatype = gdal.GetDataTypeName(band.DataType)
                ogr_ft = ogr.OFTString # default for a field is string
                if datatype in ('Float32', 'Float64'):
                    ogr_ft = ogr.OFTReal
                elif datatype in ('Int16', 'Int32'):
                    ogr_ft = ogr.OFTInteger
                # here we add the field to the PostGIS layer
```

```
            fd_band = ogr.FieldDefn('band_%s' % b, ogr_ft)
            pg_layer.CreateField(fd_band)
            print 'Field band_%s created.' % b

        # 3. iterate rows and cols
        for r in range(0, rows):
            y = yOrigin + (r * pixelHeight)
            for c in range(0, cols):
                x = xOrigin + (c * pixelWidth)
                # for each cell, let's add a point feature in the
PostGIS table
                point_wkt = 'POINT(%s %s)' % (x, y)
                point = ogr.CreateGeometryFromWkt(point_wkt)
                featureDefn = pg_layer.GetLayerDefn()
                feature = ogr.Feature(featureDefn)
                # now iterate bands, and add a value for each
table's field
                for b in range(1, bands+1):
                    band = sds.GetRasterBand(1)
                    datatype = gdal.GetDataTypeName(band.DataType)
                    value = data[b-1][r,c]
                    print 'Storing a value for variable %s in
point x: %s, y: %s, band: %s, value: %s' % (variable, x, y, b,
value)
                    if datatype in ('Float32', 'Float64'):
                        value = float(data[b-1][r,c])
                    elif datatype in ('Int16', 'Int32'):
                        value = int(data[b-1][r,c])
                    else:
                        value = data[r,c]
                    feature.SetField('band_%s' % b, value)
                # set the feature's geometry and finalize its
creation
                feature.SetGeometry(point)
                pg_layer.CreateFeature(feature)
```

4. To run the `netcdf2postgis` method from the command line, add the entry point for the script. The code will check whether the script user is correctly using the three needed parameters—the netCDF file path, the GDAL PostGIS connection string, and a prefix/suffix to use for table names in PostGIS:

```
if __name__ == '__main__':
    # the user must provide at least three parameters, the netCDF
file path, the PostGIS GDAL connection string
    # and the prefix suffix to use for PostGIS table names
    if len(sys.argv) < 4 or len(sys.argv) > 4:
```

```
        print "usage: <netCDF file path> <GDAL PostGIS connection
string><PostGIS table prefix>"
        raise SystemExit
    file_nc = sys.argv[1]
    pg_connection_string = sys.argv[2]
    postgis_table_prefix = sys.argv[3]
    netcdf2postgis(file_nc, pg_connection_string, postgis_table_
prefix)
```

5.  Run the script. Be sure to use the correct netCDF file path, GDAL PostGIS connection string (check the format from `http://www.gdal.org/ogr/drv_pg.html`), and a table prefix that has to be appended to the table names for the tables that will be created in PostGIS:

```
(postgis-cb-env)$ python netcdf2postgis.py NETCDF:"soilw.mon.1tm.
v2.nc" "PG:dbname='postgis_cookbook' host='localhost' port='5432'
user='me' password='mypassword'" netcdf
Importing from NETCDF:"soilw.mon.1tm.v2.nc":climatology_bounds the
variable climatology_bounds...
...
Importing from NETCDF:"soilw.mon.1tm.v2.nc":soilw the variable
soilw...
Table netcdf_soilw created.
Field band_1 created.
Field band_2 created.
...
Field band_11 created.
Field band_12 created.
Storing a value for variable soilw in point x: 0.25, y: 89.75,
band: 2, value: -9.96921e+36
Storing a value for variable soilw in point x: 0.25, y: 89.75,
band: 3, value: -9.96921e+36
...
```

6.  At the end of the process, check the results by opening one of the output PostGIS tables using your favorite Desktop GIS tool. The following screenshot shows how it looks in QGIS the `soilw` layer with the original netCDF dataset behind it:

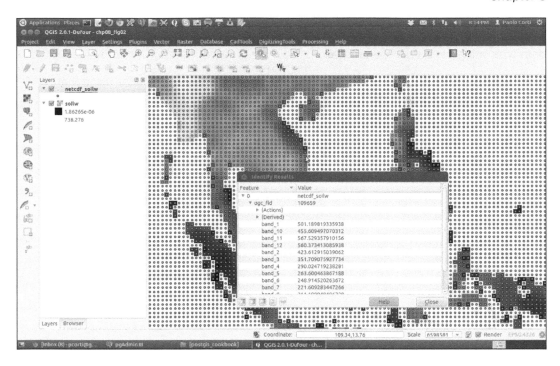

## How it works...

You have used Python with GDAL and Numpy in order to create a command-line utility to import a netCDF dataset into PostGIS.

A netCDF dataset is composed of multiple subdatasets; each subdataset is composed of multiple raster bands. Each band is composed of cells. This structure should be clear to you after investigating a sample netCDF dataset using the gdalinfo GDAL command tool.

There are several approaches to export the cell values to PostGIS. The approach you adopted here is to generate a PostGIS Point layer for each subdataset, which is composed of one field for each subdataset band. You then iterated the raster cells and appended a point to the PostGIS layer with the values read from each cell band.

The way you do this with Python is by using the GDAL Python bindings. For reading, you open the netCDF dataset and for updating, you open the PostGIS database using the correct GDAL and OGR drivers. Then you iterate the netCDF subdatasets using the GetSubDatasets method and create for each subdataset a PostGIS table named as the netCDF subdataset variable (with the prefix) using the CreateLayer method.

For each subdataset, you iterate its bands using the GetRasterBand method. For reading each band, you run the ReadAsArray method that uses Numpy to get the band as an array.

For each band, you create a field in the PostGIS layer with the correct field data type that will be able to store the band's values. To choose the correct data type, you investigate the band's data type using the `DataType` property.

Finally, you iterate the raster cells, by reading the correct *x* and *y* coordinates using the subdataset transform parameters, available via the `GetGeoTransform` method. For each cell, you create a point with the `CreateGeometryFromWkt` method and then set the fields values, read from the band array, using the `SetField` feature method.

Finally, you append the new point to the PostGIS layer using the `CreateFeature` method.

# 9
# PostGIS and the Web

In this chapter, we will cover the following topics:

- ▶ Creating WMS and WFS services with MapServer
- ▶ Creating WMS and WFS services with GeoServer
- ▶ Creating a WMS Time with MapServer
- ▶ Consuming WMS services with OpenLayers
- ▶ Consuming WMS services with Leaflet
- ▶ Consuming WFS-T services with OpenLayers
- ▶ Developing web applications with GeoDjango – part 1
- ▶ Developing web applications with GeoDjango – part 2

## Introduction

In this chapter, we will try to give you an overview of how you can use PostGIS to develop powerful GIS web applications, using **Open Geospatial Consortium** (**OGC**) web standards such as **Web Map Service** (**WMS**) and **Web Feature Service** (**WFS**).

In the first two recipes, you will get an overview of two very popular open-source web-mapping engines—**MapServer** and **GeoServer**. In both of these recipes, you will see how to implement the WMS and WFS services using PostGIS layers.

In the third recipe, you will implement a **WMS Time** service using MapServer to expose time-series data.

In the next two recipes, you will learn how to consume these web services to create a web map viewer with two very popular JavaScript clients. In the fourth recipe, you will use a WMS service with **OpenLayers**, while in the fifth recipe, you will do the same thing using **Leaflet**.

In the sixth recipe, you will explore the power of **transactional WFS** to create web-mapping applications that are able to edit data.

Finally, in the last two recipes, you will unleash the power of the popular **Django** web framework, which is based on Python, and its nice **GeoDjango** library, and see how it is possible to implement a powerful **CRUD** GIS web application. In the seventh recipe, you will create the back office for this application using the Django Admin site, and in the last recipe of the chapter, you will develop a frontend for users to display data from the application in a web map based on Leaflet.

# Creating WMS and WFS services with MapServer

In this recipe, you will see how to create a **Web Map Service** (**WMS**) and **Web Feature Service** (**WFS**) from a PostGIS layer, using the popular MapServer open-source web-mapping engine.

You will then use the services, testing their exposed requests, using first a browser and then a desktop tool such as QGIS (you could do this using other software, such as uDig, gvSIG, and OpenJUMP GIS).

## Getting ready

Follow these steps before getting ready:

1. Create a schema for this chapter within the postgis_cookbook database using the following command:

   **postgis_cookbook=# create schema chp09;**

2. Be sure to have Apache HTTP installed (MapServer will run on it as a CGI), and check whether or not it is working by visiting its home page at http://localhost (typically, an "It works!" message will be displayed if you still have not customized any features).

3. Install MapServer as per its installation guide (http://mapserver.org/en/installation/).

A handy way to have MapServer up and running in Apache for Windows is to install the OSGeo4W (http://trac.osgeo.org/osgeo4w/) or MS4W (http://www.maptools.org/ms4w/) packages.

For Linux, there are packages for almost any kind of distribution.

4. Check whether or not MapServer has been installed correctly and has `WMS_SERVER` and `WFS_SERVER` support enabled by running it as a command-line tool with the `-v` option.

   On Linux, run the `$ /usr/lib/cgi-bin/mapserv -v` command and check for the for following output:

   ```
   MapServer version 6.2.1 OUTPUT=GIF OUTPUT=PNG OUTPUT=JPEG
   SUPPORTS=PROJ SUPPORTS=GD SUPPORTS=AGG SUPPORTS=FREETYPE
   SUPPORTS=CAIRO SUPPORTS=SVG_SYMBOLS SUPPORTS=ICONV
   SUPPORTS=FRIBIDI SUPPORTS=WMS_SERVER SUPPORTS=WMS_CLIENT
   SUPPORTS=WFS_SERVER SUPPORTS=WFS_CLIENT SUPPORTS=WCS_SERVER
   SUPPORTS=SOS_SERVER SUPPORTS=FASTCGI SUPPORTS=THREADS
   SUPPORTS=GEOS INPUT=JPEG INPUT=POSTGIS INPUT=OGR INPUT=GDAL
   INPUT=SHAPEFILE
   ```

   On Windows, run the following command:

   ```
   > c:\ms4w\Apache\cgi-bin\mapserv.exe -v
   ```

5. Now, check whether MapServer is working from within httpd, using `http://localhost/cgi-bin/mapserv` (`http://localhost/cgi-bin/mapserv.exe` for Windows). If you get a `No query information to decode. QUERY_STRING is set, but empty` response message, MapServer is correctly working as a CGI script in Apache and is ready to accept http requests.

6. Download the world countries shapefile from `http://thematicmapping.org/downloads/TM_WORLD_BORDERS-0.3.zip`. A copy of this shapefile is included in the book dataset. Extract the shapefile to the `working/chp09` directory and import it in PostGIS using the **shp2pgsql** tool (be sure to specify the spatial reference system, *EPSG:4326*, with the `-s` option), as follows:

   ```
   $ shp2pgsql -s 4326 -W LATIN1 -g the_geom -I TM_WORLD_BORDERS-
   0.3.shp chp09.countries > countries.sql

   Shapefile type: Polygon

   Postgis type: MULTIPOLYGON[2]

   $ psql -U me -d postgis_cookbook -f countries.sql
   ```

## How to do it...

Carry out the following steps:

1. MapServer exposes its map services using **mapfile**, a text file format, with which it is possible to define the PostGIS layers on the Web, enable any vector and raster format supported by GDAL, and specify which services (WMS/WFS/WCS) to expose per layer. Create a new text file named `countries.map` and add the following code:

   ```
   MAP # Start of mapfile
     NAME 'population_per_country_map'
   ```

```
IMAGETYPE          PNG
EXTENT             -180 -90 180 90
SIZE               800 400
IMAGECOLOR         255 255 255

# map projection definition
PROJECTION
  'init=epsg:4326'
END

# web section: here we define the ows services
WEB
  # WMS and WFS server settings
  METADATA
    'ows_enable_request'          '*'
    'ows_title'                   'Mapserver sample map'
    'ows_abstract'                'OWS services about
                                  population per
                                  country map'
    'wms_onlineresource'          'http://localhost/cgi-
                                  bin/mapserv?map=/var
                                  /www/data/
                                  countries.map&'
    'ows_srs'                     'EPSG:4326 EPSG:900913
                                  EPSG:3857'
    'wms_enable_request'          'GetCapabilities,
                                  GetMap,
                                  GetFeatureInfo'
    'wms_feature_info_mime_type'  'text/html'
  END
END

# Start of layers definition
LAYER # Countries polygon layer begins here
  NAME             countries
  CONNECTIONTYPE   POSTGIS
  CONNECTION       'host=localhost dbname=postgis_cookbook
                   user=me
                      password=mypassword port=5432'
  DATA             'the_geom from chp09.countries'
  TEMPLATE 'template.html'
  METADATA
    'ows_title' 'countries'
    'ows_abstract' 'OWS service about population per
      country map in 2005'
    'gml_include_items' 'all'
  END
  STATUS           ON
  TYPE             POLYGON
  # layer projection definition
```

```
PROJECTION
  'init=epsg:4326'
END

# we define 3 population classes based on the pop2005
  attribute
CLASSITEM 'pop2005'
CLASS # first class
  NAME '0 - 50M inhabitants'
  EXPRESSION ( ([pop2005] >= 0) AND ([pop2005] <=
  50000000) )
  STYLE
    WIDTH 1
    OUTLINECOLOR 0 0 0
    COLOR 254 240 217
  END # end of style
END # end of first class
CLASS # second class
  NAME '50M - 200M inhabitants'
  EXPRESSION ( ([pop2005] > 50000000) AND
  ([pop2005] <= 200000000) )
  STYLE
    WIDTH 1
    OUTLINECOLOR 0 0 0
    COLOR 252 141 89
  END # end of style
END # end of second class
CLASS # third class
  NAME '> 200M inhabitants'
  EXPRESSION ( ([pop2005] > 200000000) )
  STYLE
    WIDTH 1
    OUTLINECOLOR 0 0 0
    COLOR 179 0 0
  END # end of style
END # end of third class

END # Countries polygon layer ends here

END # End of mapfile
```

2. Save the file we just created in a location that is accessible to the Apache user. For example, in Debian, it is /var/www/data, while in Windows, it can be C:\ms4w\ Apache\htdocs. Be sure that both the file and the directory containing it are accessible to the Apache user.

3. Create a file named `template.html` in the same location as the map file and enter the following code in it (this file is used by the GetFeatureInfo WMS request to output an HTML response to the client):

```
<!-- MapServer Template -->
<ul>
  <li><strong>Name: </strong>[item name=name]</li>
  <li><strong>ISO2: </strong>[item name=iso2]</li>
  <li><strong>ISO3: </strong>[item name=iso3]</li>
  <li><strong>Population 2005: </strong>[item
    name=pop2005]</li>
</ul>
```

4. With the mapfile you just created, you exposed the `countries` PostGIS layer, both as a WMS and WFS service. Both of these services expose to the user a series of requests, and you will now test them using a browser. First, without invoking any services, test whether or not the mapfile is working correctly by typing either of the following URLs in the browser:

   - `http://localhost/cgi-bin/mapserv?map=/var/www/data/countries.map&layer=countries&mode=map` (for Linux)

   - `http://localhost/cgi-bin/mapserv.exe?map=C:\ms4w\Apache\htdocs\countries.map&layer=countries&mode=map` (for Windows)

You should see the `countries` layer rendered with the three symbology classes defined in the mapfile, as shown in the following screenshot:

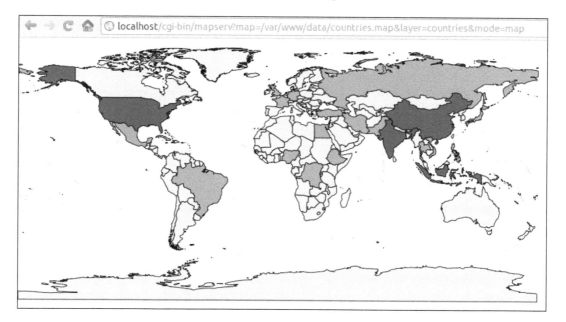

As you can see, there is a small difference between the URLs used in Windows and Linux. We will refer to Linux from now on, but you can easily adapt the URLs to Windows..

5.  Now, you will start testing the WMS service; you will try running the GetCapabilities, GetMap, and GetFeatureInfo requests. To test the GetCapabilities request, type this URL in the browser: http://localhost/ cgi-bin/mapserv?map=/var/www/data/countries.map&SERVICE=WMS& VERSION=1.1.1&REQUEST=GetCapabilities. You should receive a long XML response (shown as follows) from the server, where the more important fragments are the WMS service definitions in the <Service> section, the requests are enabled in the <Capability> section, and the layers exposed and their main details (for example, name, abstract, projection, and extent) are in the <Layer> section of each of the layers:

```
<WMT_MS_Capabilities version="1.1.1">
...
<Service>
  <Name>OGC:WMS</Name>
  <Title>Population per country map</Title>
  <Abstract>Map server sample map</Abstract>
  <OnlineResource
    xmlns:xlink="http://www.w3.org/1999/xlink"
    xlink:href="http://localhost/cgi-
    bin/mapserv?map=/var/www/data/countries.map&amp;"/>
  <ContactInformation>
  </ContactInformation>
</Service>
<Capability>
  <Request>
    <GetCapabilities>
      ...
    </GetCapabilities>
    <GetMap>
      <Format>image/png</Format>
      ...
      <Format>image/tiff</Format>
      ...
    </GetMap>
    <GetFeatureInfo>
      <Format>text/plain</Format>
      ...
    </GetFeatureInfo>
  ...
  </Request>
  ...
```

```
<Layer>
  <Name>population_per_country_map</Name>
  <Title>Population per country map</Title>
  <Abstract>OWS service about population per country map
    in 2005</Abstract>
  <SRS>EPSG:4326</SRS>
  <SRS>EPSG:3857</SRS>
  <LatLonBoundingBox minx="-180" miny="-90" maxx="180"
    maxy="90" />
  ...
  </Layer>
 </Layer>
</Capability>
</WMT_MS_Capabilities>
```

6. Now, test the WMS service with its typical `GetMap` WMS request, used on many clients to display a map to the user. Type the URL, `http://localhost//cgi-bin/mapserv?map=/var/www/data/countries.map&&SERVICE=WMS&VERSION=1.3.0&REQUEST=GetMap&BBOX=-26,-111,36,-38&CRS=EPSG:4326&WIDTH=1000&HEIGHT=800&LAYERS=countries&STYLES=&FORMAT=image/png`, in the browser and check the image that is sent back in response by the MapServer `GetMap` request, as shown in the following screenshot:

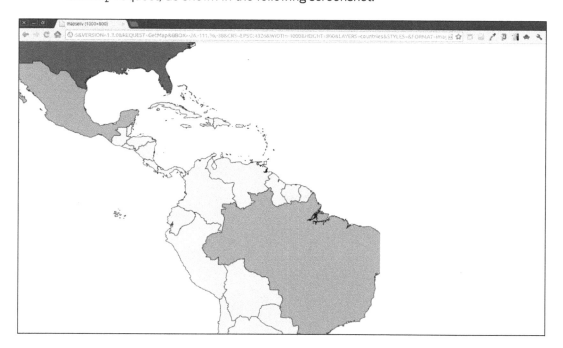

7. Another typical WMS request is `GetFeatureInfo`, used by the clients to query the map layer at the given coordinates (points). Type the following URL and you should see the field values for a given feature as the output (the output is built using the `template.html` file):

   ```
   http://localhost/cgi-bin/mapserv?map=/var/www/data/countries.
   map&layer=countries&REQUEST=GetFeatureInfo&SERVICE=WMS&
   VERSION=1.1.1&LAYERS=countries&QUERY_LAYERS=countries&S
   RS=EPSG:4326&BBOX=-122.545074509804,37.6736653056517,-
   122.35457254902,37.8428758708189&X=652&Y=368&WIDTH=1020&HEIGHT=
   906&INFO_FORMAT=text/html
   ```

8. Now you will use QGIS to use the WMS service. Launch QGIS, click on the **Add WMS layer** button (alternatively, navigate to **Layer | Add WMS Layer** or use the QGIS browser), and create a new WMS connection, as shown in the following screenshot. Type something like `MapServer on localhost` in the **Name** field and `http://localhost/cgi-bin/mapserv?map=/var/www/data/countries.map&SERVICE=WMS&VERSION=1.1.1&REQUEST=GetCapabilities` in the **URL** field, and click on the **OK** button:

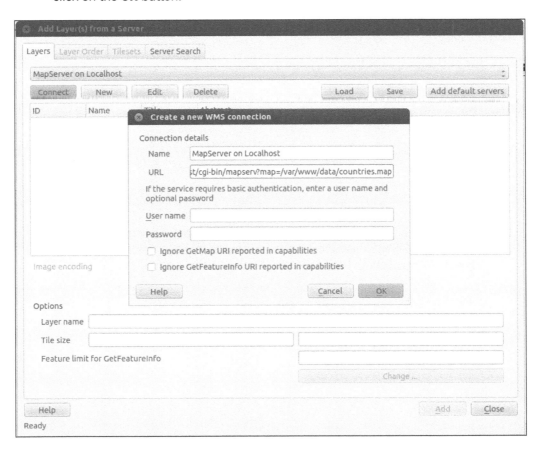

9. Now, click on the **Connect** button, as shown in the following screenshot; then, select the **countries** layer and add it to the QGIS map window using the **Add** button:

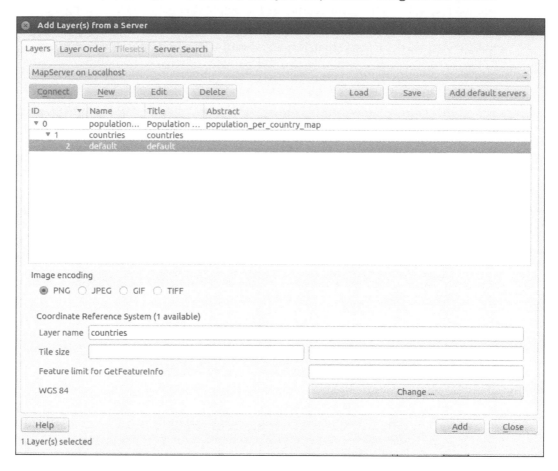

10. Now, browse to your WMS countries layer and try to perform some identification operations. QGIS will raise the needed `GetMap` and `GetFeatureInfo` WMS requests for you behind the scenes to give the following output:

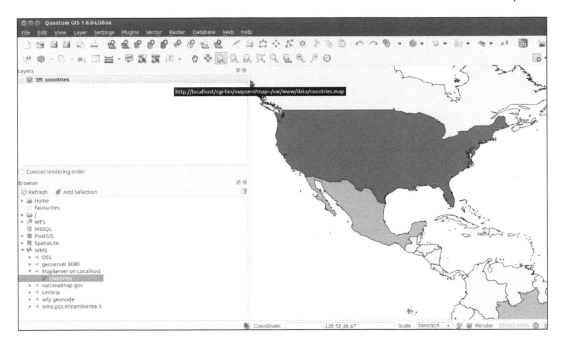

11. Having seen how the WMS service works, you will now start using WFS. Like the WMS, the WFS offers the user a `GetCapabilities` request, as well, resulting in a similar output as the `GetCapabilities` request of WMS. Type the URL, `http://localhost/cgi-bin/mapserv?map=/var/www/data/countries.map&SERVICE=WFS&VERSION=1.0.0&REQUEST=GetCapabilities`, in the browser window to inspect the XML response.

12. The main WFS request is `GetFeature`. It lets you query the map layer using several criteria, returning a collection of features in response as **GML (Geography Markup Language)** output. Test the request by typing this URL in the browser: `http://localhost/cgi-bin/mapserv?map=/var/www/data/countries.map&SERVICE=WFS&VERSION=1.0.0&REQUEST=getfeature&TYPENAME=countries&MAXFEATURES=5`.

13. You should get an XML (GML) response from the browser, as shown in the following code, with a `<wfs:FeatureCollection>` element composed of five `<gml:featureMember>` elements (as indicated in the `MAXFEATURES` parameter of the request), each representing one country. For each feature, the WFS returns the geometry and all of the field values (this behavior was specified by setting the `gml_include_items` variable in the `METADATA` layer directive in the mapfile). This is the response you should get:

```
<gml:featureMember>
  <ms:countries>
  <gml:boundedBy>
    <gml:Box srsName="EPSG:4326">
```

```
         <gml:coordinates>-61.891113,16.989719 -
           61.666389,17.724998</gml:coordinates>
       </gml:Box>
     </gml:boundedBy>

     <ms:msGeometry>
       <gml:MultiPolygon srsName="EPSG:4326">
         <gml:polygonMember>
           <gml:Polygon>
             <gml:outerBoundaryIs>
               <gml:LinearRing>
                 <gml:coordinates>
                 -61.686668,17.024441 ...
                 </gml:coordinates>
               </gml:LinearRing>
             </gml:outerBoundaryIs>
           </gml:Polygon>
         </gml:polygonMember>
         ...
       </gml:MultiPolygon>
     </ms:msGeometry>
     <ms:gid>1</ms:gid>
     <ms:fips>AC</ms:fips>
     <ms:iso2>AG</ms:iso2>
     <ms:iso3>ATG</ms:iso3>
     <ms:un>28</ms:un>
     <ms:name>Antigua and Barbuda</ms:name>
     <ms:area>44</ms:area>
     <ms:pop2005>83039</ms:pop2005>
     <ms:region>19</ms:region>
     <ms:subregion>29</ms:subregion>
     <ms:lon>-61.783</ms:lon>
     <ms:lat>17.078</ms:lat>
     </ms:countries>
   </gml:featureMember>
```

14. As a result of the WFS `GetFeature` request executed in the previous step, MapServer has returned to you only the first five features of the `countries` layers. Now, use the `GetFeature` request for making a query to the layer using a filter and getting back the corresponding features. By typing the URL, `http://localhost/cgi-bin/mapserv?map=/var/www/data/countries.map&SERVICE=WFS&VERSION=1.0.0&REQUEST=getfeature&TYPENAME=countries&MAXFEATURES=5&Filter=<Filter> <PropertyIsEqualTo><PropertyName>name</PropertyName><Literal>Italy</Literal></PropertyIsEqualTo></Filter>`, you will get the feature in the database that has the `name` field set to `Italy`.

15. After testing the WFS requests in a browser, try to open the WFS service in QGIS using the **Add WFS Layer** button (alternatively, navigate to **Layer | Add WFS Layer** or use the QGIS browser). You should see the same **MapServer on Localhost connection** you created a few steps earlier. Click on the **Connect** button and select the **countries** layer, add it to the QGIS project, and browse through it by zooming, panning, and identifying some features. The biggest difference when compared to WMS is that, with WFS, you receive the feature geometries from the server and not just an image, so you can even export the layer to a different format, such as a shapefile or spatialite!

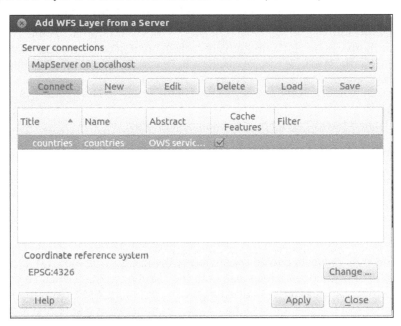

# How it works...

In this recipe, you implemented WMS and WFS services for a PostGIS layer using the MapServer open-source web-mapping engine. WMS and WFS are the two core concepts to consider when you want to develop a web GIS that is interoperable across many organizations. **Open Geospatial Consortium** (**OGC**) defined these two standards (and many others) to make web-mapping services exposed in an open, standard way. This way, these services can be used by different applications—for example, you have seen in this recipe that a GIS Desktop tool such as QGIS can browse and query those services because it understands these OGC standards (you can get exactly the same results with other tools, such as gvSIG, uDig, OpenJUMP, and ArcGIS Desktop, among others). In the same way, JavaScript API libraries, most notably, OpenLayers and Leaflet (you will be using these in the other recipes in this chapter), can use these services in a standard way to provide web-mapping features to web applications.

WMS is a service that is used to generate the maps to be displayed by clients. Those maps are generated using image formats, such as PNG, JPEG, and many others. Some of the most typical WMS requests are as follows:

- **GetCapabilities**: It offers an overview of the services offered by WMS, particularly a list of the available layers and some of the details of each layer (layer extent, coordinate reference systems, URI of the data, and so on).

- **GetMap**: It returns a map image representing one or more layers for a specified extent and spatial reference, in a specified image file format and size.

- **GetFeatureInfo**: It is an optional request by WMS that returns, in different formats, the attribute values for the features of a given point in the map. You have seen how to customize the response by introducing a template file that must be set in the mapfile.

WFS provides a convenient, standard way to access the features of a vector layer with a web request. The service response streams to the client the requested features using GML (an XML markup defined by OGC to define geographical features).

Some of the WFS requests are as follows:

- **GetCapabilities**: It gives a description of the services and layers offered by the WFS service

- **GetFeature**: It allows the client to get a set of features of a given layer, corresponding to a given criteria

These WMS and WFS requests can be consumed by the client using the HTTP protocol. You have seen how to query and get a response from the client by typing a URL in a browser with several parameters appended to it. As an example, the following WMS `GetMap` request will return a map image of the layers (using the `LAYERS` parameter) in a specified format (using the `FORMAT` parameter), size (using the `WIDTH` and `HEIGHT` parameters), extent (using the `BBOX` parameter), and spatial reference system (using `CRS`):

```
http://localhost/cgi-bin/mapserv?map=/var/www/data/countries.map&&SER
VICE=WMS&VERSION=1.3.0&REQUEST=GetMap&BBOX=-26,-111,36,-38&CRS=EPSG:4
326&WIDTH=806&HEIGHT=688&LAYERS=countries&STYLES=&FORMAT=image/png.
```

In MapServer, you can create WMS and WFS services in the mapfile using its directives. The mapfile is a text file that is composed of several sections and is the heart of MapServer. In the beginning of the mapfile, it is necessary to define general properties for the map, such as its title, extent, spatial reference, output-image formats, and dimensions to be returned to the user.

Then, it is possible to define which OWS (OGC Web Services such as WMS, WFS, and WCS) requests to expose.

Then, there is the main section of the mapfile, where the layers are defined (every layer is defined in the LAYER directive). You have seen how to define a PostGIS layer. It is necessary to define its connection information (database, user, password, and so on), the SQL definition in the database (it is possible to use just a PostGIS table name, but you could eventually use a query to define the set of features and attributes defining the layer), the geometric type, and the projection.

A whole directive (CLASS) is used to define how the layer features will be rendered. You may use different classes, as you did in this recipe, to render features differently, based on an attribute defined with the CLASSITEM setting. In this recipe, you defined three different classes, each representing a population class, using different colors.

## See also

You can find more information about using MapServer, using its extensive documentation at its project home page (http://mapserver.org/it/index.html). You will find the mapfile documentation at http://www.mapserver.org/mapfile/ very useful to read, as well.

A good tutorial to understand how to generate mapfiles can be found at http://mapserver.org/tutorial/example1-1.html.

If you want to gain a better understanding of the WMS and WFS standards, check their specifications at the OGC website. For the WMS service, go to http://www.opengeospatial.org/standards/wms, whereas, for WFS, go to http://www.opengeospatial.org/standards/wfs.

# Creating WMS and WFS services with GeoServer

In the previous recipe, you created **Web Map Services** (**WMS**) and **Web Feature Services** (**WFS**) from a PostGIS layer using MapServer. In this recipe, you will do that using another popular open-source web-mapping engine—**GeoServer**. You will then use the created services, as you did with MapServer, testing their exposed requests, first using a browser and then the QGIS desktop tool (you can do this with other software, as well, such as uDig, gvSIG, OpenJUMP GIS, and ArcGIS Desktop).

## Getting ready

While MapServer is written in the C language and uses Apache as its web server, GeoServer is written in Java, and you therefore need to install the **Java Virtual Machine** (**JVM**) in your system; it must be used from a servlet container such as Jetty and Tomcat. After installing the servlet container, you will be able to deploy the GeoServer application to it. For example, in Tomcat, you can deploy GeoServer by copying the GeoServer **WAR** (**Web archive**) file to Tomcat's `webapps` directory. For this recipe, we will suppose that you have a working GeoServer in your system; if this is not the case, follow the detailed GeoServer installation steps for your OS at the GeoServer website (`http://docs.geoserver.org/stable/en/user/installation/`) and then return to this recipe. Follow these steps:

1. Download the USA counties shapefile from the `nationalatlas.gov` website at `http://dds.cr.usgs.gov/pub/data/nationalatlas/countyp020_nt00009.tar.gz` (this archive is included in the book's code bundle). Extract the archive to `working/chp09` and import it to PostGIS using the `ogr2ogr` command, as follows:

   ```
   $ ogr2ogr -f PostgreSQL -a_srs EPSG:4326 -lco GEOMETRY_NAME=the_
   geom -nln chp09.counties PG:"dbname='postgis_cookbook' user='me'
   password='mypassword'" co2000p020.shp.
   ```

## How to do it...

Carry out the following steps:

1. Open the GeoServer administrative interface, which is typically located at `http://localhost:8080/geoserver`, in your favorite, browser and log in using your credentials—`admin` as the username and `geoserver` as the password if you are just using the GeoServer default installation and have not customized things.

2. After successfully logging in, create a workspace by clicking on the **Workspace** link under **Work** (in the left-hand side panel of the GeoServer application's main menu), and then click on the **Add new workspace** link. In the text boxes of the form that appears, specify the following values and then click on the **Submit** button:

   □ Enter `postgis_cookbook` in the **Name** field

   □ Enter the URL `http://www.packtpub.com/postgis-to-store-organize-manipulate-analyze-spatial-data-cookbook/book` in the **Namespace URI** field

3. Now, to create a PostGIS store, click on the **Stores** link under **Data** (in the left-hand side panel of the GeoServer application's main menu). Now, click on the **Add new store** link, and then on the **PostGIS** link under **Vector Data Sources**, as shown in the following screenshot:

4. In the **New Vector Data Source** page, complete the form's fields as follows:

    1. Select **postgis_cookbook** from the **Workspace** drop-down list.

    2. Enter postgis_cookbook in the **Data Source Name** field.

    3. Enter localhost in the **host** field.

    4. Enter 5432 in the **port** field.

    5. Enter postgis_cookbook in the **database** field.

    6. Enter chp09 in the **schema** field.

    7. Enter me in the **user** field.

    8. Enter mypassword in the **passwd** field.

The **New Vector Data Source** page is shown in the following screenshot:

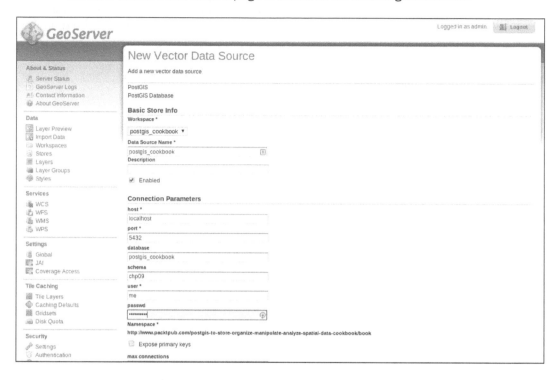

5. Now, click on the **Save** button to successfully create your PostGIS store.

6. You are now ready to publish the PostGIS `counties` layer as WMS and WFS. On the **Layers** page, click on the **Add a new resource** link. Now, select **postgis_cookbook** from the **Add layer from** drop-down list. Click on the **Publish** link to the right of the `counties` layer.

7. On the **Edit Layer** page, shown in the following screenshot, click on the links **Compute from data** and **Compute from native bounds**, and then click on the **Save** button:

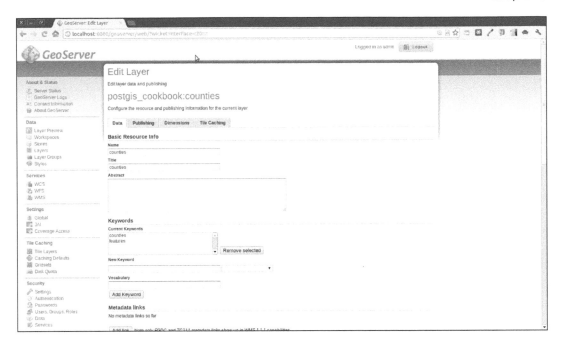

8. Now, you need to define the style used to display the layer to the user. Unlike MapServer, GeoServer uses the OGC-standard **Styled Layer Descriptor** (**SLD**) notation. Click on the **Styles** link under **Data** and then on the **Add new style** link. Fill the text fields in the form as follows:

   □ Enter Counties classified per size in the **Name** field

   □ Enter postgis_cookbook in the **Workspace** field

9. In the text area for the SLD, add the following XML code, defining the style for the counties layer; then, click on the **Validate** button to check whether or not your SLD definition is correct. Finally, click on the **Submit** button to save the new style:

```
<?xml version="1.0" encoding="UTF-8"?>
<sld:StyledLayerDescriptor xmlns="http://www.opengis.net/sld"
  xmlns:sld="http://www.opengis.net/sld"
  xmlns:ogc="http://www.opengis.net/ogc"
  xmlns:gml="http://www.opengis.net/gml" version="1.0.0">
  <sld:NamedLayer>
    <sld:Name>county_classification</sld:Name>
    <sld:UserStyle>
      <sld:Name>county_classification</sld:Name>
      <sld:Title>County area classification</sld:Title>
      <sld:FeatureTypeStyle>
        <sld:Name>name</sld:Name>
        <sld:Rule>
```

```
            <sld:Title>Large counties</sld:Title>
            <ogc:Filter>
              <ogc:PropertyIsGreaterThanOrEqualTo>
                <ogc:PropertyName>square_mil</ogc:PropertyName>
                <ogc:Literal>5000</ogc:Literal>
              </ogc:PropertyIsGreaterThanOrEqualTo>
            </ogc:Filter>
            <sld:PolygonSymbolizer>
              <sld:Fill>
                <sld:CssParameter
                  name="fill">#FF0000</sld:CssParameter>
              </sld:Fill>
              <sld:Stroke/>
            </sld:PolygonSymbolizer>
          </sld:Rule>
          <sld:Rule>
            <sld:Title>Small counties</sld:Title>
            <ogc:Filter>
              <ogc:PropertyIsLessThan>
                <ogc:PropertyName>square_mil</ogc:PropertyName>
                <ogc:Literal>5000</ogc:Literal>
              </ogc:PropertyIsLessThan>
            </ogc:Filter>
            <sld:PolygonSymbolizer>
              <sld:Fill>
                <sld:CssParameter
                  name="fill">#0000FF</sld:CssParameter>
              </sld:Fill>
              <sld:Stroke/>
            </sld:PolygonSymbolizer>
          </sld:Rule>
        </sld:FeatureTypeStyle>
      </sld:UserStyle>
    </sld:NamedLayer>
</sld:StyledLayerDescriptor>
```

The following screenshot shows how the new style looks on the **New style** GeoServer page:

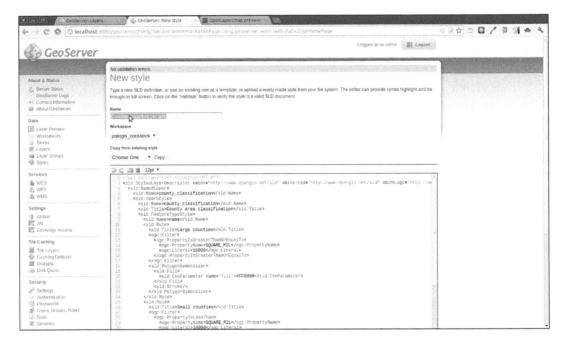

10. Now, you need to associate the created style with the `counties` layer. Go back to the layer page (**Data | Layers**), click on the `counties` layer link, and then, on the **Edit Layer** page, click on the **Publishing** section. Select **Counties classified per size** in the **Default style** drop-down list and then click on the **Save** button.

11. Now that your WMS and WFS services for the PostGIS `counties` layer are ready, it is time to start using them! First, test the `GetCapabilities` WMS request. To do this, you can click on one of the links on the right-hand side panel on the GeoServer web application home page. You can click on the link for either WMS Version 1.1.1 or WMS Version 1.3.0. Click on one of the links or type the `GetCapabilities` request directly in the browser as `http://localhost:8080/geoserver/ows?service= wms&version=1.3.0&request=GetCapabilities`.

12. Now, we will investigate the `GetCapabilities` response, which is shown as follows. You will find a lot of information about WMS that is available on your GeoServer instance, such as the WMS-supported requests, projections, and a lot of other information about each published layer. In the case of the `counties` layer, the following code is an extract from the `GetCapabilities` document. Note the main layer information such as the name, title, abstract (you could redefine all of these using the GeoServer web application), the supported **CRS** (**Coordinate Reference Systems**), the geographic extent, and the associated style:

```
<Layer queryable="1">
  <Name>postgis_cookbook:counties</Name>
  <Title>counties</Title>
  <Abstract/>
  <KeywordList>
    <Keyword>counties</Keyword>
    <Keyword>features</Keyword>
  </KeywordList>
  <CRS>EPSG:4326</CRS>
  <CRS>CRS:84</CRS>
  <EX_GeographicBoundingBox>
    <westBoundLongitude>-179.133392333984</westBoundLongitude>
    <eastBoundLongitude>-64.566162109375
      </eastBoundLongitude>
    <southBoundLatitude>17.6746921539307
      </southBoundLatitude>
    <northBoundLatitude>71.3980484008789
      </northBoundLatitude>
  </EX_GeographicBoundingBox>
  <BoundingBox CRS="CRS:84" minx="-179.133392333984"
    miny="17.6746921539307" maxx="-64.566162109375"
    maxy="71.3980484008789"/>
  <BoundingBox CRS="EPSG:4326" minx="17.6746921539307"
    miny="-179.133392333984" maxx="71.3980484008789" maxy="-
    64.566162109375"/>
  <Style>
    <Name>Counties classified per size</Name>
    <Title>County area classification</Title>
    <Abstract/>
    <LegendURL width="20" height="20">
      <Format>image/png</Format>
      <OnlineResource
        xmlns:xlink="http://www.w3.org/1999/xlink"
        xlink:type="simple" xlink:href=
        "http://localhost:8080/geoserver/
        ows?service=WMS&amp;request=GetLegendGraphic&amp;
        format=image%2Fpng&amp;width=20&amp;height=20&amp;
```

```
        layer=counties"/>
      </LegendURL>
    </Style>
  </Layer>
```

13. To test the `GetMap` and `GetFeatureInfo` WMS requests, the GeoServer web application offers you a handy way to do so with the **Layer Preview** page. Navigate to **Data | Layer Preview**, and then click on the **OpenLayers** link next to the `counties` layer. The **Layer Preview** page is based on the **OpenLayers JavaScript** library and allows you to experiment with the `GetMap` and `GetFeatureInfo` requests.

14. Try to navigate the map; at each zoom and pan action, GeoServer will stream out a new image provided by the response output to a `GetMap` request. By clicking on the map, you can perform a `GetFeatureInfo` request and the user interface will display the feature's attributes corresponding to the point on the map on which you clicked. An effective way to check how the requests are sent to GeoServer as you navigate the map is by using the Firefox Firebug plugin or the Chrome (or Chromium, if you are using Linux) Developer Tools. With these tools, you will be able to identify the `GetMap` and `GetFeatureInfo` requests that are being sent behind the scenes from the **OpenLayers** viewer to GeoServer. One such map is shown in the following screenshot:

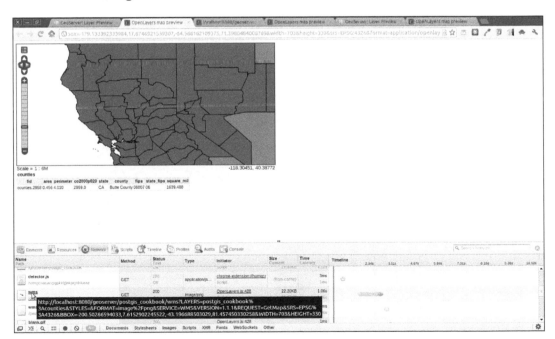

15. Now, try a WMS `GetMap` request by typing the URL,
    `http://localhost:8080/geoserver/postgis_cookbook/`
    `wms?LAYERS=postgis_cookbook%3Acounties&STYLES=&FORMAT=i`
    `mage%2Fpng&SERVICE=WMS&VERSION=1.1.1&REQUEST=GetMap&SRS`
    `=EPSG%3A4326&BBOX=-200.50286594033,7.6152902245522,-43-`
    `.196688503029,81.457450330258&WIDTH=703&HEIGHT=330`, in your browser.

16. Try a WMS `GetFeatureInfo` request, as well, by typing the URL
    `http://localhost:8080/geoserver/postgis_cookbook/wms?REQ`
    `UEST=GetFeatureInfo&EXCEPTIONS=application%2Fvnd.ogc.se_`
    `xml&BBOX=-126.094303%2C37.16812%2C-116.262667%2C41.783255&`
    `SERVICE=WMS&INFO_FORMAT=text%2Fhtml&QUERY_LAYERS=postgis_`
    `cookbook%3Acounties&FEATURE_COUNT=50&Layers=postgis_cookbook%3A`
    `counties&WIDTH=703&HEIGHT=330&format=image%2Fpng&styles=&srs=EP`
    `SG%3A4326&version=1.1.1&x=330&y=158.`

17. Now, as you did for the MapService WMS, test the GeoServer WMS in QGIS. Create
    a WMS connection named `GeoServer on localhost`, pointing to the GeoServer
    `GetCapabilities` document (`http://localhost:8080/geoserver/ows?ser`
    `vice=wms&version=1.3.0&request=GetCapabilities`). Then, connect to the
    WMS server (for example, from the QGIS browser), select `counties` from the **Layers**
    list, and add it to the map, as shown in the following screenshot; then, navigate the
    layer and try to identify some of the features:

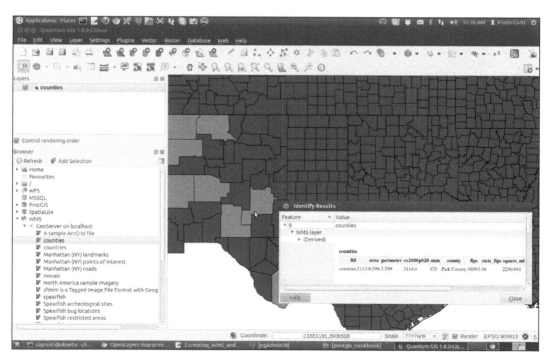

18. Having used the WMS, try to test a couple of WFS requests. A typical WFS
    `GetCapability` request can be executed by typing this URL: `http://`
    `localhost:8080/geoserver/wfs?service=wfs&version=1.1.0&request`
    `=GetCapabilities`. You could also click on one of the WFS links on the home page
    of the GeoServer web interface.

19. Investigate the XML `GetCapabilities` response and try to identify the information
    about your layer. You should have a `<FeatureType>` element, such as the following,
    corresponding to the `counties` layer:

```
<FeatureType>
  <Name>postgis_cookbook:counties</Name>
  <Title>counties</Title>
  <Abstract/>
  <Keywords>counties, features</Keywords>
  <SRS>EPSG:4326</SRS>
  <LatLongBoundingBox minx="-179.133392333984"
    miny="17.6746921539307" maxx="-64.566162109375"
    maxy="71.3980484008789"/>
</FeatureType>
```

20. As shown in the previous recipe, a typical WFS request is `GetFeature`,
    which will result in a GML response. Try it, for example, by typing the URL,
    `http://localhost:8080/geoserver/wfs?service=wfs&version=1.0.0`
    `&request=GetFeature&typeName=postgis_cookbook:counties&max`
    `Features=5`, in your browser. You will receive a GML output composed of a
    `<wfs:FeatureCollection>` element and a collection of `<gml:featureMember>`
    elements (possibly five elements, as specified in the `maxFeatures` request's
    parameter). You will get an output that is similar to the following code:

```
<gml:featureMember>
  <postgis_cookbook:counties fid="counties.3962">
    <postgis_cookbook:the_geom>
      <gml:Polygon srsName="http://www.opengis.net/
        gml/srs/epsg.xml#4326">
        <gml:outerBoundaryIs>
          <gml:LinearRing>
            <gml:coordinates xmlns:gml=
              "http://www.opengis.net/gml"
              decimal="." cs="," ts="">
            -101.62554932,36.50246048 -
              101.0908432,36.50032043 ...
            ...
            ...
            </gml:coordinates>
          </gml:LinearRing>
        </gml:outerBoundaryIs>
      </gml:Polygon>
    </postgis_cookbook:the_geom>
    <postgis_cookbook:area>0.240</postgis_cookbook:area>
```

```
<postgis_cookbook:perimeter>1.967
  </postgis_cookbook:perimeter>
<postgis_cookbook:co2000p020>3963.0
  </postgis_cookbook:co2000p020>
<postgis_cookbook:state>TX</postgis_cookbook:state>
<postgis_cookbook:county>Hansford
  County</postgis_cookbook:county>
<postgis_cookbook:fips>48195</postgis_cookbook:fips>
<postgis_cookbook:state_fips>48
  </postgis_cookbook:state_fips>
<postgis_cookbook:square_mil>919.801
  </postgis_cookbook:square_mil>
  </postgis_cookbook:counties>
</gml:featureMember>
```

21. Now, as you did with WMS, try the **counties** WFS in QGIS (or in your favorite Desktop GIS client). Create a new WFS connection, by using either the QGIS browser or the **Add WFS Layer** button, and then clicking on the **New Connection** button. In the **Create a new WFS connection** dialog box, type GeoServer on localhost in the **Name** field and add the WFS GetCapabilities URL (http://localhost:8080/geoserver/wfs?service=wfs&version=1.1.0&request=GetCapabilities) in the **URL** field.

22. Add the WFS counties layer from the previous dialog box and, as a test, select some of the counties and export them to a new shapefile using the **Save As** command from the layer's context menu, as shown in the following screenshot:

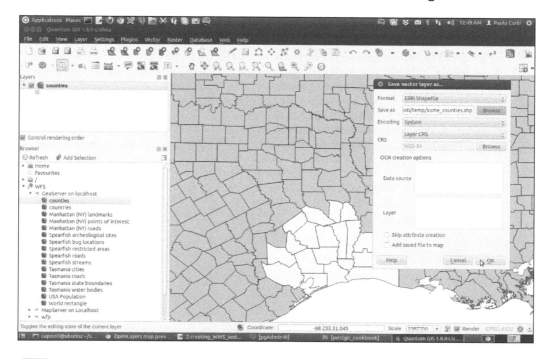

## How it works...

In the previous recipe, you were introduced to the basic concepts of the OGC WMS and WFS standards using MapServer. In this recipe, you have done that using another popular open-source web-mapping engine—GeoServer.

Unlike MapServer, which is written in C and can be used from web servers such as Apache HTTP (httpd) or Microsoft **Internet Information Server** (**IIS**) as a CGI program, GeoServer is written in Java and needs a servlet container such as Apache Tomcat or Eclipse Jetty to work.

GeoServer not only offers the user a highly scalable and standard web-mapping engine implementation, but does so with a nice user interface, the Web Administration interface. Therefore, it is generally easier for a beginner to create WMS and WFS services compared to MapServer, where it is necessary to master the mapfile syntax.

The GeoServer workflow to create WMS and WFS services for a PostGIS layer is to first create a PostGIS store, where you need to associate the main PostGIS connection parameters (server name, schema, user, and so on). After the store is correctly created, you can publish the layers that are available for that PostGIS store. You have seen in this recipe how easy the whole process of using the GeoServer Web Administration interface is.

To define the layer style to render features, GeoServer uses the **Styled Layer Descriptor** (**SLD**) schema, an OGC standard based on XML. We have written two distinct rules in this recipe to render, in a different way, the counties that have an area greater than 5,000 square miles from the others. For the purpose of rendering the counties in a different way, we have used two <ogc:Rule> SLD elements in which you have defined an <ogc:Filter> element. For each of these elements, you have defined the criteria to filter the layer features, using the <ogc:PropertyIsGreaterThanOrEqualTo> and <ogc:PropertyIsLessThan> elements. A handy way to generate an SLD for a layer is by using Desktop GIS tools that are able to export an SLD file for a layer (QGIS can do this). After exporting the file, you can upload it to GeoServer by copying the SLD file content to the **Add a new style** page.

Having created the WMS and WFS services for the counties layer, you have been testing them by generating the requests using the handy Layer Preview GeoServer interface (based on OpenLayers), and then typing the requests directly into a browser. You can modify each service request's parameters from the Layer Preview interface or just change them in the URL query string.

In the end, you tested the services using QGIS and have seen how it is possible to export some of the layer's features using the WFS service.

## See also

If you want more information about GeoServer, you can check out its excellent documentation at `http://docs.geoserver.org/`, or get the wonderful *GeoServer Beginner's Guide* book by Packt Publishing (`http://www.packtpub.com/geoserver-share-edit-geospatial-data-beginners-guide/book`).

# Creating a WMS Time with MapServer

In this recipe, you will implement a WMS Time service with MapServer. For time-series data, and whenever you have geographic data that are updated continuously in the Time and you need to expose them as WMS in a Web GIS, a WMS Time service is the way to go. This is possible by providing the `TIME` parameter a time value in the WMS requests, typically in the `GetMap` request.

Here, you will implement a WMS Time service for the hotspots, representing possible fire data acquired by NASA's **Earth Observing System Data and Information System** (**EOSDIS**). This excellent system provides data derived from MODIS images from the last 24 hours, 48 hours, and 7 days, that can be downloaded in the shapefile, KML, WMS, or text file formats. You will load a bunch of this data to PostGIS, create a WMS Time service with MapServer, and test the WMS `GetCapabilities` and `GetMap` requests using a common browser.

 If you are new to the WMS standard, please checkout the previous two recipes to get more information.

## Getting ready

1. First, download one week's worth of active fire data (hotspots) from the EOSDIS website. For example, download the data from `http://firms.modaps.eosdis.nasa.gov/active_fire/shapes/zips/Global_7d.zip`. A copy of this shapefile is included in the book code bundle. Use that if you want to use the same SQL and WMS parameters that have been used in the following steps.

2. Extract the shapefile from the `Global_7d.zip` archive to the `working/chp09` directory and import this shapefile in PostGIS using the `shp2pgsql` command, as follows:

```
$ shp2pgsql -s 4326 -g the_geom -I Global_7d.shp chp09.hotspots >
hotspots.sql

$ psql -U me -d postgis_cookbook -f hotspots.sql
```

3. When the import is completed, check the point fire data (hotspots) you just imported in PostGIS. Each hotspot contains a bunch of useful information, most notably, the geometry and acquisition date and time stored in the `acq_date` and `acq_time` fields. You can easily see that the features loaded from the shapefile span over eight consecutive days using the following command:

```
postgis_cookbook=# SELECT acq_date, count(*) AS hotspots_count
FROM chp09.hotspots GROUP BY acq_date ORDER BY acq_date;
```

The previous command will produce the following output:

```
   acq_date  | hotspots_count
------------+----------------
 2013-05-27 |           5539
 2013-05-28 |          10142
 2013-05-29 |           6688
 2013-05-30 |           7543
 2013-05-31 |           6676
 2013-06-01 |           7978
 2013-06-02 |           9228
 2013-06-03 |           3796
(8 rows)
```

## How to do it...

Carry out the following steps:

1. We will first create a WMS for the PostGIS hotspot layer. Create the mapfile named `hotspots.map` in a directory accessible to the httpd (or IIS) user, for example, `/var/www/data` in Linux, and `C:\ms4w\Apache\htdocs` in Windows, composed by the following code:

```
MAP # Start of mapfile
  NAME 'hotspots_time_series'
  IMAGETYPE        PNG
  EXTENT           -180 -90 180 90
  SIZE             800 400
  IMAGECOLOR       255 255 255

  # map projection definition
  PROJECTION
    'init=epsg:4326'
  END
```

```
          # a symbol for hotspots
          SYMBOL
            NAME "circle"
            TYPE ellipse
            FILLED true
            POINTS
              1 1
            END
          END


          # web section: here we define the ows services
          WEB
            # WMS and WFS server settings
            METADATA
              'wms_name'              'Hotspots'
              'wms_title'             'World hotspots time
                                      series'
              'wms_abstract'          'Active fire data detected
                                      by NASA Earth Observing
                                      System Data and Information
                                      System (EOSDIS)'
              'wms_onlineresource'    'http://localhost/cgi-bin/
                                      mapserv?map=/var/www/data/
                                      hotspots.map&'
              'wms_srs'               'EPSG:4326 EPSG:3857'
              'wms_enable_request' '*'
              'wms_feature_info_mime_type'  'text/html'
            END
          END


          # Start of layers definition
          LAYER # Hotspots point layer begins here
            NAME            hotspots
            CONNECTIONTYPE  POSTGIS
            CONNECTION      'host=localhost dbname=postgis_cookbook
                            user=me
                              password=mypassword port=5432'
            DATA            'the_geom from chp09.hotspots'
            TEMPLATE 'template.html'
            METADATA
              'wms_title'                     'World hotspots time
                                              series'
              'gml_include_items' 'all'
            END
            STATUS          ON
            TYPE            POINT
            CLASS
```

```
        SYMBOL 'circle'
        SIZE 4
        COLOR       255 0 0
      END # end of class

   END # hotspots layer ends here

 END # End of mapfile
```

2.  Check whether or not the WMS `GetCapabilities` request for this mapfile is working well by typing either of the following URLs in the browser:

    ❑   `http://localhost/cgi-bin/mapserv?map=/var/www/data/` `hotspots.map&SERVICE=WMS&VERSION=1.0.0&REQUEST=GetCapabi` `lities` (in Linux)

    ❑   `http://localhost/cgi-bin/mapserv.exe?map=C:\ms4w\Apache\` `htdocs\hotspots.map&SERVICE=WMS&VERSION=1.0.0&REQUEST=Ge` `tCapabilities` (in Windows)

In the following steps, we will be referring to Linux. If you are using Windows, you just need to replace `http://localhost/cgi-bin/mapserv?map=/var/www/data/hotspots.map` with `http://localhost/cgi-bin/mapserv.exe?map=C:\ms4w\Apache\htdocs\` `hotspots.map` in every request.

1.  Now, query the WMS with a `GetMap` request. Type the following URL in the browser. If everything is correct, MapServer should return an image with some hotspots as a response. The URL is `http://localhost/cgi-bin/mapserv?map=/var/www/` `data/hotspots.map&&SERVICE=WMS&VERSION=1.3.0&REQUEST=GetMap&BB` `OX=-25,-100,35,-35&CRS=EPSG:4326&WIDTH=1000&HEIGHT=800&LAYERS=h` `otspots&STYLES=&FORMAT=image/png`.

2.  Until now, you have implemented a simple WMS service. Now, to make the `TIME` parameter available for WMS Time requests, add the `wms_timeextent`, `wms_timeitem` and `wms_timedefault` variables in the `LAYER METADATA` section, as follows:

```
METADATA
  'wms_title'                    'World hotspots time
                                  series'
  'gml_include_items' 'all'
  'wms_timeextent' '2000-01-01/2020-12-31' # time extent
    for which the service will give a response
  'wms_timeitem' 'acq_date' # layer field to use to filter
    on the TIME parameter
  'wms_timedefault' '2013-05-30' # default parameter if not
    added to the request
END
```

3. Having added these parameters in the LAYER METADATA mapfile section, the WMS GetCapabilities response should change. Now, the hotspots layer definition includes the time dimension, defined by the <Dimension> and <Extent> elements. You will get a response as follows:

```
<Layer>
  <Name>hotspots_time_series</Name>
  <Title>World hotspots time series</Title>
  <Abstract>Active fire data detected by NASA Earth
    Observing System Data and Information System
    (EOSDIS)</Abstract>
  <SRS>EPSG:4326 EPSG:3857</SRS>
  <LatLonBoundingBox minx="-180" miny="-90" maxx="180"
    maxy="90" />
  <BoundingBox SRS="EPSG:4326"
    minx="-180" miny="-90" maxx="180" maxy="90" />
  <Layer queryable="1">
    <Name>hotspots</Name>
        <Title>World hotspots time series</Title>
        <Dimension name="time" units="ISO8601"/>
        <Extent name="time" default="2011-10-01"
nearestValue="0">2000-01-01/2020-12-31</Extent>
    </Layer>
</Layer>
```

4. You can finally test the WMS service with time support. You only need to remember to add the TIME parameter in the GetMap request (otherwise, GetMap will filter out the data using the default date, which is 2011-10-01, in this example) by using this URL: http://localhost/cgi-bin/mapserv?map=/var/www/data/hotspots.map&&SERVICE=WMS&VERSION=1.3.0&REQUEST=GetMap&BBOX=-25,-100,35,-35&CRS=EPSG:4326&WIDTH=1000&HEIGHT=800&LAYERS=hotspots&STYLES=&FORMAT=image/png&TIME=2013-05-28.

5. Play for a while with the TIME parameter in the preceding URL and try to see how the GetMap image response changes day by day. Remember that for the dataset we imported, the acq_date range is from 2013-05-27 to 2013-06-03. In case you didn't use the hostpots shapefile included in the book dataset, the time range will be different!

**2013-05-27**

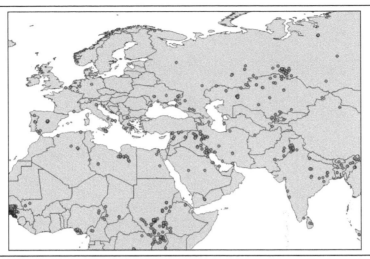

```
http://localhost/cgi-bin/mapserv?map=/var/www/data/hotspots.map&&SE
RVICE=WMS&VERSION=1.3.0&REQUEST=GetMap&BBOX=-25,-100,35,-35&CRS=EPS
G:4326&WIDTH=1000&HEIGHT=800&LAYERS=hotspots&STYLES=&FORMAT=image/
png&TIME=2013-05-27
```

**2013-05-28**

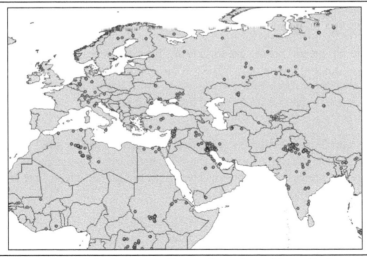

```
http://localhost/cgi-bin/mapserv?map=/var/www/data/hotspots.map&&SE
RVICE=WMS&VERSION=1.3.0&REQUEST=GetMap&BBOX=-25,-100,35,-35&CRS=EPS
G:4326&WIDTH=1000&HEIGHT=800&LAYERS=hotspots&STYLES=&FORMAT=image/
png&TIME=2013-05-28
```

| 2013-05-29 |
| --- |
| 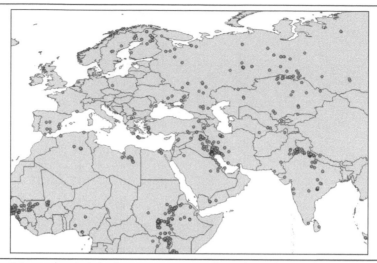 |
| `http://localhost/cgi-bin/mapserv?map=/var/www/data/hotspots.map&&SE RVICE=WMS&VERSION=1.3.0&REQUEST=GetMap&BBOX=-25,-100,35,-35&CRS=EPS G:4326&WIDTH=1000&HEIGHT=800&LAYERS=hotspots&STYLES=&FORMAT=image/ png&TIME=2013-05-29` |

## How it works...

In this recipe, you have seen how to create a WMS Time service using the MapServer open-source web-mapping engine. A WMS Time service is useful for whenever you have temporal series and geographic data varying in the Time. The WMS Time service allows the user to filter the requested data by providing a TIME parameter with a time value in the WMS requests.

For this purpose, you first created a plain WMS; if you are new to the WMS standard, mapfile and MapServer, you can check out the first recipe in this chapter. You have imported in PostGIS a points shapefile with one week's worth of hotspots derived from the MODIS satellite, and created a simple WMS for this layer.

After verifying that this WMS works well by testing the WMS GetCapabilities and GetMap requests, you have time-enabled the WMS by adding three parameters in the LAYER METADATA mapfile section: wms_timeextent, wms_timeitem, and wms_timedefault.

The wms_timeextent parameter is the time extent supported by the WMS Time service. The wms_timeitem parameter defines the PostGIS table field to be used to filter the TIME parameter (acq_date field in this case). The wms_timedefault parameter specifies a default time value to be used when the request to the WMS service does not provide the TIME parameter.

At this point, the WMS is time-enabled; this means that the WMS `GetCapabilities` request now includes the time-dimension definition for the PostGIS hotspots layer and, more importantly, the `GetMap` WMS request allows the user to add the `TIME` parameter to query the layer for a specific date.

# Consuming WMS services with OpenLayers

In this recipe, you will use the MapServer and Geoserver WMS you created in the first two recipes of this chapter using the OpenLayers open-source JavaScript API.

This excellent library help developer to quickly assemble web pages using mapping viewers and features. In this recipe, you will create an HTML page, add an OpenLayers map in it and a bunch of controls in that map for navigation, switch the layers, and identify features of the layers. We will then add to the OpenLayers map the two WMS layers pointing to the PostGIS tables, implemented with MapServer and GeoServer at the beginning of this chapter.

## Getting ready

MapServer uses *PROJ.4* (`https://trac.osgeo.org/proj/`) for projection management. This library does not exist by default with the *Spherical Mercator* projection (*EPSG:900913*) defined. Such a projection is commonly used by commercial map API providers, such as GoogleMaps, Yahoo! Maps, and Microsoft Bing, that can provide excellent base layers for your maps.

1.  As you will use a couple of Google Maps base layers in the map you are going to create in this recipe, you need to add the EPSG:900913 support to PROJ.4. Therefore, add an EPSG:900913 definition line in the PROJ.4 datafile (in Linux, generally, this is in `/usr/share/proj/epsg`, and in my Windows OS, it is in `C:\ms4w\proj\nad`). Open the PROJ.4 datafile, add the following line, and then save it:

    ```
    <900913> +proj=merc +a=6378137 +b=6378137 +lat_ts=0.0
      +lon_0=0.0 +x_0=0.0 +y_0=0 +k=1.0 +units=m
      +nadgrids=@null +no_defs
    ```

2.  Due to security restrictions in JavaScript, it is not possible to retrieve information from remote domains using `XMLHttpRequest`. You will encounter this issue in the recipe when you send a WMS `GetFeatureInfo` request to GeoServer that is typically running on Tomcat at port 8080, which is different from the HTML page running on Apache or ISS, port 80. Therefore, unless you run your GeoServer instance using httpd URL rewriting, the solution is to have a proxy script and use it in OpenLayers as suggested here at `http://trac.osgeo.org/openlayers/wiki/FrequentlyAskedQuestions#ProxyHost`.

3. Copy the proxy script `http://trac.osgeo.org/openlayers/browser/trunk/openlayers/examples/proxy.cgi?format=txt`, which is included in the book dataset as well) to the web `cgi` directory of your computer (in Linux, at `/usr/lib/cgi-bin/` and in Windows, at `C:\ms4w\Apache\cgi-bin`), open the proxy.cgi file, and add `localhost:8080` to the `allowedHosts` list.

## How to do it...

Carry out the following steps:

1. Create the `openlayers.html` file and add the `<head>` and `<body>` tags. In the `<head>` tag, import the OpenLayers and GoogleMaps Version 3 JavaScript libraries by executing the following code:

```
<html>
  <head>
    <title>OpenLayers Example</title>
    <script src="http://openlayers.org/api/OpenLayers.js">
      </script>
    <script src="http://maps.google.com/maps/api/
      js?v=3.2&sensor=false"></script>
  </head>
  <body>
  </body>
</html>
```

2. First, add a `<div>` element in the `<body>` tag that will contain the OpenLayers map. The map should be given a width of 700 pixels and a height of 400 pixels, using the following code:

```
<div style="width:700px; height:400px" id="map"></div>
```

3. Just after the map is placed in `<div>`, add a JavaScript script and create an OpenLayers `map` object. In the map constructor parameters, you will add an empty `controls` array and declare that the map has a Spherical Mercator's projection, as shown in the following code:

```
<script defer="defer" type="text/javascript">
  // instantiate the map object
  var map = new OpenLayers.Map("map", {
    controls: [],
    projection: new OpenLayers.Projection("EPSG:900913")
  });
</script>
```

4. Right after the `map` variable is declared, add some OpenLayers controls to the map. For the Web GIS viewer you are creating, you will add the `Navigation` control (which handles map browsing with mouse events, such as dragging, double-clicking, and scrolling the wheel), `PanZoomBar` control (a four-direction navigation using the arrows present above the zooming vertical slider), the `LayerSwitcher` control (which handles the switching on and off of layers added to the map), and the `MousePosition` control (which displays the map coordinates as they change while the user is moving the mouse), using the following code:

```
// add some controls on the map
map.addControl(new OpenLayers.Control.Navigation());
map.addControl(new OpenLayers.Control.PanZoomBar()),
map.addControl(new OpenLayers.Control.LayerSwitcher(
  {"div":OpenLayers.Util.getElement("layerswitcher")}));
map.addControl(new OpenLayers.Control.MousePosition());
```

5. Now, create two Google base layers: one for Google Hybrid and the other for Google Terrain Base maps, using the following code:

```
// set the Google layers
var google_hyb = new OpenLayers.Layer.Google(
  "Google Hybrid",
  {type: google.maps.MapTypeId.HYBRID, numZoomLevels: 20}
);
var google_ter = new OpenLayers.Layer.Google(
  "Google Terrain",
  {type: google.maps.MapTypeId.TERRAIN}
);
```

6. Set two variables for the WMS GeoServer and the MapServer URL that you will use (they are the URLs of the services you created in the first two recipes of this chapter).

    ❑ For Linux, add the following code:

    ```
    // set the WMS
    var geoserver_url = "http://localhost:8080/geoserver/wms";
    var mapserver_url = http://localhost/cgi-
      bin/mapserv?map=/var/www/data/countries.map&
    ```

    ❑ For Windows, add the following code:

    ```
    // set the WMS
    var geoserver_url = "http://localhost:8080/geoserver/wms";
    var mapserver_url = "http://localhost/cgi-
      bin/mapserv.exe?map=C:\\ms4w\\Apache\\
      htdocs\\countries.map&"
    ```

7. Now, create a WMS GeoServer layer to display the OpenLayers map of the counties from the PostGIS layer. You will set some opacity for this layer so that it is possible to see the other layer (counties) behind it. The `isBaseLayer` property is set to `false`, since you want to have this layer over the Google Maps base layers and not as an alternative to them (by default, all of the WMS layers in OpenLayers are considered to be base layers). Create the WMS GeoServer layer using the following code:

```
// set the GeoServer WMS
var geoserver_wms = new OpenLayers.Layer.WMS( "GeoServer WMS",
  geoserver_url,
  {
    layers: "postgis_cookbook:counties",
    transparent: "true",
    format: "image/png",
  },
  {
    isBaseLayer: false,
    opacity: 0.4
  } );
```

8. Now, create a WMS MapServer layer to display the countries from the PostGIS layer in the OpenLayers map, using the following code:

```
// set the MapServer WMS
var mapserver_wms = new OpenLayers.Layer.WMS( "MapServer WMS",
  mapserver_url,
  {
    layers: "countries",
    transparent: "true",
    format: "image/png",
  },
  {
    isBaseLayer: false
  } );
```

9. After creating the Google and WMS layers, you need to add all of them to the map, using the following code:

```
// add all of the layers to the map
map.addLayers([mapserver_wms, geoserver_wms, google_ter,
  google_hyb]);
```

10. You want to provide the user with the possibility to identify features of the counties WMS. Add the `WMSGetFeatureInfo` OpenLayers control (that will send `GetFeatureInfo` requests to the WMS behind the scenes) that point to the counties PostGIS layer served by the GeoServer WMS, using the following code:

```
var info = new OpenLayers.Control.WMSGetFeatureInfo({
  url: geoserver_url,
  title: 'Identify',
  queryVisible: true,
  eventListeners: {
    getfeatureinfo: function(event) {
      map.addPopup(new OpenLayers.Popup.FramedCloud(
        "WMSIdentify",
        map.getLonLatFromPixel(event.xy),
        null,
        event.text,
        null,
        true
      ));
    }
  }
});
map.addControl(info);
info.activate();
```

11. Finally, set the center of the map and its initial zoom level, using the following code:

```
// center map
var cpoint = new OpenLayers.LonLat(-11000000, 4800000);
map.setCenter(cpoint, 3);
```

Your HTML file should now look like the `openlayers.html` file contained in `data/chp09`. You can finally deploy this file to your web server (Apache httpd or IIS). If you are using Apache httpd in Linux, you could copy the file to the `data` directory under `/var/www`, and if you are using Windows, you could copy it to the data directory under `C:\ms4w\Apache\htdocs` (create the `data` directory if it does not already exist). Then, access it using the URL `http://localhost/data/openlayers.html`.

Now, access the `openlayers` web page using your favorite browser. Start browsing the map: zoom, pan, try to switch the base and overlays layers on and off using the layer switcher control, and try to click on a point to identify one feature from the counties PostGIS layer. A map is shown in the following screenshot:

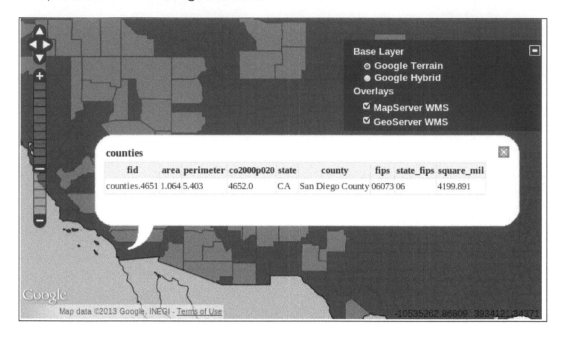

## How it works...

You have seen how to create a web map viewer with the OpenLayers JavaScript library. This library lets the developer define the various map components, using JavaScript in an HTML page. The core object is a map that is composed of *controls* and *layers*.

OpenLayers comes with a great number of controls (`http://dev.openlayers.org/docs/files/OpenLayers/Control-js.html`), and it is even possible to create custom ones.

Another great OpenLayers feature is the ability to add a good number of geographic data sources as layers in the map (you added just a couple of its types to the map, such as Google v3 and WMS), and you could add sources such as WFS, GML, KML, GeoRSS, OpenStreetMap data, ArcGIS Rest, TMS, WMTS, and WorldWind, just to name a few.

# Consuming WMS services with Leaflet

In the previous recipe, you have seen how to create a web page with a map using the OpenLayers JavaScript API and then added to the map the WMS PostGIS layers implemented with MapServer and GeoServer in the first two recipes of this chapter.

A new, lighter alternative to the widespread, venerable OpenLayers JavaScript API has emerged in the last couple of years, named **Leaflet**. In this recipe, you will see how to use this JavaScript API to create a map in a web page, add a MapServer WMS layer from PostGIS to this map, and implement an identify tool sending a `GetFeatureInfo` request to the MapServer WMS (unlike OpenLayer, Leaflet does not come with a `WMSGetFeatureInfo` control).

## How to do it...

Carry out the following steps:

1. Create a new HTML file and name it `leaflet.html`. Open it and add the `<head>` and `<body>` tags. In the `<head>` section, import the Leaflet CSS and JavaScript libraries and the jQuery JavaScript library (you will use jQuery to send an AJAX request to the `GetFeatureInfo` MapServer WMS):

```
<html>
  <head>
    <title>Leaflet Example</title>
    <link rel="stylesheet" href="http://leafletjs.com/dist/
leaflet.css" />
    <script src="http://leafletjs.com/dist/leaflet.js">
      </script>
    <script src="http://ajax.googleapis.com/ajax/
      libs/jquery/1.9.1/jquery.min.js"></script>
  </head>
  <body>
  </body>
</html>
```

2. Start adding a `<div>` tag in the `<body>` element to include the Leaflet map in your file, as shown in the following code; the map will have a width of 800 pixels and a height of 500 pixels:

```
<div id="map" style="width:800px; height:500px"></div>
```

3. Just after the `<div>` element containing the map, add the following JavaScript code. Create a Leaflet `tileLayer` object using the `tile.osm.org` service based on OpenStreetMap data:

```
<script defer="defer" type="text/javascript">
  // osm layer
  var osm = L.tileLayer('http://{s}.tile.osm.org
    /{z}/{x}/{y}.png', {
  maxZoom: 18,
  attribution: "Data by OpenStreetMap"
});
</script>
```

4. Create a second layer that will use the MapServer WMS you created a few recipes ago in this chapter. You will need to set the `ms_url` variable differently if you're using Linux or Windows.

   ❑ For Linux, use the following code:

   ```
   // mapserver layer
   var ms_url = "http://localhost/cgi-bin/mapserv?
     map=/var/www/data/countries.map&";
   var countries = L.tileLayer.wms(ms_url, {
     layers: 'countries',
     format: 'image/png',
     transparent: true,
     opacity: 0.7
   });
   ```

   ❑ For Windows, use the following code:

   ```
   // mapserver layer
   var ms_url = "http://localhost
     /cgi-bin/mapserv.exe?
     map=C:%5Cms4w%5CApache%5Chtdocs%5Ccountries.map&";
     var countries = L.tileLayer.wms(ms_url, {
       layers: 'countries',
       format: 'image/png',
       transparent: true,
       opacity: 0.7
     });
   ```

5. Create the Leaflet `map` and add layers to it, as shown in the following code:

```
// map creation
var map = new L.Map('map', {
  center: new L.LatLng(15, 0),
  zoom: 2,
  layers: [osm, countries],
  zoomControl: true
});
```

6. Now, associate the mouse-click event with a function that will perform the
GetFeatureInfo WMS request on the countries layer, by executing the
following code:

```
// getfeatureinfo event
map.addEventListener('click', Identify);

function Identify(e) {
    // set parameters needed for GetFeatureInfo WMS request
    var BBOX = map.getBounds().toBBoxString();
    var WIDTH = map.getSize().x;
    var HEIGHT = map.getSize().y;
    var X = map.layerPointToContainerPoint(e.layerPoint).x;
    var Y = map.layerPointToContainerPoint(e.layerPoint).y;
    // compose the URL for the request
    var URL = ms_url + 'SERVICE=WMS&VERSION=1.1.1&
REQUEST=GetFeatureInfo&LAYERS=countries&
QUERY_LAYERS=countries&BBOX='+BBOX+'&FEATURE_COUNT=1&
HEIGHT='+HEIGHT+'&WIDTH='+WIDTH+'&
INFO_FORMAT=text%2Fhtml&SRS=EPSG%3A4326&X='+X+'&Y='+Y;
    //send the asynchronous HTTP request using jQuery $.ajax
    $.ajax({
      url: URL,
      dataType: "html",
      type: "GET",
      success: function(data) {
        var popup = new L.Popup({
        maxWidth: 300
        });
        popup.setContent(data);
        popup.setLatLng(e.latlng);
        map.openPopup(popup);
      }
    });
}
```

7. Your HTML file should now look like the leaflet.html file contained in data/
chp09. You can now deploy this file to your web server (that is, Apache httpd or IIS). If
you are using Apache httpd in Linux, you could copy the file to the /var/www/data
directory, and if you are using Windows, you could copy it to C:\ms4w\Apache\
htdocs\data (create the data directory if it is not already existing). Then, access it
with the URL http://localhost/data/leaflet.html.

8. Open the web page using your favorite browser and start navigating the map—zoom, pan, and try to click on a point to identify one feature from the `countries` PostGIS layer—as shown in the following screenshot:

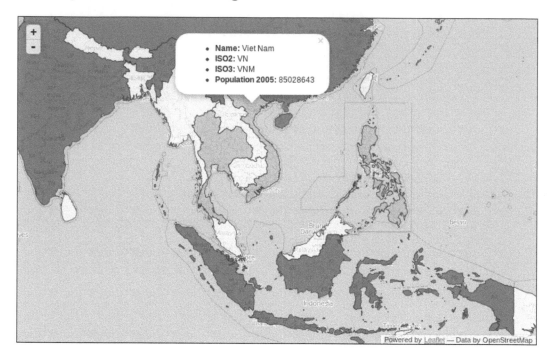

## How it works...

In this recipe, you have seen how to use the Leaflet JavaScript API library to add a map in an HTML page. First, you created one layer from an external server to use it as the base map. Then, you created another layer using the MapServer WMS you implemented in a previous recipe to expose a PostGIS layer to the Web. You then created a new map object and added it to these two layers. Finally, using jQuery, you implemented an AJAX call to the `GetFeatureInfo` WMS request and displayed the results in a Leaflet `Popup` object.

Leaflet is a very nice and compact alternative to the OpenLayers library and gives very good results when your Web GIS service needs to be used from mobile devices such as tablets and smart phones. Additionally, it has a plethora of plugins and can be easily integrated with JavaScript libraries such as Raphael and JS3D.

# Consuming WFS-T services with OpenLayers

In this recipe, you will create the **Transactional Web Feature Service** (**WFS-T**) from a PostGIS layer with the GeoServer open-source web-mapping engine, and then an OpenLayers basic application that will be able to use this service.

This way, the user of the application will be able to manage transactions on the remote PostGIS layer. WFS-T allows the creation, deletion, and updation of features. In this recipe, you will allow the user only to add features, but this recipe should put you on your way to creating more composite use cases.

If you are new to GeoServer and OpenLayers, you should first read the *Creating WMS and WFS services with GeoServer* and *Consuming WMS services with OpenLayers* recipes, and then return to this one.

## Getting ready

1.  Create the proxy script and deploy it to your web server (that is, httpd or IIS), as indicated in the *Getting ready* section of the *Consuming WMS services with OpenLayers* recipe.

2.  Create the following PostGIS points layer, named `sites`:

    ```
    CREATE TABLE chp09.sites
    (
      gid serial NOT NULL,
      the_geom geometry(Point,4326),
      CONSTRAINT sites_pkey PRIMARY KEY (gid )
    );
    CREATE INDEX sites_the_geom_gist ON chp09.sites
      USING gist (the_geom );
    ```

3.  Now, create a PostGIS layer in GeoServer for the `chp09.sites` table. For more information on this, refer to the *Creating WMS and WFS services with GeoServer* recipe in this chapter.

## How to do it...

Carry out the following steps:

1. Create a new file named `wfst.html`. Open it and add the `<head>` and `<body>` tags. In the `<head>` tag, import the `OpenLayers` library:

```
<html>
  <head>
    <title>Consuming a WFS-T with OpenLayers</title>
    <script
      src="http://openlayers.org/api/OpenLayers.js"></script>
  </head>
  <body>
  </body>
</html>
```

2. Add a `<div>` tag in the `<body>` tag to contain the OpenLayers map, as shown in the following code; the map will have a width of 700 pixels and a height of 400 pixels:

```
<div style="width:700px; height:400px" id="map"></div>.
```

3. Just after the `<div>` tag is made to contain the map, add a JavaScript script. Inside the script, start setting `ProxyHost` to the web location where you deployed your proxy script. Then, create a new OpenLayers map, as shown in the following code:

```
<script type="text/javascript">
  // set the proxy
  OpenLayers.ProxyHost = "/cgi-bin/proxy.cgi?url=";
  // create the map
  var map = new OpenLayers.Map('map');
</script>
```

4. Now, in the script, after creating the map, create an `OpenStreetMap` layer that you will use in the map as the base layer, using the following code:

```
// create an OSM base layer
var osm = new OpenLayers.Layer.OSM();
```

5. Now, create the WFS-T layer's `OpenLayers` object using the `StyleMap` object to render the PostGIS layer features with red points, as shown in the following screenshot:

```
// create the wfs layer
var saveStrategy = new OpenLayers.Strategy.Save();
var wfs = new OpenLayers.Layer.Vector(
"Sites",
{
```

```
strategies: [new OpenLayers.Strategy.BBOX(),
  saveStrategy],
projection: new OpenLayers.Projection("EPSG:4326"),
styleMap: new OpenLayers.StyleMap({
  pointRadius: 7,
  fillColor: "#FF0000"
}),
protocol: new OpenLayers.Protocol.WFS({
  version: "1.1.0",
  srsName: "EPSG:4326",
  url: "http://localhost:8080/geoserver/wfs",
  featurePrefix: 'postgis_cookbook',
  featureType: "sites",
  featureNS: "http://www.packtpub.com/postgis-
    cookbook/book",
  geometryName: "the_geom"
})
});
```

6. Add the WFS layer to the map, center align the map, and set the initial zoom. You can use the `geometry transform` method to convert a point from `EPSG:4326`, in which the layer is stored, to `ESPG:900913`, which is used by the viewer, as shown in the following code:

```
// add layers to map and center it
map.addLayers([osm, wfs]);
var fromProjection = new
  OpenLayers.Projection("EPSG:4326");
var toProjection   = new
  OpenLayers.Projection("EPSG:900913");
var cpoint = new OpenLayers.LonLat(12.5, 41.85).transform(
  fromProjection, toProjection);
map.setCenter(cpoint, 10);
```

7. Now, you will create a panel with a *Draw Point* tool (to add new features) and a *Save Features* tool (to save the features to the underlying WFS-T). We first create the panel, as shown in the following code:

```
// create a panel for tools
var panel = new OpenLayers.Control.Panel({
    displayClass: "olControlEditingToolbar"
});
```

8. Now, we will create the *Draw Point* tool, as shown in the following code:

```
// create a draw point tool
var draw = new OpenLayers.Control.DrawFeature(
  wfs, OpenLayers.Handler.Point,
  {
    handlerOptions: {freehand: false, multi: false},
    displayClass: "olControlDrawFeaturePoint"
  }
);
```

9. Then, we will create the *Save Features* tool, using the following code:

```
// create a save tool
var save = new OpenLayers.Control.Button({
  title: "Save Features",
  trigger: function() {
    saveStrategy.save();
  },
  displayClass: "olControlSaveFeatures"
});
```

10. Finally, add the tools to the panel, including a navigation control, and the panel as a control to the map, using the following code:

```
// add tools to panel and add it to map
panel.addControls([
  new OpenLayers.Control.Navigation(),
  save, draw
]);
map.addControl(panel);
```

11. Your HTML file should now look like the `wfst.html` file contained in the `chp09` directory. Deploy this file to your web server (that is, Apache httpd or IIS). If you are using Apache httpd in Linux, you could copy the file to the `data` directory under `/var/www`, whereas if you are using Windows, you could copy it to the data directory under `C:\ms4w\Apache\htdocs` (create the `data` directory if it is not already existing). Then, access it using `http://localhost/data/wfst.html`.

12. Open the web page using your favorite browser and start adding some points to the map. Now, click on the **Save** button and reload the page; the previously added points should still be there as they had been stored in the underlying `PostGIS` table by WFS-T, as shown in the following screenshot:

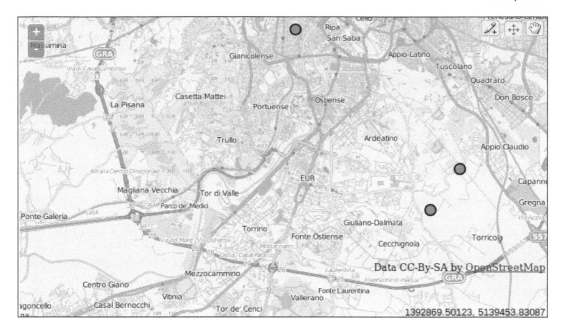

## How it works...

In this recipe, you first created a point `PostGIS` table and then published it as WFS-T using GeoServer. You then created a basic OpenLayers application using the WFS-T layer, allowing the user to add features to the underlying PostGIS layer.

In OpenLayers, the core object needed to implement such a service is the Vector layer, by defining a WFS protocol. When defining the WFS protocol, you have to provide the WFS version to use, the spatial reference system of the dataset, the URI of the service, the name of the layer (for GeoServer, the name is a combination of the layer workspace, `FeaturePrefix`, and the layer name, `FeatureType`), and the name of the `geometry` field that will be modified. You also can pass to the Vector layer constructor a `StyleMap` value to define the layer's rendering behavior.

You then tested the application by adding some points to the OpenLayers map and checked that those points were effectively stored in PostGIS. When adding the points using the WFS-T layer, with the help of tools such as Firefox Firebug or Chrome (Chromium) Developer Tools, you could dig in detail to the requests that you are making to the WFS-T and its responses.

For example, when adding a point, you will see that an `Insert` request is sent to WFS-T. The following XML is sent to the service (note how the point geometry is inserted in the body of the `<wfs:Insert>` element):

```
<wfs:Transaction xmlns:wfs="http://www.opengis.net/wfs"
  service="WFS" version="1.1.0"
  xsi:schemaLocation="http://www.opengis.net/wfs
  http://schemas.opengis.net/wfs/1.1.0/wfs.xsd"
  xmlns:xsi="http://www.w3.org/2001/XMLSchema-instance">
  <wfs:Insert>
    <feature:sites xmlns:feature="http://www.packtpub.com/
      postgis-cookbook/book">
      <feature:the_geom>
        <gml:Point xmlns:gml="http://www.opengis.net/gml"
          srsName="EPSG:4326">
          <gml:pos>12.450561523436999 41.94302128455888</gml:pos>
        </gml:Point>
      </feature:the_geom>
    </feature:sites>
  </wfs:Insert>
</wfs:Transaction>
```

The `<wfs:TransactionResponse>` response, as shown in the following code, will be sent from WFS-T if the process has transpired smoothly and the features have been stored (note that the `<wfs:totalInserted>` element value in this case is set to 1, as only one feature was stored):

```
<?xml version="1.0" encoding="UTF-8"?>
<wfs:TransactionResponse version="1.1.0" ...[CLIP]... >
  <wfs:TransactionSummary>
    <wfs:totalInserted>1</wfs:totalInserted>
    <wfs:totalUpdated>0</wfs:totalUpdated>
    <wfs:totalDeleted>0</wfs:totalDeleted>
  </wfs:TransactionSummary>
  <wfs:TransactionResults/>
  <wfs:InsertResults>
    <wfs:Feature>
      <ogc:FeatureId fid="sites.17"/>
    </wfs:Feature>
  </wfs:InsertResults>
</wfs:TransactionResponse>
```

# Developing web applications with GeoDjango – part 1

In this recipe and the next, you will use the **Django**, a Python web framework, to create a web application to manage wildlife sightings using a PostGIS data store. In this recipe, you will build the back office of the web application, based on the Django admin site.

Upon accessing the back office, an administrative user will be able to, after authentication, manage (insert, update, and delete) the main entities (animals and sightings) of the database. In the next part of the recipe, you will build a front office that displays the sightings on a map based on the **Leaflet** JavaScript library.

 You can find a copy of the whole project that you are going to build in the code bundle under `chp09/wildlife`. Refer to it if a concept is not clear, or if you want to copy and paste the code as you go through the steps of the recipe, rather than typing code from scratch.

## Getting ready

1.  If you are new to Django, check out the official Django tutorial at `https://docs.djangoproject.com/en/dev/intro/tutorial01/`, and then return to this recipe.

2.  Create a Python *virtualenv* (`http://www.virtualenv.org/en/latest/`) to create an isolated Python environment to use with the web application you will build in this recipe and the next. Then, activate the environment, as follows:

    ❏  Use the following commands in Linux:

    ```
    $ cd ~/virtualenvs/
    $ virtualenv --no-site-packages chp09-env
    $ source chp09-env/bin/activate
    ```

    ❏  Type the following commands in Windows (for steps to install virtualenv on Windows, refer to `https://zignar.net/2012/06/17/install-python-on-windows/`):

    ```
    cd c:\virtualenvs
    C:\Python27\Scripts\virtualenv.exe –no-site-packages chp09-env
    chp09-env\Scripts\activate
    ```

3. Once activated, you can install the Python packages that you will use for this recipe as well as the next, using the `pip` tool (`http://www.pip-installer.org/en/latest/`).

   ❑ In Linux, the command would be as follows:

   ```
   (chp09-env)$ pip install django==1.5.1
   (chp09-env)$ pip install psycopg2
   (chp09-env)$ pip install pil
   ```

   ❑ In Windows, the command would be as follows:

   ```
   (chp09-env) C:\virtualenvs> pip install django==1.5.1
   (chp09-env) C:\virtualenvs> pip install psycopg2
   (chp09-env) C:\virtualenvs> easy_install pil
   ```

4. If you haven't done it so far, download the world countries shapefile from `http://thematicmapping.org/downloads/TM_WORLD_BORDERS-0.3.zip`. A copy of this shapefile is included in the code bundle of this book. Extract the shapefile to the `working/chp09` directory.

## How to do it...

Carry out the following steps:

1. Create a Django project using the `django-admin` command with the `startproject` option. Name the project `wildlife`. The command for creating the project will be as follows:

   ```
   (chp09-env)$ cd ~/postgis_cookbook/working/chp09
   (chp09-env)$ django-admin.py startproject wildlife
   ```

2. Create a Django application using the `django-admin` command with the `startapp` option. Name the application `sightings`. The command will be as follows:

   ```
   (chp09-env)$ cd wildlife/
   (chp09-env)$ django-admin.py startapp sightings
   ```

   Now, you should have the following directory structure:

   ```
   wildlife/
   ├── manage.py
   ├── sightings
   │   ├── __init__.py
   │   ├── models.py
   │   ├── tests.py
   │   └── views.py
   └── wildlife
       ├── __init__.py
       ├── settings.py
       ├── urls.py
       └── wsgi.py
   ```

3. You will need to edit some of the settings in the `settings.py` file under `chp09/wildlife/wildlife`. First, the DATABASES settings should be as shown in the following code in order to use the `postgis_cookbook` PostGIS database for your application data:

```
DATABASES = {
  'default': {
    'ENGINE': 'django.contrib.gis.db.backends.postgis',
    'NAME': 'postgis_cookbook',
    'USER': 'me',
    'PASSWORD': 'mypassword',
    'HOST': 'localhost',
    'PORT': '',
  }
}
```

4. Add the two following lines of code at the top of the `wildlife/settings.py` file (PROJECT_PATH is the variable in which you will set the project's path in the settings menu):

```
import os
PROJECT_PATH = os.path.abspath(os.path.dirname(__file__))
```

5. Make sure that in the `settings.py` file under `chp09/wildlife/wildlife`, MEDIA_ROOT, and MEDIA_URL are correctly set, as shown in the following code (this is to set the media files' path and URLs for the images that the administrative user will upload):

```
MEDIA_ROOT = os.path.join(PROJECT_PATH, "media")
MEDIA_URL = '/media/'
```

6. Make sure that the INSTALLED_APPS setting looks as shown in the following code in the `settings.py` file. You will use the Django admin site (django.contrib.admin), the GeoDjango core library (django.contrib.gis), and the sightings application you are creating in this recipe and the next. For this purpose, add the last three lines:

```
INSTALLED_APPS = (
  'django.contrib.auth',
  'django.contrib.contenttypes',
  'django.contrib.sessions',
  'django.contrib.sites',
  'django.contrib.messages',
  'django.contrib.staticfiles',
  'django.contrib.admin',
  'django.contrib.gis',
  'sightings',
)
```

7.  Now, synchronize the database using the Django `syncdb` management command, using the following command; when prompted to create a *superuser*, answer `yes` and choose a preferred administrative username and password:

    **(chp09-env)\$ python manage.py syncdb**

8.  Now, you will add the models needed by the application. Edit the `models.py` file under `chp09/wildlife/sightings` and add the following code:

```python
from django.db import models
from django.contrib.gis.db import models as gismodels


class Country(gismodels.Model):
    """
    Model to represent countries.
    """
    isocode = gismodels.CharField(max_length=2)
    name = gismodels.CharField(max_length=255)
    geometry = gismodels.MultiPolygonField(srid=4326)
    objects = gismodels.GeoManager()

    def __unicode__(self):
        return '%s' % (self.name)

class Animal(models.Model):
    """
    Model to represent animals.
    """
    name = models.CharField(max_length=255)
    image = models.ImageField(upload_to='animals.images')

    def __unicode__(self):
        return '%s' % (self.name)

    def image_url(self):
        return u'<img src="%s" alt="%s" width="80"></img>' % \
          (self.image.url,
            self.name)
    image_url.allow_tags = True

    class Meta:
        ordering = ['name']

class Sighting(gismodels.Model):
    """
```

```
Model to represent sightings.
"""
RATE_CHOICES = (
    (1, '*'),
    (2, '**'),
    (3, '***'),
)
date = gismodels.DateTimeField()
description = gismodels.TextField()
rate = gismodels.IntegerField(choices=RATE_CHOICES)
animal = gismodels.ForeignKey(Animal)
geometry = gismodels.PointField(srid=4326)
objects = gismodels.GeoManager()

def __unicode__(self):
    return '%s' % (self.date)

class Meta:
    ordering = ['date']
```

9.  Each model will become a table in the database with the corresponding fields defined using the `models` and `gismodels` class. Note that the `geometry` variable in the `county` and `sighting` models will become the `MultiPolygon` and `Point` PostGIS geometry columns, thanks to the GeoDjango library. Now, we synchronize the database by executing the following code:

```
(chp09-env)$ python manage.py syncdb
Creating tables ...
Creating table sightings_animal
Creating table sightings_sighting
Creating table sightings_country
```

10. Now, for each model in `models.py`, a PostgreSQL table should have been created. Check whether or not your PostgreSQL database effectively contains the three tables created in the preceding commands using your favorite client (that is, *psql* or *pgAdmin*), and whether or not the `sightings_sighting` and `sightings_country` tables contain PostGIS geometric fields.

11. Create an `admin.py` file under `chp09/wildlife/sightings` and add the following code to it. The classes in this file will define and customize the behavior of the Django admin site when browsing the application models or tables (fields to display, fields to be used to filter records, and fields to order records). Create the file containing the following code:

```
from django.contrib import admin
from django.contrib.gis.admin import GeoModelAdmin
from models import Country, Animal, Sighting
```

```
class SightingAdmin(GeoModelAdmin):
    """
    Web admin behavior for the Sighting model.
    """
    model = Sighting
    list_display = ['date', 'animal', 'rate']
    list_filter = ['date', 'animal', 'rate']
    date_hierarchy = 'date'

class AnimalAdmin(admin.ModelAdmin):
    """
    Web admin behavior for the Animal model.
    """
    model = Animal
    list_display = ['name', 'image_url',]

class CountryAdmin(GeoModelAdmin):
    """
    Web admin behavior for the Country model.
    """
    model = Country
    list_display = ['isocode', 'name']
    ordering = ('name',)

    class Meta:
        verbose_name_plural = 'countries'

admin.site.register(Animal, AnimalAdmin)
admin.site.register(Sighting, SightingAdmin)
admin.site.register(Country, CountryAdmin)
```

12. Any web application needs the definition of URLs where the pages can be accessed. Therefore, edit your `urls.py` file under `chp09/wildlife/wildlife` by adding the following code:

```
from django.conf.urls import patterns, include, url
from django.conf import settings

from django.contrib import admin
admin.autodiscover()

urlpatterns = patterns('',
    url(r'^admin/', include(admin.site.urls)),
)

# media files
urlpatterns += patterns('',
    (r'^media/(?P<path>.*)$', 'django.views.static.serve', {
    'document_root': settings.MEDIA_ROOT})
)
```

13. In the `urls.py` file, you basically defined the location of the back office (which was built using the Django admin application), and the media (images) files' location uploaded by the Django administrator when adding new `animal` entities in the database. Now, run the Django development server using the following `runserver` management command:

```
(chp09-env)$ python manage.py runserver
```

14. Access the Django admin site at `http://localhost:8000/admin/`, and log in with the superuser credentials you furnished in an earlier step in this recipe when you initially synced the Django database.

15. Now, navigate to `http://localhost:8000/admin/sightings/animal/` and add some animals using the **Add animal** button. For each animal, define a name and an image that will be used by the frontend that you will build in the next recipe. You created this page with almost no code, thanks to the Django admin! The following screenshot shows what the **Animals** list page will look like after adding some entities:

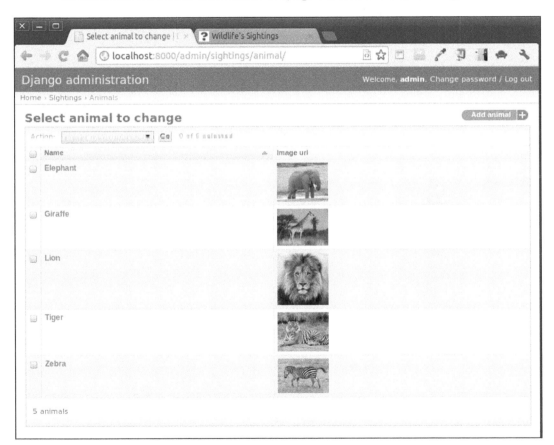

16. Navigate to `http://localhost:8000/admin/sightings/sighting/` and add some sightings using the **Add sighting** button. For each sighting, define the **Date**, **Time**, the name of the animal that was spotted, the **Rate**, and the location. GeoDjango has added the map widget to the Django Admin site for you, based on the OpenLayers JavaScript library, to add or modify geometric features. The **Sightings** page is shown in the following screenshot:

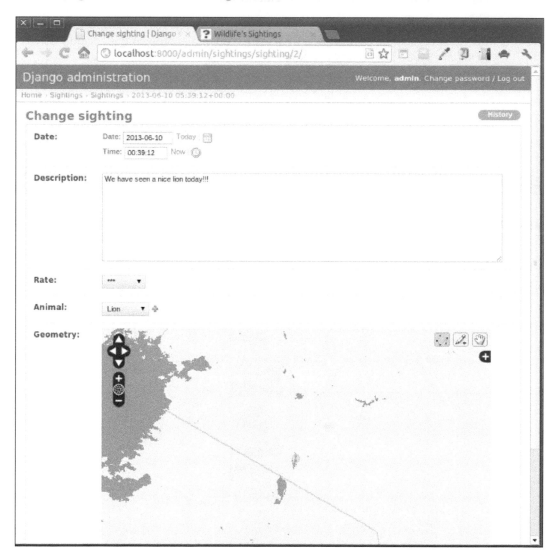

17. The **Sightings** list page, thanks to the Django admin's efficiency, will provide the administrative user with useful features to sort, filter, and navigate the date hierarchy of all of the sightings in the system, as shown in the following screenshot:

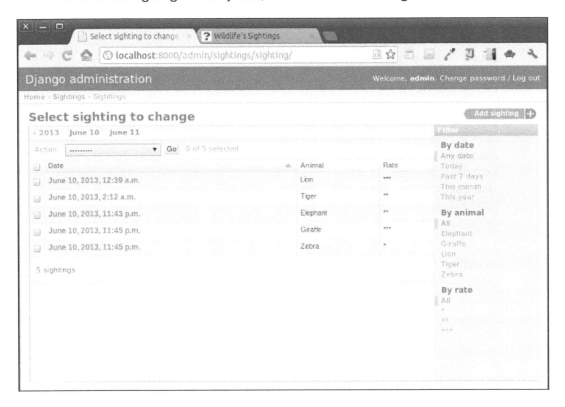

18. Now, you will import the `countries` shapefile to its model. In the next recipe, you will use this model to find out the country where each sighting occurred. Before going ahead in this recipe, investigate the shapefile structure—you will need to import just the `NAME` and `ISO2` attributes to the model as the `name` and `isocode` attributes, using the following command:

```
$ ogrinfo TM_WORLD_BORDERS-0.3.shp TM_WORLD_BORDERS-0.3 -al -so
INFO: Open of `TM_WORLD_BORDERS-0.3.shp'
        using driver `ESRI Shapefile' successful.

Layer name: TM_WORLD_BORDERS-0.3
Geometry: Polygon
Feature Count: 246
Extent: (-180.000000, -90.000000) - (180.000000, 83.623596)
```

```
Layer SRS WKT:
GEOGCS["GCS_WGS_1984",
    DATUM["WGS_1984",
        SPHEROID["WGS_84",6378137.0,298.257223563]],
    PRIMEM["Greenwich",0.0],
    UNIT["Degree",0.0174532925199433]]
FIPS: String (2.0)
ISO2: String (2.0)
ISO3: String (3.0)
UN: Integer (3.0)
NAME: String (50.0)
AREA: Integer (7.0)
POP2005: Integer (10.0)
REGION: Integer (3.0)
SUBREGION: Integer (3.0)
LON: Real (8.3)
LAT: Real (7.3)
```

19. Add a `load_countries.py` file under `chp09/wildlife/sightings`, and import the shapefile to PostGIS using the `LayerMapping` GeoDjango utility with the following code:

```python
"""
Script to load the data for the country model from a shapefile.
"""

from django.contrib.gis.utils import mapping, LayerMapping
from models import Country

country_mapping = {
    'isocode' : 'ISO2',
    'name' : 'NAME',
    'geometry' : 'MULTIPOLYGON',
}

country_shp = '../TM_WORLD_BORDERS-0.3.shp'
country_lm = LayerMapping(Country, country_shp, country_mapping,
    transform=False, encoding='iso-8859-1')
country_lm.save(verbose=True, progress=True)
```

20. Enter the Python Django shell and run the `utils.py` script. Then, check whether or not the countries have been correctly inserted in the `sightings_country` table in your PostgreSQL database:

```
(chp09-env)$ python manage.py shell
>>> from sightings import load_countries
```

```
Saved: Antigua and Barbuda
Saved: Algeria
Saved: Azerbaijan
...
Saved: Taiwan
```

Now, you should see the countries in the administrative interface. Try to browse some of the countries at `http://localhost:8000/admin/sightings/country/`.

## How it works...

In this recipe, you have seen how quick and efficient it is to assemble a back office application using **Django**, one of the most popular Python web frameworks; this is thanks to its object-relational mapper, which automatically created the database tables needed by your application and an automatic API to manage (insert, update, and delete) and query the entities without using SQL.

Thanks to the **GeoDjango** library, two of the application models, County and Sighting, have been geo-enabled with their introduction in the database tables of `geometric` PostGIS fields.

You have customized the powerful **automatic administrative interface** to quickly assemble the back office pages of your application. Using the **Django URL Dispatcher**, you have defined the URL routes for your application in a concise manner.

As you may have noticed, what is extremely nice about the Django abstraction is the automatic implementation of the data-access layer API using the models. You can now add, update, delete, and query records using Python code, without having any knowledge of SQL. Try this yourself using the Django Python shell; you will select an animal from the database, add a new sighting for that animal, and then finally delete the sighting. You can investigate the SQL generated by Django behind the scenes at any time, using the `django.db.connection` class, with the following command:

```
(chp09-env-bis)$ python manage.py shell
>>> from django.db import connection
>>> from datetime import datetime
>>> from sightings.models import Sighting, Animal
>>> an_animal = Animal.objects.all()[0]
>>> an_animal
<Animal: Lion>
>>> print connection.queries[-1]['sql']
SELECT "sightings_animal"."id", "sightings_animal"."name",
"sightings_animal"."image" FROM "sightings_animal" ORDER BY
"sightings_animal"."name" ASC LIMIT 1'
>>> my_sight = Sighting(date=datetime.now(), description='What a
lion I have seen!', rate=1, animal=an_animal, geometry='POINT(10
10)')
>>> my_sight.save()
```

```
print connection.queries[-1]['sql']
INSERT INTO "sightings_sighting" ("date", "description", "rate",
"animal_id", "geometry") VALUES ('2013-06-12 14:37:36.544268-
05:00', 'What a lion I have seen!', 1, 2, ST_GeomFromEWKB('\x01010
00020e6100000000000000000002440000000000000002440'::bytea)) RETURNING
"sightings_sighting"."id"
>>> my_sight.delete()
>>> print connection.queries[-1]['sql']
DELETE FROM "sightings_sighting" WHERE "id" IN (5)
```

Do you like Django as much as we do? In the next recipe, you will create the front end of the application. You will be able to browse the sightings in a map, implemented with the Leaflet JavaScript library. So, keep reading!

# Developing web applications with GeoDjango – part 2

In this recipe, you will create the front office for the web application you created using **Django**, in the previous recipe.

Using HTML and the **Django template language**, you will create a web page displaying a map, implemented with Leaflet, and a list to the user containing all of the sightings available in the system. The user will be able to navigate the map and identify the sightings to get more information.

## Getting ready

1.  Make sure you have gone through every single step of the previous recipe, keeping the back office of the web application working and its database populated with some entities.

2.  Activate the *virtualenv* you created in the *Developing web applications with GeoDjango – part 1* recipe, as follows:

    ❑   Use the following command for Linux:

    ```
    $ cd ~/virtualenvs/
    $ source chp09-env/bin/activate
    ```

    ❑   Use the following command for Windows:

    ```
    cd c:\virtualenvs
    > chp09-env\Scripts\activate
    ```

3. Install the libraries that you will use in this recipe; you will need `simplejson` and `vectorformats` Python libraries to produce a GeoJSON (http://www.geojson.org/) response that will feed the sighting layer in Leaflet.

   ❑ Use the following command for Linux:

      **(chp09-env)$ pip install simplejson**

      **(chp09-env)$ pip install vectorformats**

   ❑ Use the following command for Windows:

      **(chp09-env) C:\virtualenvs> pip install simplejson**

      **(chp09-env) C:\virtualenvs> pip install vectorformats**

## How to do it...

You will now create the front page of your web application, as follows:

1. Go to the directory containing the Django wildlife web application and add the following lines to the `urls.py` file under `chp09/wildlife/wildlife`:

```
from django.conf.urls import patterns, include, url
from django.conf import settings

from sightings.views import get_geojson, home

from django.contrib import admin
admin.autodiscover()

urlpatterns = patterns('',
  url(r'^admin/', include(admin.site.urls)),

  (r'^geojson/', get_geojson),
  (r'^$', home),
)

# media files
urlpatterns += patterns('',
  (r'^media/(?P<path>.*)$', 'django.views.static.serve', {
  'document_root': settings.MEDIA_ROOT}))
```

2. Open the `views.py` file under `chp09/wildlife/sightings` and add the following code. The `home` view will return the home page of your application, with the list of sightings and the Leaflet map. The `sighting` layer in the map will display the GeoJSON response given by the `get_geojson` view:

```python
from django.shortcuts import render_to_response
from django.http import HttpResponse
from vectorformats.Formats import Django, GeoJSON
from models import Sighting


def home(request):
    """
    Display the home page with the list and a map of the
      sightings.
    """
    sightings  = Sighting.objects.all()
    return render_to_response("sightings/home.html",
      {'sightings' : sightings})


def get_geojson(request):
    """
    Get geojson (needed by the map) for all of the sightings.
    """
    sightings  = Sighting.objects.all()
    djf = Django.Django(geodjango='geometry',
      properties=['animal_name',
      'animal_image_url', 'description', 'rate',
        'date_formatted',
      'country_name'])
    geoj = GeoJSON.GeoJSON()
    s = geoj.encode(djf.decode(sightings))
    return HttpResponse(s)
```

3. Add the following `@property` definitions to the `Sighting` class in the `models.py` file under `chp09/wildlife/sightings`. The `get_geojson` view will need to use these properties to compose the GeoJSON view needed from the Leaflet map and the information pop up. Note how in the `country_name` property, you are using GeoDjango, which contains a spatial-lookup QuerySet operator to detect the country where the sighting happened:

```python
@property
def date_formatted(self):
    return self.date.strftime('%m/%d/%Y')


@property
def animal_name(self):
```

```
    return self.animal.name

@property
def animal_image_url(self):
  return self.animal.image_url()

@property
def country_name(self):
  country  = Country.objects.filter(
    geometry__contains=self.geometry)[0]
  return country.name
```

4. Add a `home.html` file, containing the following code, under `sightings/templates/sightings`. Using the Django template language, you will display the number of sightings in the system, a list of these sightings with the main information for each of them, and the Leaflet map. Using the Leaflet JavaScript API, you add a base OpenStreetMap layer to the map. Then, you make an asynchronous call, using jQuery, to the `get_geojson` view (accessed by adding `/geojson` to the request URL), that in case of success of the query, will feed a Leaflet `GeoJSON` layer with the features from the sighting PostGIS layer and associate with each feature an informative pop up. This pop up will open any time the user clicks on a point on the map representing a sighting, displaying the main information for that entity:

```html
<!DOCTYPE html>
<html>
  <head>
    <title>Wildlife's Sightings</title>
    <link rel="stylesheet" href="http://leafletjs.com/dist/
leaflet.css" />
    <script src="http://leafletjs.com/dist/leaflet.js"></script>
    <script src="http://ajax.googleapis.com/ajax/libs/
jquery/1.9.1/jquery.min.js"></script>
  </head>
  <body>

    <h1>Wildlife's Sightings</h1>

    <p>There are {{ sightings.count }} sightings in the
      database.</p>
    <div id="map" style="width:800px; height:500px"></div>

    <ul>
    {% for s in sightings %}
      <li><strong>{{ s.animal }}</strong>,
        seen in {{ s.country_name }} on {{ s.date }}
        and rated {{ s.rate }}</li>
```

```
{% endfor %}
</ul>

<script type="text/javascript">

// OSM layer
var osm =
  L.tileLayer('http://{s}.tile.osm.org/{z}/{x}/{y}.png', {
  maxZoom: 18,
  attribution: "Data by OpenStreetMap"
});

// map creation
var map = new L.Map('map', {
  center: new L.LatLng(15, 0),
  zoom: 2,
  layers: [osm],
  zoomControl: true
});

// add GeoJSON layer
$.ajax({
  type: "GET",
  url: "geojson",
  dataType: 'json',
  success: function (response) {
    geojsonLayer = L.geoJson(response, {
      style: function (feature) {
        return {color: feature.properties.color};
      },
      onEachFeature: function (feature, layer) {
        var html = "<strong>" +
          feature.properties.animal_name
          + "</strong><br />"
          + feature.properties.animal_image_url
          + "<br /><strong>Description:</strong> "
          + feature.properties.description
          + "<br /><strong>Rate:</strong> "
          + feature.properties.rate
          + "<br /><strong>Date:</strong> "
          + feature.properties.date_formatted
          + "<br /><strong>Country:</strong> "
          + feature.properties.country_name
        layer.bindPopup(html);
```

```
            }
        }).addTo(map);
        }
    });

    </script>

    </body>
</html>
```

5. Now that your front end page is completed, you can finally access it at `http://localhost:8000/`. Navigate the map and try to identify some of the displayed sightings to check whether or not the pop up opens as shown in the following screenshot:

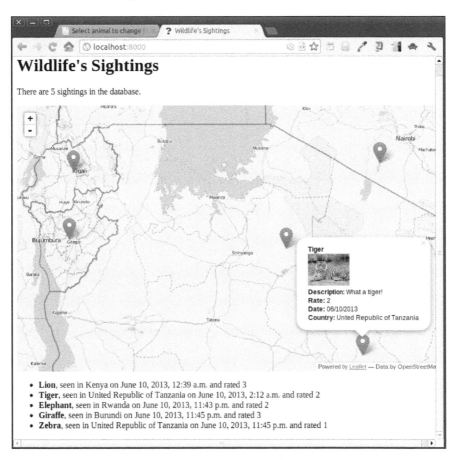

## How it works...

You created an HTML front page for the web application you developed in the previous recipe. The HTML is dynamically created using the Django Template language (https://docs.djangoproject.com/en/dev/topics/templates/), and the map was implemented with the Leaflet JavaScript library.

The Django template language uses the response from the home view to generate a list of all of the sightings in the system.

The map was created using Leaflet. First, an OpenStreetMap layer was created to be used as a base map. Then, using jQuery, you fed a GeoJSON layer that displays all of the features generated by the `get_geojson` view. You associated a popup with the layer that opens every time the user clicks on a sighting entity. The popup displays the main information for that sighting, including a picture of the sighted animal.

# 10
# Maintenance, Optimization, and Performance Tuning

In this chapter, we will cover the following recipes:

- ▶ Organizing the database
- ▶ Setting up the correct data privilege mechanism
- ▶ Backing up the database
- ▶ Using indexes
- ▶ Clustering for efficiency
- ▶ Optimizing SQL queries
- ▶ Migrating a PostGIS database to a different server
- ▶ Replicating a PostGIS database with streaming replication

## Introduction

Unlike prior chapters, this chapter does not discuss the capabilities or applications of PostGIS. Instead, this chapter focuses on the techniques for organizing the database, improving query performance, and ensuring the long-term viability of the spatial data.

These techniques are frequently ignored or set aside by most PostGIS users until it is too late, such as data loss due to user action or decreasing performance as the volume of data or users increases. Such neglect is often due to the amount of time required to learn about each technique as well as implement it. This chapter attempts to demonstrate each technique in a distilled manner that minimizes the learning curve and maximizes the benefits.

# Organizing the database

One of the most important things to consider when creating and using a database is how to organize the data. The layout of the database should be decided when you first establish the database. The layout can be decided or changed at a later date, but this is almost guaranteed to be a tedious, if not difficult, task. If it is never decided, a database will become disorganized over time and introduce significant hurdles when upgrading components or running backups.

By default, a new PostgreSQL database has only one **schema**, that is, `public`. Most users place all the data (their own and third-party modules such as PostGIS) in the `public` schema. Doing so mixes information of different origins. An easy method to separate the information is to use schemas. This enables using one schema for our data and a separate schema for everything else.

## Getting ready

In this recipe, we will create a database and install PostGIS in its own schema. We will also load some geometries and rasters for further use by other recipes in this chapter.

The following are the two methods to create a PostGIS-enabled database:

▸ Using the `CREATE EXTENSION` statement

▸ Running the installation SQL scripts with a PostgreSQL client

The `CREATE EXTENSION` method is available if you are running PostgreSQL 9.1 or a higher version and is the recommended method for installing PostGIS.

## How to do it...

Carry out the following steps to create and organize a database:

1. Create a database named `chapter10` by executing the following command:

   **`CREATE DATABASE chapter10;`**

2. Create a schema named `postgis` in the `chapter10` database, where we will install PostGIS; execute the following command:

   **`CREATE SCHEMA postgis;`**

3. Install PostGIS in the `postgis` schema of the `chapter10` database.

    1. If you are running PostgreSQL 9.1 or a newer version, use the CREATE EXTENSION statement.

```
CREATE EXTENSION postgis WITH SCHEMA postgis;
```

       The WITH SCHEMA clause of the CREATE EXTENSION statement instructs PostgreSQL to install PostGIS and its objects in the `postgis` schema.

    2. If you are not running PostgreSQL 9.1 or a higher version, run PostGIS's `postgis.sql`, `spatial_ref_sys.sql`, and `rtpostgis.sql` files. But, before doing so, make sure you set the `search_path` field to the PostGIS schema.

```
> psql -d chapter10
chapter10=# SET search_path = postgis;
chapter10=# \i /PATHTOFILE/postgis.sql
chapter10=# \i /PATHTOFILE/rtpostgis.sql
chapter10=# \i /PATHTOFILE/spatial_ref_sys.sql
```

4. Check whether or not the PostGIS installation has succeeded:

```
> psql -d chapter10
  chapter10=# SET search_path = public, postgis;
SET
  chapter10=# \dn
  List of schemas
  Name    |   Owner
----------+-----------
 postgis  | postgres
 public   | postgres
(2 rows)
chapter10=# \d
          List of relations
  Schema  |        Name        | Type  |  Owner
----------+--------------------+-------+-----------
 postgis  | geography_columns  | view  | postgres
 postgis  | geometry_columns   | view  | postgres
 postgis  | raster_columns     | view  | postgres
 postgis  | raster_overviews   | view  | postgres
 postgis  | spatial_ref_sys    | table | postgres
```

5. The `SET` statement instructs PostgreSQL to consider the `public` and `postgis` schemas when processing any SQL statements from our client connection. Without the `SET` statement, the `\d` command will not return any relation from the `postgis` schema.

6. To prevent the need to manually use the `SET` statement every time a client connects to the `chapter10` database, alter the database by executing the following command:

   ```
   ALTER DATABASE chapter10 SET search_path = public, postgis;
   ```

   All future connections and queries of `chapter10` will result in PostgreSQL automatically using both `public` and `postgis` schemas.

7. Load the PRISM rasters and San Francisco boundaries geometry, which we used in *Chapter 5, Working with Raster Data*, by executing the following command:

   ```
   > raster2pgsql -s 4322 -t 100x100 -I -F -C -Y
     C:\postgis_cookbook\data\chap5\PRISM\us_tmin_2012.01.asc
     prism | psql -d chapter10
   ```

8. As in *Chapter 5, Working with Raster Data*, we will postprocess the raster filenames to a `date` column by executing the following command:

   ```
   ALTER TABLE prism ADD COLUMN month_year DATE;
   UPDATE prism SET
           month_year = (
                   split_part(split_part(filename, '.', 1), '_', 3)
   || '-' ||
                   split_part(filename, '.', 2) || '-01'
           )::date;
   ```

9. Then, we load the San Francisco boundaries by executing the following command:

   ```
   > shp2pgsql -s 3310 -I
     C:\postgis_cookbook\data\chap5\SFPoly\sfpoly.shp sfpoly |
     psql -d chapter10
   ```

10. Copy this chapter's dataset to its own directory by executing the following commands:

    ```
    > mkdir C:\postgis_cookbook\data\chap10
    ```

    ```
    > cp -r /path/to/book_dataset/chap10
      C:\postgis_cookbook\data\chap10
    ```

11. We will use the shapefiles for California schools and police stations, provided by the USEIT program at the University of Southern California. Import the shapefiles by executing the following commands; use the spatial index flag -I only for the police stations shapefile:

```
> shp2pgsql -s 4269 -I
  C:\postgis_cookbook\data\chap10\CAEmergencyFacilities
  \CA_police.shp capolice | psql -d chapter10
```

```
> shp2pgsql -s 4269
  C:\postgis_cookbook\data\chap10\CAEmergencyFacilities
  \CA_schools.shp caschools | psql -d chapter10
```

Visit the following link to download the shapefiles for California schools and police stations:

```
http://scec.usc.edu/internships/useit/content/california-
emergency-facilities-shapefile.
```

## How it works...

In this recipe, we created a new database and installed PostGIS in its own schema. We kept the PostGIS objects separate from our geometries and rasters by not installing PostGIS in the public schema. This separation keeps the public schema tidy and reduces the accidental modification or deletion of the PostGIS objects.

In the following recipes, we will see that our decision to install PostGIS in its own schema results in fewer problems when maintaining the database.

# Setting up the correct data privilege mechanism

PostgreSQL provides a fine-grained privilege system that dictates who can use a particular set of data and how that set of data can be accessed by an approved user. Due to its granular nature, creating an effective set of privileges can be confusing and may result in undesired behavior. There are different levels of access that can be provided, from controlling who can connect to the database server itself, to who can query a view, to who can execute a PostGIS function.

The challenges to establishing a good set of privileges can be minimized by thinking of the database as an onion. The outermost layer has generic rules and each layer inward applies rules more specific than the last. An example of this is a company's database server that only the company's network can access. Only one of the company's divisions can access database A that contains a schema for each department. Within one schema, all users can run the SELECT queries against views, but only specific users can add, update, or delete records from tables.

In PostgreSQL, users and groups are known as **roles**. A role can be parent to other roles that are themselves parents to even more roles. To reduce confusion, we avoid using the term in this recipe as much as possible.

## Getting ready

In this recipe, we focus on establishing the best set of privileges for the `postgis` schema created in the previous recipe. With the right selection of privileges, we can control who can use the contents of and apply operations to a geometry, geography, or raster column.

One idea worth mentioning is that the owner of a database object (such as the database itself, a schema, or a table) always has full control over that object. Unless someone changes the owner, the user who created the database object is typically the owner of the object.

## How to do it...

In the preceding recipe, we imported several rasters and shapefiles to respective tables. By default, access to those tables is restricted to only the user who performed the import operation, also known as the owner. The following steps permit other users to access those tables:

1. By executing the following commands, we will create several groups and users in order for this recipe to demonstrate and test the privileges set on the `chapter10` database.

   ```
   CREATE ROLE group1 NOLOGIN;

   CREATE ROLE group2 NOLOGIN;

   CREATE ROLE user1 LOGIN PASSWORD 'pass1' IN ROLE group1;

   CREATE ROLE user2 LOGIN PASSWORD 'pass2' IN ROLE group1;

   CREATE ROLE user3 LOGIN PASSWORD 'pass3' IN ROLE group2;
   ```

   The first two `CREATE ROLE` statements create the groups, `group1` and `group2`. The last three `CREATE ROLE` statements create three users, with the `user1` and `user2` users assigned to `group1`, and the `user3` user assigned to `group2`.

2. We want the groups, `group1` and `group2`, to have access to the `chapter10` database. We want `group1` to be permitted to connect to the database and create temporary tables, while `group2` is granted all database-level privileges, so we use the `GRANT` statement as follows:

   ```
   GRANT CONNECT, TEMP ON DATABASE chapter10 TO GROUP group1;

   GRANT ALL ON DATABASE chapter10 TO GROUP group2;
   ```

3. Let's check whether or not the GRANT statement worked by executing the following commands:

```
> psql -d chapter10
chapter10=# \l
```

                                List of databases
```
     Name    |   Owner   | Encoding |  Collation  |   Ctype     |
Access privileges
-----------+-----------+----------+-------------+-------------+------
----------------
   chapter10 | postgres  | UTF8     | en_US.UTF8  | en_US.UTF8  | =Tc/
postgres        +
             |           |          |             |             |
postgres=CTc/postgres+
             |           |          |             |             |
group1=Tc/postgres   +
             |           |          |             |             |
group2=CTc/postgres
   postgres  | postgres  | UTF8     | en_US.UTF8  | en_US.UTF8  |
   template0 | postgres  | UTF8     | en_US.UTF8  | en_US.UTF8  | =c/
postgres        +
             |           |          |             |             |
postgres=CTc/postgres
   template1 | postgres  | UTF8     | en_US.UTF8  | en_US.UTF8  | =c/
postgres        +
             |           |          |             |             |
postgres=CTc/postgres
```

4. As you can see, group1 and group2 are present in the Access privileges column of the chapter10 database.

   **group1=Tc/postgres**

   **group2=CTc/postgres**

5. There is one thing in the privileges of chapter10 that may be of concern to us.

   **=Tc/postgres**

6. Unlike the privilege listings for group1 and group2, this listing has no value before the equal sign (=). This listing is for the special public metagroup, which is built into PostgreSQL and to which all users and groups automatically belong.

7. We don't want everyone to have access to the chapter10 database. So, we need to use the REVOKE statement to remove privileges from the public metagroup by executing the following command:

   **REVOKE ALL ON DATABASE chapter10 FROM public;**

8. Let's see what the initial privileges are for the schemas of the chapter10 database by executing the following command:

```
chapter10=# \dn+
```

```
                                       List of schemas
            Name        |   Owner   |   Access privileges    |
Description
-------------------+----------+------------------------+----------
----------------------
 postgis            | postgres  |                         |
 public             | postgres  | postgres=UC/postgres+  | standard
public schema
                    |           |  =UC/postgres           |
```

9. The postgis schema has no privileges listed. This does not mean that no one can access the postgis schema though. Only the owner of the schema—postgres, in this case—can access it. We will grant access to the postgis schema to both group1 and group2 by executing the following command:

```
GRANT USAGE ON SCHEMA postgis TO group1, group2;
```

We generally do not want to grant the CREATE privilege in the postgis schema to any user or group. New objects (such as functions, views, and tables) should not be added to the postgis schema.

10. If we want all users and groups to have access to the postgis schema, we can grant the USAGE privilege to the public metagroup by executing the following command:

```
GRANT USAGE ON SCHEMA postgis TO public;
```

11. Before continuing further, we should check that our privileges have been reflected in the database.

```
chapter10=# \dn+
```

```
                                       List of schemas
            Name        |   Owner   |   Access privileges    |
Description
-------------------+----------+------------------------+----------
----------------------
 postgis            | postgres  | postgres=UC/postgres+  |
                    |           | group1=U/postgres    + |
                    |           | group2=U/postgres      |
 public             | postgres  | postgres=UC/postgres+  | standard
public schema
                    |           |  =UC/postgres           |
```

Granting the USAGE privilege to a schema does not allow the granted users and groups to use any objects in the schema. The USAGE privilege only permits viewing the schema's child objects. Each child object has its own set of privileges, which we establish in the remaining steps.

12. PostGIS comes with more than 1,000 functions. It would be unreasonable to individually set privileges for all those functions. Instead, we grant the EXECUTE privilege to the public metagroup and then grant and/or revoke privileges to specific functions, such as management functions.

13. First, grant the EXECUTE privilege to the public metagroup by executing the following command:

    **GRANT EXECUTE ON ALL FUNCTIONS IN SCHEMA postgis TO public;**

14. Now, revoke the EXECUTE privileges of the public metagroup for some functions, such as postgis_full_version(), by executing the following command:

    **REVOKE ALL ON FUNCTION postgis_full_version() FROM public;**

15. The GRANT and REVOKE statements do not differentiate between tables and views. So, care must be taken to ensure that the applied privileges are appropriate for the object.

16. We will grant the SELECT, REFERENCES, and TRIGGER privileges to the public metagroup on all postgis tables and views by executing the following command; none of these privileges give the public metagroup the ability to alter the tables' or views' contents:

    **GRANT SELECT, REFERENCES, TRIGGER ON ALL TABLES IN SCHEMA
      postgis TO public;**

17. We want to allow group1 to be able to insert new records into the spatial_ref_sys table, so we must execute the following command:

    **GRANT INSERT ON spatial_ref_sys TO group1;**

    Groups and users that are not part of group1 (such as group2) can only use the SELECT statements on spatial_ref_sys. Groups and users that are part of group1 can now use the INSERT statement to add new spatial reference systems.

18. Let's give user2, which is a member of group1, the ability use the UPDATE and DELETE statements on spatial_ref_sys by executing the following command; we are not going to give anyone the privilege to use the TRUNCATE statement on spatial_ref_sys:

    **GRANT UPDATE, DELETE ON spatial_ref_sys TO user2;**

19. After establishing the privileges, it is always good practice to check that they actually work. The best way to do so is by logging into the database as one of of the users. We will use the user3 user to check by executing the following command:

    **> psql -d chapter10 -u user3**

20. Now, check that we can run a `SELECT` statement on the `spatial_ref_sys` table by executing the following commands:

```
chapter10=# SELECT count(*) FROM spatial_ref_sys;
count
-------
  3911
(1 row)
```

21. Let's try inserting a new record in `spatial_ref_sys` by executing the following commands:

```
chapter10=# INSERT INTO spatial_ref_sys VALUES (99999, 'test',
    99999, '', '');
ERROR:  permission denied for relation spatial_ref_sys
```

22. Excellent! Now update records in `spatial_ref_sys` by executing the following commands:

```
chapter10=# UPDATE spatial_ref_sys SET srtext = 'Lorum ipsum';
ERROR:  permission denied for relation spatial_ref_sys
```

23. Run a final check on the `postgis_full_version()` function by executing the following commands:

```
chapter10=# SELECT postgis_full_version();
ERROR:  permission denied for function postgis_full_version
```

## How it works...

In this recipe, we granted and revoked privileges based on the group or user, with security increasing as a group or user descends into the database. This resulted in `group1` and `group2` being able to connect to the `chapter10` database and use objects found in the `postgis` schema. The `group1` group could also insert new records into the `spatial_ref_sys` table. Only the `user2` user was permitted to update or delete the records of `spatial_ref_sys`.

The `GRANT` and `REVOKE` statements used in this recipe work, but they can be tedious to use with a command-line utility such as `psql`. Instead, use a graphical tool, such as pgAdminIII, that provides a grant wizard. Such tools also make it easier to check the behavior of the database after granting and revoking privileges.

For additional practice, set up the privileges on the `public` schema and child objects such that, although `group1` and `group2` will be able to run the `SELECT` queries on the tables, only `group2` will be able to use the `INSERT` statement on the `caschools` table. You will want to make sure that an `INSERT` statement executed by a user of `group2` actually works.

# Backing up the database

Having functional backups of your data and work is probably the least appreciated, yet the most important thing you can do for your productivity (and stress level). You may think that you don't need to have backups of your PostGIS database because you have the original data imported to the database. But, do you remember all the work you did to develop the final product? How about the intermediary products? Even if you remember every step in the process, how much time will it take to create the intermediary and final products?

If any of these questions gives you pause, you need to create a backup for your data. Fortunately, PostgreSQL makes the backup process painless or at least less painful than the alternatives.

## Getting ready

In this recipe, we use PostgreSQL's `pg_dump` utility. The `pg_dump` utility ensures that the data being backed up is consistent, even if it is currently in use.

## How to do it...

Use the following steps to back up a database.

1. Start by backing up the `chapter10` database by executing the following command:

   ```
   > pg_dump -f chapter10.backup -F custom chapter10
   ```

   We use the `f` flag to specify that the backup should be placed in the `chapter10.backup` file. We also use the `-F` flag to set the format of the backup output as custom by default, the most flexible and compressed of `pg_dump`'s output formats.

2. Inspect the backup file by outputting the contents onto a SQL file by executing the following command:

   ```
   > pg_restore -f chapter10.sql chapter10.backup
   ```

   After creating a backup, it is good practice to make sure that the backup is valid. We do so with the `pg_restore` PostgreSQL tool. The `-f` flag instructs `pg_restore` to emit the restored output to a file instead of a database. The emitted output comprises standard SQL statements.

3. Use a text editor to view `chapter10.sql`. You should see blocks of SQL statements for creating tables, filling created tables, and setting privileges shown as follows:

```
SET statement_timeout = 0;
SET client_encoding = 'UTF8';
SET standard_conforming_strings = on;
...
CREATE TABLE capolice (
   gid serial NOT NULL,
   objectid integer,
   policestat character varying(8),
...
REVOKE ALL ON SCHEMA postgis FROM PUBLIC;
REVOKE ALL ON SCHEMA postgis FROM postgres;
GRANT ALL ON SCHEMA postgis TO postgres;
...
```

4. Because we backed up the `chapter10` database using the custom format, we have a fine-grained control over how `pg_restore` behaves and what it restores. Let's extract only the `public` schema using the `-n` flag as follows:

```
> pg_restore -f chapter10_public.sql -n public
  chapter10.backup
```

5. If you compare `chapter10_public.sql` to the `chapter10.sql` file exported in the preceding step, you see that the `postgis` schema is not restored.

## How it works...

As you can see, backing up your database is easy in PostgreSQL. Unfortunately, backups are meaningless if not performed on a regular schedule. If the database is lost or corrupted, any work done since the last backup is also lost. It is encouraged that backups be done at intervals that minimize the amount of work lost. The ideal interval will depend on the frequency of changes done to the database. The `pg_dump` utility can be scheduled to run at regular intervals by adding a job to the operating system's task scheduler, with instructions available in the PostgreSQL wiki at `http://wiki.postgresql.org/wiki/Automated_Backup_on_Windows` and `http://wiki.postgresql.org/wiki/Automated_Backup_on_Linux`.

The `pg_dump` utility is not adequate for all situations. If you have a database undergoing constant changes or one that is larger than a few tens of gigabytes, you will need a backup mechanism far more robust than that discussed in this recipe. Information regarding these robust mechanisms can be found in the PostgreSQL documentation at `http://www.postgresql.org/docs/current/static/backup.html`.

The following are several third-party backup tools available for establishing robust and advanced backup schemes:

▸ Barman, which is available at `http://www.pgbarman.org`

▸ pg-rman, which is available at `http://code.google.com/p/pg-rman`

# Using indexes

A database index is very much like the index of a book (such as this one). While a book's index indicates the pages on which a word is present, a database column index indicates the rows in a table containing a searched value. Just as a book's index does not indicate exactly where on the page a word is located, the database index may not be able to denote the exact location of the searched value in a row's column.

PostgreSQL has several types of indexes, such as `B-Tree`, `Hash`, `GIST`, `SP-GIST`, and `GIN`. All these index types are designed to help queries find matching rows faster. What makes the indexes different is the underlying algorithms. Generally, to keep things simple, almost all PostgreSQL indexes are of the `B-Tree` type. PostGIS (spatial) indexes are of the `GIST` type.

Geometries, geographies, and rasters are all large, complex objects, and relating to or among these objects takes time. Spatial indexes are added to the PostGIS data types to improve search performance. The performance improvement comes not from comparing potentially complex, actual spatial objects, but rather the simple bounding boxes of those objects.

## Getting ready

For this recipe, `psql` will be used as follows to time the queries:

```
> psql -d chapter10
chapter10=# \timing on
```

We will use the `caschools` and `sfpoly` tables loaded in this chapter's first recipe.

## How to do it...

The best way to see how a query can be affected by an index is by running the query before and after the addition of an index. The following steps will guide you through the process of optimizing a query with an index:

1. Run the following query, which returns the names of all the schools found in San Francisco:

```
SELECT
  schoolid
FROM caschools sc
JOIN sfpoly sf
  ON ST_Intersects(sf.geom, ST_Transform(sc.geom, 3310));
```

2. The results from the query do not matter. We are more interested in the time it took to run the query. When we run the query three times, it runs with the following elapsed times; your numbers may be different from these numbers:

```
Time: 540.228 ms
Time: 585.835 ms
Time: 516.888 ms
```

3. The query ran quickly. But, if the query needs to be run many times (say 1,000 times), it would take more than 500 seconds to run it those many times. Can the query run faster? Use EXPLAIN ANALYZE to see how PostgreSQL runs the query, as follows:

```
EXPLAIN ANALYZE
SELECT
    schoolid
FROM caschools sc
JOIN sfpoly sf
    ON ST_Intersects(sf.geom, ST_Transform(sc.geom, 3310));
```

4. Adding EXPLAIN ANALYZE before the query instructs PostgreSQL to return the actual plan used to execute the query, as follows:

```
                                                        QUERY PLAN
----------------------------------------------------------------------
-------------------------------------------------------------

Nested Loop  (cost=0.00..4160.93 rows=4 width=9) (actual
   time=99.872..678.103 rows=234 loops=1)

   Join Filter: ((sf.geom && st_transform(sc.geom, 3310)) AND _st_
intersects(sf.geom, st_transform(sc.geom, 3310)))

   Rows Removed by Join Filter: 13254

   ->  Seq Scan on sfpoly sf  (cost=0.00..1.01 rows=1 width=32)
(actual time=0.016..0.017 rows=1 loops=1)

   ->  Seq Scan on caschools sc  (cost=0.00..551.88 rows=13488
       width=41) (actual time=0.009..13.671 rows=13488 loops=1)
```

5. What is significant in the preceding QUERY PLAN is Join Filter, which has consumed most of the execution time. This may be happening because the caschools table does not have a spatial index on the geom column.

6. Add a spatial index to the geom column, as follows:

```
CREATE INDEX caschools_geom_idx
    ON caschools
    USING gist
    (geom);
```

7. Rerun the query from step 1 three times so as to minimize one-time anomalies. With a spatial index, the query ran with the following elapsed query times:

```
Time: 451.231 ms
Time: 490.250 ms
Time: 469.842 ms
```

The query did not run much faster with the spatial index. What happened? We need to check the QUERY PLAN.

8. See if the QUERY PLAN changed in PostgreSQL using EXPLAIN ANALYZE as follows:

```
                                                        QUERY PLAN
--------------------------------------------------------------------
--------------------------------------------------------
Nested Loop   (cost=0.00..4160.93 rows=4 width=9) (actual
   time=95.485..588.466 rows=234 loops=1)
   Join Filter: ((sf.geom && st_transform(sc.geom, 3310)) AND
     _st_intersects(sf.geom, st_transform(sc.geom, 3310)))
   Rows Removed by Join Filter: 13254
   -> Seq Scan on sfpoly sf   (cost=0.00..1.01 rows=1 width=32)
      (actual time=0.018..0.019 rows=1 loops=1)
   -> Seq Scan on caschools sc   (cost=0.00..551.88 rows=13488
      width=41) (actual time=0.008..12.511 rows=13488 loops=1)
```

The QUERY PLAN table is the same as that in step 4. The query is not using the spatial index. Why?

If you look at the query, we used ST_Transform() to reproject caschools.geom to the spatial reference system of sfpoly.geom. The ST_Transform() geometries used in the ST_Intersects() spatial test were in SRID 3310, but the geometries used for the caschools_geom_idx index were in SRID 4269. This difference in spatial reference systems prevented the use of the index in the query.

9. We can create a spatial index that uses geometries projected in the desired spatial reference system. An index that uses a function is known as a **functional index**. It can be created as follows:

```
CREATE INDEX caschools_geom_3310_idx
   ON caschools
   USING gist
   (ST_Transform(geom, 3310));
```

10. Rerun the query from step 1 three times to get the following output :

```
Time: 279.548 ms

Time: 263.896 ms

Time: 238.668 ms
```

That's better! From about 500 ms to 260 ms.

11. Check the QUERY PLAN table as follows:

```
QUERY PLAN
-------------------------------------------------------------------
-------------------------------------------------------------------
--------------
 Nested Loop  (cost=0.00..9.55 rows=4 width=9) (actual
   time=92.553..272.146 rows=234 loops=1)
   ->  Seq Scan on sfpoly sf  (cost=0.00..1.01 rows=1 width=32)
       (actual time=0.013..0.016 rows=1 loops=1)
   ->  Index Scan using caschools_geom_3310_idx on caschools sc
       (cost=0.00..8.53 rows=1 width=41) (actual
       time=91.762..270.965 rows=234 loops=1)
     Index Cond: (sf.geom && st_transform(geom, 3310))
     Filter: _st_intersects(sf.geom, st_transform(geom, 3310))
   Rows Removed by Filter: 34
```

12. The plan shows that the query used the caschools_geom_3310_idx index. The Index Scan command was significantly faster than the previously used Join Filter command.

## How it works...

Database indexes help us quickly and efficiently find the values we are interested in. Generally, a query using an index is faster than one that is not, but the performance improvement may not be to the degree found in this recipe.

Additional information about PostgreSQL and PostGIS indexes can be found at the following links:

► http://www.postgresql.org/docs/current/static/indexes.html

► http://postgis.net/docs/using_postgis_dbmanagement.
  html#id607043

We will discuss query plans in greater detail in a later recipe in this chapter. By understanding query plans, it becomes possible to optimize the performance of deficient queries.

# Clustering for efficiency

Most users stop optimizing the performance of a table after adding the appropriate indexes. This usually happens because the performance becomes "good enough". But what if the table has millions or billions of records? This amount of information may not fit in the database server's RAM, thereby forcing hard drive access. Generally, table records are stored sequentially on the hard drive. But, the data being fetched from the hard drive for a query may be accessing many different parts of the hard drive. Having to access different parts of a hard drive is a known performance limitation.

To mitigate hard drive performance issues, a database table can have its records reordered on the hard drive so that similar record data are stored next to or near each other. The reordering of a database table is known as **clustering** and is used with the CLUSTER statement in PostgreSQL.

## Getting ready

We will use the California schools (caschools) and San Francisco boundaries (sfpoly) tables for this recipe. If neither table is available, refer to the first recipe of this chapter.

The psql utility will be used for this recipe's queries as follows:

```
> psql -d chapter10
chapter10=# \timing on
```

## How to do it...

Use the following steps to cluster a table:

1. Before using the CLUSTER statement, check the time at which the query used in the previous recipe was executed by executing the following commands:

   ```
   SELECT
      schoolid
   FROM caschools sc
   JOIN sfpoly sf
      ON ST_Intersects(sf.geom, ST_Transform(sc.geom, 3310));
   ```

2. We get the following performance numbers for three query runs:

   ```
   Time: 274.619 ms
   Time: 255.102 ms
   Time: 295.135 ms
   ```

3. Cluster the `caschools` table using the `caschools_geom_3310_idx` index as follows:

```
CLUSTER caschools
  USING caschools_geom_3310_idx;
```

4. Rerun the query from the first step three times for the following performance timings:

```
Time: 242.878 ms
Time: 220.739 ms
Time: 238.378 ms
```

5. The performance improvements were not significant.

## How it works...

Using the `CLUSTER` statement on the `caschools` table did not result in a significant performance boost. The lesson here is that there is no guarantee that query performance will improve on a clustered table. Clustering should be reserved for tables with many large records and only after adding the appropriate indexes to and optimizing queries for the tables in question.

# Optimizing SQL queries

When a SQL query is received, PostgreSQL runs the query through its planner to decide the best execution plan. The best execution plan generally results in the fastest query performance. Though the planner usually makes the correct choices, on occasion, a specific query will have a suboptimal execution plan.

For these situations, the following are several things that can be done to change the behavior of the PostgreSQL planner:

▶ Add appropriate column indexes to the tables in question

▶ Update the statistics of the database tables

▶ Rewrite the SQL query by evaluating the query's execution plan and using capabilities available in your PostgreSQL installation

▶ Consider changing or adding to the layout of the database tables

▶ Change the query planner's configuration

Adding indexes (item 1) is discussed in a separate recipe found in this chapter. Updating statistics (item 2) is generally done automatically by PostgreSQL after a certain amount of table activity. But, the statistics can be manually updated using the `ANALYZE` statement. Changing the database layout and the query planner's configuration (items 4 and 5, respectively) are advanced operations used only when the first three items have already been attempted and thus, will not be discussed further.

This recipe only discusses item 3, that is, optimizing performance by rewriting SQL queries.

## Getting ready

For this recipe, we will find the nearest police station to every school and the distance in meters between each school in San Francisco and its nearest station, as fast as possible. This will require us to rewrite our query many times to be more efficient and take advantage of new PostgreSQL capabilities.

## How to do it...

The following steps will guide you through the iterative process required to improve query performance:

1. To find a school's nearest police station and the distance between each school in San Francisco and its nearest station, we will start by executing the following query:

```
SELECT
    di.school,
    police_address,
    distance
FROM ( -- for each school, get the minimum distance to a
    police station
    SELECT
        gid,
        school,
        min(distance) AS distance
    FROM ( -- get distance between every school and every police
    station in San Francisco
        SELECT
            sc.gid,
            sc.name AS school,
            po.address AS police_address,
            ST_Distance(po.geom_3310, sc.geom_3310) AS distance
        FROM ( -- get schools in San Francisco
            SELECT
                ca.gid,
                ca.name,
                ST_Transform(ca.geom, 3310) AS geom_3310
            FROM sfpoly sf
```

```
            JOIN caschools ca
              ON ST_Intersects(sf.geom, ST_Transform(ca.geom, 3310))
          ) sc
          CROSS JOIN ( -- get police stations in San Francisco
            SELECT
               ca.address,
               ST_Transform(ca.geom, 3310) AS geom_3310
            FROM sfpoly sf
            JOIN capolice ca
              ON ST_Intersects(sf.geom, ST_Transform(ca.geom, 3310))
          ) po
              ORDER BY 1, 2, 4
      ) scpo
      GROUP BY 1, 2
      ORDER BY 2
  ) di
  JOIN ( -- for each school, collect the police station addresses
  ordered by distance
    SELECT
       gid,
       school,
       (array_agg(police_address))[1] AS police_address
    FROM ( -- get distance between every school and every police
    station in San Francisco
      SELECT
         sc.gid,
         sc.name AS school,
         po.address AS police_address,
         ST_Distance(po.geom_3310, sc.geom_3310) AS distance
      FROM ( -- get schools in San Francisco
        SELECT
           ca.gid,
           ca.name,
           ST_Transform(ca.geom, 3310) AS geom_3310
        FROM sfpoly sf
```

```
        JOIN caschools ca
          ON ST_Intersects(sf.geom, ST_Transform(ca.geom, 3310))
      ) sc
      CROSS JOIN ( -- get police stations in San Francisco
        SELECT
          ca.address,
          ST_Transform(ca.geom, 3310) AS geom_3310
        FROM sfpoly sf
        JOIN capolice ca
          ON ST_Intersects(sf.geom, ST_Transform(ca.geom, 3310))
      ) po
      ORDER BY 1, 2, 4
    ) scpo
    GROUP BY 1, 2
    ORDER BY 2
  ) po
    ON di.gid = po.gid
ORDER BY di.school;
```

2. Generally speaking, this is a crude and simplistic query. The scpo subquery occurs twice in the query because it needs to compute the shortest distance from a school to its nearest police station and the name of the police station closest to each school. If each instance of scpo took 10 seconds to compute, two instances of scpo would take 20 seconds. This is very detrimental to performance.

3. The query output looks as follows:

```
                      school            |        police_address
|      distance
----------------------------------------+-----------------------
------+-----------------
ABRAHAM LINCOLN HIGH                    | 2345 24th Ave
| 348.311916238521
ADDA CLEVENGER JUNIOR PREPARAT          | 2345 24th Ave
| 1851.38147290568
AIM HIGH ACADEMY                        | 3401 17th St
| 976.082872160513
...
(234 rows)
```

4. The query results do provide the addresses of the schools in San Francisco, the addresses of the closest police station to each of those schools, and the distance from each school to its closest police station. But, we are also interested in getting the answer as fast as possible. With timing turned on in `psql`, we get the following performance numbers for three runs of the query:

```
Time: 10873.610 ms

Time: 10560.931 ms

Time: 10754.971 ms
```

5. Just by looking at the query in step 1, we see that there are redundant subqueries. Let's get rid of those duplicates using **Common Table Expressions (CTEs)**, introduced in PostgreSQL 8.4. CTEs are used to logically and syntactically separate a block of SQL from subsequent parts of the query. Since CTEs are logically separated, they are run at the start of the query execution and their results are cached for subsequent use.

```
WITH scpo AS ( -- get distance between every school and every
  police station in San Francisco
  SELECT
    sc.gid,
    sc.name AS school,
    po.address AS police_address,
    ST_Distance(po.geom_3310, sc.geom_3310) AS distance
  FROM ( -- get schools in San Francisco
    SELECT
      ca.*,
      ST_Transform(ca.geom, 3310) AS geom_3310
    FROM sfpoly sf
    JOIN caschools ca
      ON ST_Intersects(sf.geom, ST_Transform(ca.geom, 3310))
  ) sc
  CROSS JOIN ( -- get police stations in San Francisco
    SELECT
      ca.*,
      ST_Transform(ca.geom, 3310) AS geom_3310
    FROM sfpoly sf
    JOIN capolice ca
      ON ST_Intersects(sf.geom, ST_Transform(ca.geom, 3310))
```

```
   ) po
   ORDER BY 1, 2, 4
)
SELECT
   di.school,
   police_address,
   distance
FROM ( -- for each school, get the minimum distance to a police
station
   SELECT
     gid,
     school,
     min(distance) AS distance
   FROM scpo
   GROUP BY 1, 2
   ORDER BY 2
) di
JOIN ( -- for each school, collect the police station
   addresses ordered by distance
   SELECT
     gid,
     school,
     (array_agg(police_address))[1] AS police_address
   FROM scpo
   GROUP BY 1, 2
   ORDER BY 2
) po
       ON di.gid = po.gid
ORDER BY 1;
```

6. Not only is the query syntactically cleaner, the performance improved as follows:

```
Time: 4192.614 ms
Time: 4651.967 ms
Time: 4329.707 ms
```

The execution times went from more than 10 seconds to less than 5 seconds.

7. Though some may stop optimizing this query at this point, we will continue to improve the query performance. We can use the window functions, which are another PostgreSQL capability introduced in v8.4. Using the window functions as follows, we can get rid of the JOIN expression:

```sql
WITH scpo AS ( -- get distance between every school and every
  police station in San Francisco
  SELECT
    sc.name AS school,
    po.address AS police_address,
    ST_Distance(po.geom_3310, sc.geom_3310) AS distance
  FROM ( -- get schools in San Francisco
    SELECT
      ca.name,
      ST_Transform(ca.geom, 3310) AS geom_3310
    FROM sfpoly sf
    JOIN caschools ca
      ON ST_Intersects(sf.geom, ST_Transform(ca.geom, 3310))
  ) sc
  CROSS JOIN ( -- get police stations in San Francisco
    SELECT
      ca.address,
      ST_Transform(ca.geom, 3310) AS geom_3310
    FROM sfpoly sf
    JOIN capolice ca
      ON ST_Intersects(sf.geom, ST_Transform(ca.geom, 3310))
  ) po
  ORDER BY 1, 3, 2
)
SELECT
  DISTINCT school,
  first_value(police_address) OVER (PARTITION BY school ORDER
    BY distance),
  first_value(distance) OVER (PARTITION BY school ORDER BY
    distance)
FROM scpo
ORDER BY 1;
```

8. We use the `first_value()` window function to extract the first `police_address` and `distance` values for each school sorted by the distance between the school and a police station. Though the readability of the SQL improves even more, it does not look like the query improves with the use of the window functions, as seen in the following elapsed times:

```
Time: 4268.268 ms
```

```
Time: 4493.860 ms
```

```
Time: 4490.656 ms
```

9. We should inspect the execution plan with `EXPLAIN ANALYZE VERBOSE` to see what is decreasing the query performance. Due to the verbosity of the output, we've trimmed it to just the following lines of interest:

```
                QUERY PLAN
-----------------------------------------------------------------
-----------------------------------------------------------------
--
  Unique  (cost=19.43..19.45 rows=1 width=204) (actual
time=4224.661..4230.587 rows=234 loops=1)
    Output: scpo.school, (first_value(scpo.police_address) OVER
(?)), (first_value(scpo.distance) OVER (?)), scpo.distance
    CTE scpo
      -> Sort  (cost=19.36..19.37 rows=1 width=104) (actual
time=3977.815..3986.504 rows=7956 loops=1)
        Output: ca.name, ca.address, (st_distance(st_transform(ca.
geom, 3310), st_transform(ca.geom, 3310)))
        Sort Key: ca.name, (st_distance(st_transform(ca.geom,
3310), st_transform(ca.geom, 3310))), ca.address
        Sort Method: external merge  Disk: 496kB
        -> Nested Loop  (cost=0.01..19.35 rows=1 width=104)
(actual time=174.856..3858.436 rows=7956 loops=1)
          Output: ca.name, ca.address, st_distance(st_
transform(ca.geom, 3310), st_transform(ca.geom, 3310))
          -> Nested Loop  (cost=0.00..10.56 rows=1 width=81)
(actual time=90.613..108.940 rows=34 loops=1)
            Output: ca.address, ca.geom, sf.geom
            -> Nested Loop  (cost=0.00..9.54 rows=1 width=49)
(actual time=90.576..108.221 rows=34 loops=1)
              Output: ca.address, ca.geom
  ...
```

10. In the `EXPLAIN ANALYZE VERBOSE` output, we want to inspect the values for the actual time, which provide the actual start and end times for that part of the query. Of all the actual time ranges, the value actual time, 174.856..3858.436, for the `Nested Loop` (highlighted in the preceding output) is the worst. This query step consumes at least 80 percent of the total execution time, so any work done to improve performance must be done in this step.

11. The columns returned from the slow `Nested Loop` utility is found in the value for the output. Of these columns, `st_distance()` is present only in this step and not in any inner step. This means we will need to mitigate the number of calls to `ST_Distance()`.

12. At this step, further query improvements are not possible without running PostgreSQL 9.1 or a higher version. PostgreSQL 9.1 introduced indexed nearest-neighbor searches using the `<->` and `<#>` operators to compare the geometries' convex hulls and bounding boxes, respectively. For point geometries, both operators result in the same answer.

13. Let's rewrite the query to take advantage of the `<->` operator. The following query still uses the CTEs and window functions:

```
WITH sc AS ( -- get schools in San Francisco
  SELECT
    ca.gid,
    ca.name,
    ca.geom
  FROM sfpoly sf
  JOIN caschools ca
    ON ST_Intersects(sf.geom, ST_Transform(ca.geom, 3310))
), po AS ( -- get police stations in San Francisco
  SELECT
    ca.gid,
    ca.address,
    ca.geom
  FROM sfpoly sf
  JOIN capolice ca
    ON ST_Intersects(sf.geom, ST_Transform(ca.geom, 3310))
)
SELECT
  school,
```

```
    police_address,
    ST_Distance(ST_Transform(school_geom, 3310), ST_
Transform(police_geom, 3310)) AS distance
FROM ( -- for each school, number and order the police stations by
how close
    each station is to the school
    SELECT
        ROW_NUMBER() OVER (PARTITION BY sc.gid ORDER BY sc.geom <->
po.geom) AS r,
            sc.name AS school,
            sc.geom AS school_geom,
            po.address AS police_address,
            po.geom AS police_geom
    FROM sc
    CROSS JOIN po
) scpo
WHERE r < 2
ORDER BY 1;
```

14. The query has the following performance numbers:

```
Time: 511.360 ms
Time: 535.226 ms
Time: 517.626 ms
```

Wow! Using indexed nearest-neighbor searches with the `<->` operator, we reduced our initial query from 10 seconds to almost half a second.

## How it works...

In this recipe, we optimized a query that users may commonly encounter while using PostGIS. We started by taking advantage of the PostgreSQL capabilities to improve the performance and syntax of our query. Once performance could no longer improve, we ran EXPLAIN ANALYZE VERBOSE to find out what was consuming most of the query-execution time. We learned that the ST_Distance() function consumed the most time from the execution plan. Finally, we used the `<->` operator of PostgreSQL 9.1 to dramatically improve the query-execution time to under a second.

The output of `EXPLAIN ANALYZE VERBOSE` used in this recipe is not easy to understand. For complex queries, it is encouraged that you use the visual output in pgAdminIII (discussed in a separate chapter's recipe) or the color coding provided by the `http://explain.depesz.com/` web service shown in the following screenshot:

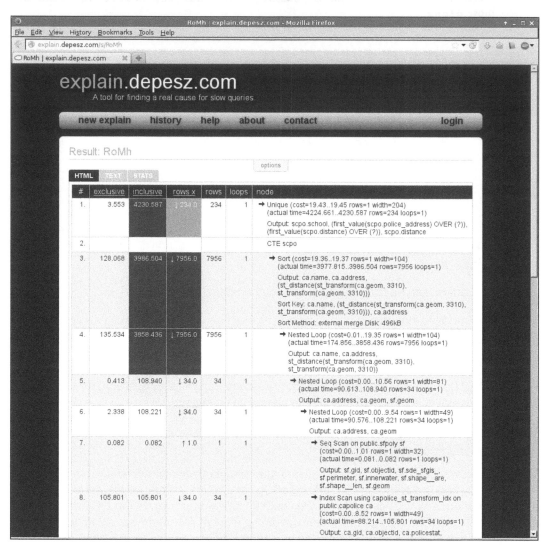

# Migrating a PostGIS database to a different server

At some point, user databases need to be migrated to a different server. This need for server migration could be due to a new hardware or database-server software upgrade.

The following are the three methods available for migrating a database:

▸ Dump and restore the database with `pg_dump` and `pg_restore`

▸ Perform an in-place upgrade of the database with `pg_upgrade`

▸ Perform streaming replication from one server to another

## Getting ready

In this recipe, we will use the `dump` and `restore` methods to move user data to a new database with a new PostGIS installation. Unlike the other methods, this method is the most foolproof, works in all situations, and stores a backup in case things don't work as expected.

## How to do it...

On the command line, perform the following steps:

1. Though a backup file was created in this chapter's third recipe, create a new backup file by executing the following command:

   ```
   > pg_dump -f chapter10.backup -F custom chapter10
   ```

2. Create a new database to which the backup file will be restored by executing the following commands:

   ```
   > psql -d postgres

   postgres=# CREATE DATABASE new10;
   ```

3. Connect to the `new10` database and create a schema for PostGIS as follows:

   ```
   postgres=# \c new10

   new10=# CREATE SCHEMA postgis;
   ```

4. If your PostgreSQL server supports `CREATE EXTENSION`, execute the following command:

   ```
   new10=# CREATE EXTENSION postgis WITH SCHEMA postgis;
   ```

Otherwise, run the following commands:

```
new10=# SET search_path = postgis;
new10=# \i /PATHTOFILE/postgis.sql
new10=# \i /PATHTOFILE/rtpostgis.sql
new10=# \i /PATHTOFILE/spatial_ref_sys.sql
```

5. Make sure you set the `search_path` parameter to include the `postgis` schema, as follows:

```
new10=# ALTER DATABASE new10 SET search_path = public,
   postgis;
```

6. Restore only the `public` schema from the backup file to the `new10` database by executing the following command:

```
> pg_restore -d new10 --schema=public chapter10.backup
```

7. The `restore` method runs, but throws error messages such as the following:

```
pg_restore: [archiver (db)] Error while PROCESSING TOC:
pg_restore: [archiver (db)] Error from TOC entry 3781; 0
   3496229 TABLE DATA prism postgres
pg_restore: [archiver (db)] COPY failed for table "prism":
   ERROR:  function st_bandmetadata(postgis.raster, integer[])
   does not exist
LINE 1:   SELECT array_agg(pixeltype)::text[] FROM
   st_bandmetadata($1...
```

We installed PostGIS in the `postgis` schema, but the database server can't find the `ST_BandMetadata()` function. If a function cannot be found, it is usually an issue with `search_path`. We will fix this issue in the next step.

8. Check what `pg_restore` actually does by executing the following command:

```
pg_restore -f chapter10.sql --schema=public chapter10.backup
```

9. Looking at the `COPY` statement for the prism table, everything looks fine. But the `search_path` parameter preceding the table does not include the `postgis` schema as follows:

```
SET search_path = public, pg_catalog;
```

10. Change the `search_path` value in `chapter10.sql` to include the `postgis` schema by executing the following command:

```
SET search_path = public, postgis, pg_catalog;
```

11. Run `chapter10.sql` with `psql`, as follows; the original `chapter10.backup` file can't be used because the necessary change can't be applied with `pg_restore`:

    ```
    > psql -d new10 -f chapter10.sql
    ```

## How it works...

This procedure is essentially the standard PostgreSQL backup and restore cycle. It may not be simple, but has the benefit of being accessible in terms of the tools used and the control available in each step of the process. Though the other migration methods may be convenient, they typically require faith in an opaque process or the installation of additional software.

# Replicating a PostGIS database with streaming replication

The reality of the world is that, given enough time, everything will break. This includes the hardware and software of computers running PostgreSQL. To protect data in PostgreSQL from corruption or loss, backups are taken using tools such as `pg_dump`. However, restoring a database backup can take a very long time during which users cannot use the database.

When downtime must be kept to a minimum or is not acceptable, one or more standby servers are used to compensate for the failed primary PostgreSQL server. The data on the standby server is kept in sync with the primary PostgreSQL server by streaming data as frequently as possible.

In addition, you are strongly discouraged from trying to mix different PostgreSQL versions. Primary and standby servers must run the same PostgreSQL version.

## Getting ready

In this recipe, we will use the streaming replication capability introduced in PostgreSQL 9.0. This recipe will use one server with two parallel PostgreSQL installations instead of the typical two or more servers, each with one PostgreSQL installation. We will use two new database clusters in order to keep things simple.

## How to do it...

Use the following steps to replicate a PostGIS database:

1. Create directories for the primary and standby database clusters by executing the following commands:

   ```
   > mkdir C:\postgis_cookbook\db
   > mkdir C:\postgis_cookbook\db\primary
   > mkdir C:\postgis_cookbook\db\standby
   > mkdir C:\postgis_cookbook\db\primary\archive
   > mkdir C:\postgis_cookbook\db\standby\archive
   ```

2. Initialize the database clusters with `initdb` as follows:

   ```
   > cd C:\postgis_cookbook\db
   > initdb --encoding=utf8 --locale=en_US.utf8 -D primary
   > initdb --encoding=utf8 --locale=en_US.utf8 -D standby
   ```

3. Edit the `pg_hba.conf` authentication file of the primary cluster by running the following command:

   ```
   > notepad primary\pg_hba.conf
   ```

4. If you're running PostgreSQL 9.0, add the following text to the end of `pg_hba.conf`:

   ```
   local    replication    postgres                        trust
   host     replication    postgres       127.0.0.1/32     trust
   host     replication    postgres       ::1/128          trust
   ```

5. For PostgreSQL 9.1 or a higher version, the script in the previous step is already provided in `pg_hba.conf`. You just need to remove the comment character (#) from the beginning of each matching line.

6. Edit the primary cluster's `postgresql.conf` configuration file to set the streaming replication parameters. Search for each parameter and replace the assigned value to the following:

   ```
   port = 5433
   wal_level = hot_standby
   max_wal_senders = 5
   wal_keep_segments = 32
   archive_mode = on
   archive_command = 'copy "%p"
     "C:\\postgis_cookbook\\db\\primary\\archive\\%f"' # for Windows
   ```

7. Start PostgreSQL on the primary database cluster by executing the following command:

```
> pg_ctl start -D primary -l primary\postgres.log
```

8. Create a base backup of the primary database cluster and copy it to the standby database cluster. Before performing the backup, create an exclusion list file for xcopy (Windows only) by executing the following command:

```
> notepad exclude.txt
```

9. Add the following to exclude.txt:

```
postmaster.pid
```

```
pg_xlog
```

10. Run the base backup and copy the directory contents from the primary to the standby database cluster, as follows:

```
> psql -p 5433 -d postgres -c "SELECT
  pg_start_backup('base_backup', true)"
> xcopy primary/ standby /e /exclude:exclude.txt
> psql -p 5433 -d postgres -c "SELECT pg_stop_backup()"
```

11. Make the following changes to the standby cluster's postgresql.conf configuration file:

```
port = 5434
```

```
hot_standby = on
```

```
archive_command = 'copy "%p"
  "C:\\postgis_cookbook\\db\\standby\\archive\\%f"' # for
  Windows
```

12. Create the recovery.conf configuration file in the standby cluster directory by executing the following command:

```
> notepad standby\recovery.conf
```

13. Enter the following in the recovery.conf configuration file:

```
standby_mode = 'on'
```

```
primary_conninfo = 'port=5433 user=postgres'
```

```
restore_command = 'copy
  "C:\\postgis_cookbook\\db\\standby\\archive\\%f" "%p"'
```

14. Start PostgreSQL on the standby database cluster by executing the following command:

```
> pg_ctl start -D standby -l standby\postgres.log
```

15. Run some simple tests to make sure the replication is working.

16. Create the `test` database and the `test` table on the primary database server by executing the following commands:

```
> psql -p 5433 -d postgres

postgres=# CREATE DATABASE test;

postgres=# \c test

test=# CREATE TABLE test AS SELECT 1 AS id, 'one'::text AS
  value;
```

17. Connect to the standby database server by executing the following command:

```
> psql -p 5434 -d postgres
```

18. See if the `test` database is present by executing the following commands:

```
postgres=# \l
```

```
                              List of databases
     Name     |   Owner   | Encoding |  Collate   |   Ctype    |
  Access privileges
-----------+-----------+----------+------------+------------+------
-----------------
  postgres  | postgres  | UTF8     | en_US.utf8 | en_US.utf8 |
  template0 | postgres  | UTF8     | en_US.utf8 | en_US.utf8 | =c/
  postgres        +
            |          |          |            |            |
  postgres=CTc/postgres
  template1 | postgres  | UTF8     | en_US.utf8 | en_US.utf8 | =c/
  postgres        +
            |          |          |            |            |
  postgres=CTc/postgres
  test      | postgres  | UTF8     | en_US.utf8 | en_US.utf8 |
```

19. Connect to the `test` database and get the list of tables by executing the following commands:

```
postgres=# \c test

test=# \d
```

```
        List of relations
 Schema | Name | Type  |  Owner
--------+------+-------+----------
 public | test | table | postgres
```

20. Get the records, if any, in the `test` table by executing the following commands:

```
test=# SELECT * FROM test;

 id | value
----+-------
  1 | one
```

Congratulations! The streaming replication works.

## How it works...

As demonstrated in this recipe, the basic setup for streaming replication is straightforward. Changes made to the primary database server are quickly pushed to the standby database server.

There are third-party applications to help establish, administer, and maintain streaming replication on production servers. These applications permit complex replication strategies, including multimaster, multistandby, and proper failover. A few of these applications include the following:

▶ Pgpool-II, which is available at `http://www.pgpool.net`

▶ Bucardo, which is available at `http://bucardo.org/wiki/Bucardo`

▶ Postgres-XC, which is available at
`http://postgresxc.wikia.com/wiki/Postgres-XC_Wiki`

▶ Slony-I, which is available at `http://slony.info`

# 11
# Using Desktop Clients

In this chapter, we will cover the following topics:

- ▶ Adding PostGIS layers – QGIS
- ▶ Using the Database Manager plugin – QGIS
- ▶ Adding PostGIS layers – OpenJUMP GIS
- ▶ Running database queries – OpenJUMP GIS
- ▶ Adding PostGIS layers – gvSIG
- ▶ Adding PostGIS layers – uDig

## Introduction

At a minimum, Desktop GIS programs allow you to visualize data from a PostGIS database. This relationship gets more interesting with the ability to edit and manipulate data outside of the database and in a dynamic "play" environment.

Make a change, see a change! For this reason, visualizing the data stored in PostGIS is often critical for effective spatial database management—or at least as a now-and-again sanity check. This chapter will demonstrate both dynamic and static relationships between your database and desktop clients.

Regardless of your experience level or role in the geospatial community, you should find at least one of the four GIS programs serviceable as a potential intermediate staging environment between your PostGIS database and end product.

In this chapter, we will connect to PostGIS using the following Desktop GIS programs: QGIS, OpenJUMP GIS, gvSIG, and uDig.

Once connected to PostGIS, extra emphasis is placed on some of the more sophisticated functionality offered by QGIS and OpenJUMP GIS using the **DB Manager plugin** and **run datastore queries**, respectively.

# Adding PostGIS layers – QGIS

In this recipe, we will establish a connection to our PostGIS database in order to add a table as a layer in **QGIS** (formerly known as **Quantum GIS**). Viewing tables as layers is great for creating maps or simply working on a copy of the database outside the database.

Please navigate to the following site to install the latest version of QGIS (2.0 as of writing this book):

```
http://qgis.org/en/site/
```

On this page, click on **Download Now** and you will be able to choose the suitable operating system and settings. QGIS is available for Android, Linux, Mac OS X, and Windows. You might also be inclined to click on **Discover QGIS** to get an overview of some basic information about the program, along with features, screenshots, and case studies.

## Getting ready

To begin, let's download data from the following U.S. Census Bureau's FTP site:

```
ftp://ftp2.census.gov/geo/tiger/TIGER2012/EDGES/tl_2012_39035_edges.zip
```

The shapefile consists of roads, streams, and other line features found within Cuyahoga County, Ohio.

Extract the ZIP file to your working directory and then load it into your database using `shp2pgsql`. Be sure to specify the spatial reference system, EPSG/SRID: 4269. When in doubt about using projections, use the wonderful service provided by the folks at OpenGeo, located at the following website:

```
http://prj2epsg.org/search.
```

## How to do it...

Now, it is time to take a look at the data we downloaded using QGIS. We must first create a connection to the database in order to access the table. Get connected to PostGIS and add the table as a layer with the following steps:

1.  Click on the **Add PostGIS Layers** icon:

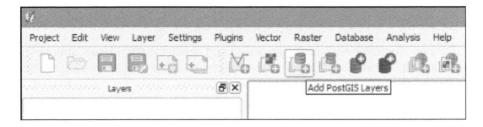

2.  Click on the **New** button below the empty **Connections** drop-down menu:

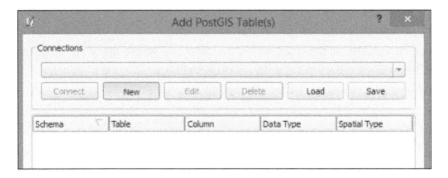

3.  Create a new PostGIS connection. After the **Add PostGIS Table(s)** window opens, create a name for the connection and fill in a few parameters for your database—**Host**, **Port**, **Database**, **Username**, and **Password**:

4. Once you have entered all of the pertinent information for your database, click on the **Test Connect** button to verify that the connection is successful. If the connection is not successful, double check for typos and errors. Additionally, make sure you are attempting to connect to a PostGIS-enabled database.

5. If the connection is successful, go ahead and check the **Save Username** and **Save Password** checkboxes. This will prevent us from having to enter our login information multiple times throughout the exercise.

6. Click on **OK** at the bottom of the menu to apply the connection settings. Now, you can connect!

   Make sure the name of your PostGIS connection appears in the drop-down menu, and then click on the **Connect** button. If you choose not to store your username and password, you will be asked to submit this information every time you try to access the database.

   Once connected, all schemas within the database will be shown and the tables will be made visible by expanding the target schema.

 Export your connection details in an XML file by clicking on the **Save** button located below the **Connections** drop-down menu. Select your connection and export it to a file. You can then load the XML content from that file rather than entering all of your database parameters over again.

7. Select the table(s) to be added as a layer by simply clicking on the table name or anywhere along its row to select. Selection(s) will be highlighted in blue. To deselect a table, click on it a second time and it will no longer be highlighted. Select the tl_2012_39035_edges table that was downloaded at the beginning of the chapter and click on the **Add** button:

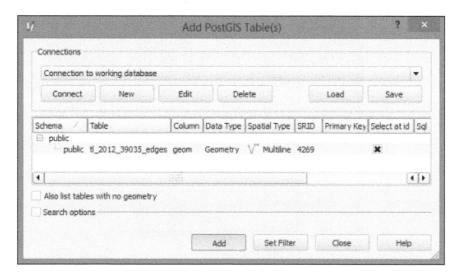

8. A subset of the table can also be added as a layer. This is accomplished by double-clicking below the **Primary Key** column in the row of the table we will be using.

9. The **Query Builder** window will open, which aids in creating simple SQL WHERE clause statements. Add the roads by selecting the records where roadflg = Y. This can be done by typing a query or using the buttons within **Query Builder**:

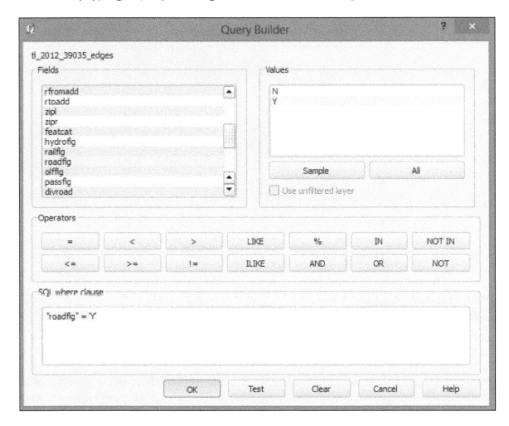

10. Click on the **OK** button followed by the **Add** button. A subset of the table is now loaded into QGIS as a layer. The layer is strictly a static, temporary copy of your database. You can make whatever changes you like to the layer and it will not affect the database table.

The same holds true the other way around. Changes to the table in the database will have no effect on the layer in QGIS.

If needed, you can save the temporary layer in a variety of formats, such as DXF, GeoJSON, KML, or SHP. Simply right-click on the layer name in the **Layers** panel and click on **Save As**. This will then create a file, which you can recall at a later time or share with others.

The following screenshot shows the Cuyahoga County road network:

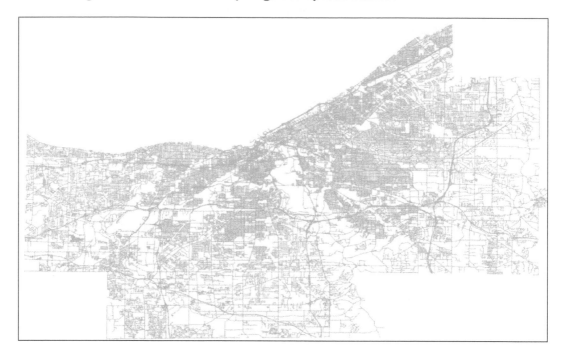

## How it works...

You have added a PostGIS layer into QGIS using the built-in **Add PostGIS Table** GUI. This was achieved by creating a new connection and entering your database parameters.

Any number of database connections can be set up simultaneously. If working with multiple databases is more common for your workflows, saving all of the connections into one XML file (see the tip in the preceding section) would save much time and energy when returning to these projects in QGIS.

# Using the Database Manager plugin – QGIS

The **Database Manager** (**DB Manager**) allows for a more sophisticated relationship with PostGIS by allowing users to interact with the database in a variety of ways. The plugin mimics some of the core functionality of pgAdmin with the added benefit of data visualization.

In this recipe, we will use DB Manager to create, modify, and delete items within the database and then tinker with the SQL window. By the end of this section, you will be able to do the following:

- Navigate to the DB Manager menu
- Create, modify, and delete database schemas and tables
- Run SQL queries to add new QGIS layers or create new tables in the database

QGIS needs to be installed for this recipe. Please refer to the first recipe in this chapter for information on where to download the installer.

## Getting ready

Let's make sure the plugin is enabled and connected to the database.

1. Click on the **Plugins** menu located on the QGIS menu bar and select **Manage and Install Plugins** from the drop-down menu:

2. The QGIS **Plugin Manager** window will open. Search for **DB Manager** in the list of plugins and make sure it is checked (enabled):

3.  Now that **DB Manager** is enabled, let us open the plugin and check the status of the database connection. Open **DB Manager** by navigating to **Database | DB Manager** from the QGIS menu bar:

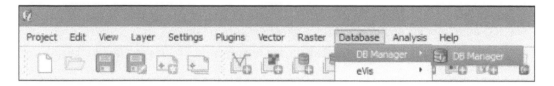

4.  Expand the **PostGIS** directory within the **Tree** window of DB Manager. The PostGIS connection created in the last recipe will appear. Expand the connection to view your schema(s) and table(s). You will be asked for a username and password if you opted not to save your credentials.

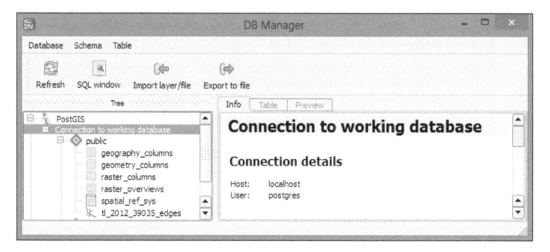

A PostGIS connection is not in place if you are unable to expand the **PostGIS** menu. If you need to establish a connection, refer to steps 1 to 4 in the *Adding PostGIS layers – QGIS* recipe. The connection must be established before using the DB Manager.

## How to do it...

Navigate to the **DB Manager** menu and carry out the following steps:

1.  Select the t1_2012_39035_edges table in the **Tree** window.

2.  Click on the **Info** tab above the main window to view information about the data, such as spatial reference, geometry type, field names, field types, and much more, as shown in the following screenshot:

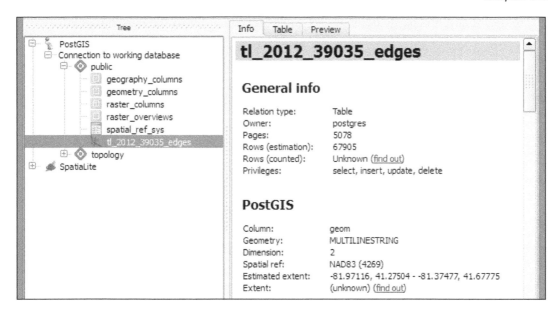

3. Next, click on the **Table** tab to view the actual data table:

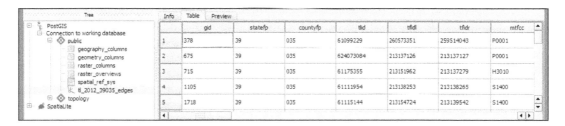

4. The final tab, **Preview**, is for visualizing the data:

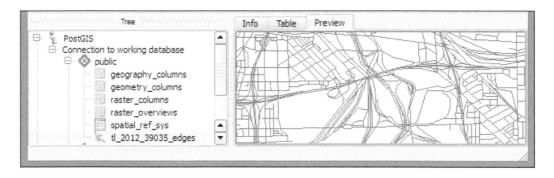

To create, modify, and delete database schemas and tables, follow the ensuing steps:

1.  First, let's create a new schema in the database to store data for this chapter. Select **Schema** | **Create schema** from the menu bar:

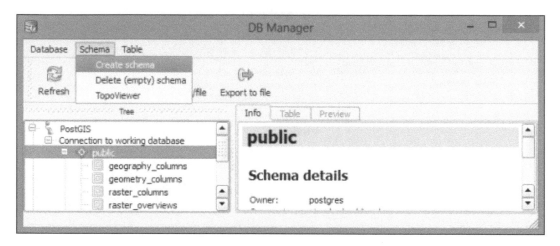

2.  Enter Chp11 as the schema name and then click on **OK**. The schema has been created, but will not be visible until you refresh the connection to the database. Select the database connection in the **Tree** window once you've clicked on the **Refresh** button:

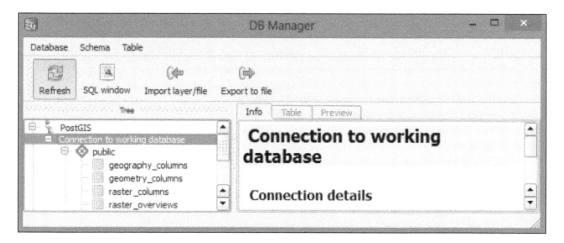

3.  Your new, empty schema will now be visible in the **Tree** window. Let's move the tl_2012_39035_edges table to the Chp11 schema. Simply select the table in the **Tree** window and then click on **Table** in the menu bar. Go to **Move to schema** | **Chp11**, as shown in the following screenshot:

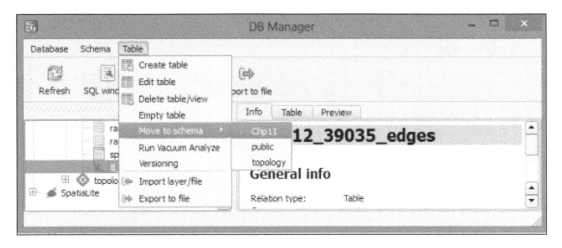

4. Next, let's modify the table name to something more generic. How about "lines"? You can change the table name by clicking on the table in the **Tree** window. As soon as the text is highlighted and the cursor flashes, you can delete the existing name and enter the new name, lines.

Right now, our lines table's data is using degrees as the unit of measurement for its current projection (*EPSG: 4269*). Let's add a new geometry column using EPSG: 3734, which is a State Plane Coordinate system that measures projections in feet. To run SQL queries, follow the ensuing steps:

1. Click on the **SQL window** button in the DB Manager:

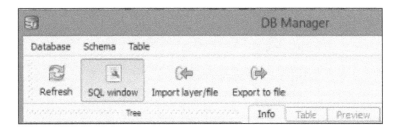

2. Copy the following query into the SQL window and then click on **Execute**:

```
SELECT AddGeometryColumn('Chp11', 'lines','geom_sp',3734,
'MULTILINESTRING', 2);

UPDATE "Chp11".lines SET geom_sp = ST_Transform(geom,3734);
```

The query creates a new geometry column named `geom_sp`, and then updates the geometry information by transforming the original geometry (`geom`) from EPSG 4269 to 3734:

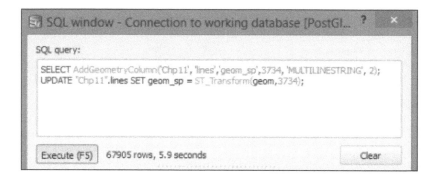

3. Refresh the `Chp11` schema and you'll notice that the table in the database now has two geometry columns that are treated independently in the **Tree** window:

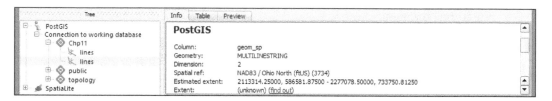

The preceding screenshot shows the created geometry. The following screenshot shows the original geometry.

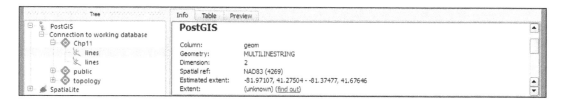

4. For our next query, let us take a subset of the `lines` table. Similar to what we did in the preceding section, we will only look at the data about the roads. However, this time, we can limit the columns that we want to load with the layer, as well as perform more complicated spatial queries. We'll apply a buffer of 10 feet using the new geometry column (`geom_sp`), by executing the following command:

```
SELECT gid, ST_Buffer(geom_sp, 10) AS geom, fullname, roadflg FROM
"Chp11".lines WHERE roadflg = 'Y'
```

Check the **Load as new layer** checkbox, and then select **gid** as the unique ID and **geom** as the geometry. Create a name for the layer and then click on **Load Now!**:

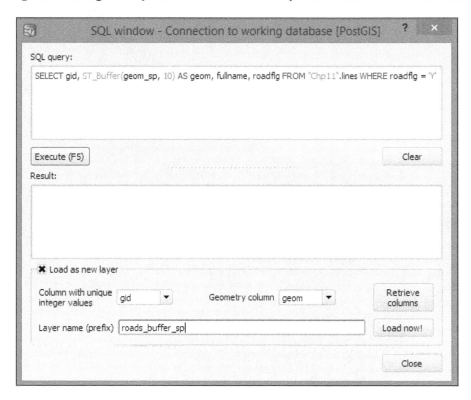

The query adds the result in QGIS as a temporary layer.

5.  Now, let us modify the query to create a table in the database rather than load the query as a layer, by executing the following command:

```
CREATE TABLE "Chp11".roads_buffer_sp AS SELECT gid, ST_
Buffer(geom_sp, 10) AS geom, fullname, roadflg FROM "Chp11".lines
WHERE roadflg = 'Y'
```

The following screenshot shows the Cuyahoga Country Road Network:

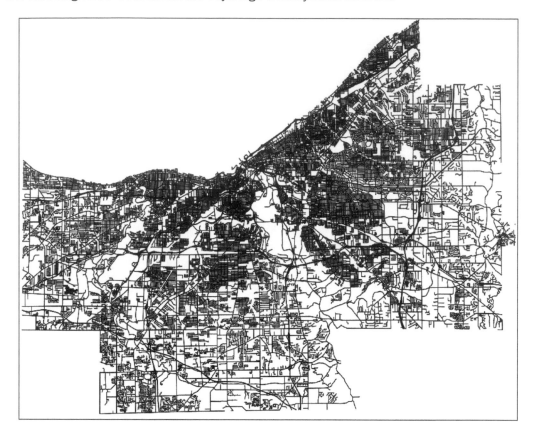

## How it works...

Connecting to a PostGIS database (see the *Adding PostGIS layers – QGIS* recipe in this chapter) allows you to utilize the DB Manager plugin. Once the DB Manager was enabled, we were able to toggle between the **Info**, **Table**, and **Preview** tabs to efficiently view metadata, tabular data, and data visualization.

Next, we made changes to the database by adding a new schema and moving an existing table to the new schema. A query was then run on the table in order to transform the projection. Note the autocomplete feature in the **SQL Window**, which makes writing queries a breeze.

Changes to the database were made visible in the DB Manager by refreshing the database connection. So, while changes are being made in the database, they can only be seen in QGIS after clicking on the **Refresh** button. This is a minor inconvenience in an otherwise very powerful tool.

# Adding PostGIS layers – OpenJUMP GIS

In this section, we will connect to PostGIS with OpenJUMP GIS (OpenJUMP) in order to add spatial tables as layers. Next, we will edit the temporary layer and update it in a new table in the database.

The *JUMP* in OpenJUMP stands for **Java Unified Mapping Platform**. To learn more about the program, or if you need to install the latest version, go to:

```
http://www.openjump.org/.
```

Click on the **Download it here** link on the previously mentioned page to view the list of installers. You can click on the **View Details** icon next to an installer to make sure you select the version that suits your operating system. Detailed directions for installing OpenJUMP, along with other documentation and information, can be found on the OpenJUMP Wiki page at the following link:

```
http://sourceforge.net/apps/mediawiki/jump-pilot/index.
php?title=Main_Page.
```

## Getting ready

We will be reusing and building upon data used in the *Adding PostGIS layers – QGIS* recipe. If you skipped over this recipe, you will want to do the following:

1. Download the following ZIP file from the U.S. Census Bureau's FTP site:

   ```
   ftp://ftp2.census.gov/geo/tiger/TIGER2012/EDGES/tl_2012_39035_
   edges.zip.
   ```

   The shapefile consists of roads, streams, and other line features found within Cuyahoga County, Ohio.

2. Extract the ZIP file to your working directory and then load it into your database using `shp2pgsql`. Be sure to specify the spatial reference system, which is *EPSG: 4269*, and name the table `lines`.

## How to do it...

The data-source layer can be added by performing the following steps:

1. Click on the **Open** (folder) icon or go to **File | Open**.

2. Select **Data Store Layer** from the left-hand-side menu:

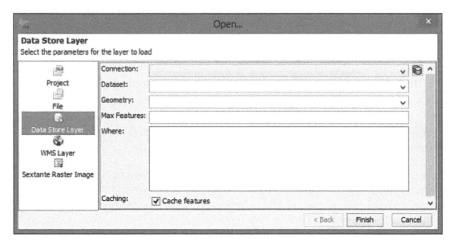

3. Click on the icon to the right of the **Connection** dropdown to open the Connection Manager.

4. Click on the **Add** button. This will prompt a new window in which you must enter your database parameters:

5. Enter a name for the connection and then enter values for the following database parameters:

   ❑ **Server/Host**

   ❑ **Port**

   ❑ **Database**

   ❑ **Username**

   ❑ **Password**

6. Then, click on **OK**:

7. We are now connected to the database; you can see a green circle to the left of the connection name:

The copy of the connection we added here has a typo for contrast (port 54321 instead of 5432). A red **x** mark next to the connection name means the connection was not successful. Check for typos and errors if a red **x** mark is next to your connection. If the connection is successful, select the connection and click on **OK**.

8. Click the **Dataset** drop-down menu to select the **lines** table to add:

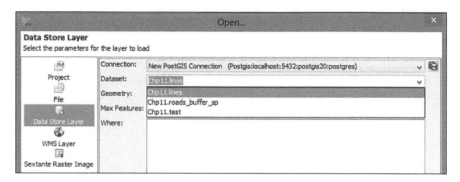

If multiple geometry columns exist, you may choose the one you want to use with the **Geometry** drop-down menu. Add the data's State Plane Coordinator geometry (geom_sp), as shown in the *Using the Database Manager plugin – QGIS* recipe.

Simple SQL WHERE clause statements can be used if only a subset of a table is needed.

9. Click on **Finish** to load the dataset into the main window:

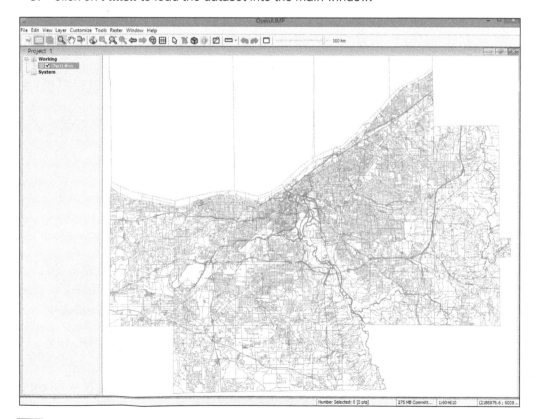

10. Now, let us make a quick edit to the temporary layer and save it back to the database. Select the **Editing Toolbox** button:

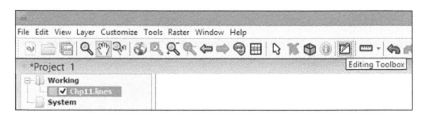

11. The toolbox will be loaded over the main menu. Click on the **Select Features Tool** button (to the top-left corner of the screen):

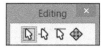

12. Select some of the lines, as shown in the following screenshot, that look out of place on the map. In particular, the lines to the North of the county; these actually jet out into Lake Erie. You can select multiple lines by clicking-and-dragging a rectangle with the cursor or holding *Shift* while clicking on line segments. Hit the *Delete* key once you have selected some lines to remove them from the data.

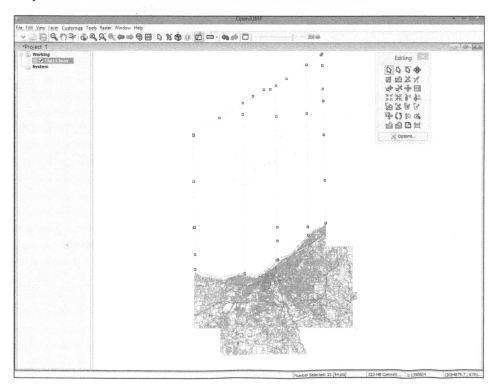

13. Save the changes made to the layer and replace the existing table in the database with the edited copy. Right-click on the layer name on the left panel and then select **Save Dataset As**.

14. Select your PostGIS connection with the **Connection** drop-down menu, choose the appropriate table name, and then make sure that the **Create new or replace existing table** option is selected:

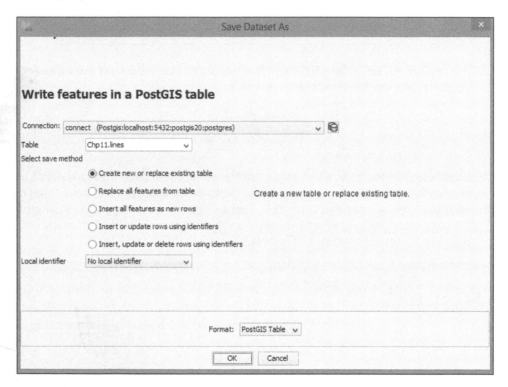

15. Click on **OK**; now you have successfully edited a PostGIS table in OpenJUMP.

## How it works...

We added a PostGIS layer in OpenJUMP using the **Open Data Store Layer** menu. This was achieved after creating a new connection and entering our database parameters.

In the example, census data was added that included the boundary of Cuyahoga County. Part of the boundary advances into Lake Erie to the International Boundary with Canada. While technically correct, the water boundary is typically not used for practical mapping purposes. In this case, it's easy to visualize which data needs to be removed.

OpenJUMP allows us to easily see and delete records that should be deleted from the table. The selected lines were deleted and the table was saved to the database.

# Running database queries – OpenJUMP GIS

Executing ad hoc queries in OpenJUMP is simple and offers a couple of unique features. Queries can be run on specific data selections, allowing for the manual control of the queried area without considering the attribution. Similarly, temporary **fences** (areas) can be drawn on the fly and the geometry of the surface can be used in queries. In this recipe, we will explore each of those cases.

## Getting ready

Refer to the preceding recipe if you need to install OpenJUMP or require assistance connecting to a database.

## How to do it...

Carry out the following steps to run the data store query:

1.  Navigate to **File | Run Datastore Query**:

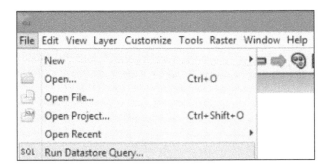

2.  Choose the PostGIS connection from the **Connection** drop-down menu, or use the Connection Manager utility if you are not linked to the database.

3.  We'll create and name a polygon layer of the main streams in the region by executing the following query:

```
SELECT gid, ST_BUFFER("Chp11".lines.geom_sp, 75) AS the_geom,
fullname FROM "Chp11".lines WHERE fullname <> ''

AND hydroflg = 'Y'
```

The preceding query is shown in the following screenshot:

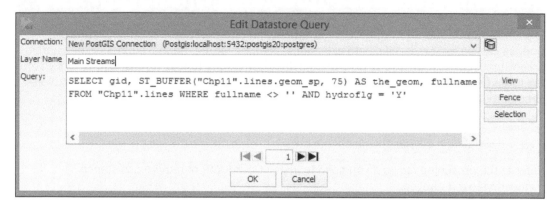

The preceding query selects the lines on the map that represent hydrology units such as "hydroflg" = 'Y' and streams. The selected stream lines (which use the State Plane geometry) are buffered by 75 feet, which should yield a result like that shown in the following screenshot:

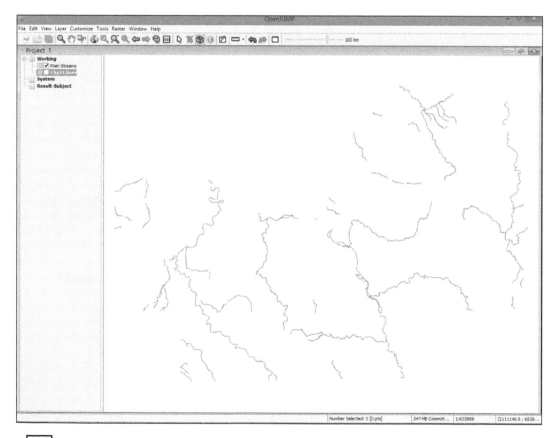

4. The `ST_Buffer` function uses the units of the data projection for bufferring. So, if your data still has the original spatial reference, *EPSG: 4269*, you will be buffering the lines by 75 degrees, and this will lead to very strange results indeed! Modify the following SQL query to transform your geometry:

```
SELECT AddGeometryColumn('Chp11', 'lines','geom_sp',3734,
'MULTILINESTRING', 2);

UPDATE "Chp11".lines SET geom_sp = ST_Transform(geom,3734);
```

5. You'll then want to go back to step 3 in order to create the buffer measured in feet.

6. Next, pan and zoom on the map and find two separate polygons that are near each other.

7. Select the **Fence** icon on the main menu:

8. Draw a connection (overlapping a connection is fine) between the two unconnected polygons using the **Fence** tool. Click once on the **Fence** button to create a vertex, and double-click on it once your polygon is complete.

9. Switch over to the **Select Features Tool**, as shown in the following screenshot, and select polygons that you drew on either side of the **Fence** bridge; select multiple features by holding down the *Shift* key:

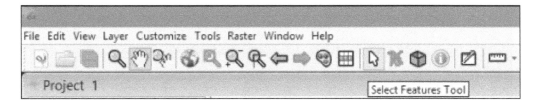

You should now have a fence junction between the selected polygons. You should see something similar to the following screenshot:

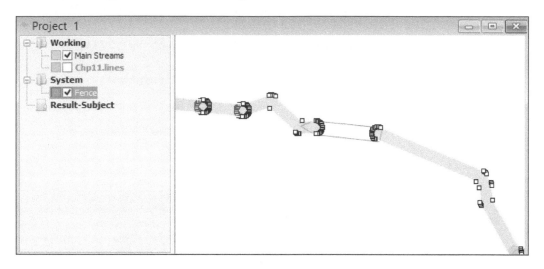

10. Navigate to **File | Run Datastore Query** again.

11. This time, we will utilize the buttons to the right-hand side of the window to connect.

    Run ST_UNION on the selection and fence together so that the gap is filled. We do this with a query, as follows:

    ```
    SELECT ST_UNION(geom1, geom2) AS geom
    ```

    Use the **selection** and **fence** buttons in place of geom1 and geom2 so that your query looks like that shown in the following screenshot:

12. Click on **OK** and view the query result by turning off the **Main Streams** and **Fence** layers, as shown in the following screenshot:

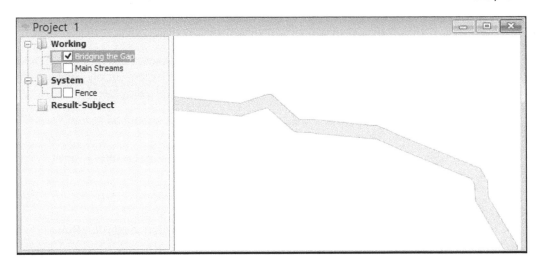

## How it works...

We added a buffered subset of a PostGIS layer in OpenJUMP using the **Run Datastore Query** menu. We took lines from a database table and converted them to polygons, to viewing them in OpenJUMP.

We then manually selected an area of interest that had two representative stream polygons disjointed from one another. The idea being that the streams would be or are connected in a natural state.

The **Fence** tool was used to draw a freehand polygon between the streams. A union query was then performed to combine the two stream polygons and the fences. Fences allow us to create temporary tables for use in spatial queries executed against a database table.

# Adding PostGIS layers – gvSIG

gvSIG is a GIS package developed for the **Generalitat Valenciana** (**gv**) in Spain. SIG is the Spanish equivalent of GIS. Intended for use all over the world, gvSIG is available in more than a dozen languages.

Installers, documentation, and more details for gvSIG can be found at the following website:

`http://www.gvsig.org/web/`

To download gvSIG, click on the latest version (gvSIG 2.0, as of this writing). The all-included version is recommended on the gvSIG site. Be careful while selecting the .exe or .bin versions; otherwise, you may download the program in a language that you don't understand.

## Getting ready

Before we begin, we have to deal with the incompatibility between PostGIS 2.0 and gvSIG. Older functions that have been left out of PostGIS 2.0 are needed for this recipe. Luckily, dealing with incompatibility issues is a quick and easy fix when you perform the following steps:

1. Search for `legacy.sql` in your `PostgreSQL` directory. It should be at the following location:

   `C:\Program Files\PostgreSQL\9.2\share\contrib\postgis-2.0`

2. Open the file with Notepad select all and copy.

3. Load pgAdmin III and open a SQL window.

4. Paste the contents from `legacy.sql` into the SQL window, and click on **Run**.

A second or so later, you should be all set!

## How to do it...

The GeoDB layer can be added by following the ensuing steps:

1. Select **View** as the document type in the **Project manager** section and then click on the **New** button. A blank view (canvas) will open.

2. Click on the **Add Layer** button on the menu bar:

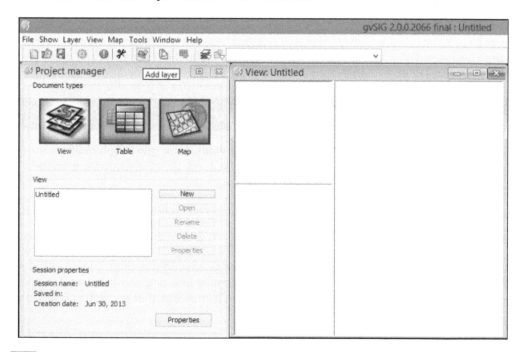

3. Next, select the **GeoDB** tab and click on the button to the right of the **Choose connection** drop-down menu.

4. Enter the values in **Connection parameters** and make sure to select **PostgreSQLExplorer** as the value for **Driver**:

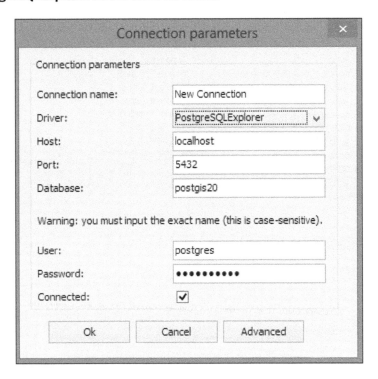

5. Click on **OK**. All of your tables should appear in **Choose table**. One or many tables can be added at a time. You can also do the following:

   ❑ Choose the columns you want to add in each layer

   ❑ Select the geometry column to be used in the event of multiple geometries being present

   ❑ Give each layer a unique name

   ❑ Perform SQL WHERE clause queries to load a subset of a dataset

You can see these steps performed in the following screenshot:

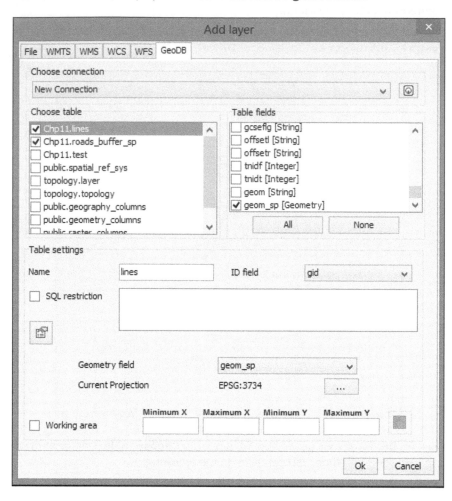

6. Click on **OK** when you're ready. The data will load in the new view that was created, as shown in the following screenshot:

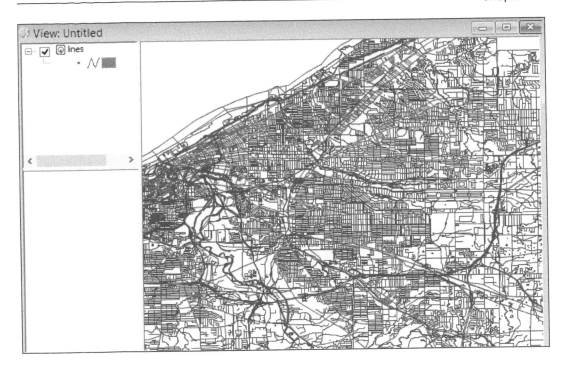

## How it works...

PostGIS layers were added to gvSIG using the **Add Layer** menu. The **GeoDB** tab allowed us to set the PostGIS connection. After choosing a table, many options are afforded with gvSIG. The layer name can be aliased to something more meaningful, and unnecessary columns can be omitted from the table.

## Adding PostGIS layers – uDig

A hallmark of the **User-friendly Desktop Internet GIS (uDig)** program is that it can be used as a standalone application or plugin for existing applications. Details on the uDig project, as well as installers, can be found at the following website:

```
http://udig.refractions.net/
```

Click on **Downloads** on the preceding website to view the list of versions and installers. As of this writing, 1.4 is the latest stable version. uDig is supported by Windows, Mac OS X, and Linux.

In this recipe, we will quickly connect to a PostGIS database and then add a layer to uDig.

## How to do it...

Carry out the following steps:

1. Navigate to **Layer | Add** from the main menu:

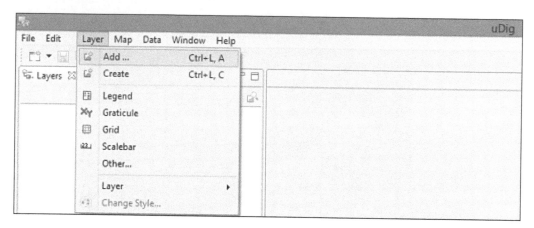

2. Select **PostGIS** as the data source and click on the **Next** button to continue:

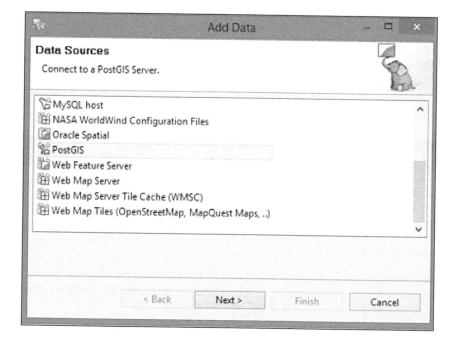

3. Fill in your PostGIS connection parameters and then click on the **Next** button:

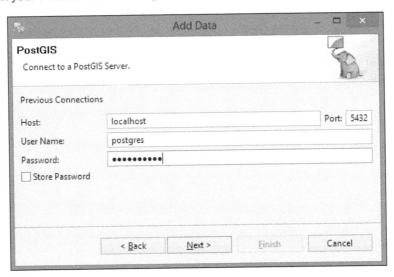

4. Select the target database in the **Database** drop-down menu. Click on the **List** button to view all of the tables from the database that have valid geometries. Then, check the checkboxes for one or more tables to add them as layers:

5. Click on **Finish** and your data will be loaded in the **Map** window.

## How it works...

The **Add Layer** menu in uDig generates a hefty list of possible sources that can be added. PostGIS was set as the database, and your database parameters were entered. uDig was then connected to the database. Clicking on **List** calculates the total number of tables available in the connected database. Any number of tables can be added at once.

# Index

## Symbols

## A

## B

## C

## D

data
  exporting, to shapefile with pgsql2shp PostGIS
    command 33, 34
  loading, from OSM 220
database
  backing up 403, 404
  organizing 394-397
database index
  about 405, 406
  working 408
Database Manager. *See* DB Manager plugin
database queries
  running 449-453
data deployment
  geometries, clipping for 116-119
DataType property 324
DB Manager plugin
  using 435-441
  working 442
demographics
  calculating, driving distance used
    229-232
DEM operations
  executing 206-209
Dijkstra
  routing 215-219
  using 216
distances
  measuring 107-110
distance/service area calculation
  driving 224-228
django-admin command 376
Django template language
  about 386
  URL 392
Django URL Dispatcher 385
Django web framework 326
driving distance
  used, for demographics calculations 229-232

## E

Editing Toolbox button 447
Enhanced Vegetation Index (EVI) 200
EOSDIS (Earth Observing System Data and
    Information System) 12

error tolerance 198
European Forest Fire Information System
    (EFFIS) 8
European Petroleum Survey Group (EPSG) 58
EVI 200
Exchangeable Image File format (EXIF) 258
external scripts
  bundling, as function 166, 167
  input text, preparing 160-164
  results, returning 164
  test table, preparing 159
  translating, into geometry 167, 168, 172
  used, for functionality embedding 152-155
  used, for other library embedding 156-159

## F

Fence tool 453
Find_PlaceNames function 305
functional index 407

## G

GDAL
  about 12
  used, for netCDF datasets import 316-324
  used, for nonspatial tabular data (CSV) import
    12-16
gdalbuildvrt command 45
gdalbuildvrt utility 197
gdalinfo command 41
gdalinfo command-line utility 39
GDAL OGR virtual format 12
GDAL Python bindings 282
gdal_translate command
  used, for raster exporting 51-53
GDAL utilities
  gdalbuildvrt 174
  gdalinfo 174
  gdal_translate 174
GDAL VRT format 194
gdalwarp GDAL command
  used, for raster exporting 51-53
geocode method 312
geocoding
  GeoNames datasets, using 302-305
  OSM datasets, using with trigrams 306-312
  with geopy 312-316

# Thank you for buying
# PostGIS Cookbook

## About Packt Publishing

Packt, pronounced 'packed', published its first book "*Mastering phpMyAdmin for Effective MySQL Management*" in April 2004 and subsequently continued to specialize in publishing highly focused books on specific technologies and solutions.

Our books and publications share the experiences of your fellow IT professionals in adapting and customizing today's systems, applications, and frameworks. Our solution based books give you the knowledge and power to customize the software and technologies you're using to get the job done. Packt books are more specific and less general than the IT books you have seen in the past. Our unique business model allows us to bring you more focused information, giving you more of what you need to know, and less of what you don't.

Packt is a modern, yet unique publishing company, which focuses on producing quality, cutting-edge books for communities of developers, administrators, and newbies alike. For more information, please visit our website: www.packtpub.com.

## About Packt Open Source

In 2010, Packt launched two new brands, Packt Open Source and Packt Enterprise, in order to continue its focus on specialization. This book is part of the Packt Open Source brand, home to books published on software built around Open Source licenses, and offering information to anybody from advanced developers to budding web designers. The Open Source brand also runs Packt's Open Source Royalty Scheme, by which Packt gives a royalty to each Open Source project about whose software a book is sold.

## Writing for Packt

We welcome all inquiries from people who are interested in authoring. Book proposals should be sent to author@packtpub.com. If your book idea is still at an early stage and you would like to discuss it first before writing a formal book proposal, contact us; one of our commissioning editors will get in touch with you.

We're not just looking for published authors; if you have strong technical skills but no writing experience, our experienced editors can help you develop a writing career, or simply get some additional reward for your expertise.

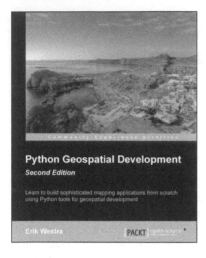

# PostgreSQL Replication

ISBN: 978-1-84951-672-3        Paperback: 250 pages

Understand basic replication concepts and efficiently replicate PostgreSQL using high-end techniques to protect your data and run your server without interruptions

1. Explains the new replication features introduced in PostgreSQL 9

2. Contains easy to understand explanations and lots of screenshots that simplify an advanced topic like replication

3. Teaches PostgreSQL administrators how to maintain consistency between redundant resources and to improve reliability, fault-tolerance, and accessibility

# PostgreSQL Server Programming

ISBN: 978-1-84951-698-3        Paperback: 264 pages

Extend PostgreSQL and integrate the database layer into your development framework

1. Understand the extension framework of PostgreSQL, and leverage it in ways that you haven't even invented yet

2. Write functions, create your own data types, all in your favourite programming language

3. Step-by-step tutorial with plenty of tips and tricks to kick-start server programming

Please check **www.PacktPub.com** for information on our titles

CPSIA information can be obtained
at www.ICGtesting.com
Printed in the USA
LVHW062027081221
705492LV00016B/231